Baltic Capitals

TALLINN • RIGA • VILNIUS • KALININGRAD

contributing editor
Neil Taylor

additional authors
Stephen Baister
Gordon McLachlan
Chris Patrick

Bradt Travel Guides Ltd, UK
The Globe Pequot Press Inc, USA

First published in 2001 by Bradt Travel Guides Ltd
19 High Street, Chalfont St Peter, Bucks SL9 9QE, England
Published in the USA by The Globe Pequot Press Inc,
246 Goose Lane, PO Box 480, Guilford, Connecticut 06437-0480

This second edition published in 2003

The author and publishers have made every effort to ensure the
accuracy of the information in this book at the time of going to press.
However, the publishers cannot accept any responsibility for any loss,
injury or inconvenience resulting from the use of information contained in this guide.

British Library Cataloguing in Publication Data
A catalogue record for this book is available from the British Library

ISBN 1 84162 071 8

Photographs *Front cover* Tallinn door (Tricia Hayne), Cosmonaut Memorial,
Kaliningrad (Matt Rudd), Vilnius street scene (Rachel Russell), House of the Cat, Riga
(Mark Wadlow/Russia & Eastern Images)
Text Stephen Baister and Chris Patrick (SC); Tricia Hayne (TH); Gordon McLachlan
(GM); Matt Rudd (MR); Rachel Russell (RR); Jonathan Smith (JS)
Maps Alan Whitaker

Typeset from the author's disc by Wakewing
Printed and bound in Italy by Legoprint SpA, Trento

Authors

Neil Taylor is director of Regent Holidays, a British tour company that has specialised in travel to the Baltic States and Kaliningrad since 1991. He visits the area about four times a year and in 1999 his Bradt guide to Estonia was published. He is on the Board of the Association of Independent Tour Operators (AITO) and writes and broadcasts on general travel trade topics.

In 2000, Neil was awarded the Lifetime Achievement Award by the British Guild of Travel Writers.

Stephen Baister studied modern languages at Oxford and London universities and worked as a publisher before becoming a solicitor. While in practice, he represented a number of clients with interests in eastern and central Europe. He was co-author of the *Bradt Guide to East Germany*, published in 1990, and a contributor to *Eastern Europe by Rail* (Bradt Publications 1994). He has a doctorate in East European law from University College London. He is now a Registrar in Bankruptcy in the High Court.

Gordon McLachlan was born in Edinburgh. Following graduation from Edinburgh University, he worked for several years on the sales side of publishing, then assumed a full-time writing career in 1987. His many published books include guides to Germany, Berlin, Poland and Edinburgh, and it was his long professional association with the southern Baltic region which inspired him to add Lithuania to this list. His special interests include music, photography, art and architecture, reading, hiking and gastronomy.

Chris Patrick has a degree in French and German from Oxford University. After graduation she lived and worked in Japan and travelled extensively in the Far East. She works now in international research and consultancy and is Director of the Europe Japan Centre. She has assisted a number of organisations from Eastern Europe in doing business in the Far East. She first visited Latvia in 1989 and has returned many times since. She was co-author of the *Bradt Guide to East Germany*, published in 1990, and a contributor to *Eastern Europe by Rail* (Bradt Publications 1994).

Contents

Introduction

The late 1990s saw the term 'short break' take on a totally new dimension in the travel business. Tourists who previously limited their horizons to Paris and Amsterdam were suddenly offered shopping weekends in Minneapolis or a glimpse at the Taj Mahal. The three Baltic capitals soon realised that they could fill a gap between these two extremes. With a flying time of three hours from London or four from Birmingham, Manchester and Glasgow, with the abolition of visas, and with the 'Westernisation' of hotels, each offers a fulfilling three or four days either on their own or as part of a longer visit to two or three of them. Except perhaps in December and January, the weather is good enough for walking between the major attractions, all of which now cater for the English-speaking visitor.

The time difference is one or two hours from Britain, the airports are close to the city centre and immigration procedures are very quick so a visitor might well reach a hotel in one of the Baltic capitals more quickly than one in Berlin or Rome.

Kaliningrad took longer to realise the potential of catering for short-stay visitors. Only in 1999 were visas issued on arrival at both the land borders and at the airport. Travel was often an obstacle course with little non-Russian material available and in the early 1990s tourists had been treated with suspicion and fear. Neither the shops nor the few open museums could really offer any temptations. Seeing, however, the success of Vilnius to the north and Krakow to the south has been a major stimulus to compete. There is much still to do and older visitors will quickly find some parallels with the Soviet Union but regular visitors point to the month by month changes. There is now a genuine need for a guidebook; five years ago this claim could not have been made.

Parallels with many other parts of Europe will immediately strike the visitor. The towering Gothic steeples in Tallinn, Riga and Kaliningrad emphasise the importance of the Baltic German community. The domes and colour of the Russian orthodox churches are constant reminders of the two hundred years the Baltic Republics spent in the Russian Empire. The use of mobile phones by all generations is one of many habits picked up by the renewed links to Sweden and Finland. France, Italy and Spain have made their mark in the local restaurants, whilst Britain has concentrated on the pubs. Local footballers, of course, play not only in Europe but for teams all over the world!

Allow time in all four capitals for evening concerts; in the winter the architecture of the buildings will be as much an attraction as the music. Most date from the late 19th century and avoided damage both from bombing and from over-zealous modernisers during the Soviet period. In the summer, music moves to the lakes, to the parks, to the riverside and to the coast. The concert repertoire will mix local music with Western classics and high standards can be guaranteed. Allow time too for shopping since local materials and craftsmanship stand out in all the local markets. Wool, linen, copper and amber are all transformed into original gifts. Local photographers, historians and translators have now finally got together to publish excellent souvenirs of each city. With efficient postal services, they can easily be sent home. Above all, take in the changes that have taken place in the last ten to twelve years. There is no longer the need to look on a visit to the Baltics as an adventure. The best compliment that can be paid to them is to regard them as ordinary European capitals.

ACKNOWLEDGEMENTS

In preparing the text on Königsberg, I must give particular thanks to Lorenz Grimoni, Director of the Königsberg Museum in Duisburg. He gave me access to the museum archives which cover all aspects of pre-war life in the city and which house research done by Germans in Kaliningrad since 1990 when they were able to return there. Future generations in particular will be grateful for all the work done in the museum to preserve the memory of what had been an important German city. In Kaliningrad itself, my guide, Olga Danilova, has shared her enthusiasm, realism and knowledge on each of my visits. I owe Olga a great debt, as do most English-speaking visitors. The staff at Baltma Tours always seemed to meet my increasingly complicated requests and must be congratulated on cutting out much of the Soviet visa bureaucracy that still plagues the rest of Russia.

Practical Information

WHEN TO GO

Most tourists to the Baltic States visit in the summer months between late April and early October. July and early August are very busy in the cheaper hotels since this is the German and Scandinavian school holiday period. Temperatures in the summer can reach 25°C/80°F quite regularly, though they often hover around 20°C/70°F. Good weather can never be guaranteed in this area. Clouds can quickly congregate, turning a sunny morning into a dismal afternoon, but the reverse is equally true, too. Day trips should never be undertaken without a coat and strong shoes. Tallinn hardly sees a night around midsummer on June 23 and the days are long in all four countries from May until September. The deluxe and business-class hotels often reduce their prices in July and August to attract tourists at a time when their normal clientele is absent.

More tourists are now seeing the attractions of winter visits to these four cities. Culture flourishes then, temperatures do not drop much below freezing, and queues are non-existent at the major sites. From western Europe winter air fares have now dropped to a level which makes weekend breaks in these cities very popular. January and early February should be avoided because of the short hours of daylight then and the occasional bitter day, but other months should offer a pleasant stay. Christmas is now taken seriously in the Baltics and a well-planned short shopping trip should more than cover the air fare.

TIME ZONES

Before World War II, Estonia and Latvia were two hours ahead of GMT and Lithuania one hour ahead, as was East Prussia. During the Soviet occupation the three Baltic republics and the Kaliningrad region were forced to use Moscow time which is three hours ahead of GMT. Courageous local nationalists during this period would often keep their watches an hour behind Moscow time as an act of defiance to the USSR and of loyalty to the former regime. On regaining independence changing back the time was one of the first acts of the new governments and in the early 90s they all kept in step, to be joined later by Kaliningrad. From 1997, however, they have not always acted in tandem for a variety of reasons. In summer 2000 Kaliningrad adopted summer time two hours ahead of Britain and one hour ahead of Western Europe, but the other three did not, so are now one hour ahead of Britain and have the same time as most of the rest of Europe throughout the year. As these decisions are often taken at relatively short notice, it is important to reconfirm timings of international travel shortly before departure. Tickets may have been issued abroad before a change was announced.

RED TAPE

Estonia, Latvia and Lithuania abolished the Soviet visa system immediately after their independence in 1991. Nationals of all EU countries and the United States do not need visas at all. Australians, Canadians and New Zealanders need one for Latvia. Canadians also need one for Estonia, and New Zealanders for Lithuania. However, for these nationalities a visa for one Baltic state is valid for the other two as well so they never need obtain more than one visa, even if they plan to visit more than one country.

Kaliningrad initially followed Russia by adopting the former Soviet visa system but a fall in the number of tourists forced them to break away from this in 1999. All tourists still need a visa, which is only granted on the basis of pre-booked accommodation, but it is now issued on arrival. This can be at Kaliningrad airport or on the road crossings from Poland and Lithuania. This is easily arranged by travel agents abroad in conjunction with their agents in Kaliningrad. The only exception is for visitors planning to arrive by train. They will have to obtain their visas from Russian embassies abroad, but given the difficulties of this procedure and the state of the international trains that serve Kaliningrad, few visitors are likely to choose this method. Visas are for specific dates and accommodation so must be arranged several weeks in advance. It is not possible to backpack in Kaliningrad or to have an open-dated visa. In summer 2002, this simplified visa system became restricted to the Polish border crossing points and travellers arriving at the airport or from Lithuania had to obtain visas abroad. Given the drastic fall in tourists which resulted from this, it is expected that the simplified system will be reintroduced in 2003.

Consular help in the Baltics

Australia, Britain and the United States have consulates in each of the Baltic capitals except Kaliningrad. The British consulates can provide assistance to nationals of most Commonwealth countries in emergencies and also to nationals of EU countries that do not have their own consulates. Kaliningrad has four consulates representing Belarus, Denmark, Lithuania and Poland. The Danish one, situated in the Scandinavian Airlines office at Sovietsky 1, tel: 0112 55 0105, handles emergencies for all Western tourists. The German government has expressed interest in opening a consulate in Kaliningrad but Moscow has remained unwilling to allow this. See also pages 26, 62, 123 and 168.

MONEY MATTERS

Each country has its own currency and payment in any other one is impossible. All four are convertible and can be exchanged throughout the Baltic countries. As banks and exchange bureaux do not usually charge commission, small amounts left over can be re-exchanged without difficulty. In Tallinn, Riga and Vilnius, banks and exchange bureaux change all major Western currencies. Those at airports are always open for incoming flights but at land borders and at railway and bus stations they tend to close between 20.00 and 08.00, even though many international buses and trains travel through the night. Exchange bureaux in the towns are usually open seven days a week from around 09.00 to 19.00. Most hotels change money, some at any time of day, but rates are always better in exchange bureaux. On day trips out of town, remember to change sufficient money before departure since exchange and credit card facilities may not be available en route. In the Kaliningrad *oblast*, apart from at the land border with Lithuania, it is often only possible to exchange euros or US dollars into roubles. It is forbidden to make any payments in foreign currency. Thomas Cook and HKSB sell all four currencies in the UK, but it is otherwise difficult to obtain them in advance in western Europe.

Estonia
The Estonian kroon is fixed at a rate of 15.65 kroon to the euro, so in early 2003 there were about 23 kroon to the UK pound and 16 to the US dollar. The lowest note is for one kroon and the highest for 500, but those for one and two kroon are likely to be completely withdrawn during 2003. Coins are minted for 10, 20 and 50 cents, and for one, two and five kroon.

Latvia
The Latvian lat (Ls) is tied to a range of Western currencies and is worth around £1.10 or US$1.80. In contrast to Estonia, coins are issued up to Ls2 and notes from Ls5 upwards. As the lat is worth a little more than £1, the money there is very convenient for British tourists to calculate as coins and notes match their British counterparts fairly closely. Coins are issued for 1, 2, 5, 10, 20 and 50 santimi and for Ls1 and Ls2; notes for Ls5, Ls10, Ls20 and Ls50. (Gamblers and money-launderers may also find the Ls100 and Ls500 notes of use.) Outside Latvia, it is sometimes difficult to exchange coins so these should be re-exchanged before departure, and on the Latvian side of land borders.

Lithuania
Having for nine years been tied to the US dollar, since February 2002, the lit has been tied instead to the euro. The fixed rate is 3.45Lt = €1, so in late 2002 the pound was worth about 5.40Lt and the dollar about 3.70Lt. There are coins for 1, 2, 5, 10, 20 and 50 cents and also for 1Lt, 2Lt and 5Lt. There are coins for 5, 10, 20 and 50 cents and for 1Lt, 2Lt, and 5Lt. There are notes for 10, 20, 50 and 100 lits and some still in circulation for 1, 2, and 5 lits but these are gradually being replaced by coins.

Kaliningrad
Through much of the 1990s the Russian rouble fluctuated wildly against other currencies, but since 1998 it has been very stable against the US dollar at a rate of US$1 = RUB27.00. In late 2002, the pound was worth about RUB40. Coins are issued for 10, 20 and 50 kopeks and for 1, 2 and 5 roubles. Given the very low prices for most items of interest to tourists, the only notes likely to be of use are those for 10, 20 and 50 roubles, although higher denominations are issued.

Cash machines
These are easily found all over Tallinn but are less common in Riga and Vilnius. Their use is, however, spreading all the time in these three cities. In Kaliningrad they remain rare and the few that exist often do not work.

Credit cards
In Tallinn, Riga and Vilnius the use of cards is as widespread as elsewhere with all major shops, restaurants and hotels taking them. They can be used in hotels in

Kaliningrad, but not in shops and only in a few restaurants. The Eurolines offices at Tallinn and at Riga bus stations accept credit cards, but otherwise they cannot be used at railway or bus stations. As even long-distance fares are very low, this is not a major problem.

Travellers' cheques

These are useless throughout the Baltics. Only a very few banks can exchange them; shops hotels, restaurants and exchange bureaux will invariably refuse them. The easy availability of cash machines in Estonia, Latvia and Lithuania, and the very low cost of incidentals in Kaliningrad, makes their use superfluous. (Many local people do not write cheques anymore as they only use electronic banking.)

COSTS

Whilst hotel costs are similar to those in western Europe, other expenses will be much lower, except at restaurants and clubs clearly geared to affluent foreigners. A bus or train ride of 200km may well cost only £3/US$5, a light lunch £2/US$3 and a taxi across town £3/US$4.50. With low sales taxes, petrol is about half the UK price and a carton of 200 cigarettes costs scarcely more than the price of a packet in Britain. In Kaliningrad, prices are even lower than in the other three cities. Museums do charge admission fees, usually with reductions for children and for the elderly. The full charge is rarely more than £1/US$1.50 and often much less. Locally produced books and maps in English often offer good value. On day trips out, incidental costs will be much lower than in the capitals and on these occasions it is worth looking out for souvenirs since their prices will be geared to local consumers.

Shoppers visiting more than one of the cities will save money by finishing their tour in Kaliningrad, where all the obvious souvenirs are much cheaper than further north. Amber is of course the obvious buy there, together with linen and vodka. Lithuania and Estonia produce tasteful items carved from juniper wood, whereas the best china and glass is sold in Riga.

WHAT TO TAKE

The shops are now so well stocked in all four countries, with prices usually much lower than those in western Europe, that there is no need to stock up with supplies before departure. Long-gone are the days when travellers took iron rations and a medicine chest to safeguard their survival. An umbrella is essential year-round as clouds can suddenly appear on even the nicest of days. Be prepared similarly for changes in temperature: a sweater may be needed in summer and a spring day can revert to being a winter one. Tough footwear is always essential because of the uneven pavements and the number of sites away from main roads. Relatively formal wear is still the custom for concerts and plays. Westerners attending performances often stand out with their untidy, casual dress.

The foreign-language bookshops in three of the Baltic capitals are well supplied with English-language light and serious reading matter but few English (or even German) books are sold in Kaliningrad. Local guides in Kaliningrad are always pleased to receive books in English and many find their way into school and college libraries.

GETTING THERE
Tour operators
Exodus Travels 9 Weir Rd, London SW12 OLT; tel: 020 8673 0859; fax: 020 8673 0779; email: sales@exodustravels.co.uk; web: www.exodustravels.co.uk. Organise cycling groups to Latvia and Estonia which start in Riga and finish in Tallinn, also general tours covering the three Baltic States. About half the time is spent in the capitals and half in the countryside.

Explore Worldwide 1 Frederick St, Aldershot, Hants GU11 1LQ; tel: 01252 760100; fax: 01252 760001; email: info@exploreworldwide.com; web: www.exploreworldwide.com. Operate an extensive general itinerary through the three Baltic States which includes the capital cities.

Martin Randall Travel 10 Barley Mow Passage, Chiswick, London W4 4PH; tel: 020 8742 3355; fax: 020 8742 7766; email: info@martinrandall.co.uk; web: www.martinrandall.com. Have an extensive programme of group tours to the Baltic States for those interested in art, architecture and music. Guest lecturers accompany every tour. There is a tour each year to the Riga Opera Festival.

Regent Holidays 15 John St, Bristol BS1 2HR; tel: 0117 921 1711; fax: 0117 925 4866; email: regent@regent-holidays.co.uk; web: www.regent-holidays.co.uk. The only UK operator to promote Kaliningrad as well as the Baltic States. Group tours cover the four capitals; city breaks are available to each of them and tailor-made individual itineraries can cover any combination of the cities with the surrounding areas. Itineraries can also include Belarus, Finland, Poland and Russia.

Scantours 47 Whitcomb St, Leicester Square, London WC2H 7DH; tel: 020 7839 2927; fax: 020 7839 5891; email: info@scantoursUK.com; web: www.scantoursuk.com. Offer city breaks, group tours and individual arrangements to three of the Baltic capitals and also combinations with Denmark, Sweden and Finland.

Specialised Tours 4 Copthorne Bank, Copthorne, Crawley, West Sussex RH10 3QX; tel: 01342 712785; fax: 01342 717042; web: www.specialisedtours.com. Arrange short breaks to three of the Baltic capitals, a Classical Baltics tour linking the three, and individual arrangements throughout the Baltics.

By air
Most tourists are likely to start and to finish their tours in this way. SAS Scandinavian Airlines used to serve all four capitals but they withdrew their daily Copenhagen–Kaliningrad service in autumn 2001. However, they still have several services a day from the three other capitals to both Copenhagen and Stockholm and then these connect with flights to Britain and to the USA. SAS offer 'open-jaw' fares, which allow travel into one city and back from another. This facility is also available to towns in Poland and Russia, so that it is possible to fly into Gdańsk, for example, and out of Tallinn. SAS is particularly convenient for travellers from Great Britain and Ireland as it serves seven airports – London Heathrow, London Gatwick, Birmingham, Manchester, Edinburgh, Glasgow and Dublin so a journey from any of them to the Baltics should not take more than five hours.

Shortly after SAS withdrew their Kaliningrad service, LOT Polish Airlines introduced one from Warsaw three times a week, which connects in both directions with most of their flights to western Europe. They also serve the other three Baltic capitals from Warsaw. Apart from some charter flights to Germany in the summer, other flights from Kaliningrad go only to Russia.

Finnair have several flights a day to Tallinn from Helsinki and also daily services to Riga and Vilnius. These connect with the services they jointly operate with BA between Helsinki, London and Manchester. British Airways also fly direct between London Heathrow and Riga. The service they operated to Vilnius between 1999 and 2000 did not return in 2002, but Lithuanian Airlines have successfully operated a daily service for many years from Vilnius to either Heathrow or Gatwick. In 2002, this flight switched from Heathrow to Gatwick. Estonian Air flies daily except on Saturdays between Gatwick and Tallinn. A popular way to travel from Britain is to take Estonian Air in one direction and Lithuanian Airlines in the other. Visitors wanting to combine a visit to the Baltic States with one to central Europe can use the services of Czech Airlines or of Austrian Airlines.

Flights between Vilnius, Riga and Tallinn are operated by Estonian Air, Lithuanian Airlines and by Air Baltic. Air Baltic is a subsidiary of SAS. Because of the very high taxes at Riga Airport, the future of intra-Baltic flights involving that destination was uncertain in late 2002, but those between Tallinn and Vilnius were likely to continue. Fares on these routes are high when booked on their own, but good discounts are available from specialist travel agents when they are booked in conjunction with flights to other countries.

Minimal air services now operate from the Baltics to Russia and Ukraine. Flights from Germany increased in 2002 so it is easy to fly from Berlin, Frankfurt and Hamburg to the Baltics.

Although the no-frills airlines had not shown interest in the Baltics by 2002, air fares have dropped, as has happened on most European routes. By summer 2004, when three of the Baltic States are in the EU, the no-frills airlines may well begin services. Major discounts are often available if flights and hotels are booked at the same time with tour operators active in this area. Airport taxes are becoming an increasingly large component of fares so it is important to check these before making any commitment. If possible, do not leave from Riga Airport, as taxes there are much higher than at Tallinn or at Vilnius. From November 1, 2002 visitors from the UK benefited from a drop in APD (Airport Passenger Duty). The previous rate of £20 went down to £5.

By train

With the continuing reduction in air fares and the worsening services on international trains, this is unlikely to be a means of transport used by many visitors to reach this area. Customs and immigration procedures can take many hours, usually in the middle of the night. Trains still operate from Kaliningrad to Warsaw and from Tallinn to St Petersburg. There are also trains from Kaliningrad and the Baltic cities to Moscow and Kiev. Belarussian transit visas are now needed for these, as well as the appropriate Russian or Ukrainian visas. In summer 2000 a Russian visa was no longer valid for transit across Belarus. In 2001, train services between Vilnius, Riga and Tallinn were finally abandoned and this was threatened in 2002 for the Tallinn–St Petersburg service, although it was in the end retained.

By bus

Eurolines has an extensive network of services to western Europe from the Baltics and some services to Russia. Eurolines and other local companies also run express buses between the Baltic States. These operate several times a day and are the most practical way of land travel between the major cities. They jump the queue at the frontiers so timings are virtually guaranteed. The journey takes around five hours from Riga to either Vilnius or Tallinn. There is a through service from Vilnius to Tallinn and also routes from Riga to Kaunas and to Tartu. Reservations can be made abroad through travel agents (see page 5) but tickets are collected from the Eurolines office in the relevant bus station. The fare from Riga to either Tallinn or Vilnius is around £7/US$10 one-way. English is spoken in all Eurolines offices.

Local companies operate services from Kaliningrad to Nida, Vilnius and Riga which should be prebooked in view of the visa stipulations. These, too, jump border queues so passengers who may have spent around £5/US$8 for their fare can have the pleasure of overtaking rich businessmen fuming in their Mercedes. There are some similar services to Poland but these are less regular nowadays as local travellers now require visas.

By car

It is virtually impossible to obtain insurance valid for cars brought into the Baltic States and Kaliningrad from the rest of Europe. This stems from the high rate of theft that used to be prevalent in the area and which to some extent continues. Car hire is possible locally but for visitors staying largely in the capital cities is unlikely to be of use. Many of the sites are within walking distance of hotels and others are within easy reach by bus or taxi. For day trips off the beaten track hiring may be worthwhile but as prices for local guides and drivers are very reasonable it is often sensible to consider hiring a car on this basis. Minor roads are not well signposted and local people in the countryside do not usually speak foreign languages.

By ferry

In the summer, hovercrafts and catamarans take between an hour and 90 minutes to link Tallinn and Helsinki. Larger boats, taking about three hours, operate year-round. Services start around 08.00 in the morning and finish around 21.00 at night. Competition between the many companies operating these routes and the profits they make selling duty-free goods on board keeps prices down to about£12 one-way and £20 return. Some carriers offer a business-class for about double this price and this offers a private lounge and free refreshments. An overnight ferry operates between Tallinn and Stockholm and a day one between Riga and Stockholm. Visitors from Britain and Ireland wanting to visit Sweden and the Baltic States can obtain a three-sector ticket from SAS agents and then use one of these ferries. Several cruise liners visit Kaliningrad, Riga and Tallinn as part of a tour around the Baltic Sea.

GETTING AROUND
By air

Domestic flights in Estonia operate between Tallinn and the islands of Hiiumaa and Saaremaa. In Lithuania they operate in the summer between Vilnius and Palanga on the coast. None operate in Latvia. From Monday to Friday there are morning flights and evening flights from Riga to, and between, Tallinn and Vilnius. There are no flights to Kaliningrad from the other Baltic capitals.

By train

Most tourists never use the rail services in the Baltic States as so few meet their needs. There is one overnight train between Vilnius and Riga but none by day and no trains at all between Riga and Tallinn. Normally buses are quicker and more regular, both between the countries and on domestic routes. The only train routes likely to be of use to tourists are from Tallinn to Paldiski, from Riga to Jurmala, and from Kaliningrad to Svetlogorsk, in each case from the capital to a nearby town on the coast. Day trains do, however, operate between Vilnius and Kaliningrad and can be considered as an alternative to the bus.

English is not often spoken in railway stations but timetables are clearly displayed, although in Kaliningrad this is of course in the Cyrillic alphabet. Russian is in fact the first language of most railway employees throughout the Baltics. Tickets for the suburban services mentioned above are sold on the train.

By bus

The most convenient way to travel between all four cities is by bus. Most services are run by Eurolines and Baltic specialists abroad can prebook these. In the winter, it is often possible to buy a seat on the spot before departure. The journey time between Tallinn and Riga and also between Riga and Vilnius is around five hours. Buses operate about six times a day on both sectors and the one-way fare is around £7/US$10. There is a daily bus from Kaliningrad to Riga which takes around nine hours and one night bus between Kaliningrad and Vilnius which takes eight hours. The one-way fare on these routes is also around £7/US$10. For those in no rush between Kaliningrad and Vilnius, there are six buses a day between Kaliningrad and Klaipeda which run along the Curonian Spit. These then connect with hourly services between Klaipeda and Vilnius. Allow about ten hours for the whole journey.

Extensive services operate in all four cities and local maps will give details of current routings. In Tallinn, where several competing companies operate, service numbers change quite frequently so it is important to get an up-to-date map. In the other cities, a regular pattern has now been set so few changes are likely in the near future. In Riga and Vilnius, the airports are served by a good local bus service. This is less regular in Tallinn, but as several hotels have a minibus service and a taxi into town should not cost more than £3/US$5, this does not matter so much. In Kaliningrad the local bus that serves the airport does not pass close to any of the hotels so most tourists are collected by their local travel agent.

At the time of writing in summer 2002, tickets bought at kiosks in Tallinn and Vilnius are a little cheaper than those bought on the bus. Visitors staying for several days at hotels in the outskirts should investigate season tickets. Riga and Tallinn have tourist passes which include free local transport as part of the total package but, as the price of these is rather high, visitors will normally save money by paying fares and admission charges as they go.

Buses link the capitals with all other major cities in their respective countries on a very regular basis. For instance between Tallinn and Tartu, or Vilnius and Kaunas, services operate every half-hour. Timetables are displayed in the bus stations and in most cases the fare is paid directly to the driver.

By taxi

Taxis used to be a nightmare throughout the Baltics but are now properly regulated in all four cities. Within city limits, meter fares apply and this is also the case to and from the airports. Taxis can be easily hailed in the streets and with the lively nightlife for which all four cities are now renowned, they operate almost round the clock. Taxis ordered by phone are usually cheaper than those hailed on the street so visitors planning to make many such journeys should enquire on arrival about reliable companies. These all use meters. Some of the deluxe hotels operate their own fleets. These are metered; prices tend to be higher but then so is the comfort of the vehicles! Lengthy journeys which would be unthinkable by taxi in western Europe can be undertaken in the Baltics with costs being so much lower.

ACCOMMODATION

A massive programme of hotel renovation took place throughout the area following the demise of the Soviet Union. The cities approached this task in different ways. Tallinn and Riga started by renovating the large tower blocks bequeathed by the Soviet Union and several have now gone through two separate renovations since 1991. From the mid-nineties, smaller hotels opened in the old town centres and also in the more affluent suburbs. In Vilnius, the reverse process operated with new small hotels opening first and only in 2002 did renovation begin at the Lietuva Hotel. In all three cities, visitors have now, for many years, taken for granted proper plumbing, satellite television, English-speaking reception staff and varied menus in the restaurants. In Kaliningrad, the lack of investment incentives and the lower number of visitors has let modernisation proceed at a much slower pace so most hotels remain large and impersonal.

The bigger hotels rarely expect visitors to pay the prices given on their websites as most book through agents who have negotiated lower rates. Many smaller hotels now also prefer to use agents since the volume of regular business they provide compensates for the lower prices they pay. Four-five star hotels reduce their prices at weekends, over public holidays and in July–August when business traffic drops. Three-star hotels tend to raise their prices then since they cater largely for tourists.

It is always wise to prebook hotels not only for the lower prices but also simply to secure a room. A relatively small conference or sporting event may lead to the whole town being full. The publicity generated by Eurovision gave Tallinn an excellent 2002 and Riga is expecting likewise in 2003. Vilnius, with fewer rooms, has seen similar success, even without a major event taking place there. Prebooking in Kaliningrad is in any case essential to secure a Russian visa.

In their renovations many hotels are only putting in showers and not baths in the rooms. Tourists who prefer baths should ask their tour operator to stipulate this when making the booking.

EATING AND DRINKING

It is perhaps in restaurants and bars that the transformation from the old days is most apparent in Tallinn, Riga and Vilnius. *In Your Pocket* and the *City Paper* now list hundreds of choices in each city and what is gratifying is the number that still exist five or six years after opening. Every major cuisine is represented and, with the numbers of restaurants now available, advance booking is often not necessary. It is worth venturing outside the old city areas: the best food is often to be found in modest suburban surroundings. One has to be brutally honest about local food. Whilst there are many perfectly acceptable dishes, few are memorable. However, they should at least be made from fresh ingredients, now that these are available year-round. Thick soups can be recommended in winter as meals in themselves, and pancakes are served with a variety of savoury or sweet fillings. The ranges of coffee, cakes and ice-cream available are one positive legacy of Soviet and German times.

Kaliningrad has made progress recently and there is sufficient choice to cover a stay of a week or so. Prices are so low that it would be invidious to complain about the quality; a wide menu can now be taken for granted but do not yet expect many non-Russian restaurants.

Wine is quite expensive throughout the region and the quality unexciting. It is often better (and much cheaper) to drink local beer. Spirits are good everywhere with a wide local and international choice. Tourists who knew the old USSR will still find it hard to adjust to a small café in the Baltics offering a choice of malt whisky, at prices half those charged in Scotland.

MEDIA AND COMMUNICATIONS
Telephones and post
Public telephones in all four countries are operated by cards which can be bought at local kiosks. Cards are not interchangeable so new ones have to be bought for each country. It is not possible to use credit cards, nor do any phones accept coins. Instructions are usually given in English in the phone booths. The procedure is the same in all four countries: the receiver is lifted, the card inserted and then the number dialled. As the call continues, the reducing value of the card is shown on the screen. Calls to western Europe cost around £0.60/US$1 a minute with reductions in the evenings and at weekends. With competition from mobile phone companies, prices are tending to fall. Prices from hotel rooms are of course higher than this but they are rarely exorbitant. Calls to local mobile phones can cost almost as much as international calls, particularly in Estonia. Calls can be made from all major post offices and, except in Vilnius, they are open all night.

Dialling codes and information specific to the various countries are given in the individual city chapters later in the book.

Post from the three Baltic States is transmitted quickly, reaching western Europe or America within four or five days. From Kaliningrad, post has to travel via Moscow so tends to take at least two weeks. Postage rates are fairly similar in all four countries, with higher charges applying for cards and letters sent out of Europe. As they sell thick envelopes and parcel paper, it is easy to send home books and other bulky items bought during a tour. Post offices sell cards at very reasonable rates. Stamps can naturally only be used in their country of origin so do not forget to use them before moving on!

All major courier companies such as DHL, Fedex and UPS have offices in each of the capitals.

Newspapers and magazines
The *In Your Pocket* series of mini-guides to each of the capitals provides invaluable information for each city, including listings of restaurants, museum opening hours, postage rates and details of public transport. Their irreverent style is a

pleasant contrast to the minimal official tourist material that is produced locally. Where appropriate they can be highly critical. For Tallinn, Riga and Vilnius the guides are produced locally every couple of months, so are always up to date. The Kaliningrad one is produced on an irregular basis, if at all, from Vilnius so is less reliable. Guides cost the equivalent of £1.50/US$2.50 and are available at many hotels and kiosks. They are published in full on the website www.inyourpocket.com so this site is worth consulting before departure.

The *Baltic Times* is published weekly in Riga (in English) and covers contemporary politics in the three main Baltic countries. The *Königsberg Express*, published monthly in German in Kaliningrad, fulfils a similar role there. European editions of the main American and British newspapers are available on the morning of publication in Tallinn, Riga and Vilnius. German papers occasionally reach Kaliningrad. In the winter they are sold in the Kaliningrad Hotel, in the summer also in Svetlogorsk.

The *City Paper*, published in Tallinn bimonthly, in a sense combines the *Baltic Times* and the *In Your Pocket* guides. Each issue costs about £1.30/US$2. It combines useful background articles on politics with thoughtful restaurant reviews and excellent practical information on the three main Baltic capitals. It is an excellent introduction to the area and earlier issues are covered on its website www.balticsworldwide.com.

Television

All hotels used regularly by foreign tourists now have satellite television, offering at least one English-language channel. Many offer both American and British channels, realising that most visitors have a clear preference for one or the other.

MUSEUMS

In all four countries, museums tend to have short opening hours and close at least one day a week. Monday is the most likely day for closure. Although opening times tend to change frequently, the *In Your Pocket* guides carry this information, as do the local tourist offices. It is rare for museums to open before 10.30 in the morning. Smaller ones are happy to open specially for groups and tour operators usually arrange this so that their party can have the building to themselves. This arrangement is particularly attractive at the Mentzendorf House and at the Rozentals Museum in Riga both of which can take around 25 people in comfort, but not more. Most have an admission charge, though this is rarely higher than the equivalent of £1/$1.50. Pensioners are often admitted free of charge.

HEALTH

No inoculations are required for visits to this area and hygiene standards in hotels and restaurants are high. Tap water should not be drunk in Kaliningrad but is safe elsewhere in the Baltic States. Local hospitals can be trusted to deal with any emergency; long gone are the days when foreigners flew to. Helsinki or Stockholm for any minor ailment. Sometimes treatment is free but foreigners are now normally charged a small sum to cover costs.

CRIME

This is much less of a problem than in most European capitals, although pickpockets are a threat in Tallinn and Riga old towns where the maze of small streets makes for an easy get-away. There have recently been attacks on rich foreigners in Tallinn leaving clubs late at night. Car theft is common throughout the area and cars should always be left overnight in a guarded hotel parking lot.

Passports and air tickets can fairly safely be left in hotel rooms, locked in cases. Otherwise usual sensible precautions apply. Do not take out large sums of cash when walking around the main tourist areas. What might be a modest sum to a Western tourist can be a month's pay for a local youngster so it is not surprising that some will succumb to temptation when offered the chance.

MAJOR DATES IN BALTIC HISTORY

1201	Riga founded.
1221	First recorded demonstration in Riga against occupation.
1323	Vilnius documented for the first time in a letter by Grand Duke Gediminas, who made it Lithuania's capital.
1386	Royal union of Poland and Lithuania.
1410	Polish-Lithuanian army defeats the Teutonic, ending German hegemony over the Baltic region.
1544	Founding of Königsberg University.
1569	Polish-Lithuanian Commonwealth formed.
1579	Founding of Vilnius University.
1581	Riga falls to the Polish-Lithuanian Commonwealth.
1600	Tallinn seized by the Swedes.
1621	Riga seized by the Swedes.
1710	Riga and Tallinn seized by the Russians.
1758–62	Russians occupy Königsberg for four years.
1794	Vilnius seized by the Russians.
1795	Polish-Lithuanian Commonwealth is wiped off the map; Vilnius becomes a provincial capital of the Tsarist Empire.
1812	Napoleon seizes Vilnius but his forces are driven back a few months later. Riga's wooden suburbs were burnt to prepare to defend the Old Town against Napoleon, who instead advanced towards Moscow.
1836	Richard Wagner moves to Königsberg from Magdeburg to marry and to escape his creditors. The following year he would move to Riga to take up an appointment as Director of Music (and also to be further from his creditors).
1873	First Song Festival held in Riga.
1918	Lithuanian independence is declared in Vilnius on February 16, Estonian independence declared on February 24 in Tallinn, and Latvian independence in Riga on November 18.
1920	In the Treaty of Tartu of February 2 1920, the Treaty of Moscow of July 12, and the Treaty of Riga of August 1, the Soviet Union recognises the independence of each of the Baltic States. Polish troops seize Vilnius on October 9 and it will remain under Polish occupation until autumn 1939. Kaunas is established as a temporary capital of Lithuania.
1924	On December 1 an attempted coup d'état by the Communist Party of Estonia fails.
1933	In elections held on March 5, the Nazis win 53% of the vote in Königsberg, one of the highest percentages anywhere in Germany.
1939	Molotov-Ribbentrop pact signed on August 23.

1939   On October 9, Hitler summons the Baltic-German communities of Tallinn and Riga 'back home' even though most had been settled in the Baltics for centuries.

1940   Between June 14 and 16, Tallinn, Riga and Vilnius are occupied by Soviet troops. The three Baltic States would be formally incorporated into the USSR on July 21.

1941   The Baltic capitals each fall to the German army as it advances into Russia; Vilnius on June 23, Riga on July 1 and Tallinn on August 28.

1944   Reoccupation by Soviet troops of Vilnius on July 7, of Tallinn on September 22 and of Riga on October 13.

1945   On April 10, General Lasch surrenders Königsberg to the Red Army.

1946   In July Königsberg is renamed Kaliningrad.

1947   In October the deportation begins of all remaining Germans in Kaliningrad.

1960   Tallinn, Riga and Vilnius are opened to foreign tourists for stays of no more than three nights. Kaliningrad will stay closed until 1988.

1965   A twice-weekly ferry service opens between Tallinn and Helsinki, which will remain the only link with the West until 1989.

1980   Olympic Games sailing and yachting events held in Tallinn.

1986   On June14, the first demonstration since the return of Soviet power in 1944 is held beside the Freedom Monument in Riga.

1988   On September 11 Trivimi Velliste, a future Foreign Minister, publicly demands Estonian independence in front of an audience of 300,000 at the Song Festival Amphitheatre in Tallinn.

1989   A human chain of two million people link Vilnius, Riga and Tallinn on August 23, the 50th anniversary of the signing of the Molotov-Ribbentrop Pact.

1990   March 11 The restoration of Lithuanian independence is declared in Vilnius by Vytautas Landsbergis from the same balcony used on February 16 1918.

1991   Fourteen protestors defending the Vilnius Television Tower are killed by Soviet troops on January 13. On January 20 five protestors would be similarly killed in Riga.

   August 20–21 Following the unsuccessful coup in Moscow against President Gorbachev, Estonia and Latvia declare independence. Worldwide diplomatic recognition for all three Baltic States follows within the next few days.

1993   On August 31 the last Soviet troops leave Lithuania; they would finally leave Latvia and Estonia in 1994.

2002   Eurovision Song Contest held in Tallinn. The 2003 one takes place in Riga.

2004   Likely entry of three of the Baltic States into the EU.

Tallinn

Neil Taylor

Whether approached by air, land or sea, Tallinn is immediately identifiable as a capital that looks west rather than east. The departure board at the airport lists London, Copenhagen and Stockholm but rarely St Petersburg. The boats that fill the harbour, be they massive ferries or small yachts, head for Finland and Sweden, not Russia. The traffic jams that are beginning to block the main streets are caused by Volkswagens, Land Rovers and Saabs, not by Ladas. Links with the west are celebrated, those with Russia are commemorated. In May 1998, Tallinn celebrated its 750th anniversary since on May 15 1248 it adopted Lübeck Town Law, which united most members of the Hanseatic League. A month later, as on every June 14, flags were lowered in memory of those deported to the Soviet Union on June 14 1941.

Immediately after independence Western goods started pouring into the shops, and Russian ones are now very hard to find. There is a similar reluctance to buy from any of the other former Soviet Republics. Travel agents offer the same tempting prices for holidays in Turkey, Greece and Italy that are available in western Europe, but nobody is interested in St Petersburg or the Crimea. Architecturally, with the exception of the Alexander Nevsky Cathedral, it is the Germans, Swedes and Danes who have left their imposing mark on the churches and fortifications of the Old Town. Tallinn was always ready to defend itself but in the end never did so. The nearest it came to a major battle was at the conclusion of the Northern War in 1710, but plague had reduced the population from 10,000 to 2,000 so the Swedes offered little resistance to the army of Peter the Great. It has suffered many occupations but, apart from a Soviet bombing raid in 1944, the city has not been physically harmed as no battles were ever fought there.

The division in Tallinn between what is now the Old Town on the hill (Toompea) and the newer town around the port has survived political administrations of every hue. It has divided God from Mammon, Tsarist and Soviet governors from their reluctant Estonian subjects, and now the Estonian parliament from successful bankers, merchants and manufacturers who thrive on whatever coalition happens to be in power. Tallinn has no Capitol Hill or Whitehall. The parliament building is one of the most modest in the Old Town, dwarfed by the town walls and surrounding churches. When fully restored, the Old Town will be an outstanding permanent monument to Gothic and baroque architecture, and a suitable backcloth to formal political and religious activity. Outside its formidable wall, contemporary Tallinn will change rapidly according to the demands of the new business ethos.

HISTORY

Written records on Tallinn date only from the 12th century although it is clear that a small port existed well before then. In 1219 the Danes occupied Tallinn and much of what is now northern Estonia on the pretext of spreading Christianity. The name Tallinn dates from this time and in Estonian actually means 'Danish city'. Although this name was chosen to suggest only temporary occupation, it has been maintained. The first German merchants settled in 1228 and they were to maintain their economic domination until 1919, even during the long periods of Swedish and Tsarist rule. When for instance the Swedes surrendered to the Russians in 1710, the capitulation documents confirmed that German would remain the official language of commerce. Reval, the German name for Tallinn, is sometimes seen in English publications; it probably comes from *Revala*, the old Estonian name for the surrounding area. A more colourful explanation is that it comes from the two German words *Reh* and *Fall*, meaning the falling of the deer as they attempt to escape the Danish occupation.

Peter the Great visited Tallinn on 11 different occasions, so crucial was the city as an ice-free port to his empire. He instigated the permanent expansion of Tallinn beyond the city walls by building Kadriorg Palace; the previous history of constant warfare in the vicinity of the town had led to all buildings being

A DESCRIPTION OF TALLINN IN LATE SOVIET TIMES

I spent last week in one of the saddest cities in the world, Tallinn in Estonia, famed for its medieval and 18th century architecture. Extraordinarily, this tiny backwater of the Soviet empire has been in the news recently as its people were warned by the voice of Pravda (Moscow's main daily newspaper at the time) that they were not Soviet enough.

Suddenly the secrets of this benighted land began to emerge. So last week, determined to find out about the real Estonia, I became the first Western journalist in the country for many, many months, and certainly the first since Estonia came back into the news.

At issue in Estonia is the enforced Russification of their land and the disappearance of their language and all their customs. The blue, black and white flag of independent Estonia was banished in 1944. Today the Russian flag is everywhere. So is the huge figure of 40, accompanied by a hammer and sickle to remind everyone that the yoke has been in place for 40 years and is intended to be there in excess of 40 x 40. Already more than half the population, 52%, is Russian rather than Estonian and by 1987, when the vast military harbour outside Tallinn is finished, the proportion will rise to 65%.

About 65,000 Estonians fled to the West in 1944. Thousands more were deported to remote parts of the Soviet Union and most of the present-day dissidents now rot in Russian labour camps. As Ernst Jaakson, Estonian Consul-General in New York, told me: 'There is hardly an Estonian family in existence that has not been separated from its loved ones or nearest relatives as a result of the Soviet occupation.

Kate Wharton 'The Mail on Sunday' September 2 1984

makeshift wooden houses which could easily be burnt as a preliminary defence to the city. Tallinn was then to enjoy 200 years of peace and increasing prosperity. Architecturally, though, the Old Town has always remained the centre of Tallinn and its main attraction. Gert Walter, a Baltic German who settled in East Germany and could therefore return to Tallinn during the Soviet period, describes the Old Town as having half a per cent of the surface area of Tallinn but giving it its entire magic.

The completion of the railway link with St Petersburg in 1870 turned Tallinn into a major city. The port was enlarged to handle the increasing volume of goods that could now be brought there and factories were established to take advantage of the larger markets. Fortunately they could adapt quickly in the 1920s to selling westwards rather than eastwards; a similar process took place in the early 1990s, though with more difficulty. Between 1945 and 1990 the city doubled in size and its population is now 400,000, about a third of the total population of Estonia.

PRACTICAL INFORMATION
Communications
The *Baltic Times*, published weekly on a Thursday is the best English-language source of news for the three main Baltic Republics. It also lists exhibitions and concerts. *Tallinn In Your Pocket* published every two months is invaluable for its independent, and therefore irreverant reviews on restaurants, museums and other sites. *The City Paper*, also published every two months, covers Tallinn, Riga and Vilnius together, in a similar way to *Tallinn In Your Pocket* but with the addition of political articles. European editions of British and American newspapers are on sale in Tallinn at the larger hotels on the day of publication.

Telephones
To reach Tallinn by phone from abroad, dial the Estonia country code 372, the Tallinn city code of 6 and then the six-digit number. Many Estonians now have mobile phones which are operated by a number of different companies. They each have a separate access code which is dialled after the 372 and which replaces the city code of 6. To reach phones abroad from Tallinn, dial 00 and then the relevant country code. Public phone boxes only take phone cards which can be bought at kiosks. They do not take cash or credit cards. Calls can also be made from post offices.

Post
The Central Post Office is at Narva mnt 1, opposite the Viru Hotel. It has relatively short opening hours, 08.00–20.00 Monday–Friday and 08.00–18.00 on Saturday. It is closed on Sunday. It sells postcards, exchanges money and provides telephone services. Tourists often use the post office at the top of the Old Town at Lossi Plats 4 beside the Alexander Nevsky Cathedral but this is only open 09.00–17.00 Monday–Friday.

Internet
All major hotels have a business centre offering a full range of services including internet access but the charges are high – usually around 100EEK (£4/US$6) per

half hour. Terminals are free of charge, but therefore often in use, at the airport and at the National Library. Kaubamaja, the department store at the back of the Viru Hotel, charges 40EEK (£1.75/US$3) an hour, and they are open seven days a week, Monday-Friday 09.00–21.00, Saturday 09.00–20.00 and Sunday 10.00–18.00.

Tours

For tourists who arrive without having pre-booked any excursions, the Tourist Office on the corner of Kullasepa 4/Niguliste 2 can advise on local operators with regular programmes.

Tourist information

The two 'bibles' for any English-speaking visitor are *The City Paper* and *Tallinn In Your Pocket*, both of which are published six times a year. *The City Paper* covers Riga and Vilnius as well. It mixes cerebral but amusing articles on the local political scene with reminiscences on earlier times and detailed current listings. *Tallinn In Your Pocket* has extremely detailed listings on everything in Tallinn and each edition has a supplement on another Estonian town. It is particularly helpful for opening hours and current transport information. Both publications should be available at hotel kiosks and at the airport on arrival. Their irreverence is a welcome contrast to other more turgidly written local guidebooks. Serious Baltic tour operators abroad stock these publications and both have websites (see page 215).

For general current affairs information the *Baltic Times* is a weekly political newspaper covering the three main Baltic countries. The fierce and bitter parliamentary debates it summarises contrast with the seeming stability of the world outside.

Tallinn Tourist Board has a shopfront office on the corner of Kullasepa and Niguliste which sells a good range of books, maps and cards. They always have up-to-date editions of *Tallinn In Your Pocket* and *The City Paper*. There is also a large reference folder with timetables for ferries to Finland, buses out of Tallinn and local railways. There is a similar office in the ticket hall by the harbour. This office, like all other tourist offices around Estonia, has a website: visitestonia.com. Visiting these sites before departure will save a lot of time on arrival.

Public holidays

Independence Day	February 24
Midsummer	June 23–24
Restoration of Independence Day	August 20

The Tallinn Card

Since its introduction in 1998, it has never really met the needs of many tourists. It offers free admission to most museums, free use of public transport and a free sightseeing tour in the summer. However, the price is the same on Mondays and Tuesdays, when many museums are closed, and in the winter when the sightseeing tour does not operate. Except for those who wish to make hurried visits to a large number of museums and who perhaps are staying out of the town centre, it probably makes better sense to pay each entrance or each fare individually. The cost in 2002 was 205EEK (£8/US$12) for 24 hours, 275EEK

(£11/US$16.50) for 48 hours and 325EEK (£13/US$18.00) for 72 hours. To check the current price and exactly what is offered, visit their website on www.tallinn.ee/tallinncard.

Banks and money

The Estonian currency is the kroon, abreviated as EEK. It is tied to the euro at a rate of 1∈ = 15.65EEK. In October 2002 the pound bought 24.50EEK and the dollar 16.00EEK. Exchange booths are open seven days a week in Tallinn, banks normal office hours. Banks usually offer slightly better exchange rates and they handle travellers' cheques which exchange bureaux do not. The Sampo Bank on the Town Hall Square normally gives good rates. They also have a branch outside the customs hall on the arrival side of the airport. Cash machines are available throughout the town. Kroon can be obtained abroad, through several UK banks, in Helsinki, and in the neighbouring Baltic States. Neither banks nor exchange bureaux usually charge any commission so quite small amounts of currency can be exchanged at the land border, harbour, or airport on departure.

Transport

Tallinn airport

The airport is only 3–4km from the town centre. It was built for the Moscow Olympics in 1980 (sailing events were held in the Baltic) and has adapted well to the demands of Western travellers since independence. A local bus service operates to the town centre every quarter of an hour with the final stop behind the Viru Hotel. This costs 10EEK if tickets are bought from kiosks before boarding the bus. Tickets bought from the driver cost 15EEK. The Central, Mercure, Olympic, Park and Viru Hotels operate a shuttle bus that meets each flight and the cost is 20EEK with tickets being bought from the driver. During the day taxis are easily available. They are all metered and cost about 100EEK into town. Passengers arriving on late evening flights should pre-book a transfer through their travel agent as few taxis operate then and the bus service usually finishes around 22.30. The local bus from the airport passes the main bus station (*Autobussijaam*), which is useful for those wanting to continue journeys beyond Tallinn. Local buses, transfer coaches and taxis must be paid for in local currency.

There is an **exchange bureau** air-side and also one land-side in the arrivals area. The land-side one offers much better rates for incoming travellers. For travellers arriving from Britain on an Estonian Air flight from Gatwick, the Thomas Cook exchange bureau at Gatwick handles Estonian kroon. There is a cashpoint in the arrivals area. There is no tourist information office or hotel booking agency at the airport. American and British tourists plagued by high airport taxes at home will be relieved to hear that at Tallinn airport they are minimal. Flights schedules are available on the website: www.tallinn-airport.ee.

Taxis

Taxis are all metered and start at around 20EEK. Journeys within town should not cost more than 50EEK. As taxis are reasonably priced and always metered, they can be considered for long journeys. For instance, one to Lahemaa National Park, about 100km from Tallinn, is unlikely to cost more than 750EEK.

Local buses

Many tourists to Tallinn never take either a bus or a taxi during their stay as the Old Town is very close to most of the hotels and the steep narrow roads conveniently restrict traffic to walkers. Such visitors, however, miss everything which is cheaply and easily accessible by bus outside the Old Town. There are competing bus companies so exact routes and numbers change from time to time but services are frequent and the public transport map *Tallinn Uhistranspõrdi Kaart* is reprinted sufficiently often to be up to date. In summer 2002 the flat fare was 10EEK for tickets bought from kiosks or 15EEK for tickets bought on the bus. Passes are available for stays of four days or longer. (See also *Tallinn Card* page 20) Good services operate to Pirita and Rocca Al Mare and also to the cheaper suburban hotels such as the Dzingel and Susi.

Bus tour

Currently bus route 7 is the equivalent of New York's M4 or the 38 in London as the route to take instead of an organised sightseeing tour. It starts in the affluent suburb of Nomme, then passes through the now declining 1930s commercial quarter before skirting the Old Town. It then passes the Estonian Theatre, parts of the city wall, Viru Gate, and the main post office before reaching the new commercial quarter where glass and steel are replacing concrete and brick as the main construction materials.

Car hire

This is not advisable within Tallinn. Distances are so short and parking so difficult that public transport and taxis are the sensible way to travel around.

Leaving Tallinn

The long-distance bus station (*Autobussijaam*) is on Lastekodu, off the Tartu Road which leads to the airport. The enquiry number is 643 2857 but do not expect English to be spoken. There are no printed timetables but all services are listed on a large departure board. It gives arrival times and also buses for the return journey. Write down the destination, date and time to present at the booking office since few staff speak English. As a bus or taxi takes only a few minutes from the town centre, it is advisable to go a day ahead to book a specific bus and to check timings. Whilst in the winter and mid-week it may often be easy to catch a bus without pre-booking, around the holiday periods and on less frequent services it is essential. Remember to book on an express for the longer journeys. Prices are very cheap – £6/US$9 to Saaremaa and Hiiumaa islands (including the ferry), Narva or Voru, or £4/US$6 to the nearer towns of Pärnu or Tartu. At least every two hours en route, stops of ten minutes are made which allow time for a cigarette, use of the toilets and purchase of refreshments. Smoking is not allowed on buses.

On most routes, the first bus leaves around 06.00 and the last one around 21.00. To **Tartu**, they operate every half-hour, and the journey takes 2 hours. To **Narva** (3 hours) the service is hourly. Buses go every two hours to **Pärnu** and **Viljandi** and the journey time in both cases is around two hours. Buses to **Kuressaare**, the capital of Saaremaa, operate six times a day and a space on the ferry is always guaranteed. Every town in Estonia, plus many villages such as those in Lahemaa National Park, has a bus service from Tallinn, so it is not usually necessary to change en route.

Accommodation

Tallinn now has about 60 hotels but they are often fully booked at weekends, during trade fairs and in the peak summer season. Prebooking is therefore always advisable. Specialist travel agents abroad often have access to lower prices than those quoted by the hotels directly. They may also have allocations at several hotels specifically reserved for them. February 2001 saw the opening of the Radisson and during 2002 several smaller hotels opened in the Old Town. No new major chain is planning to open during 2003 in Tallinn but it can only be a matter of time before they do.

The recommendations that follow are obviously rather arbitrary and omission of a hotel should be taken as resulting from lack of space rather than necessarily as a criticism. It can be assumed that, in all cases, rooms in these hotels have private facilities, the hotel accepts credit cards, and it has a restaurant and bar. Many hotels have saunas which guests can use free of charge. Baths are rare in Estonian hotels, even in four-star establishments, so should be specifically requested. In luxury hotels, expect to pay around £100/US$150 a night, in first class £70/US$110 and in tourist class £30–50/US$50–80. The more expensive hotels sometimes reduce prices at weekends and in July, the local holiday season, whereas the cheaper hotels usually increase them then. Prices always include buffet breakfast.

Luxury

Parkconsul Schlössle Puhavaimu 13/15; tel: 699 7700; fax: 699 7777, email: schossle@consul-hotels.com; web: www.consul-hotels.com.
For the time being, this hotel is in a class on its own, though envious competitors must soon try to emulate it. A townhouse owned by many successful Baltic Germans over the years has been converted into Tallinn's first truly luxurious hotel. At present it has just 27 rooms so still maintains the air of a gracious private residence. There is a small conference centre, but it seems incongruous. The hotel is a setting for constant but unostentatious indulgence, for cigars rather than cigarettes, for champagne rather than wine. The restaurant, like all the best ones in Tallinn, is in a cellar and has an extensive menu. For those able briefly to abandon indulgence, the hotel is within walking distance of all the attractions in the Old Town.

First class

Domina City Vana-Posti 11-13; tel: 681 3900; fax: 681 3901; email: city @domina.ee; web: dominahotels.com.
As one of the few hotels to open in 2002, the Domina with its Old Town location, its size and its standards, was bound to succeed. It is a pity that only six rooms have baths as well as showers, but the computers built into the television sets will be more than adequate compensation for most visitors. The British will like the choice of Sky as well as BBC television. The Italian management is reflected in the ample use of marble in the reception area and with the range of wildly abstract art in the restaurant. What is distinctly not Italian is the fact that two whole floors are non-smoking. Like all good restaurants in Tallinn, the one here is built into a brick-lined cellar.
Grand Hotel Tallinn Toompuiestee 27; tel: 667 7000; fax: 667 7001; email: hotel@grandhotel.ee; web: www.grandhotel.ee
Travellers who came to Tallinn in the early 1990s will remember the grim Hotel Tallinn that used to besmirch this site. Luckily all traces of it were removed before this new hotel opened in 1999. Being immediately below the Old Town and having 165 rooms, it

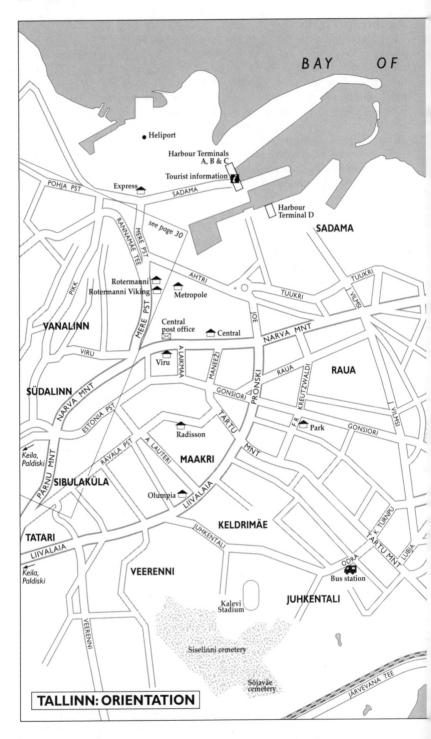

BAY OF

Heliport

Harbour Terminals
A, B & C

Tourist information

Express

POHJA PST

SADAMA

Harbour
Terminal D

SADAMA

RANNAMÄE TEE

MERE PST

PIKK

see page 30

TUUKRI

VILMSI

AHTRI

TUUKRI

Rotermanni
Rotermanni Viking

Metropole

VANALINN

JOE

VIRU

Central
post office

Central

NARVA MNT

Viru

A LAIKMAA

MANEEZI

PRONSKI

RAUA

KREUTZWALDI

RAUA

SÜDALINN

NARVA MNT

ESTONIA PST

GONSIORI

TARTU

F.R

Park

GONSIORI

VILMSI

RAVALA PST

Radisson

MNT

A LAUTERI

MAAKRI

PÄRNU MNT

Keila,
Paldiski

SIBULAKÜLA

Olümpia

LIIVALAIA

KELDRIMÄE

K. TÜRNPU

TATARI

JUHKENTALI

TARTU MNT

LUBJA

LIIVALAIA

ODRA

Keila,
Paldiski

VEERENNI

Bus station

JUHKENTALI

VEERENNI

Kalevi
Stadium

Siselinni cemetery

Sõjaväe
cemetery

JÄRVEVANA TEE

TALLINN: ORIENTATION

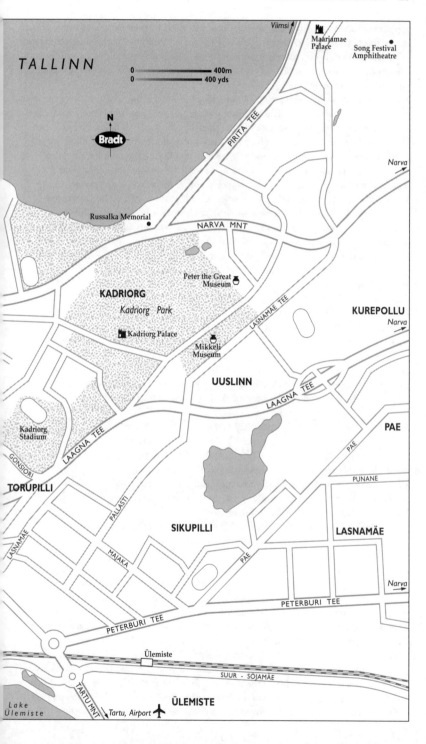

appeals both to business travellers and to tourist groups. It is tempting to spend much of a stay in this hotel in the lift, since it offers one of the best views of Toompea Hill at the top of the Old Town. British tourists are drawn by the high proportion of rooms with baths.

Olümpia Livalaia 33; tel: 631 5333; fax: 631 5325; email: olympia@revalhotels.com; web: www.revalhotels.com.

Built originally for the Olympic Games in 1980, this hotel is now the firm favourite of foreign business visitors to Tallinn. With the range of restaurants and conference facilities it offers, some never leave the hotel during their stay in Tallinn. They are often joined by the local ex-pat community which has a particular affinity for the 60s' music played in the Bonnie and Clyde nightclub. At weekends and during the summer, rates drop to attract tourists paying their own way. All 400 rooms are now at least of four-star standard and reception staff work very quickly during the arrival and departure 'rush hours'. The restaurant on the top floor offers excellent views of the Old Town and many rooms do so as well. The newspaper shop always stocks up-to-date British newspapers, a rarity in Tallinn. The hotel operates its own bus service to the airport, particularly useful for passengers arriving on late night flights when taxis at the airport are in short supply. Tourists who want to arrive or leave in greater style hire the hotel's 9m-long Lincoln which costs about £50/US$80 an hour.

Reval Park Kreutzwaldi 23; tel: 630 5305; fax: 630 5315; email: sales@revalhotels.com; web: www.revalhotels.com.

Formerly the dreaded Kungla Hotel which could barely claim two-star status, the site transformed itself within a few weeks during the summer of 1997 and has never looked back. It has pioneered rooms for non-smokers, for the disabled and for those with allergies as well as round-the-clock gambling, fortunately in a casino with a separate entrance. Rooms are larger here than in most other hotels, and the restaurant has very low prices for excellent food. Walking to the Old Town is just about possible, and essential as the surroundings are very bleak. The guarded car park is free of charge to hotel guests.

St Petersbourg Rataskaevu 7; tel: 628 6500; fax: 628 6565; email: stpetersbourg@consul-hotels.com; web: www.consul-hotels.com.

The St Petersbourg (spelt as in the Estonian) is under the same management as the deluxe Schlössle Hotel and suits those who want a comfortable Old Town address but who do not miss luxury. Its location near to many famous clubs and restaurants appeals to visitors who can dispense with sleep for much of the night. It is one of the very few hotels in Tallinn to offer a baby-sitting service.

Santa Barbara Roosikrantsi 2a; tel: 631 3991; fax: 631 3992; email: st_barbara.res@scandic-hotels.ee; web: www.scandic-hotels.com.

An austere limestone façade from the turn of the century hides a very professional operation which is run by the Scandic group who also operate the nearby Palace Hotel. The cellar restaurant is completely German, with no intrusion from Estonia or anywhere else. It has 53 rooms so staff get to know all the guests, many of whom are now regulars, which makes the hotel difficult to book for first-time visitors.

Scandic Palace Vabaduse Valjak; tel: 640 7300; fax: 640 7299; email: palace@scandic-hotels.com; web: www.scandic-hotels.com

The hotel brochure claims it has offered 'excellent service since 1937' and this is probably true. Although many other hotels now match its facilities, Estonians are very loyal to it as the hotel was one of the few links from the first independence period that remained throughout the Soviet era. Embassies were briefly set up in the hotel in 1991 before foreign legations could reclaim their pre-war buildings. It is now equally conveniently situated for tourists interested in the Old Town and business visitors needing the government ministries. In 1997 President Meri opened the new Presidential Suite which will doubtless remain one of the most expensive in Tallinn at £250/US$400 per night, but the remaining 86 rooms are more modestly priced. The hotel is run by the Scandic Hotel Group that also operates the Santa Barbara in Tallinn, the Ranna in Pärnu and the Karupesa in Otepää.

Viru Viru Valjak 4; tel: 630 1390; fax: 630 1303; email: reservation@viru.ee; web: www.viru.ee.

Being the centre of the tourism trade for much of the Soviet era, the enormous Viru initially found it hard to redefine its role in the face of competition and ever-rising standards. By 2000 it had finally undergone a complete renovation and can now serve both business clients and fastidious tourists. It has become very biased towards Finnish clients, some of whom can provide unwanted liveliness late on Friday and Saturday evenings. Its location is excellent for the Old Town and for local shops. Tourists determined to have a bath rather than a shower are more likely to succeed here. Although the hotel has over 400 rooms, construction began in 2002 of an extension into Viru Square.

Tourist class

Central Narva mnt 7; tel: 633 9800; fax: 633 9900; email: central@revalhotels.com; web: www.revalhotels.com

This hotel became an immediate favourite of tour operators from abroad when it opened in 1995 as it had no Soviet past to eliminate. Staff were immediately aware of the demands and eccentricities of Western tourists and the Primavera Restaurant was, and still is, one of the best Italian restaurants in Tallinn. The hotel offers disabled access and one room in the new wing is adapted for use by disabled guests. It is within easy walking distance of the Old Town and the main post office. Having opened in what was then a rundown part of town, the surrounding area is becoming increasingly attractive, with more shops and restaurants opening every year. The supermarket in the hotel complex is particularly convenient.

Dzingel Manniku 89; tel: 610 5201; fax: 610 5245; email: hotell@dzingel.ee; web: www.zingel.ee.

Situated in Nomme, Tallinn's most exclusive suburb, the Dzingel is in fact one of its simplest hotels. Regular long-stay visitors find its facilities perfectly adequate in view of the low prices charged, and many tourists are happy both in winter and in summer with its quiet location beside a pinewood. The bus journey into the town centre takes about 20 minutes. It is one of the few hotels where the staff happily and openly speak Russian although they can manage basic English. The restaurant is dull and surprisingly expensive. There is a late-night supermarket in the same block which can provide the ingredients for a varied picnic.

Mihkli Endla 23; tel: 666 4800; fax: 666 4888.

The location on one of the main roads leading from the town centre is certainly drab and the hotel itself used to be as well. From around 1998 however, serious attempts were made to improve the décor and the staff and these have been largely successful. It is within walking distance of the Old Town, and on the doorstep of the National Library. Long-stay visitors are now here, always a good sign, and the repeat business that the hotel enjoys is also evidence of a complete turn-around.

Old Town Maestro Suur-Karja 10; tel: 626 2000; fax: 631 3333; email: maestro@maestrohotel.ee; web: www.maestrohotel.ee.

Having opened in 2001, this small hotel now has its regulars who want straightforward furnishings, peace and quiet and yet an Old Town location. Rooms are much bigger than might be expected from a converted town house but the lift is much smaller – it can only take one person with a case at a time. The road is traffic-free, but that does mean wheeling cases along the cobbles on arrival and departure. The reception area doubles up as a bar, which adds to the family atmosphere. The sauna and the business centre are surprisingly side by side on the top floor.

Rotermanni Tel: 613 7900; fax: 613 7999; email: hotell@rotermanni.ee; web: www.rotermanni.ee; and **Rotermanni Viiking** Tel: 660 1934; fax: 613 7901; email: bookings@vikinghotels.ee; web: www.vikinghotel.ee.

These two hotels share the same address, Mere pst 6a, and are very similar. Just 200m from the Viru Gates, this modest complex opened in summer 1998 and immediately became popular amongst individual tourists. It has been converted from an abandoned factory site and both hotels have about 35 rooms. Fortunately only the exterior shows signs of this past. Estonia, like Britain, is rapidly replacing losses in manufacturing with profits in tourism. From 2002, the surrounding area was undergoing considerable redevelopment. Be ready for construction noise, but also for exciting buildings next door.

Susi Peterburi 48; tel: 630 3200; fax: 630 3400; email: susi@susi.ee; web: www.susi.ee. An estate agent would probably describe the location as 'unprepossessing' since it is surrounded by factories and a petrol station, and is on the wide St Petersburg motorway. It is literally the high-point of Tallinn at 55m above sea level. On May 14 1343, the St George's Day rebellion took place here. It had started further north on April 23 and this was the nearest point to Tallinn that Estonian forces would reach. Over 10,000 were killed in a desperate attempt to overthrow the Teutonic Knights. A plaque in the hotel lobby commemorates the battle. The hotel is more comfortable and more modern than any of the other tourist-class hotels outside the centre and is easily accessible by tram. The pictures displayed on its staircase put many of Tallinn's museums to shame. There are oils, lithographs, and watercolours showing contemporary and historical Tallinn; other pictures are of country scenes. They are well-lit and sensibly framed and of course can be seen 24 hours a day. Should the lift break down, this gallery is more than adequate compensation.

Taanilinna Uus 6; tel: 640 6700; fax: 646 4306; email: info@taanilinna.ee; web: www.taanilinna.ee.

Perhaps they were daring, perhaps they were foolish, but in June 2002 Tallinn saw its first hotel with Russian-speaking reception staff and with brochures in English and Russian. The spelling 'Hotell' was the only concession made to Estonia at the time, although the website now has an Estonian section. Visitors who do not care about this will like the prices, the location in one of the few quiet streets in the Old Town and the use of wood rather than of stone. The terrace sadly looks out on to the back of a supermarket and a dreary block of flats, but in future years this view may well change. The wine-cellar is an unexpected bonus in a hotel of this size and category, but most welcome given the lack of other watering holes in the immediate vicinity.

Vana Wiru Viru 11; tel: 669 1500 fax: 669 1501; email: hotel @vanawiru.ee; web: www.vanawiru.ee.

Viru Street is always full of tourists but most will not know of the existence of this hotel as its entrance is at the back. It was one of the very few hotels to open in Tallinn during 2002. Its vast marble lobby suggests luxury but in fact the 80 rooms are of a standard size and mostly with showers rather than baths. Few have good views, but with a location beside the City Wall, one can forgive anything. Groups will like the convenient coach park right beside the entrance.

Food and drink

There is now such a choice of restaurants in Tallinn that it is invidious to attempt a short list. Every major nation is represented, and more unusual ones include Argentina, Georgia, Lithuania and Scotland. Hawaiian and Thai food appeared for the first time in 2000, Czech and Arabic food followed in 2002 and by then Russian food had also staged a come-back, having been completely rejected in the years immediately following independence.

Detailed descriptions of restaurants appear in *The City Paper*, shorter ones in *Tallinn In Your Pocket*. A dark entrance, down poorly maintained stairs in a side street, is usually a clear lead to good food and value. Bright lights at street level should be avoided. Exploration need no longer be limited to the Old Town; competition there is driving many new entrants to open up in the suburbs. At the time of writing, nobody has opened a revivalist Soviet restaurant, though the success of such ventures in Riga and in former East Berlin must in due course tempt some embittered members of the Russian-speaking community in Tallinn. Pleasant cafés have been mentioned when they coincide with a walking itinerary, as most fortunately do. Most of the following restaurants have been open for several years and are popular with tourists, ex-pats and local residents. Apologies in advance to the many other excellent restaurants which, with more space, would also have been included.

Balthasar Raekoja Plats 11; tel: 627 6400; web: www.restaurant.ee. Garlic dominates every course here, even the ice-cream, but above all in the salads. Whilst other dishes do appear on the menu, they tend to be as appetising as a vegetarian option in a steakhouse. Opening in early 2000, the restaurant took over the top floor of the former pharmacy (see page 38) and has kept as much of the original wooden furnishings as was practical. With its views over the Town Hall Square, it is tempting to linger here but it also offers a quiet respite over lunch between morning and afternoon sightseeing tours. The range of short drinks at the bar can be equally tempting at other times of day.

Controvento Katariina käjk; tel: 644 0470; web: www.controvento.ee. Uniquely in Tallinn, this restaurant could maintain a review written when it first opened in 1992. It has maintained the same menu, the same décor and probably many of the same clients, who want no-nonsense home cooking in an Italian bistro and no attempts to emulate temporary culinary fads. Prices have had to increase somewhat but they remain modest in comparison with the competition in the Old Town.

Eeslitall (The Donkey's Stable) Dunkir 4; tel: 631 3755; web: www.eeslitall.ee. In the early days after independence, this restaurant was an immediate indication of changing times. Whilst its easy-going service, French sauces, enormous menus and wine-lists may now seem normal for Tallinn, it then set a trend which other restaurants took several years to emulate. Young and old both dine happily here (an unusual combination in Tallinn), although only the young would consider staying in the spartan hostel of the same name upstairs.

Eesti Maja Lauteri 1; tel: 645 5252; web: www.eestimaja.ee. Do not expect quick service here or even staff with much English, but instead be ready for enormous portions and rich food at each course. It will be hard to spend more than £6/US$10 a head and many eat their fill for much less. The vegetable soup makes a good meal in itself at lunch time. The building also houses *Global Estonian*, an English-language bi-annual magazine well worth buying for the tough interviews they give to local politicians willing to meet them.

Karl Friedrich Raekoja Plats 5; tel: 627 2413. The grand location on Town Hall Square might suggest ostentation and prices to match but fortunately this has not happened. Each floor caters for a different age-group but it is the top floor that is recommended. Oldies should book well in advance for a table overlooking the square and enjoy a lingering lunch or dinner. Its fish salads are to be recommended and it has its own beer, called Karl Friedrich. The long walk up and down is well worthwhile.

Klafira Vene 4; tel: 667 5144. If Soviet Russia has been banished for good from Estonia, the Tsarist aristocracy is making an effective come-back here instead. Perhaps they were wise to wait until 2000, nine years after the re-establishment of Estonian independence, before doing so. Their food is strictly Russian, their wine is sensibly French. That rich Estonians are firstly willing to come and then secondly even to speak Russian to the staff shows the high standards the restaurant has set. Allow a full evening here and do not consider the cost beforehand. It will be expensive by Estonian standards, but not by London or New York ones.

Kuldse Notsu Korts (The Golden Pig) Dunkri 8; tel 628 6567. Although this restaurant belongs to the luxury St Petersbourg Hotel next door, the two establishments have nothing in common. This country restaurant, with low ceilings and long wooden tables, seems pleasantly incongruous in the middle of the Old Town. However this is precisely its appeal. It offers surprisingly varied Estonian fare – thick mushroom soups, pork in innumerable guises and apples in almost as many. Drink apple juice or beer rather than wine. Few tourists venture in, but many Estonians do and this must be its best recommendation.

Must Lammas (The Black Sheep) Avatud 12–23; tel: 644 2031; web: www.mustlammas.ee. For years this Georgian restaurant was called Exit but it changed its name in early 2001. Luckily little else has changed. All guests are greeted with portions of firewater and strips of salted beef as the menus are handed out. Eat meat, meat and more meat all evening, topped if you did not have lunch with some ice-cream drenched in brandy. Start with stuffed vine leaves and move on to beef and pork stews. Vegetarians keep out.

Olde Hansa Vanaturg 1; tel: 627 9020; web: www.oldehansa.com. Ignore the silly name and enjoy the candles (there is no electric light). Some tables are for two, but don't come here for a quiet, intimate evening. This is really a party venue so come as a group and with a very empty stomach. Portions are enormous, even for soup and ice-cream.

Primavera Narva 7; tel: 633 9891. The bland façades that still blight much of this road out of Tallinn hide a number of bars and restaurants. This one has already been mentioned under the Central Hotel as it is in the same building, but a second listing needs no apology. Mediocre Italian food is spreading across Estonia at an alarming rate, but standards here for all courses remain excellent, even if the quality of the wine does not always match that of the food.

Toomkooli Toomkooli 13; tel: 644 6613. Those who are not deterred by the awkward location at the back of the Old Town are rewarded on arrival with an extensive international menu and wine list but prices that have stayed Estonian. Minimal music and very heavy wooden chairs give a more formal air to the surroundings than is now common in many Tallinn restaurants, but in a town now so geared to the young, this should be taken as a compliment.

Vanaema Juures (Grandma's Place) Rataskaevu 10/12; tel: 631 3928. This is probably Tallinn's most famous restaurant, but not even a visit from Hillary Clinton has gone to its head. The valid and repeated descriptions – good home cooking, a traditional décor, a cosy atmosphere – degenerate into cliché but few would dispute them. The furnishings and photographs from the previous independence period (1918–40), together with discreet music from that time, deter the young and raucous, but others will immediately appreciate the originality of total Estonian surroundings.

Entertainment

Young people congregate at Linnahall, the Concert Hall beside the Heliport near the harbour. Live pop music is staged most evenings.

Classical concerts are held in the Old Town Hall, the Estonia Concert Hall, the House of Blackheads and in St Nicholas Church. In most cases tickets are only sold on the day or the day before the concert so there is no need to prebook from abroad.

Films are always subtitled and never dubbed so tourists can see films missed at home without any problem. The Soprus Cinema in the Old Town at Vana-Post 8 is easily accessible from many hotels.

Shopping

Monday to Friday most shops open 10.00–18.00 and on Saturday they close earlier, usually around 16.00. On Sunday they stay closed. However, those in the Old Town of interest to tourists open in the summer 10.00–19.00 seven days a week. Supermarkets open seven days a week, usually 09.00–21.00.

For **books** and postcards, the Tourist Information Centre on the corner of Kullasepa and Niguliste has a good selection, all reasonably priced. The widest selection of books in English on Estonia is at Apollo Raamatumaja Viru 23, web: www.apollo.ee.

A one-stop shop for **souvenirs**, since it stocks linen, woollen jerseys, ceramics, and wooden toys, is Puupood, Lai 5. Although in the Old Town, it is just off the main tourist circuit so prices are very reasonable.

For those who can restrict themselves to wooden dolls, Nukupood on Town Hall Square (Raekoja Plats 18) is conveniently located and has an enormous choice.

Kaubamaja is Tallinn's largest **department store** and is situated halfway between the Viru and Radisson Hotels at Gonsiori 2. It will supply any forgotten toilet article or item of clothing, and is worth visiting for its CDs of Estonian music and for its porcelain.

Medical services

Emergency services Fire: 112; Ambulance: 112; Police: 110.
Dentist Kentmanni Hambaravi, Kenmanni 11a; open 08.30–20.00 seven days a week.
Hospital Tallinn Central Hospital, Ravi 18.
Pharmacy None are open 24 hours, but Koduapteek, in the Kaubamaja Department Store, is open seven days a week; Mon–Fri 10.00–21.00, Sat 10.00–20.00 and Sun 10.00–18.00.

Embassies

Canada Toom-Kooli 13; tel: 627 3311, fax 627 3312
Ireland Demini Building, Viru 1; tel: 681 1888; fax: 681 1899
Latvia Tõnismägi 10; tel: 646 1313; fax: 631-1366
Lithuania Uus 15; tel: 631 4030; fax: 641 2013
UK Wismari 6; tel: 667 4700; fax: 667 4723
USA Kentmanni 20; tel: 668 8100; fax: 668 8134

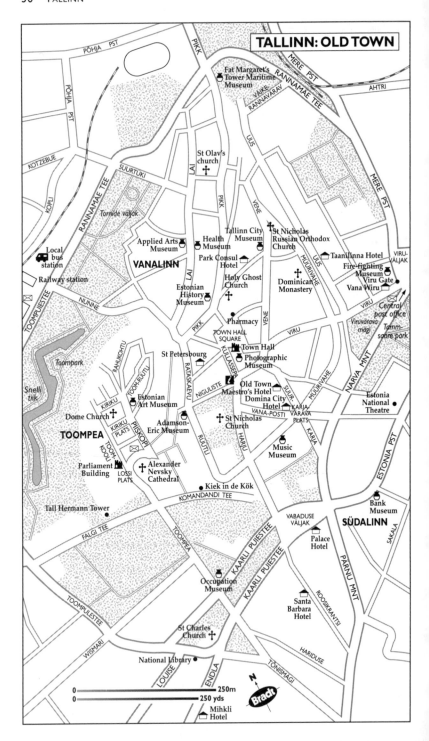

TALLINN: OLD TOWN

Fat Margaret's Tower Maritime Museum

St Olav's church

Tornide väljak

Applied Arts Museum

Local bus station

Railway station

VANALINN

Health Museum

Tallinn City Museum

St Nicholas Russian Orthodox Church

Park Consul Hotel

Holy Ghost Church

Dominican Monastery

Taanilinna Hotel

Fire-fighting Museum

Viru Gate

Vana Wiru

VIRU-VÄLJAK

Central post office

Estonian History Museum

Pharmacy

TOWN HALL SQUARE

Viruvärava mägi

Tammsaare park

Toompark

St Petersbourg

Town Hall

Photographic Museum

Snelli tiik

St Nicholas Church

Old Town Maestro's Hotel

Domina City Hotel

Estonia National Theatre

Estonian Art Museum

Dome Church

TOOMPEA

Adamson-Eric Museum

Music Museum

Parliament Building

Alexander Nevsky Cathedral

Kiek in de Kök

KOMANDANDI TEE

Tall Hermann Tower

Bank Museum

SÜDALINN

VABADUSE VÄLJAK

Palace Hotel

Occupation Museum

Santa Barbara Hotel

St Charles Church

National Library

0 ___ 250m
0 ___ 250 yds

N

Bradt

Mihkli Hotel

Places of worship

Church services are held in English every Sunday at the Holy Ghost Church (Pühavaimu).

WHAT TO SEE

Tourists tend to concentrate on the Old Town but many modern buildings are of interest too. The main sights in the Old Town can be covered in one day but more time would be needed for other visits. A route for a day-long walking tour is suggested and then another day should be allowed for Pirita and Kadriorg. Several sights outside Tallinn warrant a half-day on their own.

Museums usually close on Mondays though some close on Tuesdays as well. Opening hours tend to be 11.00–17.00, but for pre-booked groups they can open specially on closed days. Admission charges vary between 5EEK and 30EEK so are still quite low by Western standards.

A walking tour through Tallinn

The tour starts at the final Soviet architectural legacy to Estonia – the **National Library** (Eesti Rahvusraamatukogu) – begun in 1986 and completed in 1993. It is situated on the intersection of Endla and Tonismägi close to the Mihkli and Santa Barbara hotels. Its predecessor was opened in 1918 in the parliament building on Toompea and had 2,000 books, a number that only increased to 6,000 during the 1930s. After World War II, the history of the library mirrored that of the country as a whole. Its bleakest period was until 1953 when most of the collection was of Russian books translated into Estonian. On Stalin's death, the library was renamed after one of Estonia's most famous authors, Friedrich Kreutzwald, a clear sign of a more liberal climate. By 1967 funds were specifically allocated for books in the Estonian language and in 1988, shortly before this new building was supposed to open, it was renamed the National Library and the formerly restricted sections were opened to all. The design seems to symbolise *glasnost*: light streams in through many massive windows, and large open shelves display a wide cross-section of the two million books stored there. It will remain a grandiose memorial to massive public sector investment. Yet it was almost not completed. The fading Soviet government was not eager to continue funding projects outside Russia and the new Estonian one was faced with bills it could not pay. On June 28 1989, between four and five thousand volunteers joined the building works under the slogan 'Dig a grave for Stalinism'. The director, Ivi Eenmaa, later to become mayor of Tallinn, single-handedly fought Moscow and then each new Estonian government for adequate funds and was finally able to open the library on February 22 1993, two days before National Day.

Day tickets can be bought in the entrance hall, which is decorated with prints by one of Estonia's most famous contemporary artists, Eduard Wiiralt. To encourage regular use, the library has several music rooms, shops, a café and even piped music. On a bitter winter's day, tourists may wish to await a change in the weather amongst the many English-language books and journals now available there. As one of Estonia's many preparations for entry into the EU, there are also large French, German and Scandinavian reading rooms. Normally, however, visitors should head straight for the 8th floor to view two contrasting Tallinns. To the north and east is the Tallinn of the posters – the spires, turrets and golden domes. In the other direction is a part of the town best seen at this distance, consisting of abandoned factories and fading tower blocks, with minimal intrusion of any colour.

Cross the road to **St Charles's Church** (Kaarli Kirik). In its almost Episcopalian simplicity, it is the perfect antidote to what is to come later in the walk. It is a massive and austere late 19th-century limestone building which seats 1,500 people and is the centre of the Estonian Orthodox Church. At a time when Russian rule was becoming more oppressive, its size discreetly symbolised Estonian nationalism. The name comes from an original wooden church built in the late 17th century during the reign of the Swedish King Charles XI. Although the church took 20 years to build, the large altar fresco was completed in ten days in 1879 by the well-known artist Johann Köler.

On leaving the church, turn right into Kaarli and then take the first road on the left, Toompea. The Occupation Museum is due to open at this crossroads in summer 2003. At the first crossroads, note the simple **monument** to August 20 1991, the date Estonia declared independence during the failed Moscow coup. Had it been necessary, Estonians were ready to use the walls and towers to defend the Old Town from possible Soviet attack but the quick collapse of the coup and the immediate recognition by the USSR of Estonian independence prevented this. Looking ahead is a monument that dates from the 15th century, **Pikk Hermann** (Tall Hermann Tower). It has withstood numerous invasions and remains intact. Its height of nearly 50m is supported by foundations 15m deep. The first Estonian flag was flown from here in 1884, 34 years before the country was to become independent. Subsequent conquerors always marked their success by raising a flag here. A German guidebook printed in 1942 lists 12 major dates in Tallinn's history, the last being August 28 1941 when the German flag was raised over Pikk Hermann. During the Soviet occupation, the Estonian SSR flag was flown, but the Estonian national flag returned in 1989. It is raised at sunrise and lowered at sunset, except at midsummer when it is not lowered at all on the night of June 23/24. The blue in the flag represents the sky, black the soil, and white the aspirations of the Estonian people.

Turn right down the hill (Komandandi) to **Kiek in de Kök** (Peep in the Kitchen). The reason for the name becomes obvious as one climbs the 45m to the sixth floor and peers into more and more houses; only the steeples of St Nicholas and St Olav are higher. From its initial construction in the 15th century until completed in the late 17th century, the tower grew in height and width with walls and floors as thick as 4m, but ironically, after a Russian attack in 1577, it never saw military action again. The last time it was prepared for war was in the 1850s when the Russians feared a British invasion during the Crimean War. On the top floor, note the model of the 'plague doctor' with a waxed tunic and cape impregnated with herbs. He carries a cane with which to touch patients to avoid any risk of infection. The main exhibition on the top three floors covers Tallinn's military history. The lower floors are now used as an art gallery. Kiek in de Kök does not have any catering, but the nearest tower to it, **Megedi**, can be recommended in this respect. This tower, like most in the city wall, dates from the late 14th century and was continually enlarged during the 15th century. From around 1800 when its defensive potential declined, it was converted into a barracks. In 1980, the top floor became a café which uses the name Megedi, and the ground floor a restaurant, called Neitsitorn.

On leaving Kiek in de Kök turn back up the hill and turn right into Toompea, which ends in the square between the **Parliament building** and the **Alexander Nevsky Cathedral**. The juxtaposition of these two buildings appropriately contrasts official Estonian and Russian architecture. The one is simple, small and functional, the other elaborate, and deliberately powerful. Ironically, the Tsarist power that it represented was to last only a further 17 years. Entering the cathedral represents a symbolic departure from Estonia. No-one speaks Estonian and no books are sold in Estonian. It is a completely Russian architectural outpost dominating the Tallinn skyline and was built between 1894 and 1900 at a time when the Russian Empire was determined to stifle the burgeoning nationalistic movements in Estonia. It was provocatively named after Alexander Nevsky since he had conquered much of Estonia in the late 13th century. The icons, the mosaics and the 15-ton bell were all imported from St Petersburg. Occasionally plans are discussed, as they were in the 1930s, for the removal of the cathedral as it is so architecturally and politically incompatible with everything else in Toompea, but it is unlikely that any government would risk the inevitable hostility that would arise amongst the Russian-speaking population of Tallinn.

The Parliament building, most of which dates from 1921, is one of very few in the Old Town to have seen frequent reconstruction, the last one resulting from a fire in 1917 which may have been started by the Bolsheviks. The façade is a simple classicist one, and all the stone and wooden materials are local. Earlier buildings on this site had usually served as a governor's residence although, in the late 19th century, the building became a prison. The earliest fort was built on this site in 1227 and the northern and western walls date from this time.

The most famous room within the building is the White Hall, with a balcony overlooking the square. The current décor, with white cornices and a yellow ceiling, dates from 1935. From 1922 there had been a more elaborate neo-classicist design, including ceiling mirrors and elaborate panelling. The current Parliamentary Chamber was rebuilt in 1998 and members of the public can attend debates there, but no interpretation from Estonian is provided. There are 101 members of Parliament, representing ten parties and around 20% of its members are women. Visitors are forbidden to enter 'with cold steel, firearms and pungent-smelling substances'.

Continue up the hill along Toomkooli with the post office on your right. By the end of 2003, this street should be completely restored, the first one to be back to its 1920s glory. Straight ahead, on Kiriku Square, is the **Dome Church** (Toomkirik), sometimes called St Mary's Cathedral. Work started soon after the Danish invasion in the early 13th century and the first church was consecrated by King Waldemar II in 1240. It was slowly enlarged over the next four centuries as funds became available but much of the interior was destroyed in the fire of 1684 which devastated the whole of the Old Town. The Swedish King Charles XI imposed a special tax for the rebuilding of Tallinn and within two years the church had been largely restored. The baroque spire was added in 1778 so in all the church has an architectural history of over 600 years. The altarpiece, painted in 1866, is the work of the Baltic-German artist Eduard von Gebhardt. The organ, probably the most powerful in Estonia, was made in Frankfurt an der Oder in 1913 so is the last to have been imported from Germany before World War I.

The Dome Church was the religious centre for the main families of the Tallinn Baltic-German community; their coats of arms cover the church walls and their tombstones cover the floor, although a few are of Swedish origin. At the back of the church are two tombstones commemorating the butchers and the shoemakers guilds. The most impressive tomb, which is beside the altar, is that of the French mercenary Pontus de la Gardie, who served in the Swedish army in many battles with the Russians. In the north aisle is a monument to Samuel Greig, a Scots admiral who served in the Tsarist navy from 1763 until his death in 1788. The inscription expresses the sorrow of Catherine II at his death. Like many Scots predecessors and successors, he had a distinguished career in this navy. He helped to destroy the Turkish fleet at the battle of Chesme in 1770 and to build up Kronstadt into a major naval base. Next to this monument is one to Adam von Krusenstern, the Baltic-German who led the first Russian expedition to sail around the world, in 1803. Note the two globes, both of which omit New Zealand.

Turning left out of the church, the **Estonian Art Museum** dominates the opposite side of Kiriku Plats. Although it looks as though it was built as an art gallery, it was first used in the 19th century as the headquarters of the Estonian Knighthood, a major business guild. During the first independence period (1920–40) it was the Foreign Ministry and for much of the Soviet period served as the National Library. The names of the 19th- and 20th-century artists displayed here are sadly unknown outside Estonia, but many styles will be recognised by visitors. Both in the Tsarist period and under independence, most Estonian artists of note studied in Paris so the prevalent style there is reflected in their pictures. Konrad Mägi (1878–1925) is the most famous landscape artist and his pictures here are of many regions in Estonia. There is no catalogue available in English at present, perhaps because the collection may move to a new National Museum planned to open in the Kadriorg Park area in 2005 or 2006.

Turning sharp right from the museum along Toom Rüütli leads, after 150m, to the main viewpoint across Tallinn. It is inevitably crowded during the tourist season so an alternative can be recommended along Rahukohtu, on the corner of Rüütli. Rahukohtu also starts on the right-hand side of the gallery. To reach the lower town, it is necessary in either case to return along Piiskopi towards the Russian cathedral and then to walk down the steps of Lühike Jalg ('Short Leg'), rather a misnomer as there are in fact about 100 steps. At the top, though, are several tempting cafés, souvenir shops and well-maintained toilets which can provide a respite before continuing the walk. Before starting the descent, look to the left along Pikk Jalg ('Long Leg'). The façade which commands one of the best views over Tallinn is modelled on the main building of Tartu University. Perhaps appropriately, in view of the current strength of the Estonian economy, this imposing building houses the Ministry of Finance.

On the right at the end of Lühike Jalg is the **Adamson-Eric Museum**. Adamson-Eric (1902–68) was without doubt the most famous Estonian artist who worked during both the independence period and the Soviet era. This house has no links with him, although before being used as a museum it did have workshops for coppersmiths. The museum opened in 1983 and the collection is based on around 1,000 works bequeathed by his widow. These cover his whole life in both painting and applied art. Gifts from abroad have recently been added to the collection. Labels are in English. Adamson-Eric's parents were able to pay for long periods of study during the 1920s in both Paris and Berlin. Elements of Fauvism and Cubism can be seen in many of his pictures but he was equally drawn to the Bauhaus and worked closely with Walter Gropius, George Grosz and Otto Dix. On his return to Estonia he first specialised in portraits, then added landscapes and broadened into applied arts. In this field, his work became as diverse as his painting. Around 1930, he began with tapestries and textiles and then added ceramics and metalwork to his range. Shortly before the war, he diversified even more, starting to work with leather and to design stage sets. He retreated with the Soviet army in 1941 and managed to maintain his artistic integrity despite the stringent demands of Soviet officialdom. With the inevitable lack of materials for applied art at this time, he concentrated again on painting. In 1949, the political tide finally turned against him and he was expelled from the Communist Party, forced to give up his posts and sent into factory work. Although released in 1953 on Stalin's death, his health had deteriorated and he suffered a stroke in 1955. His reaction was simply to learn to paint as well with his left hand as he had previously done with his right! His health slowly improved and he was able to add porcelain painting and tile design to his work in the field of applied art. He remained active until shortly before his death in 1968.

Continuing down the hill, the steps become a road which continues to a junction. To the left is Rataskaevu and to the right, Rüütli, both roads which house some of Tallinn's most famous restaurants. On the corner of Lühike Jalg and Rataskaevu is **Bakhos**, one of Tallinn's best-value wine merchants. Many are the angry tourists who have shopped abroad at a so-called duty-free shop only to find the same bottle here at half the price. Ahead is **St Nicholas Church, Niguliste**. It is unusual in Tallinn in having been a military installation as well as a church with ample hiding places and secret exits to the city walls. In common though with other churches, it was first built in the 13th century and then expanded over the next 400 years. The original spire dated from 1696 and, being outside the town walls, the church was spared from the 1684 fire. It was, however, badly damaged during the Soviet air raid on Tallinn of March 9 1944 and the spire was only restored in 1984. Fortunately the carvings, chandeliers and pictures, many dating from the 16th century, had been removed before the raid. They are all now on display again and are particularly valuable given that so much similar work was either destroyed in the 1684 fire or suffered from neglect in more recent times. The interior of the church was slowly restored during the Soviet period from 1953 onwards. A small exhibition describes this work but captions are only in Russian and Estonian. St Nicholas has kept its role as a museum and concert hall so has not been reconsecrated. The life of St Nicholas is portrayed in the altarpiece, over 6m wide and painted in Lübeck by Hermen Rode between 1478 and 1482. Note the one very modern addition – a stained glass window by the contemporary artist, Rait Prääts, whose glass can also be seen at the National Library and the Sakala Conference Centre.

On leaving the church, turn right to the memorial to the writer Eduard Vilde (1865–1933). The illustrations depict scenes from his novels and plays. The two stones represent an open book. Proceed down the steps to Harju and then turn right again. This bombed site has deliberately been left as it was after the raid of March 9 1944. The inscription commemorates the 463 people killed by the raid. Returning along Harju and then Kullassepa brings one into Raekoja Plats, or Town Hall Square. Just before reaching the square, it is worth turning right for a few minutes into the small alley, Raekoja. The building on the right, which now houses the **Photographic Museum**, was the town's main prison until the early 19th century. Estonia has always had a strong photographic tradition and this museum displays not only cameras produced in the country but photographs from the 19th and early 20th century. It is fortunate that many pictures from the first independence period have survived. The basement is a gallery for the display and sale of contemporary photographs.

Town Hall Square (Raekoja Plats) is similar to many in northern Germany as it was the commercial centre for the Baltic-Germans. In the 16th century, the Germans accounted for about 1,500 of Tallinn's total population of around 5,000. They maintained all positions of authority, ruling from the Town Hall and the surrounding buildings. The square was the centre for all major events in the town, happy and tragic. Carnivals, weddings and Christmas have all been regularly celebrated here and the Tallinn Old Days Festival, held each year in early June, recreates the carnival atmosphere with its musical and artistic events. What was probably the world's first Christmas tree was displayed here in 1441. Yet the square was also the site for frequent executions and floggings, its grimmest day being in 1806 when 72 peasants were executed following a failed uprising. Nowadays it is hard to imagine such a background as work and punishment have given way to total relaxation. Cafés surround the square and spread into it during the summer. From 2001, a Christmas market has taken place here throughout December. The Café Tristan and Isolde, in the Town Hall building but with an entrance from the square, is hardly noticed by tourists so offers a quiet respite from all the activity elsewhere, as well as much lower prices. One of the few buildings on the square that has kept its original function is the **pharmacy**, which dates from 1422. Tour guides often like to point out that this is 70 years before Columbus discovered America. The coat of arms of the Burchart family, who ran the pharmacy for 400 years, can be seen over the entrance. Amongst the medicines they dispensed which are unlikely to find contemporary favour were fishes eyes, lambswool and ground rubies, but patients were at least offered these potions with a glass of hot wine to help digestion. In 1725 Peter the Great summoned Burchart to St Petersburg, but he died before Burchart could reach him. In 2000 the pharmacy was extensively refurbished.

The **Town Hall** is the only late Gothic building still intact in Estonia, dating largely from the 15th century. The exterior and the interior are equally impressive. It was the administrative and judicial centre of the town and the extensive range of woodwork and paintings in the Council Chamber mainly reflect judicial themes. Six centuries of Tallinn's history have been determined in this room and, with the restoration of independence, its role will now increase. For much of this time, there were clearly ample funds in the public treasury, as is shown by the opulence of the candelabra, the money-chests and the size of the wine cellars. One of the carvings on the magistrates' bench of David and Goliath is often taken to symbolise the relationship between Tallinn Council and its nominal masters on Toompea in the Old Town. The Council Chamber has always been heated, unlike the neighbouring Citizens Hall. Dancing, eating and drinking at winter receptions tend to be particularly vigorous to compensate for this. The original weathervane on the top of the spire, known as Old Thomas, was destroyed in the 1944 raid but the rest of the building was spared. German architects, artists and craftsmen were employed for the Town Hall and all documents were written only in German, even during the long periods of

Swedish and Russian rule. Only the tapestries have a non-German origin, being Flemish. It is sometimes possible to climb up the spire; the view from the top offers excellent shots of the Old Town for photographers but the stairs are steep and in poor condition so this is only recommended for the fit and determined.

Across the square, opposite the Town Hall, are several short streets which lead to Pikk. On the corner of Mündi and Town Hall Square is a millennium clock which counted down the seconds until midnight on December 31 1999. Saiakäik is the smallest street in Tallinn. Take either of these and turn right to the junction of Pikk and Pühavaimu for Pühavaimu, the **Holy Ghost Church**. That it does not face due east suggests that there was already a complex street layout by 1300 when building began. It was the first church to hold services in Estonian and the first extracts from the catechism in the Estonian language were printed for use here in 1535. The 1684 fire destroyed much of the interior and the original spire but the current spire is now the oldest in Tallinn, dating from 1688. Of the same age inside the church is the large wooden clock on the north wall, carved by Christian Ackermann from Königsberg. Spared from the fire was the folding altar carved in 1483 by the Lübeck artist Bernt Notke. Only the organ is modern, dating from 1929; it is one of the few in Tallinn's churches built by an Estonian and not imported from Germany. Sadly fire was to strike again on May 29 2002 and the spire was seriously damaged, although most of the interior woodwork was saved. Hopefully the spire will be fully repaired by summer 2003.

Cross Pikk for the Ajaloomuuseum, the **Estonian History Museum**. The building is as impressive as any of the contents, perhaps more so. Dating from 1410, it was the headquarters of the Great Guild and has changed little since. Visitors who arrive when the museum is shut can at least be consoled by the sight of the 15th-century door knockers. Exhibits inside are well labelled in English and concentrate on archaeology and costumes. Of more contemporary interest is the coin collection and a section on the founding of the local freemasons in the late 1770s. They were later banned by Alexander I in 1822. As you turn left into Pikk, the new Russian Embassy is on the left and on the right is Maiasmokk, a café that has deliberately stayed old-fashioned both in decor and in prices. The name translates appropriately as 'sweet tooth'. Pikk has two of the few notable **Jugendstil buildings** in Tallinn, both designed by Jacques Rosenbaum. Number 18, next to Maiasmokk, has a flamboyant Egyptian theme; number 25 on the corner of Hobusepea is more modest. Number 61, built across Pagari, and probably the blandest building in the Old Town, was the KGB headquarters in Soviet times, and now houses the Interior Ministry. Unlike its opposite number in Vilnius, it has not been opened to the public. Next on the left is **St Olav's Church** (Oleviste) named after the king of Norway and now a Baptist church. When first built in 1267, its 140m-high steeple made it one of the tallest buildings in the world. This steeple caught fire in 1820, having been struck by lightning, and its replacement 'only' reaches 120m. It is still, however, a major feature of the Tallinn skyline. Much of the interior of the church was destroyed in the subsequent fire, as it had been in an earlier one in 1625. The rebuilding, completed in 1840, provides a contrast to most other churches in Tallinn for its plain interior. Tsar Nicholas I donated a large bell in 1850 and his generosity is noted in an inscription written, with no trace of irony, in German. The organ dates from this time but the chandeliers are earlier and have been donated from other buildings.

A few yards further down on the right is **Fat Margaret's Tower** which houses the **Maritime Museum** (Meremuuseum). Outside is a plaque unveiled by Prince Andrew in May 1998 which commemorates British naval involvement in the battles between Estonian forces and the Bolsheviks from 1918 to 1920. The tower was built between 1510 and 1529. Some walls are as much as 6m thick. In 1830 it became a prison but after being stormed in 1917 it was left as a ruin for the next 60 years. Polish restorers, famous throughout the former Soviet block, finally came to the rescue in 1978. Climb to the roof for very photogenic views of St Olav's and the town gates. The museum covers shipbuilding, cartography, port-construction and fish-breeding. There is a recent exhibit on the *Estonia* which sank off the Finnish coast on September 28 1994 with the loss of 850 lives. A model of one of the boats has political interest. It was named first after Viktor Kingisepp, leader of the underground Estonian communist party in the early 1920s and then in 1990 was renamed after Gustav Sule, who was Estonian javelin champion in the 1930s.

Turn right out of the museum and leave the Old Town on Suur Rannavarara, the continuation of Pikk. On the right is the monument to those who died in the *Estonia* tragedy in 1994. It can be interpreted in a number of ways, perhaps symbolising the boat breaking into two or the total divide between life and death. Cross Pohja Puiestee to the disused power station, now ironically the **Energy Museum** (Energeetikamuuseum). Built originally in the late 1920s, it then had some claim to Jugendstil influence but many subsequent alterations have completely removed any hint of beauty and style. For tourists who never had the chance to visit Tirana's 'Albania Today' or Chinese museums during the Cultural Revolution, this is a splendidly flamboyant substitute. Ironically for an energy museum, many of the lights do not work but those that do illuminate graphs that all start at zero in 1945 and shoot up to the stratosphere throughout the 1950s, 1960s and 1970s. Engineers will be interested in the various meters and generators on display. The only hint of modern Estonia is in an occasional photograph. The basement could not provide a greater contrast with all its striplights working and its displays of contemporary abstract art. Modern Estonia does indeed have energy but it is now portrayed more metaphorically than literally. Demonstrations of the machinery take place several afternoons a week. Check at the entrance for details.

Return into the Old Town and walk behind Fat Margaret along Uus. Number 31 is the Scottish club, in fact a restaurant open to all which has the best-maintained lawn in Estonia. Next door is a whisky shop, a clear testimony to Tallinn's affluence and passion for Western consumer goods. It is hard to believe that until 1989 whisky was only available in foreign currency shops. Turn right into Olevimägi and then left into Vene. On the left is a smaller, but no less Russian version of the Alexander Nevsky Cathedral, **St Nicholas Russian Orthodox Church**. Again no concessions are made to Estonia; everything is written, spoken and sung in Russian. It dates from the early 19th century. On the right at number 17 is the **City Museum** (Linnamuuseum). As with the History Museum, the building is as of much interest as the contents. Having escaped the fires that ravished so many buildings in the Old Town, this 14th-century merchant's house still has examples of 16th-century wooden panelling, windows and furniture. Many of the exhibits would now be regarded as politically incorrect in the West as they concentrate on the accoutrements of the rich; life below stairs and outside the guilds and churches is ignored. Part of the museum is quite understandably called the 'Treasury', given the quantity of tapestries, silverware, pewter and porcelain displayed there. Nonetheless the collection shows the breadth of industry and culture that developed in Tallinn from 1860 onwards. The arrival in 1870 of the railway from St Petersburg led to an increase in the population from 30,000 to 160,000 by 1917. One anniversary the Estonians were forced to celebrate in 1910 was the 200th anniversary of the Russian conquest. The museum was closed in 2000 for extensive renovations. It now shows videos of pre-war and Soviet Estonia, of the 1944 bombing, the 1980 Olympics and the 1989 demonstrations that would in due course lead to independence. A room of Soviet posters has also been added. The café on the top floor is unusual in only offering home-made food. This museum is well labelled in English and the postcard sets they sell are excellent value.

On the right are the ruins of the **Dominican Monastery**, founded in 1246 but destroyed during the Reformation in 1524 when the monks were forced to flee. Extensive archaeological excavations were carried out between 1954 and 1968 when the ruins were first opened to the public. Take a torch and wear sturdy shoes as the surviving ambulatories are poorly lit. Of most interest are the stone carvings by the 16th-century Dutch sculptor Arent Passer. Chamber-music concerts take place here during the summer. On leaving the monastery, turn left into Vene and left again into Katariina Kaik. This tiny alleyway is where local ex-pats buy their souvenirs of Tallinn, as few tourists find it. Turn right at the end into Muurivahe, which runs below the city wall. Elderly Russians have stalls here, selling woollen sweaters, gloves and socks both in midsummer and in midwinter. The walk ends at the junction with Viru Street. To the left is the 15th-century Viru Gate, as formidable as the fortifications seen at the start of the walk. To the right is McDonald's; will it also last five centuries?

Elsewhere in Tallinn

Visitors with more time can see many other museums. Close to the Viru Gate at Vana Viru 14 and opposite the Viru Hotel is the **Fire-Fighting Museum**. Like the Energy Museum, it has not changed since the Soviet era so combines the didactic with the heroic. Dolls' houses show every possible cause of an accident in each room. Macabre photos abound of charred bodies, exploding television sets and open fires out of control. A panel lists medals awarded to local firemen until 1988 but none are listed after that year. It is a cruel comment to suggest that heroism in the Estonian fire service ceased at the restoration of independence in 1989. A number of horse-drawn and early motor fire engines are displayed. Although captions to all exhibits are only in Estonian and Russian, the staff hand out translation cards in English and German.

Back in the Old Town, in Lai, are the **Applied Arts Museum** at number 17 and the **Health Museum** at number 28–30. The former still sells the Soviet guidebook which boasts that the exhibits 'are really wonderful, conspicuous in their originality and can bear comparison with the best items of the world'. Exhibits from the Soviet period are now on the upper floors, and modern ones on the ground floor, so visitors can judge the changes for themselves and whether such hyperbole applies to either era. In all fields the collections are extensive and show the Estonian dedication to pottery, weaving, glassmaking and woodwork that has surmounted all political regimes.

TALLINN IN 1960
Michael Bourdeaux

For 15 years after World War II, Tallinn was a closed city, nestling amongst the forest of defensive (offensive) weaponry trained on the NATO countries. Suddenly in 1960 it was opened to Western visitors. I was lucky enough to have been a student at Moscow University at the time, so in May 1960 I was perhaps the first British visitor. Diplomats kept away until independence in 1991 because according to the bureaucrats a visit would have implied recognition of the Soviet occupation. I not only went there by train from Leningrad but stayed illegally in a private house for the first and only time during the 25 years that I knew the Soviet Union. Far from being worried that I would bring trouble on their heads, the occupants barred the exit and refused to let me out until I had agreed to stay for three nights, having found my photograph displayed on their wall!

How did this come about? In 1958 the Soviet authorities allowed a few hand-picked theological students to study abroad. One from Riga and one (Pastor Kaide Ratsep) from Tallinn arrived at Wycliffe Hall, Oxford while I was there. As I was a graduate in Russian, we gravitated towards each other. The next year, the door suddenly opened to me to study in Moscow as a member of the first-ever exchange programme with the USSR and I finally met Pastor Ratsep there when he was in transit to London. I promised I would call on his family if ever the opportunity arose.

It did. On arriving in Tallinn, I took a suburban train to the (as it still is) upmarket suburb of Nomme with its large wooden houses among the trees, looking more like Scandinavia than the Soviet Union. Maps of any practical use were unobtainable, being considered items of military intelligence, so I had to ask my way to the Ratsep's house. A rare Russian speaker eventually pointed me down one of the many paths cut into sand and I found a two-storey house separated from its neighbours by a wooden fence and a strip of pine trees. I knocked on the bright green door. A man with grey hair put his head out of an upstairs window before coming down. We had no common language, but I mentioned the name of the person who turned out to be his son. He invited me in, and there on the wall was the photograph of the Wycliffe Hall student body of 1958.

The Health Museum is one of the few totally contemporary museums in Tallinn and uses a range of models, toys, visual aids and colourful charts to show both adults and children the importance of healthy living. It is a brightly lit and well-thought-out display, a vivid contrast to many other museums. It may well be the only museum in the country with a hands-on element – two exercise bicycles are available for visitors. One section has been translated into Russian – that on sexually transmitted diseases.

Next to the Applied Arts Museum is the **Natural History Museum** at Lai 29, much of which is in fact contemporary rather than historical. Whilst there is an impressive collection of stuffed animals, of far greater interest is the collection of photographs of the Estonian countryside, all well lit and well labelled in English.

He simply would not allow me to leave and I somehow understood that I must await the return of his daughter-in-law. I was anticipating a conversation of a few words, knowing how elementary Kaide's knowledge of English had been when he arrived in Oxford. On the contrary, Enid Ratsep was bilingual, having been born in free Estonia of an English mother. The family at home had always spoken English, a tradition not entirely dead in 1960. Their 12-year-old daughter spoke it quite well. Later I would meet Enid's brother who sang me Harry Lauder songs while marching me through the streets of medieval Tallinn. Thirty years later I reflected on whether this might have been a preview of the Singing Revolution. I could hardly believe I was in the Soviet Union. Lampshades and bedspreads were of British pre-war manufacture. I slept in Kaide's study with a bookcase of German and English theology behind my pillow.

All of us, as if by common agreement, steered clear of the topic of the Soviet occupation but the family thoroughly organised my time for the next three days. After eight months in drab winter Moscow, the elan of ancient Tallinn in its bright spring colours took me into a new world. A visit on Sunday to Kaide's Lutheran Church, St Charles Church, left mixed impressions. Strangely, the family did not want to accompany me. This huge church was about half full, with 40% of the congregation younger people, a far higher proportion than one saw in Russia. I tried to see the pastor after the service, but the corridor was blocked by dozens of young people waiting outside his door. None of these, to my surprise, would speak to me, although most must have known Russian. I surmised they were waiting for religious instruction, illegal under the Soviet system at the time, and were unwilling for a foreigner (or a Russian if they took me for one) to intrude.

On my final day, having purchased an air ticket to Riga, I was waiting on the tarmac beside a small aeroplane. An official came up to me, demanded my documents, took me inside and told me my intended flight was illegal for a foreigner. 'Our rules are less strict than yours in Britain for Soviet citizens,' he said. 'When I was there, I was prevented from visiting many places. You can go where you like, but not always by your chosen route. Visit Riga by all means, but you must do so by train via Leningrad.'

The **Theatre and Music Museum** at Müürivahe 12, despite its name, only covers music. A violin-maker's workshop has been reconstructed and the display covers most instruments of the orchestra, all of which have at some time been made in Estonia. The production of violins and pianos has a long and distinguished history in Tallinn. Very few labels are in English but fortunately this does not matter too much given the self-explanatory nature of the exhibits. Estonians are often accused of taking themselves too seriously; from the cartoons on the stairs, it is clear that musicians at least do not. No famous 20th-century conductor is spared portrayal in irreverent clothes. One violinist, Hugo Schuts, is even drawn in a bathing costume.

Just outside the Old Town, behind the railway station at Kotzebue 16, is the **Dolls' Museum**. Opened in 1985 as a memorial to one of Lenin's closest colleagues, Mikhail Kalinin, it nonetheless even then had a small collection of toys. Kalinin is now forgotten and toys have taken over completely. The collection of dolls and dolls' houses goes back as far as the 18th century, but there are also board games, teddy bears and general toys from 1900 onwards since this is one of the few elements of Estonian life unaffected by the changing political environment. The walk from the Old Town offers a completely changed architectural environment; Tallinn on the wrong side of the tracks becomes a town of poorly maintained wooden houses and an abandoned factory. The market beside the station is worth a stop of a few minutes. Excellent light refreshments are available at prices well below those elsewhere in the town and the choice of clothes, CDs and gadgets is a good reflection of mass Estonian taste.

A walk from the Viru Gate along either Pärnu mnt or Estonia pst, and then along Kaarli pst back to the National Library, passes the main buildings that remain from the end of the Tsarist period and the first independence period, so from 1900 until 1940. Jugendstil, neo-classicism and functionalism are all represented here and it is to be hoped that developers do not get permission to make drastic changes. The **Estonian National Theatre** was in fact designed by a Finnish architect, Armas Lindgren, and opened in 1913, although the rebuilding that followed the bombing of Tallinn in 1944 was carried out under the Estonian architect Alar Kotli. The money for the original building was raised by private subscription and the Tsarist authorities attempted to block the project. They did briefly succeed in preventing the Estonian language from being used in any production. In 1918 The Estonian National Assembly met there.

On the opposite side of Estonia pst from the theatre is the **Estonian Bank Museum** which was modernised in the summer of 1998. The political history of the country is mirrored in this museum through the currency. In 1928 the kroon was tied to the British pound but it floated after 1933 when Britain had left the Gold Standard. The current building dates from 1935 and manages to combine elements of neo-Gothic, neo-renaissance and functionalism. In its predecessor, Estonian independence was proclaimed on February 24 1918 and in this one, a temporary government was formed in September 1944 between the German and the Russian occupations.

The **Sakala Conference Centre** behind the bank is best known for the stained glass of Rait Präts whose work can also be seen in St Nicholas Church and in the National Library. This area is likely to be developed soon with many office and hotel projects now under consideration. On Vabaduse Väljak (Freedom Square), the Palace Hotel and the Town Hall beside it both date from the 1930s. Their size and the imposing nature of similar buildings along Pärnu mnt testify to the confidence of the regime at the time. Behind them are a number of functionalist buildings that survived the 1944 bombing raid. There was a statute of Peter the Great in the Square from 1910 to 1923, when it was removed. Nobody knows what happened to the top, but the metal from the base was used to mint Estonian coins.

A walk again from Viru Gate across Viru Square gives an appropriately unflattering picture of the construction that took place between 1960 and 1980. Looking back towards Narva mnt, the **Viru Hotel** is a major eyesore and the inevitable result of conflicting Soviet policies in the early 1970s. On the one hand, tourists needed to be admitted to Tallinn to boost the country's international image; on the other, they must not be allowed serious contact with the local population. An isolated tower block was obviously the answer, and until 1980, when some of the Olympic Games were held in Tallinn, the Viru was the only hotel for foreigners. Many probably only saw Tallinn from the bar on the 22nd floor. Estonians console themselves with the knowledge that the Viru Hotel did at least spare them a 'Stalinist cathedral' which was one proposal for this location, or an enormous memorial to Mikhail Kalinin which was another. Kalinin, a member of Lenin's Politburo, lived in Tallinn for three years between 1901 and 1904 whilst he was banished from St Petersburg. A Soviet guidebook published in 1987 blames the lack of 'artistic and economic means' for the failure of both projects. One published a year or two later might have given the true reason: the intense local opposition. A more modest statue of Kalinin was instead erected on Tower Square, a park between the Old Town and the railway station. Behind the Viru Hotel is a department store built in the 1960s. In the Soviet period it was crudely divided between a shop for the local population and one for foreigners. Both were flagships in their different ways. The local shop was better supplied than most in St Petersburg and Moscow and the notorious 'Berioshka', which took only precious *valuta* (hard foreign currencies) in exchange for vodka, wooden dolls and fur hats, was the only Soviet shop that thousands of tourists would ever enter. Before the war, the main Tallinn synagogue stood on this site.

The current **synagogue** shares premises with the **Jewish School** on Karu, near the harbour and was opened in December 2000. It is the only active synagogue in Estonia and replaced a temporary building used in Soviet times, on Magdaleena Street in the southern part of the city. Sadly, the occasional brutal attack on the premises has meant that they carry no outside identification. The building is now the headquarters for the small Jewish community in Tallinn. Visitors, both Jewish and non-Jewish, are welcome to visit the synagogue.

Returning towards town, Karu becomes Ahtri which skirts the harbour. Now very dwarfed by the huge boats that ply between Helsinki and Tallinn, the icebreaker **Suur Töll** still stands out as a boat clearly moored here for good. Having been delivered to the Tsarist navy in 1914 from the Stettin shipyards in Germany, it would inevitably have a complicated history over the next eight years, being based in Tallinn all that time. The Finns and Estonians who operated it wanted to prevent its fall into either White Russian or Bolshevik hands and, under the Tartu Treaty signed between the USSR and Estonia in February 1920, it was finally given to the Estonians. It could break ice a metre thick when launched, and it was still doing so with the same equipment in the late 1980s. Visitors can see the engines, the living quarters and the two separate kitchens from which food for the officers and for the men was prepared.

In December 2000, the **Kalev Chocolate Museum** opened at the Kalev factory on the Pärnu Road, beside the tram terminus. Whilst it gives a thorough coverage of the different production techniques used in its 200-year history and visitors have the chance to smell eight different flavours, the real interest is in the political history revealed in the designs on the boxes issued during the Soviet period. In 1950, the 10th anniversary of Estonia 'joining' the USSR warranted a special box-top, even though three of those years had been spent under German occupation. Later in the 1950s pre-war pictures of Narva were used, even though it was the Soviet army that destroyed the city in 1944. By the 1980s the authorities became aware of the knowledge Estonians now had of the West so

Mickey Mouse and Finnish television characters were allowed to join traditional Russian role models.

The history of chewing-gum in the former USSR deserves a book to itself since different politburos all devoted endless sessions to this topic. Puritans wanted it banned, but the realists wanted to prove that whatever the USA could do, the USSR could do better. Production was first authorised in 1968, banned again and then reintroduced for the Olympics. Only the Kalev factory ever received the necessary authorisation.

The factory is proud that following independence in 1991 it has been able to re-establish export markets, even as far away as the United States. Perhaps a few elderly consumers there remember the Shirley Temple portrait used on boxes produced in the 1930s. Not even famous German factories are likely to be able to match the 237 varieties of marzipan produced here now. The factory shop is in a different building next door, so no hard-sell can follow a visit. As prices are about 20% lower than those charged in town or at the airport, the short tram ride could result in considerable savings.

EXCURSIONS FROM TALLINN
Rocca al Mare Open Air Museum
This deserves a half day to itself, ideally in balmy summer weather. Take the 21 or 21b bus from the railway station and also take a sweater as protection against the wind on the many non-balmy days. A winter excursion on a sunny day is worthwhile to get some impression of what most Estonians used to endure month in, month out, every winter. Visitors at midsummer on June 23 can enjoy the all-night celebrations held here. The name in Italian means 'cliff beside the sea' and was given by the original owner of the estate when it was bought in 1863. The museum was founded in 1957 and first opened to the public in 1964. The descriptive panels throughout are in English. It now consists of around 70 buildings and when complete should have a hundred. The aim is to show all aspects of Estonian rural architecture, with houses of both rich and poor. Most date from the 19th century but one of the chapels was built in 1699. The whole of Estonia is represented – windmills are of course from the island of Saaremaa but in contrast there are fishermen's cottages from Lake Peipsi on the Russian border. Even the poorest families managed to afford a sauna since to Estonians it is as crucial to living as a cooking pot. The interiors have all been appropriately furnished with kitchen utensils, weaving looms and chests of drawers. Amongst the more unusual buildings are a tabernacle from the Herrnhut movement, a strict offshoot of the Lutheran church. Future plans include the restoration of a Swedish cottage – about 8,000 Swedes lived in Estonia before World War II. There is already a Swedish church here, brought from the formerly Swedish-speaking village of Sutlepa. The exterior is 17th century and the interior 19th century. Inside there is a permanent exhibition of drawings from all the other Swedish churches in Estonia. In bad weather, finish your tour at the Kolu Tavern. Kolu is a village between Tallinn and Tartu. The tavern still has two separate bars, one originally for the gentry and one for the peasants. It serves filling, hot food such as pea soup and mashed potatoes with bacon, but do not expect any concessions to the 21st century; it remains firmly in the 19th, although a more conventional restaurant will in due course be built for more fastidious diners.

Paldiski

Since independence, an uneasy quiet has descended on this former Soviet naval base situated 40km west of Tallinn. Unusually for Estonia, a regular train service operates from here to Tallinn, with eight services a day, the journey lasting a little over one hour. However, individual tourists would be well advised to take a car and guide for a half-day excursion as several en route stops can be made. Estonians are more than happy to see the back of the Russian sailors but have yet to find a new role for this harbour. A daily car-ferry service to Kappelskär in Sweden started in summer 2000 and the switching of cargo services from Tallinn is being considered.

Peter the Great inspected the site personally in 1715 before authorising the building of a harbour which was originally planned as the largest in the Russian Empire. He was not to live to see its final completion which was not until 1768 as financial problems had led to frequent delays. Much of the labour was supplied by prisoners; so many died of ill-treatment that Paldiski became known as the 'second Siberia'. In September 1939 the USSR imposed a mutual assistance pact on Estonia under which Paldiski was seized as a naval base. In May 1940, shortly before the full occupation of the country, all Estonians were expelled from the town, a practice that would be repeated all too often from 1945 in many other towns and villages along the coast. Paldiski is now the largest Soviet blot on the Estonian landscape; only the dustbins, brightly coloured and modelled on penguins with their beaks open, provide relief from piles of rubble, barbed wire and ransacked blocks of flats. The first building to be seen on the way into the town is the former prison, but it can hardly be distinguished from much of what follows. When the Russian forces finally left in September 1995, having been granted dispensation to stay after independence, a population of around 4,000 was left with only 10% of them speaking Estonian. The remainder were Russian-speaking civilians. A curtain behind a window, an occasional light or even the sight of an occasional human being, shows that life has not totally died out here but the slogan in the town's English-language brochure, 'A Town with a Future', seems a joke in particularly bad taste. However, in 2000 a new hotel was opened, the **White Ship** (Valge Laev) at Rae 32 (tel: 674 2095; web: www.weekends.ee). 'Welcome aboard' mats are behind each entrance, a porthole is on the door of every room and maritime memorabilia cover all the walls. It would be possible to commute into Tallinn from here and when Tallinn hotels are full, late bookers will have no choice.

Returning to Tallinn, two very contrasting stops can be made. Shortly after independence, a monument was erected in the forest at **Klooga** to commemorate the massacre of 2,000 Jews there on September 19 1944, just before the German withdrawal. The small Estonian-Jewish community had already been killed by then; these victims were largely from other Eastern European countries. The former village of **Tabasalu** is now the first of Tallinn's suburbs. It has a nickname of 'idiots village' in view of those who live there, most of whom have much more money than sense or taste. The money stands out, but it is well protected by high walls and rottweilers. A few poultry farmers remain on the outskirts of the village but it cannot be long before they are bought out.

Aegna, Pirita and Kadriorg

Allow a full day to visit the island of Aegna, the yacht harbour at Pirita and the park at Kadriorg. Boats to and from Aegna operate out of Pirita harbour from a small jetty beside the café, not from the larger jetty beside the hotel and yacht club. Several buses serve Pirita from the town centre and the journey takes about ten minutes. Boats leave for Aegna around nine in the morning, at midday and in the early evening. Check timings at the tourist office or via a hotel reception before setting off and do not forget an umbrella in case the weather suddenly changes. Tickets cost 80EEK (£3.50/US$5.50) for the round trip.

Aegna

Aegna is so quiet that even Estonians are prepared to turn off their mobile phones, and neither the Germans nor the Russians were able to leave their mark. Conifer trees abound, as do minute beaches, and the few open areas have been made available for camping. Much of the island can be seen in the three hours allowed by the morning boat schedule though a full day of peace and quiet is what most local visitors seek. Paths are clearly marked and a detailed map is displayed at the harbour.

Pirita and Viimsi

Pirita was built as the Olympic village for the yachting and sailing events of the 1980 Olympics. For a precious three weeks, Tallinn briefly returned to being an international city. An array of consumer goods, Western newspapers and direct international telephone dialling suddenly came to Tallinn and left equally suddenly when the Games were over. Only the buildings have remained and they are so obviously of Soviet design that the harbour hardly seems to belong to modern Estonia. On returning to Pirita, visitors of Estonian origin may wish to take the 34 bus for 2km inland to **Metsakalmistu**, the **Forest Cemetery**. Most famous Estonians are buried in this pine forest, including the writer A H Tammsaare, the poetess Lydia Koidula and the chess player Paul Keres. Since independence, the body of Konstantin Päts, president until the Soviet occupation, has been returned and he is now buried here together with his immediate family. He died in a Soviet psychiatric hospital in 1956. The body of General Laidoner, however, still lies in 2001 in a communal grave in Vladimir Prison where he died in March 1953, despite strong pressure from the Estonian government for it to be formally identified and returned. Laidoner was Commander in Chief for much of the pre-war period and his former house on the Viimsi Peninsula, about five kilometres from Pirita, is now the **Laidoner Museum**.

The most moving exhibit is a French–Russian dictionary given to him during his imprisonment in 1944; he used several pages of it to compose his political testament. It ends, in English, with the words 'Estonia, with all thy faults, I love thee still. Johan Laidoner'. Considering how jealous Stalin was of his reputation, it is remarkable how many items associated with him and with this house have survived. During Soviet times, the KGB had taken it over in order to break completely the links with Estonian independence.

The museum was greatly expanded in 2001. With the help of the Imperial War Museum in London, there is now a British Room, covering the navy's role in helping to establish Estonian independence in 1918–20. It is expected that many more exhibits will soon come from Britain. This would be appropriate in view of Laidoner's often quoted remark, 'Without the arrival of the British fleet in Tallinn in December 1918, Estonia and the other Baltic States would have found themselves in the hands of the Bolsheviks.' The Poles have likewise opened a room in honour of Marshal Pilsudski who played a similar role to Laidoner in ensuring his country's independence from Russia.

Other visitors will head for the main harbour and the entrance to the *Lembit* submarine, beside the petrol station. No brochures are available but the sailors on board speak reasonable English and their enthusiasm on meeting the few English-speaking visitors who bother to come more than compensates for any linguistic failings. Two submarines were originally commissioned from Barrow-in-Furness by the Estonian navy in 1936. *Kalev*, the second one, was sunk in October 1941, by which time both had been taken over by the Soviet navy and taken from Tallinn before it fell to the Germans. The *Lembit* saw service throughout World War II, being used mainly to attack German cargo ships en route to Sweden. Its torpedoes had a range of 12km and it could sink below the surface for up to 24 hours. Its speed reached 60km/h. It remained in service until 1955, after which it was used for training. The Soviets made no attempt to conceal the British origin of the submarine, so many of the original features remain.

The walk back to the centre of Tallinn is two or three miles. Cross the main road from the harbour to the site of **St Birgitta's Convent**. Although the convent is included in most sightseeing tours, walking here can be a precarious experience as the ruins are so badly maintained. The convent lasted intact for only 170 years, from 1407 until the siege of 1577. The outline of the main body of the church, the western gable together with the vestry, cloister and refectories, is clear.

Staying on the land side of the main road, after half a mile is the **Soviet War Memorial**. It could hardly be anything else, given its size and the military themes of the bronze statues. The Estonians carry out minimal maintenance here but, as with all Soviet war memorials, they are not removed and Russians congregate on the days of the old Soviet holidays such as May Day and November 7. The text is particularly offensive to Estonians as the monument is dedicated to 'Fighters for Soviet Power'. It was completed only in 1975. A Soviet guidebook excuses this long delay by claiming 'at last Estonian artists had enough skill and adequate economic means to complete such an ensemble'. The obelisk dates from 1960 and commemorates the hurried departure from Tallinn of the Bolshevik fleet in 1918 when German forces occupied the town.

An even more dominant landmark from the Soviet era is the **TV Tower**, about a mile inland from Pirita on Kloostrimetsa. Going there by bus, expect to be surrounded by elderly Russians with flowers, since the Russian cemetery and crematorium are nearby. The few tourists who now visit the tower also seem to be Russian. This is a pity as it does provide an extensive view of the town and port not available elsewhere. The entrance is as flamboyant as one would expect; the windows are of stained glass, with portraits of valiant industrial workers; covered aisles surround basins of fountains and they in turn are surrounded by lawns. However nothing has been maintained properly (except for the lifts inside) so moss and weeds become ever more prominent. Nobody has bothered to put Estonian signs in the lift or change the menu in the revolving tower restaurant from smoked fish and chicken kiev. The telescope still takes kopek coins.

A few hundred yards further along this road is **Maarjamäe Palace**, which has probably had one of the most turbulent ownership histories of any site in Tallinn.

Maarjamäe means 'Mary's Hill' but the German name, Streitberg ('Hill of Strife'), was for many centuries more appropriate. The only consolation is that the blood shed here spared Tallinn itself from many battles. The final one took place in the early 18th century as Russia seized the Baltics from the Swedes during the Northern Wars. To set the seal on his conquest, Peter the Great established Kadriorg Park as a summer residence, so many of the St Petersburg nobility felt obliged to followed suit. Those who could not immediately afford the luxury of a suitable building, subsidised it with a factory, so lime kilns and sugar refineries adjoined the manor houses. The sugar was sold in Riga and St Petersburg and the plant was run on British coal. A fire in 1868 destroyed much of the factory and it was never rebuilt. In the 1870s, when the estate was bought by Count Anatoli Orlov-Davydov from St Petersburg, the rebuilding he ordered came to deserve the title 'palace'. Terraces, a gateway decorated with copper eagles, and the Gothic tower gave it an almost regal air. The Dutch Consulate bought it in the 1920s when the Orlov-Davydovs emigrated to France and continued its use as a summer residence. It was to lose its appeal in this role when in 1926 the road to Pirita was built across the grounds, cutting off the manor house from direct and private access to the sea. However, the road brought with it commercial potential realised in a hotel and restaurant called the Riviera Palace. In 1937 the Estonian air force took it over as a training school and they are sadly responsible for the dreary façade at the front of the building. From 1940 until 1975, when Maarjamäe became a museum, the Soviet military used, but did not abuse it. During the 1980s, Polish restorers finally brought the building back to its turn-of-the-century glory, turning their attention to the chandeliers, fireplaces, parquet floors and ceilings. It is ironic that one of the last Soviet legacies to Tallinn should be the perfect surroundings for a museum which chronicles Estonian independence.

Although few labels are in English and the one available guidebook is now badly out of date, this is without doubt the best museum in Tallinn. New rooms are constantly being added, exhibits are generously displayed, layout is sensibly planned and there is the complete absence of benign neglect that seems to permeate so many other Tallinn museums. It covers Estonian history from the mid 19th century until the present day. It amply contrasts the lifestyles of rich and poor and shows the diversity of industrial products and international contacts that the country enjoyed during the first period of independence between the two world wars. It even had a thriving tourist board whose brochures displayed here sold Estonia as 'The Cheapest and Most Interesting Country in Europe'. One room opened in the summer of 1998 is devoted to the life of Konstantin Päts, Estonia's president between the two world wars. On more contemporary themes, the anti-Soviet guerrilla movement and the return to independence are covered movingly but not bombastically. Amongst new themes covered in rooms opened in 2000 are the battle for Tallinn in early 1918 and the German occupation from 1941–44.

Behind the palace is one of the few late-1950s constructions of which Estonians can be fiercely proud – the **Song Festival Amphitheatre**. It has the massive grandeur to be expected from that time but is not wasteful of materials and does not dominate the surrounding area. The parabola provides cover for 5,000 singers and up to 20,000 more have often taken part. The most famous recent festival took place in 1989, when the previously banned national anthem, the *Song of Estonia*, was sung by an audience of around 300,000 people, 20% of the entire population of the country. In winter, the steep slope at the back of the parabola provides Tallinn's only ski- and toboggan-run. Note the plaques at the top of the slope which commemorate each of the Song Festivals held every five years since 1869. The tower was opened to the public in 2000, and gives photographers good shots of the Old Town and the port combined.

Returning to the shoreline, at the junction of the roads to Pirita and to Narva, note the **Russalka** (Mermaid) **Memorial**, which commemorates the sinking of a battleship with this name in 1893. It depicts an angel looking out to sea. The sculptor, Amandus Adamson, is one of Estonia's most famous, and perhaps because of this monument he was granted official respect in the Soviet period and a memorial bronze bust of him stands in Kadriorg Park. The park is the next stage of the walk and one corner is just behind the Russalka Memorial. The park, and **Kadriorg Palace**, which forms its centrepiece, was built immediately following Peter the Great's first visit to Tallinn in 1718 with his Italian architect Niccolo Michetti. Sadly it was not completed by 1725 when Peter the Great died and no subsequent Tsar ever showed the commitment that he did. In fact Catherine I never came to Tallinn again after his death. Perhaps the description often given of the palace as a 'mini-Versailles' is fair, as what was carried out does show some French and Italian influence. A fire destroyed much of the interior in 1750 and it was subsequently never again used by the Russian royal family. Kadriorg Palace became the official residence of the Estonian presidents, but now houses the **Foreign Art Museum**, the collection being mainly Flemish and Baltic German. However, the room devoted to Soviet art from the 1920s is likely to be of most interest to visitors. The designs on the porcelain show the most immediate break with the past as all the themes are 100% political. It would take another ten years before painting was similarly controlled. Some of this porcelain was prepared for the first Soviet Art Exhibition held in St Petersburg in 1923, by which time the St Petersburg Imperial Porcelain Factory had become the State Porcelain Factory. It came to be known as 'agitation porcelain'. Many rooms have been restored to their original 1930s layout, when President Päts lived here. The Danzig-baroque library is the most elaborate room and was only completed in 1939, a year before the Soviet take-over.

Kadriorg Park is a year-round joy for local people and tourists alike. In winter the combination of sun and snow amidst the trees and sculptures offers a peaceful contrast to the hectic commercial life of Tallinn just a few hundred metres away. Spring brings out the blossom of the cherry and ash trees, summer the swans, the squirrels and the fountains and autumn the blends of gold and red as the trees shed their leaves. A cottage in the park used by Peter the Great during the construction of the palace now poses as a museum but the paucity of exhibits perhaps redefines the word 'minimalist'. A bare main room, a few p
hotographs and some haphazard items of furniture would be best concealed from tourists entitled to expect much more.

A hundred metres back towards town, on Weizenbergi opposite the main entrance to Kadriorg Palace, the **Mikkeli Museum** will quickly restore the enthusiasm of a visitor. This building was the palace kitchen but in 1997 was opened to house the collection of Estonia's most fortunate private art collector, Johannes Mikkel. Born in 1907, he was able to start buying during the first independence period when departing Baltic-Germans and Russian nobles abandoned enormous quantities of paintings, porcelain and prints. He was allowed to trade during the Soviet period and enhanced his collection with items bought in the Caucasus and Central Asia. There is no predominant theme, but the quality and taste of every item stands out, be it a piece of Kangxi or Meissen porcelain, a Dürer woodcut, a Rembrandt etching or any one of his 20 Flemish paintings. Folders in English are available in every room with descriptions of all major exhibits, and modern lighting ensures that each item is viewed as well as possible.

On leaving the museum and turning left, a slight detour can first be made to the far side of the lake behind the Mikkeli building. The splendidly isolated house at Roheline 3 is the **Eduard Vilde House Museum** where Estonia's most prolific writer, both at home and in exile all over Europe, spent the final six years of his life between 1927 and 1933. Typically for most established Estonians at that time, the furnishings are simple and there are many empty spaces. Return to Weizenbergi to continue back into town. At the corner of Poska on the left, house number 20a has some baroque imitation of the palace although it was built only in 1939. A good place to rest is the Café Omabi on the other corner. Apart from one microwave, modern Estonia has passed it by so the food is freshly prepared for each order, there is no menu in English and no piped music. Beside it is Kasitoo, a souvenir shop sensibly patronised by overseas Estonians as its prices are not geared to cruise passengers or Finnish day trippers. Weizenbergi lasts a further 300m or so before joining Narva mnt. Every house is probably now owned, or was before World War II, by a famous Estonian. Ladas or small Toyotas may be parked in the street, but considerable wealth is discreetly hidden behind the lace curtains. The turn-of-the-century, four-storey houses display hints of Jugendstil, whilst the wooden ones are characteristic of middle-class suburbs throughout Estonia. On a neighbouring street, Koidula, one of the largest wooden houses belonged to Estonia's most famous author, A H Tammsaare, who died in March 1940. In his honour it is now the **Tammsaare Museum** but labelling is only in Estonian and Russian. The only English translations of his work were published in Moscow in the 1970s and are now out of print. The exhibition has hardly been changed since the Soviet era so presents him as far more of a 'man of the people' than was really the case. Tammsaare is depicted on the 25EEK note and it is perhaps significant that it is his farm that is pictured on the reverse, not this town house. Some downstairs rooms are now used for modern art exhibitions, which contrast a much-needed splash of colour to the gloom upstairs.

At the junction of Weizenbergi and Narva mnt there is a taxi rank and bus stop. A large Methodist church has recently been built on the far side; otherwise Narva mnt from here back to the Viru Gate is totally devoted to mammon. There is no point in describing any of the buildings since they are mainly being pulled down to give way to glass skyscrapers. This area will soon be Tallinn's Wall Street or Square Mile. A Japanese restaurant has already opened to ensure a serious and affluent gastronomic ambience.

Riga

Stephen Baister and Chris Patrick
updated by Neil Taylor

Riga is the largest and most cosmopolitan of all the Baltic capitals and is by a long way the most interesting town or city in Latvia. It is located on the Daugava River about 15km from the point where the Daugava meets the Baltic Sea in the southeastern corner of the Gulf of Riga. Riga can trace its history to the beginning of the 13th century, but it was in the course of the Middle Ages that it developed into a Hanseatic city, and by the 18th and 19th century it had grown into one of Europe's leading ports and industrial centres. By the late 19th/early 20th century it had also become a cultural centre, famous for its opera, theatre and music. Riga celebrated its 800th anniversary in 2001 with a year-long series of special events and also with the rebuilding of the House of Blackheads (see page 87).

THE CITY

The modern city is divided into two parts by the city canal which flows through the elegant parks that separate the historic Old Town from most of the New Town, with its shops, offices and suburbs. The air of elegance and spaciousness created by the area of open space in what is otherwise the centre of a busy capital has led to Riga being compared to Paris by a number of guide books and travel writers. There is some justification in the comparison. Even when Latvia was part of the Soviet Union, Riga was more sophisticated than Russian Soviet cities and towns, since it had better shops and the odd decent restaurant and café. Now its medieval and art nouveau architecture and well-kept parks allow the comparison to continue. There are modern international hotels, many good cafés and restaurants, and small and pleasant shops stocking local art and international brands. In 1992–3 the local authority privatised about 90% of Riga's shops, from the old GUM (State Universal Store) in the Old Town, to the small bookshops and tobacconists.

Between 1945 and 1991 Riga grew enormously, largely as a result of Soviet expansion which generally took the form of building large, drab, low-quality blocks of flats in the suburbs. One of the first, called Kengarags, can be seen along the Daugava and plenty can also be seen on the trip from the airport to the city centre.

The present population is estimated at just under 800,000, but even now about 40% is Latvian and about 55% Russian (the balance is made up of Poles, Belarussians and Ukrainians). Over half the population (about 54%) is female.

Until Latvia's independence from the Soviet Union in 1991 Russian was the predominant language heard in Riga. Now, as can be seen from the signposts, Latvian is regaining ground, but Russian is still widely spoken (as are English and German, as second languages).

History
Neil Taylor
Foundation
In the centre of Riga Old Town, on the corner of Gleznotāju and Vāgnera streets, is a signpost showing the distance west to Berlin as 1,226km and east to Moscow as 1,011km. A neighbouring antiquarian bookshop displays mainly German books, as perhaps is only to be expected in a street named after Richard Wagner. Outside the tourist season, many of the passing pedestrians will, however, be speaking Russian. The empty building on one corner is a Soviet legacy, since an empty space was then preferred to a replacement for an earlier German building.

Riga's 800 years of recorded history has been largely a battle for dominance between the Germans and the Russians, with Latvians always being the underdogs. Other colonial powers, such as the Swedes, did conquer the area from time to time and the French under Napoleon almost succeeded in doing so. It is, however, the Germans and the Russians who between them have left such a firm architectural stamp on Riga that visitors from cruise ships spending just a few hours there may well wonder if they have seen anything Latvian. Riga has, after all, only been the capital of an independent country for a little over 30 years, between 1920 and 1940 and again from 1991 until the present. Although the British never conquered Riga, they provided it between 1904 and 1912 with a mayor, George Armistead. Only in 1916 was the first Latvian mayor elected.

The date for Riga's founding is traditionally given as 1201 when Bishop Albert established his residence there on a crusade against the local Livs. There had clearly been a port which had already been developed but later German, Russian and Swedish historians had no wish to credit 'pagans' with the ability to establish and to run a trading post. This obvious natural harbour at the confluence of two rivers and near to the sea may well have had a previous history of several centuries but it has not been chronicled.

Bishop Albert quickly recognised the commercial and military potential of Riga so encouraged traders from Bremen and Gotland to settle there whilst ensuring for his soldiers a safe base to return to from their forays into the surrounding countryside. A city wall was built 10m high and 2.5m thick. The Dom Cathedral was begun in the 13th century, although none of the present building dates from before the 14th century. (Some 790 years later, traders from Bremen would again be pioneers as they were amongst the first business people to establish contacts in Riga after the collapse of the USSR.) Allegiances in the countryside would change frequently and violently but Riga remained in Teutonic hands until 1561 when it fell to the Polish/Lithuanian Empire. Around that time too the Reformation took hold in Riga and Lutheranism has been a dominant religion ever since. Its many churches literally tower over the small number of Catholic and Orthodox churches built more recently.

Polish rule was to last only 40 years, as in 1601 King Gustav Adolphus of Sweden conquered Riga after a six-week battle. The area outside the town where he prepared his troops for this is now called Mezaparks or King's Wood. (The Baltic-

German name of Kaiserwald was often used by foreigners before World War II.) Yet under both regimes, economic power remained in the hands of the Baltic Germans as it would under the Russians who drove out the Swedes in 1710. The Russians delegated the running of Riga to the Baltic Germans and would profit from this arrangement for the next two hundred years. The town soon spread well beyond the traditional city walls, although many of the suburbs were unnecessarily burnt down in 1812 to prepare for a defence of the city should Napoleon's forces attack. These forces in fact headed east towards Moscow. (Napoleon condescendingly referred to Riga as a 'suburb of London' and realised that, had he captured it, he would have eliminated the extensive trade between Russia and Britain that the port serviced.)

During the 19th century, as a result of effective delegation to the Baltic Germans from St Petersburg, Riga became a cosmopolitan city that could rival any other on the Baltic coast. Many foreigners settled there and the Jewish community became increasingly prominent in commerce and in medicine. The advent of large-scale industrial production at the beginning of the 19th century, followed by the introduction of the railways 50 years later, were just the most obvious in a wide range of developments that made Riga prosperous and envied. The population increased from around 100,000 in 1860 to over 250,000 just 40 years later. Only once during the 19th century did Riga face a military threat; this was in 1855 when the British failed in an attempt to block the harbour during the Crimean War.

In the arts field, German influence is clear from the presence in Riga of the writer Johann Herder and the composer Richard Wagner, amongst many others. In architecture first eclecticism and then Jugendstil would add in the suburbs to the German Gothic of the Old Town. The removal in 1857 of what remained of the medieval walls brought these former suburbs into what is now the town centre. As wide boulevards stretched north, east and west, the new buildings that lined them became the fashionable addresses for flats and offices. The introduction of planning controls in 1866 and the strengthening of these regulations in 1881 have bequeathed Riga acres of architectural excellence. In Jānis Baumanis (1834–1891), Riga found the perfect but rare combination of architect and politician, and his skills can still be appreciated. Amongst his many buildings that have changed little since his time are the university on Raina Boulevard and the Riga Regional Court on Brīvības (Freedom) Avenue.

These new roads all required names and from then until 1990 contemporary politics would always be reflected in those chosen. Initially all the Tsars, their consorts and their governor-generals were remembered in this way, but Latvian authors and artists replaced them during the first independence period between 1920 and 1940. Although the Nazis ruled Riga for only three years, it was long enough for all major roads to be named after Hitler and his immediate entourage. Soviet leaders and Red Army generals quickly took their place in 1945 and only in 1990 did Latvian names start to return.

By the start of World War I, Riga was the third largest city in the Russian Empire. The Germans reached the outskirts of the city in 1915 but the Russians would surrender only in September 1917 and this was without a fight. Latvian independence was proclaimed in Riga on November 18 1918 but the Red Army seized it on January 3 1919 and the fledgling government fled to Liepāja. During the following year, Riga might well have fallen to the Germans, the White Russians or the Bolsheviks. It was only in December 1919 that Latvian power was restored.

BALTIC COUNTDOWN: A NATION VANISHES

Peggy Benton worked in the British Embassy in Riga from 1938 until the Russians ordered its closure in 1940. She then had to return to Britain via Vladivostok and Canada. Here she describes the arrival of the Soviet troops in June 1940, just when the West was pre-occupied with the fall of France to the Germans.

On June 17th there was thunder in the air and everyone's nerves were on edge. Communications with the outside world were cut, and there was a general feeling of uneasiness. As we returned to the office after lunch, we heard a distant rumbling. People were hurrying, like leaves before the wind, down the broad Brīvības iela (Freedom Avenue) towards the centre of the town. As we crossed the corner of Raina Boulevard, the first Russian tanks came into sight. There was no time to be lost; we had to start burning our confidential documents at once. Within a few minutes, black smoke was rising from the chimneys of all the legations.

When we returned to Town Hall Square, the mood of the crowd was ugly. Men were prising up paving stones and throwing them at the police, two of whom stood at the corner, back to back, their faces grey, their revolvers swinging in a slow arc in an attempt to intimidate the crowd. At this moment a Russian tank rumbled up the street. A machine gun was mounted on the roof. A soldier emerged from the turret of the tank and motioned to the policeman to step back. With an angry rattle, the gunner swung his weapon, sending a swathe of bullets into the densely-packed crowd. There was a moment of total silence and then screams as the onlookers struggled to push past the dead and dying. The soldier watched dispassionately, his hand on the trigger. Within moments the square was empty but for the bodies on the ground, some still, some writhing. 'I think the local Communists are in for a surprise'

With the Russian hinterland suddenly cut off in 1920, Latvia had to look west to find new markets. Dairy products and timber quickly became the backbone of the export drive and new impetus was given to the port of Riga as the crucial new link with the outside world. From the mid 1920s, it started to take on the role of listening post for the Soviet Union, as normal diplomatic and commercial life became so difficult for Westerners in Moscow very soon after the Revolution. It also became in many respects the capital of the Baltic States as embassies there were often accredited to Kaunas and to Tallinn as well. It was, though, much larger than either of these towns and in Tsarist times had already enjoyed a dominant role. Crucially it continued to maintain a high standard of living and the shops offered a wide range of consumer goods. What was taken for granted at that time would later become cherished memories.

June 1940 saw the Soviet occupation of Riga, which the Latvian government decided not to resist militarily. It took only a few months to destroy the business community and for Stalinism at its most brutal to be imposed. Yet far worse was to come; June and July 1941 were undoubtedly the worst two months in the 800 years of Riga's history. On June 14, several thousand Latvians were arrested without warning and deported to Siberia. Hardly any of them would ever return home. On June 22, the Germans invaded the USSR and within a few days were able to occupy my husband said. 'The Russian army isn't going to stand for disorder here any more than it would at home.'

As we walked to the office next morning, we saw that the Russians had roped off the vast Esplanade and turned it into a military camp with field kitchens and improvised washing arrangements. Rows of tanks and lorries were drawn up on the perimeter. All around the square, people crowded to the ropes, watching the scene like visitors to a zoo. Suddenly my hat was snatched from my head. I whipped round in alarm, but it was only an old peasant woman. 'Better not wear a hat, my dear', she cautioned. 'These Russians are not used to ladies and gentlemen.'

In a few days, the aspect of Riga was completely altered without any revolutionary changes having been carried out. The police vanished from the streets, their place being taken by soldiers directing traffic with improvised red flags. Illuminated signs, advertisements for a capitalist economy, were turned off and had not yet been replaced by the giant red stars so beloved of the Russian administration. Shop windows, nearly empty now, were unlit. People who normally dressed smartly now wore their oldest clothes. There was a pervading drabness, an almost tangible depression.

The Russians now faced an awkward problem. Ever since the Revolution, there had been an acute shortage of consumer goods and dwelling space in the USSR. The evidence of Latvian prosperity could not be eliminated overnight, but in the meantime the armed forces needed to be given some explanation as to why a small country under a 'corrupt capitalist administration' could achieve for its people a standard of living so much higher than that in Russia. The story was put about, and was actually believed, that Riga was part of a great exhibition and that the city would shortly return to normal.

Riga as the Soviet forces provided minimal resistance. On June 30, Latvian radio played the national anthem again and the Germans were seen by many in Riga as liberators. Their true colours were quickly revealed; on July 4 they hoarded about 1,500 Jews into the main synagogue and set it alight. Concentration camps were then set up around Riga for the murder of most of the 90,000 Jewish community in Latvia. A similar fate awaited anyone who offered the slightest resistance to the Nazi regime. An independent Latvia was as alien a concept to the Germans as it was to the Soviets. When Soviet forces retook Riga in October 1944, there were a few Latvians fighting on both sides; most regarded the two occupiers with equal contempt.

There could not be a greater contrast between the Tsarist regime and the Soviet one that ruled between 1944 and 1991. The latter one, by ineffective and sometimes brutal centralisation under Moscow, converted Riga into an embittered backwater with no links abroad. German culture was largely banned and Latvian culture restricted to painting and fiction. No references were made to the many Latvian writers and artists by now working abroad. No attempt was made to acknowledge or revive the contributions made by the murdered Jewish community to Riga's science, music and architecture. With no transport links to the West by either sea or air, Riga was more isolated than it had been in the days of the Vikings a thousand

RIGA IN 1992
Frances Samuel

Riga in February 1992 was dark, secretive, intense; winter was long and cold and there was little street lighting; rooms were lit with 40-watt light bulbs; the few shops open were smelly and empty; a few sad white cabbages in the market; black smoky buses, sweaty and steamy inside; muddy trams with tinkly warning bells; almost no private phones, no telephone directory, no local maps; practically no private cars. The dingy airport provided connexions to only three Western destinations. People hurried along the wet pavements, eyes down, guarded. But if you looked closely, the passing women often had a style about them, interesting hats worn at just the angle, well-cut – albeit well-worn – coats and suits in a post-war New Look style. With no modern make-up available, they plucked their eyebrows and wore one red lipstick, Edith Piaf-like. I came to admire these women greatly, particularly ones in their fifties, who were often living, eating and sleeping in one room, shared with an old difficult mother, bringing up a child, with a husband long gone away. They worked all day, made the best of their cramped quarters, queued for hours for basics, cooked and washed in primitive conditions, could not travel abroad – and yet they kept their spirits alive with poetry and music, taught their children the truth, preserved their belief in freedom in spite of the decades of oppression – and wore their hats just so. One middle-aged apolitical grandmother told me later that when, the previous summer, word had gone around that Soviet tanks were coming to the main square she realised that she was ready to lie down in front of them to defend her new-found freedom.

I was told the best café in town was just along the street from the hotel – the Kafejnica Luna. I had high hopes of somewhere cosy and welcoming to escape to from the hotel. I took the children with me. The café door was banged in my face, and when I did manage to open it, the strip lighting revealed peeling paint, asbestos tiles sagging from the ceiling, solitary women standing, gazing at the wall, snatching a hasty cup of coffee and, it had to be admitted, some really good cakes, slammed down on the counter by a none too obliging manageress.

We took our family car with us. Western cars were a rarity, and we had to remember to take the windscreen wipers off the car every time we left it: otherwise they would be gone by the time we got back. One colleague forgot this rule and duly found her blades had disappeared. It was snowing hard. She became increasingly desperate and finally had the brilliant idea of putting her mittens on to the remains of the wipers. The only petrol supply, apart from the Russian army trucks by the side of the road selling

years earlier. A lot of money was indeed spent in Latvia on education and in the arts, but this was always with a Russian and a political agenda.

The Soviet regime was at its most brutal in the immediate aftermath of the war. Visually, the most dramatic display of its power took place early in the morning of May 23 1948 when the ruins of the House of Blackheads on Town Hall Square were blown up. This was a Sunday, so few people would have been around as gritty petrol, was to be found – if you could find the place at all – well out of the city centre, run from a kiosk by a large grumpy lady from behind a net curtain, who might or might not agree to sell you some from her one rusty pump. A few months after we arrived, we drove off for a wintry trip to the sea at Saulkrasti and to our amazement saw a brand new Nordic petrol station, Riga's first – selling not just fuel but also the previous day's *Financial Times* and Oreo chocolate biscuits. Best of all, it provided somewhere cheerful and bright to have a cup of coffee. 'Hang the freezing beach walk,' we said, 'we'll spend the rest of the day at the petrol station.'

The English Church of St Saviour's, built for the British community in Riga in 1859, had been used in Soviet times as a disco, painted a depressing purple, and was now closed up and empty. A visiting Anglican clergyman, a friend of the then US Ambassador in Riga, offered to hold a communion service in the derelict building. Ten or so of us joined in the first such celebration for 50 years or more, standing in a semicircle in front of a plain wooden table which served as an altar, with a cross made from two wooden poles tied together propped up in a camera tripod, and bread from a local baker's shop. The chalice was an ordinary wineglass we borrowed from the hotel bar. Our vicar had a fine actor's voice, which swept us along as we gave our hesitant and emotional responses; it was an extremely moving experience. Some months later a young American Lutheran minister began to hold regular services. The church in those early days was a lifeline for the tiny group of foreign diplomats, traders, students and others, as well as a few brave Latvians, and one splendid old Russian lady. We would gather after a stressful week, stand in a comforting circle for communion and say the Lord's Prayer together, each in her or his own language. Before we left Riga we got a young Latvian silversmith to put a silver collar on the humble wineglass. It is still sometimes used by the now thriving congregation of the fully re-established Anglican church.

Unlike our own people in London, the Latvians had never forgotten that the old British Legation building from before World War II was still ours. Soon after we arrived we were invited to a mysterious meeting at which a presentation would be made. After a speech of welcome to us a package was handed to Richard with great ceremony: inside was the brass plate from the old British Legation which had been secretly preserved through the Soviet occupation by an old lady, and now, in free Latvia, was proudly being handed back. It was a deeply touching gesture. Before we left in 1993 we moved into an annexe which later became the consul's offices. Now this supposedly over-large building is already bursting at the seams.
Richard and Frances Samuel reopened the British Embassy in Riga in 1991.

witnesses to what was taking place in broad daylight. Two years later there would be a similar tragedy in Berlin with the Royal Palace and as late as 1969 yet another in Kaliningrad with the castle. The aim on the three occasions was the same: all evidence of German imperialism had to be eliminated. In Riga, the whole Town Hall Square would subsequently be 'Sovietised' leaving no memories of what it had been like in early 1941. Fortunately, there was no further destruction in Riga, but it was only in the 1980s that serious attempts were begun to maintain and restore the Old Town.

During the Soviet era, the city's population increased from 250,000 at the end of the war to nearly a million in 1990 and much of this increase was amongst the Russian ethnic community who quickly represented more than 50% of this population. Massive industrial projects were begun around Riga to provide a pretext for bringing in more and more workers from outside with a consequent decline in the Latvian language. Refrigerators, washing machines and radiograms were amongst the bulky consumer durables produced in Riga and for which the USSR became so notorious. Most Soviet train carriages likewise came from Riga. Had the Soviet Union lasted longer, Riga would probably have had a metro built, since central funds were always found for this when towns grew to over a million people. The project was resisted, when this became possible during the 'perestroika' era of the late 1980s. This was partly out of fears for the Old Town under which it would be built, and partly to prevent further Russian immigrants desperate to enjoy the 'window on the West'. Perestroika was also the time when Riga would see many peaceful demonstrations for Latvian independence and when the Latvian flag could reappear in public.

Sadly the Soviet Union could not leave Latvia without bloodshed. Despite the worldwide ignominy suffered by Moscow after the January 13 1991 shootings in Vilnius, a similar tragedy took place in Riga a week later on January 20. Barricades had been put up by the local population around crucial buildings, but Soviet troops were determined to seize the Latvian Radio building opposite the Dom Cathedral, and five civilians were killed; thanks to foreign journalists, the whole world immediately knew. During the short-lived coup attempt on August 19 and 20, Soviet troops were again seen on the streets of Riga, but this was for the last time. On the 21st, Riga became the capital of a truly independent Latvia.

What did not return to Riga was its status as a regional capital with influence beyond Latvia. In contrast to 1920, foreign governments and international companies regarded the three Baltic States equally so foreign embassies and offices are as prevalent in Tallinn and Vilnius as they are in Riga. The other two countries would never have accepted a Baltic currency, controlled largely from Riga, which was initially suggested as an alternative to the dying Russian rouble. Riga is, and will stay, a Baltic capital but will never again be the Baltic capital. Even within Latvia, its trading status is constantly under threat from the port of Ventspils, ever eager to take business from Riga, be it the 2003 Eurovision Song Contest or transit shipping from Russia. Until 1940 business came automatically to Riga since its supremacy was never in doubt. Now it always has to be won.

It took until 2002 before a decision was made to have a totally new public building designed by a Latvian. Gunars Birkerts, who has spent all his working life in the United States, provided a design as early as 1989 for a new national library which would bring together the many collections scattered around Riga. It took 13 years to guarantee the funding and it will be 2008 before it is fully functional. Let us hope it is the precursor to many more such buildings, if Riga is to become a truly Latvian capital.

PRACTICAL INFORMATION
Communications
Telephones
The country code for international calls to Latvia is 371. Riga numbers with seven digits do not require an additional area code. Six digit numbers require the

area code 2. To call foreign numbers from Latvia the international access code is the standard 00 which should be followed by the relevant country code.

Post office

The main post office (*Latvijas Pasts*) is at 19 Brīvības iela and is open 24 hours. It sells phonecards and postcards, and can help with international calls. Other post offices are at Stacijas laukums (Station Square), 41–43 Elizabetes iela and 24 Aspāzijas bulvāris between the two bookshops Valters un Rapa and Globuss. This last sells packaging materials so is convenient for posting books abroad.

Internet cafés

Prices vary enormously throughout the town and are particularly high on the main streets frequented by tourists. Elsewhere it should be possible to pay around Ls1 an hour during the day and around 0.80 lats an hour at night. Some centres have an all-night rate of around 2 lats applicable for any length of time between 22.00 and 06.00. There is a 24-hour internet centre in the underpass linking the railway station and the Old Town which has good rates, and also one at the bus station which is open for about 12 hours a day. In the Old Town itself, **Dualnet** at Peldu 17 is open 24 hours a day and is probably the cheapest outlet there.

Banks and money

Changing money in Riga is not a problem: most banks have a bureau de change, and there are ATMs all over the city. In addition, there are exchange booths (*valutas maina*) in many streets and in shops in the city centre, and of course most hotels will change money. All are reliable, although rates do vary, so it can be worth shopping around, especially if you are changing a large sum. Hotels tend not to give such a good rate as the bureaux.

Rates for British pounds and for Estonian kroon are particularly erratic. In summer 2002, two casinos and a wine merchant gave consistently good rates for sterling. They are the **Renaissance** Casino at Kaļķu 22 close to the Hotel de Rome, the **Arkelins** Casino at Teātra 12, beside the Hotel de Rome, and **Arka** at Tērbatas 12.

There is a 24-hour currency exchange bureau called **Ahāts** at 26 Brīvības bulvāris, 90 Brīvības iela and on Stacijas laukums, the square in front of the railway station. The other, **Marika**, has branches at 14 Basteja bulvāris and 30 Brīvības iela.

Cash machines are also becoming more common in Riga, and a large number accept Visa and Mastercards. (Most machines have English-language instruction options.)

Eurocheques and **travellers' cheques** can be changed at many banks, but are never accepted in restaurants. It is best to carry a certain amount of cash for drinks and to pay admission charges, but almost everything else can be put on a credit card.

Tourist information

The Riga **Tourist Information Centre** is centrally located on Town Hall Square at Rātslaukums 6. It is open 10.00–19.00 every day. The phone number is 703 7900, email: tourinfo @rcc.lv and website: www.rigatourism.com. This office has limited free material to hand out, but sells a range of maps and guidebooks.

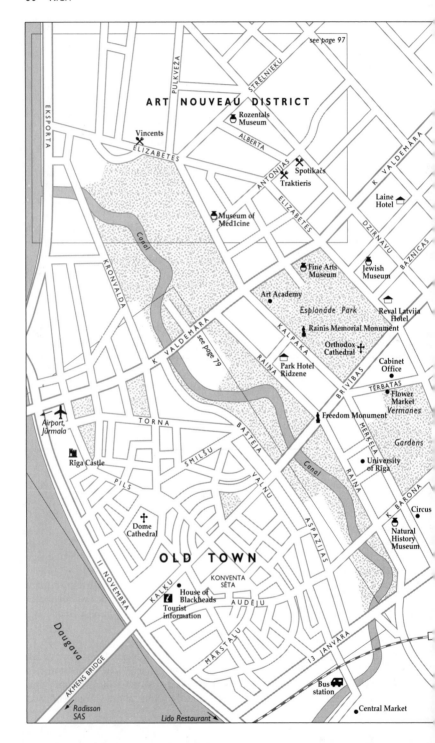

see page 97

ART NOUVEAU DISTRICT

EKSPORTA

PULKVEŽA

STRĒLNIEKU

Rozentals
Museum

Vincents

ALBERTA

ELIZABETES

K VALDEMĀRA

ANTONIJAS

Spotikačs

Traktieris

ELIZABETES

Laine
Hotel

DZIRNAVU

BAZNĪCAS

Museum of
Medicine

KRONVALDA

Fine Arts
Museum

Jewish
Museum

Art Academy

Esplanāde Park

Reval Latvija
Hotel

K VALDEMĀRA

see page 79

KALPAKA

RAINA

Rainis Memorial Monument

Orthodox
Cathedral

Cabinet
Office

Park Hotel
Ridzene

BRIVIBAS

TĒRBATAS

Flower
Market

Vērmanes

Airport,
Jūrmala

TORŅA

BASTEJA

MERKELA

Freedom Monument

Gardens

Rīga Castle

SMILŠU

VALNU

RAINA

University
of Riga

PILS

Canal

K BARONA

Circus

Dome
Cathedral

Natural
History
Museum

OLD TOWN

KONVENTA
SĒTA

KALKU

House of
Blackheads

Tourist
information

AUDĒJU

ASPAZIJAS

Daugava

II NOVEMBRA

MĀRSTALU

13 JANVĀRA

AKMENS BRIDGE

Bus
station

Radisson
SAS

Lido Restaurant

Central Market

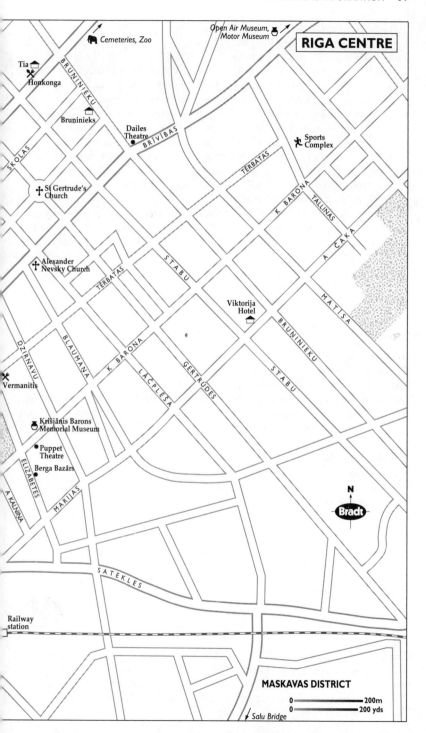

There are no offices at the airport or at the harbour, so it is not possible to book hotels on arrival at either place. If you'd like a guide to the city, ask at the tourist office.

The bimonthly magazine *Riga In Your Pocket* provides a pleasantly irreverent contrast to the many more formal guidebooks now around and to the plethora of free listings magazines that have sprouted in the last few years. It costs Ls1.20 and lists all the major hotels, restaurants, clubs and tourist attractions, plus some ideas for travel outside Riga. It also gives details of the bus, tram and trolleybus services. It covers the opening hours of the many Riga museums and is a mini yellow pages for any other services visitors and local foreign residents may need. The guide is also published in full on the website, www.inyourpocket.com.

The **Riga Card** is sold by the Tourist Information Centre and at a number of hotels. It offers free local transport and free admission to some museums but few visitors are likely to reach the cost of the card by paying as they go. They may also find that the card is not recognised by some drivers and museum attendants. There is no reduction in cost on Monday and Tuesday when many museums are closed. In spring 2003 the price was Ls8 for one day, Ls12 for two days and Ls16 for three days.

Jāņa Sēta is the best known map publisher in the Baltics and they publish many detailed **maps** of Riga and the surrounding area. Their shop at Elizabetes iela 83–85 sells these at lower prices than those in other shops. For a general range of guidebooks and maps, and also for the more lavish architectural guides to Riga, **Pie Doma** at Krāmu 3 can be recommended as its prices are considerably lower than those at the more famous bookshops near the Riga Hotel.

Lattelkom provides an information service which can be obtained by calling 118. The service costs Ls0.09 a minute. Operators speaking Latvian, Russian and English can give the usual directory enquiries kind of information, but also give out information on what is on in theatres and cinemas and so on; you can also dial the number to obtain directions if you are lost.

Public holidays

Good Friday	
Midsummer	June 23–24
Independence Day	November 18
Christmas	December 24–26
New Year	January 1

Tours

A number of firms offer city tours by coach. It is probably best to organise these through your hotel if you are staying in one that offers this facility. Otherwise you can contact one of the agencies below:

Impro Merķeļa 13; tel: 722 1312; fax: 722 1256; email: impro@impro.lv; web: www.impro.lv

Latvia Tours 8 Kaļķu iela; tel: 708 5001; fax: 782 0020; email: hq@latviatours.lv; web: www.latviatours.com; also at 13 Marijas iela; tel: 724 3391. Does city tours and also offers trips to the Open Air Musuem, Rundāle Palace, Sigulda, Cēsis, Kurzeme and Latgale. Bookings can also be made at the Hotel Latvijā (tel: 722 1040) and at the Hotel de Rome (tel: 721 6168).

Norvista Elizabetes 63; tel: 728 3338; fax: 728 7977; email: info@norvista.lv; web: www.norvista.lv

Riga City Tour by double decker bus, leaves from Raiņa bulvāris, just by the Freedom Monument, every day at 10.00, 12.00, 15.30 and 18.00 for a city tour of 2½–3 hours.

Student and Youth Travel Bureau Lacplesa 29; tel: 728 4818; fax: 728 3064; email: sjcb@sjcb.lv; web: sjcb.lv

TAS (Travel Agency Satellite) 21–22 Raina Blvd; tel: 722 2901 or 781 4045; fax: 782 0285; email: tas@blatnet.lv. Offers group and individual tours and general travel agency services.

VIA Hansa Tours Alunāna 3; tel: 722 7232; fax: 782 0294; email: Riga@viahansa.com; web: www.viahansa.com

Transport

Riga has a well-developed transport system of eight **tram** lines, 24 **trolleybus** lines and 39 **bus** lines. The fare is charged at a flat rate of Ls0.20 a journey. Different tickets are needed for each mode of transport. Tickets can only be bought on board from the *konduktors*. Unlike in Tallinn and Vilnius, they cannot be bought in advance at kiosks. An extra ticket has to be bought for a suitcase. In addition to the bus, tram or trolleybus, there is another form of transport, the *taksobuss* or *mikroautobuss*, which covers longer distances and costs more depending on the length of the journey.

The maps in *Riga in Your Pocket* and the yellow Jāņa Sēta Riga map contain information showing public transport routes.

Taxis are fairly reliable provided you use official ones which have a meter (though ensure it is on). Some have orange and black markings and all have yellow number plates. Rates are about Ls0.30 per kilometre during the day, rising to 40 per kilometre between 22.00 and 06.00. There is usually a surcharge to pay for entry into the Old Town. To avoid this, take taxis from just outside, at the Hotel de Rome, Town Hall Square or Riga Castle.

The **bus station** (*autoosta*) is in Prāgas iela, close to the main market and on the other side of the railway station (under the bridge) away from the city centre. You can try to phone for information; tel: 721 3611, but may find it advisable to attend in person: timetables are on display; otherwise apply to window 1. The timetables posted often list only the final destination, not en-route stops. **Eurolines** have an office in the bus station which sells tickets on all its international services to neighbouring countries. From 2002, rival companies began to compete with Eurolines on services to Tallinn and Vilnius, usually with lower prices. Check the various offices at the bus station for prices and schedules.

The **railway station** is at Stacijas laukums; tel: 723 3397 for bookings and 237 2134 for information.

Airport

The airport is about 8km from the city centre and the 22 and 22a link the two, the 22 going to the bus stop on 13 Janvāra, just outside the Old Town and the 22a going to the Orthodox Church close to the Latvia Hotel. The fare is Ls0.20 on both routes with a second ticket being needed for suitcases. The buses do not stop directly outside the terminal but about 100m away across the car park. The service, which runs every half-hour, stops around 22.30 so passengers arriving later are advised to pre-book a transfer with their tour operator in case insufficient taxis are available. Taxis cost about 8 lats (£9/US$14). Currency exchange offices are open whenever flights arrive and leave.

Port
The tram stop is about 300m from the terminal and trams run every few minutes. The fare for any distance is Ls0.20 (£0.23/US$0.36).

River boats
From May to September, several companies offer one- or two-hour river trips on the Daugava. At weekends they also offer trips to Mezaparks, for the zoo and funfair. It is possible to travel one way by boat to Mezaparks and then to return by no 11 tram or to do this journey in reverse. The pier is on 11th November, opposite Town Hall Square, near to the Akmens Bridge. The cost is usually Ls1 in each direction and catering is available on board.

Car hire
Visitors restricting their itinerary to Riga will have little need for a car as public transport is so good and so cheap and can be supplemented with the occasional taxi. Equally those visiting other towns will find the local bus service quite sufficient. Obviously for visits to smaller places, and for a rushed itinerary to several towns, a car is ideal. During the peak travel season of June–August it is essential to pre-book and at other times advisable, if only to secure the lower prices that tour operators abroad can normally negotiate.

The major international companies all have offices at the airport and can arrange delivery there or to a hotel. A local company based at the airport that may be able to help at the last minute is **Sixt** (tel: 720 7121; fax: 720 7131; email: car.rent@carlease.lv; web: www.sixt.lv).

Accommodation
This last few years have seen an enormous expansion in the range of accommodation available in Riga. Old hotels have been renovated and many new ones built. The years 1999–2000 saw concentration on four- to five-star hotels, and more recently many smaller ones in the three-star category have opened. In 2001,with the celebrations surrounding the 800th anniversary of the founding of Riga, hotels filled up easily and charged accordingly. In 2002, although published prices remained high, there was massive discounting through tour operators both for groups and for individuals. The Eurovision Song Contest will ensure full occupancy and high prices at the end of May 2003, but otherwise tourists on package holidays should be able to enjoy rates previously only available in Tallinn and Vilnius. Prices always include a buffet breakfast. Visitors happy to stay outside the Old Town will benefit from much lower hotel prices, both for rooms and for the other services such as minibars, laundry and room phones. Tram services ensure quick links into the Old Town at all times of day. They have dedicated tracks so are unaffected by rush hours.

Hotel websites and brochures may quote prices in lats, US dollars or euros, but payment will always be in lats. There is little difference in price between single and twin rooms as single travellers will usually be given a twin room anyway. In superior hotels, rooms booked direct are likely to cost around £100/US$160 a night; in the medium range ones, about £60/US$95 a night in the town centre and £40/US$65 elsewhere. Rates are reduced in several hotel chains if bookings are made at the same time for partner hotels in Tallinn and Vilnius.

Superior hotels

Ainavas Peldu 23; tel: 781 4316; fax: 781 4317; email: reservations@ainavas.lv; web: www.ainavas.lv.
This hotel opened to great acclaim in 2000. The side-street location in the Old Town was welcome as was the acceptance of both summer and winter, a courtyard for the former and a real open fire in the lounge for the latter. Ainavas means 'landscape' and each of the 23 rooms has an original painting showing a different aspect of the Latvian countryside. In 2000, the computer technology provided in each room was seen as novel. Soon it will probably be standard, as other hotels catch up.

Eurolink 22 Aspāzijas bulvāris; tel: 722 0531; fax: 721 6300; email: eurolink@brovi.lv; web: www.brovi.lv.
This is actually the third floor of the Hotel Riga (see below) but is run as a separate hotel under joint Latvian-Swedish management. It was the first four-star hotel in the capital when it was set up, and offers modern conference and meeting rooms as well as accommodation of a high standard (59 rooms) and Scandinavian cuisine in the restaurant. It is conveniently located, right next to the Opera House and within easy reach of the Old and New Towns. Whatever changes are made to the Hotel Riga, the Eurolink will always be one step ahead.

Hotel Grand Palace 12 Pils iela; tel: 704 4000; fax: 704 4001; email: hotel@grandpalace.lv; web: www.schlossle-hotels.com.
Following the success of their Park Consul and St Petersbourg hotels in Tallinn, the Schlossle Hotel group opened this hotel in Riga Old Town in May 2000. The clientele immediately became the similar cross section of the great and perhaps the good, but certainly the famous. As in Tallinn, an ancient façade on a narrow cobbled street hides a hotel of discreet but extensive luxury in both the public areas and in the 56 rooms. An open fire during the winter is a hallmark of these hotels but unique to Riga is the Orangerie where a traditional afternoon tea is served.

Gutenbergs Doma Laukums 1; tel: 781 4090; fax: 750 3326; email: hotel@gutenbergs.lv; web: gutenbergs.lv.
The building dates from 1880 and was designed as a book depository and printing works by the architect Jānis Baumanis, the first ethnic Latvian to gain recognition in a field previously dominated by the Baltic Germans. It would then publish the plays of Rūdolf Blaumanis, who played a similar role in Latvian literature and ensured that Latvian would never again be seen as a 'peasant's language'. The current displays on each floor emphasise this literary past and although he had no links to Riga, facsimiles from pages of the Gutenberg Bible are on display. In certain rooms, heritage has had to take precedence over convenience as vast wooden beams stretch across desks and sinks. Some rooms are rather small for a hotel of this class, but the location beside the cathedral, the ambience and the décor more than make up for this. The rooftop 'Summer Garden' offers views of 17 nearby churches.

Konventenhof or **Konventa Sēta** 9–11 Kalēju iela; tel: 708 7501; fax: 708 7506; email: reservation@konventa.lv; web: www.konventa.lv.
This hotel is housed in a complex of restored buildings in the heart of Old Riga (see

page 90 for an account of the restoration of the Konventa Sēta). It has 80 rooms and 61 apartments. The background to the hotel undoubtedly still gives it some appeal, although the many competitors it now has in the Old Town have long since withdrawn its former exclusivity. Rooms are large, but some on the ground floor are perhaps too close for comfort to the outside world. Noise on Kalēju can intrude late in the evenings. The restaurant is surprisingly and unnecessarily modest about what it offers, both at breakfast and for dinner.

Man-Tess 6 Teātra iela; tel: 721 6056 or 721 0225; fax: 782 1249; email: man-tess@binet.lv.

This charming hotel in the centre of Old Riga is an elegant 18th-century house once owned by Kristofs Hāberlands (1750–1803) who designed a number of houses in the Old Town. It has only six rooms (three doubles, one single, two suites and four offices), each one in a different style (the so-called white room is light and modern, the 18th-century room is furnished in the style of the Hanseatic period). The ground floor restaurant is exotically decorated (marble, water and even caged birds) and is one of the best in the Old Town.

Maritim Park Slokas 1; tel: 706 9000; fax: 706 9001; email: info.rig@maritim.lv; web: www.maritim.lv.

This was for many years the rather seedy Hotel Turist but it reopened as a totally new four-star hotel with 240 rooms in May 2000. The waterfall in the lobby immediately sets the tone of the building. Its location 'over the river' may put off some visitors but others will appreciate the extra space, the quieter environment, the access to cheap local shops and above all its much lower prices. The Old Town is in any case only a ten-minute tram-ride away and in the summer this is a pleasant walk of half an hour. The 11th-floor restaurant is an excellent venue for a sunset dinner during the summer.

Metropole 36–38 Aspāzijas bulvāris; tel: 722 5411; fax: 721 6140; email: metropole@metropole.lv; web: www.metropole.lv.

Run by the same Latvian-Swedish management team as the Eurolink, the Metropole is suitable for both tourists and the business traveller. Built in 1871, it is the oldest hotel in Riga. It has 80 rooms and was completely refurbished before reopening in 1992. Another refurbishment would not go amiss now, as many other hotels can now compete on location, design and certainly on facilities. Double rooms are generous, singles rather tight, and rooms at the front are exposed to the noise of trams. As with the Europa, it is conveniently located next to the Opera House and within easy reach of the Old and New Towns. Single rooms cost US$109–160, doubles US$129–185 and suites about US$240. All rooms are equipped with satellite phone and cable TV.

Park Hotel Ridzene 1 Reimersa iela; tel: 732 4433; fax: 732 2600; email: park.hotel@ridzene.lv; web: parkhotelridzene.com.

In Soviet times, senior foreign guests were housed here and the hotel has tried to maintain a similar air of exclusivity. The exterior clearly reveals its past, although the inside certainly does not. Only in 1999 was it properly modernised and for a long time it tried to maintain prices that no government, Latvian or foreign, was willing to pay. The 100 rooms here are smaller than might be expected in a business hotel but they are frequently updated and the underground car park is a rare bonus for a town-centre hotel. All rooms and facilities are accessible by wheelchair. From September 11 2001 its location behind the American Embassy became a nuisance rather than an advantage and this was amongst a number of factors leading to a change in policy. Although published prices stayed high, massive discounts became available through agents.

Radisson SAS Daugava Hotel 24 Kugu iela; tel: 706 1111; fax: 706 1100; email: reservations.riga@radissonsas.com; web: www.radissonsas.com.
This is the leading business hotel in the Baltics and claims to be the only real conference hotel. It has 361 large rooms and suites, all with individually controlled air conditioning, including two floors of executive rooms which have their own lounge for drinks and a fully equipped business centre. There is security parking, 24-hour room service and cable TV. With 10 air-conditioned conference rooms the hotel can arrange meetings for up to 360 delegates. A business service offers translation, secretarial and other commercial services. The Mediterranean Talavera restaurant is a restful alternative to the all-day American Grill, while the Vienna Café offers pastries and coffee. In April 2003, the Olympia Casino was opened. For those seeking exercise, there is a modern fitness centre, a sauna and the only sensibly large swimming pool in any Riga hotel.

Published prices reflect the hotel's business focus, but tourists can get excellent rates at weekends, and in July and August. Agents who specialise in the Baltics can often offer competitive prices year-round. The building is a rather unimaginative white block on 'the wrong side' of the Daugava away from the main part of the city, but it is quiet and has spectacular views over the river. For these reasons, together with the size of its rooms, it has now attracted a regular clientele of business visitors and tourists. It offers free transfers from the airport and an hourly shuttle bus to the Old Town.

Reval Latvija Elizabetes 55; tel: 777 2222; fax: 777 2332; email: latvia.sales@revalhotels.com; web: revalhotels.com.
Formerly known just as the Latvia Hotel, and in Soviet times almost the only place tourists could stay in Riga, the Reval group have brought about as complete an alteration as they did with the similarly large Hotel Olümpia in Tallinn and which they are also expected to do with the Lietuva in Vilnius. The staff have been transformed as much as the building and given its size the clientele is ironically as varied now as it was in the Soviet era. Business visitors mix with tourists, Latvians mix with long-lost relatives now happy to return home. In winter, some visitors never leave as the shops and different restaurants cover every likely need. The bar on the 26th floor and the sauna on the 27th are both of obvious appeal and neither overcharges. Higher charges of course apply for the high rooms looking towards the Old Town but few rooms are without some sort of view.

Riga Hotel 22 Aspāzijas bulvāris; tel: 704 4222; fax: 704 4223; email: info@hotel.Riga.lv; web: www.hotelriga.lv.
A very necessary renovation began in autumn 2002 but perhaps because of the hotel's Soviet past, no information was offered on what could be expected in 2003. The website must be one of the blandest in Riga. In the past, the hotel has always been three or four years behind its competitors in the facilities that it offers, but perhaps this time they will finally leap ahead. The location of the hotel, opposite the Opera House, is ideal, as is the size of the rooms. All it now needs is imaginative redesigning and imaginative restaffing. To see what the staff got up to before 1991, visit the Occupation Museum which displays the bugging devices they used to monitor phone calls.

Rolands Kaļķu 3a; tel: 722 0011; fax: 728 1203; email: info @hotelrolands.lv; web: www.hotelrolands.lv.
Without doubt, the opening of this hotel in summer 2002 was one of the most publicised events in the tourism calendar of Riga that year. Naming it after the town's patron saint and a location in the heart of the Old Town were sensible moves, but it is the broad glass frontage which was bound to attract attention. Equally, the artist Lilia Dinere at work on the murals in the restaurant for several weeks after the opening was

certain to keep journalists interested. She is probably better known in Latvia for her stained glass but the medieval themes she has chosen will fit well into a cellar with walls dating from the 16th century and a well from the 12th century. Fillet of deer marinated in gin, breast of duck with baked parsnips and raspberry tart with ginger sauce are amongst the many unusual dishes offered.

The rooms use birch wood (all from Latvia) extensively and have ample cupboard space. The waterfall beside the lift gives the interior a further rural feel. Standard rooms are quite small, though adequate for a short stay. Long-stay visitors will find the higher charge for a bigger room worthwhile.

Hotel de Rome 28 Kaļķu iela; tel: 708 7600, fax 708 7606; email: reservation@derome.lv, web: www.derome.lv.

The hotel is now better known for its top-floor restaurant **Otto Schwarz** than for its accommodation. The political elite started to eat there immediately after independence, and they still do. The food and the enormous wine list certainly deserve this attention and the view across to the Freedom Monument makes the location politically very correct indeed. Prices are much lower at lunch-time. The ground-floor entrance used to match the grandeur of the restaurant but no longer does. The arcade of antique shops and jewellers through which it is now reached perhaps reflects the current standard of the hotel. It is a good business-class hotel, but no longer exclusive. Rates fall drastically in the summer and at weekends as it does not enjoy regular tourist traffic.

Medium-range hotels

Brigita 11 Saulkalnes; tel: 762 3000; fax: 762 3190; email: hotel.brigita@delfi.lv.
Unlike many other hotels that opened in the early 1990s, the Brigita has always changed with the times. If it can do nothing about its location, about 25 minutes by trolleybus from the centre, it regularly updates its furnishings and now offers suites for prices which barely secure rooms elsewhere. It will not suit the rushed tourist but many will take advantage of its low rates to extend their stay in Riga.

Bruņinieks (The Knight) Bruņinieku 6; tel: 731 5140; fax: 731 4310; email: hotel@bruninieks.lv.
As no foreigner can pronounce this name, it is due to change to City in 2003, when an extra wing will also open. A suit of armour is displayed in the foyer, but otherwise this is a perfectly normal three-star hotel. Some may find the location near the theatre of help and it is sufficiently far from the town centre for the neighbouring shops all to offer Latvian rather than Western prices and for peace and quiet to be assured in the evenings. The lack of a restaurant is a bonus in this respect too. The hotel caters in particular for families, with adjoining rooms available and – for those with smaller children – triple rooms with a roll-up bed. Being just off Brīvības, the main road leading to the Freedom Monument, the hotel has a wide range of buses within walking distance.

Hotel Centra Audēju 1; tel: 722 6441; fax: 750 3281; email: centra@hotel.lv.
This welcome addition to the small hotels in the Old Town opened in June 2000 with 24 rooms so is well suited to individual travellers. Access by taxi is easy as it is near one of the Old Town entry points and the baths in every room will be welcomed by many. Each room has an original Latvian painting in it, and the hotel prides itself on the fact that all the furniture and fabrics are produced in Latvia too. Good soundproofing fortunately protects guests from the lively nightlife in the surrounding streets. Photographers should try for a room on the higher floors, to get a novel angle on the Old Town streets. Prices are usually much lower than those in similar hotels in the Old Town.

Forums Vaļņu 45; tel: 781 4680; fax: 781 4682, email reservations@hotelforums.lv; web: www. hotelforums.lv

A very modest exterior and gloomy entrance hall in fact disguises a well-appointed hotel which opened under Russian management in 2000. All rooms are large, with a bath, and some on the higher floors have good views. It is on the edge of the Old Town, in a quiet street, yet within easy walking distance of the bus and train stations, so also close to the airport bus stop. Breakfast is served but there is no restaurant or bar, which helps to ensure a quiet environment. For those who need to break with this calm, the hotel offers its guests free admission to an Old Town night club.

Karavella 27 Katrīnas dambis; tel: 732 3130; fax: 783 0187; email: hotel@karavella.lv; web: www.karavella.lv.

This is one of the few Riga hotels that does not seriously discount its individual rate to tour operators so attracts visitors who prefer to book direct and who are drawn by its low published rates (£40–60/US$65–100). The harbour location is however a major disadvantage as there are no close public transport links and no congenial walks nearby. The area is certainly 'Riga in the raw'.

Laine Hotel 11 Skolas iela; tel: 728 8816 or 728 9823; fax: 728 7658; email: info@laine.lv; web: www.laine.lv.

In the early 1990s backpackers tended to drift in here as there was no system for prebooking. It was a hostel then and some rooms still come into that category. Others can now definitely be called hotel rooms but the past continues to make its presence felt. A brighter entrance would be welcome as would the disappearance of communal showers.

Māra 186 Kalnciema iela; tel: 790 1316; fax: 790 1315; email: mara@mailbox.Riga.lv.

Part of the Best Western chain, the Māra has 24 rooms at prices from US$125–175 per night. It is out of the centre on the way to the airport but operates a shuttle bus to both the airport and the city centre. More of a business hotel than one for tourists.

OK Slokas 12, tel 786 0050; fax: 789 2702; email: service@:okhotel.lv; web: www.okhotel.lv.

Given the effort the hotel makes, it could perhaps have chosen a more positive name. Each floor has a different colour scheme and the terrace at the back is an ideal place to relax after a full summer's day. The hotel was completely new in 2000, and seems determined to maintain a freshly painted ambience. This hardly applies to some of the neighbouring shops and cafés, but the very low prices they charge more than makes up for this. The trams can be heard in the rooms at the front, but they are very convenient for the 15-minute journey into town. More active guests enjoy the 20-minute walk across the river to the castle.

Oma 33 Ernestīnes iela; tel: 761 3388 or 761 2388; fax: 761 3233; email: oma@com.latnet.lv; web: www.oma.lv.

A former private house in what was one of the more fashionable quarters of Riga before the war, this tastefully converted hotel has just 17 rooms plus meeting rooms for business clients. Located about 15 minutes from the city centre by bus and 20 minutes from the airport, this hotel is again more likely to appeal to the business user than the tourist, although long-stay visitors will appreciate the lower prices and the quiet location.

Radi un Draugi 1–3 Mārstaļu iela; tel: 722 0372; fax: 724 2239; email: radi@draugi.lv; web: www.draugi.lv.

Beloved by the British-Latvian community, the hotel for many years saw little need to modernise or to promote itself. It has recently extended to 76 rooms and may find it

difficult to fill them if modernisation does not keep pace with that of its many competitors. Corridors remain gloomy and the breakfast room cramped. Noise can also be a problem, with both a British and Irish pub too close for comfort.
Tia 63 Kr Valdemāra; tel: 733 3918 or 733 3396; fax: 783 0390; email: tia@tia.lv; web: www.tia.lv.
One local review says that 'it's reasonably priced with some amenities' and there is really little more to say. The concrete exterior is off-putting, but not enough has been done inside to make it welcoming, a particular lapse given the lack of amenities in the surrounding area. If budgets are critical, this is the place to stay, but a small extra outlay will provide much happier memories of Riga. The Old Town is walkable in 15 minutes.
Viktorija 55A Čaka iela; tel: 701 4111; fax: 701 4140; email: info@hotel-victorija; web: www.hotel-viktorija.lv.
Like several hotels that opened soon after independence, the Viktorija rather lost its way when many others opened later on. It now combines adequate rooms having full facilities with budget floors where bathrooms are shared. Even double-glazing does not keep out all the traffic noise from Čaka but a bus and tram stop outside has its uses, particularly for links to the bus and train stations.

Bed and breakfast and apartments

Bed and breakfast is still not common in Riga, as few Latvians have spare rooms in their very cramped flats. Apartments are now fairly easy to rent for a period of a week or more and these are usually adapted to the requirements of foreign business visitors, although tourists can of course use them as well. Agencies include:

Patricia Elizabetes 22-6; tel: 728 4868; fax: 728 6650; email: mike@rigalatvia.net; web: www.rigalatvia.net. This private tourist office handles both bed and breakfast and apartments for 3 days or more, from £45 per night.
Apartments Brīvības 183; tel: 733 9955; fax: 737 3608; email: briv183@latnet.lv. This agency is so sure about the furnishings and services in the 17 apartments it represents that it advertises under the slogan 'All You Need is Your Toothbrush'.
Dolce Vita Stabu 59, tel/fax: 727 0265; email: hoteldolcevita@inbox.lv. Whole apartments and individual rooms in them are offered.

Youth hostels

For up-to-date information, contact the **Hostel Association** at 2a Laimdotas iela; tel: 755 1271.

Placis 2a Laimdotas iela; tel: 755 1824. Prices are Ls3–6 a night. There are double and single rooms. Take the number 4 trolleybus or the number 1, 14 or 32 bus to the Teika stop.
Studentu Kopmītne 10 Basteja bulvāris; tel: 721 6221. Student rooms above the Baltika travel agency at Ls3–4 per person per night.
Technical University Hostel 22a Āzenes iela; tel: 203395 or 613843. Basic accommodation at Ls3 per person per night. Located on the Ķīpsala island, take the trolleybus (number 7 or 21) across the Daugava.
Turība 68 Graudu iela; tel: 790 1471. 158 beds at Ls5–7 per night. Take the number 8 trolleybus from Strēlnieku laukums to the Graudu stop.

Restaurants

Walking around the Old Town, deciding between an Armenian, a Japanese or a Swiss restaurant (amongst several hundred others), it is difficult to believe that hardly any existed 12 years ago. A pleasant stability has now arrived, with few failures and many successes. The famous grand restaurants of five years ago still have the same status and following. Those of a more casual nature, specialising in just one cuisine, are equally still in business, able to serve fastidious customers who are now at liberty to taste these cuisines at first hand in their countries of origin. All the superior hotels, without exception, have good restaurants and several of these are mentioned in the hotel descriptions. They are therefore not mentioned again below.

Many tourists never leave the Old Town for a meal but they miss a lot as a result. Whilst nobody has yet set up a good restaurant in the suburbs, within a mile of the Freedom Monument an extensive choice has emerged. The list below features a variety of locations, including several chosen specifically because they are out of the Old Town, but it should in no way be seen as comprehensive.

Hongkonga Valdemāra 61; tel: 781 2292. What a relief to find a Chinese restaurant in the Baltics where what you see is what you get. The ambience is straightforward but the cooking more elaborate. It is clear that Chinese are in control of the whole operation and are catering for their colleagues; if others wish to come, they are welcome to have a meal that makes no concessions to so-called Western tastes.

Ķirbis Doma Laukums 1; tel: 949-5409. That a vegetarian restaurant can thrive in a prime location beside the Stock Exchange and the Cathedral shows how broad-minded Latvia has quickly become since 1991. Portions are sold by weight and even the greediest will find it hard to spend more than Ls2 (£2.30/US$3.50). Have plenty of wild mushrooms to start with and always leave space for yoghurt and cake; otherwise, have a main course at lunch time and return for these during the afternoon. An array of artists and designers have been let loose indoors; walk around for a quick tour of the Latvian countryside.

Lido Atpūtas Centrs Krasta 76; tel: 781 2187. This is undoubtedly Riga's success story of 2002 in the restaurant world. To take over an out-of-town estate rather than a house in an area barely accessible by public transport required considerable daring but the gamble has paid off as the crowded car park proves every evening. Family groups are the main target, as large play areas are available, and service is cafeteria-style with trays along the counter. Yet more and more foreigners are now coming; they enjoy, as the Latvians do, the space, the light and the wooden tables, not to mention food of a variety and quality rarely obtainable in a self-service restaurant, and a micro-brewery in the cellar. They enjoy the broad clientele too; Latvia mixes here in a way it hardly does elsewhere. To get there take bus 17A from the railway station or a short taxi ride (Ls2–3).

Livonīja Meistaru 21; tel: 722 7824. There are few restaurants in Riga where an identical review could be written year after year. For the Livonīja, this is the case and it has always been positive. Nothing changes, and why should it? A broad international menu, with a wine list to match, is offered, the service remains subtly unobtrusive and the Jugendstil chairs will never be forgotten, even if the menu might be. The restaurant is in a cellar well underneath the hurly-burly of Livu laukums; this position shelters it not only from noise but also from the climate: it stays cool in summer and warm in winter.

Melnia Mūki (The Black Monk) 1–2 Jāņa sēta; tel: 721 5006. Dark and rather formal, this highly respected restaurant is rapidly gaining popularity for international food at prices that, if high for Riga, are by no means off the scale for the overseas visitor.

Nostalgija Kaļķu 22; tel: 722 2328. If everything here really belonged to the Soviet era, the name would be appropriate, but fortunately that is not the case. The marble décor, the chandeliers, and the wide open spaces are from that time, but the menu is too comprehensive and the service far too quick for these two aspects to generate memories. Order caviar and think back much further, probably to Tsarist times, and then the name may fit.

Ole Audēju 1. The food is so good here that one can hardly believe the restaurant is totally self-service. Perhaps as a reaction to the vegetarian Ķirbis on the other side of Cathedral Square, this is a place for carnivores. The size of the portions may be German or American, but the clientele is much wider. At the long wooden tables, ordinary Latvians may find themselves sitting next to tourists who have just bedecked themselves in amber at the next-door jewellery shop. All will be tucking into chicken or steak.

Otto Schwarz see Hotel de Rome, page 68.

Palete Gleznotāju 12; tel: 721 6037. Given its reputation for seafood, this restaurant should be nearer to the harbour, but it is in fact situated on a very short street in the Old Town. The entrance is narrow, but there is plenty of ground-floor space once inside and even a garden and courtyard. Few tourists find it, despite its proximity to several large hotels, which makes it pleasantly uncrowded during the summer and a relaxing environment for unwinding after a day's sightseeing. The background music, if on at all, is never oppressive.

Spotikačs Antonijas iela 12; tel: 750 5709. The somewhat childish décor of this Ukrainian restaurant, complete with floral friezes and strategically placed puppets, is at odds with its straightforward cuisine, offering excellent-value dishes of the 'meat and potatoes' variety.

Symposium 84/1 Dzirnavu iela; tel: 724 2545. This well-recommended restaurant is in the new Berga Bazārs. The décor has a distinctly southern European feel, as befits the good Mediterranean food and attentive service.

Traktieris Antonijas 8; tel: 733 2455. Hearing Russian and Ukrainian spoken here by other diners is clearly a good sign. The Russia to which this restaurant wants to link is of course the one that died in 1917, not the later variant that died in 1991. Although in the heart of the Jugendstil area, the décor is from rural Russia, as are the costumes worn by the staff. The menu is from aristocratic St Petersburg but the prices appeal to quite a range of classes. In 2002, a buffet was opened, presumably for architecture fanatics determined to miss nothing in the surrounding neighbourhood, but a stay of at least two hours is recommended in the main restaurant.

Vermanitis Elizabetes 65; tel: 728 6289. If Latvians meet each other, this is often the place they will choose. Prices are certainly not 'Old Town' and it manages to bridge the generation gap better than many other restaurants. Probably the self-service elements and the wooden dance floor help to do this. Older folk will be soothed by the stained glass and stone in much of the decoration. It is supposed to recall the first independence period from 1920 to 1940. Pizza and salad are always popular dishes here amongst foreigners but Latvians stick to the dependable local meat dishes.

Vincents Elizabetes 19; tel: 733 2634; web: www. vincents.lv. It is a pity that the massive advertising this restaurant undertakes always has to include the celebrities who have dined there. Their portraits unnecessarily dominate the foyer, and if anyone wants to know when the 'Archibishop' of Canterbury, or the Prince of 'Whales' dined there, the website will tell them. Luckily the food is of a higher standard than the English spelling, though steer clear of the 'gastronomic menu' in favour of individual dishes. The prices would certainly pass muster in central London though they drop to Bristol and Birmingham levels for several dishes at lunchtime, and the wine list is outrageous, so consider the house wines. Those unable to go at all can always try to make the dishes themselves, following the many recipes given on the website.

1739 Skārņu 6; tel: 721 1398. Many tourists are appalled at the sight of the tourist menu displayed on the street and quickly walk by. This is a mistake, since they then miss Riga's best Italian restaurant. It passes the ultimate test, which is with the pasta, rather than with the meat or fish. The sweets and coffee maintain this high standard. Slimmers and vegetarians should probably keep away and others can simply miss lunch and tea to make the most of the dinner here.

Bars and cafés

There is less of a distinction in Latvia than in other countries between bars, cafés and restaurants. Included below are places to visit for a snack, light meal or just a drink. To all intents and purposes, there are no licensing laws in Latvia, so alcohol can be sold and consumed anywhere. As with the restaurants, places listed below are just a minimal selection of what could have been included. No disrespect is intended to the many international fast-food chains now represented in Riga but not mentioned here. Their standards are well-known and they now have prime sites in Riga so addicts will have no difficulty in finding them.

Apsara Tea House Tērbatas 2. The architecture has a southern USA feel, with the stress on the white painted wood. The ambience is more Chinese, with the stress on the tea, rather than on any food. The leisurely approach to drinking could come from either culture. It is hard to say what links there are to Latvia, but perhaps the lack of any is the appeal to the many locals seen here regularly. A much smaller outlet can be found in the Old Town at Šķūņu 10, but it does seem sadly ordinary in comparison with its 'head office'.

Café Opera Aspāzijas. A suitably ornate café has been inside the Opera House since it opened in 1995, with plenty of marble and wood. It never advertises, which suits the regulars who prefer the peace and quiet and the absence of tourists even in July and August. An open-air café opened to a cacophony of silence in 2002, but because of its location and the photo opportunities it gives, soon filled up during the summer. A thick soup followed by a light salad makes a good lunch here. The waiters are well-trained for the local weather; at the first drop of rain, up go the parasols.

Jāņa Sēta Jāņa sēta. Do not look for this out of the summer season since it is entirely open-air, although well covered. The Hotel Konventa Sēta borders one side and they in fact operate it. The food comes in substantial portions and the quality of the garnishes and sauces warrants the slightly higher prices than would be paid elsewhere. However, given its size, nobody will mind if you linger over a beer and fail even to order garlic toast with it.

Kafe Inese Šķūņu 6. Given its Old Town location, the surroundings are surprisingly modest and the prices very low. The long opening hours until 02.00 can be useful, given the lack of choice in this area after midnight. Do not expect haute cuisine here, but the rapid service of a basic menu and the cheapest beer for miles have their own appeal.

Meingalvju nama kafejnica ... Rāts laukums 7. With a name like this (it means 'House of Blackheads Café), marketing to visitors was clearly not seen as a priority, but its location beside the House of Blackheads on Town Hall Square ensures a regular stream of clients. The staff work at the pace and with the enthusiasm of a Russian immigration officer, so anyone wanting coffee within 20 minutes of arrival goes to the counter inside to get it and probably still waits 10 minutes. In a town where tea is usually of a higher quality than coffee, it is good to find the reverse here, particularly with the cappuccino. If the delays do not matter and the weather is good, look around the square at leisure from an outdoor table and admire its quick architectural return from the Soviet Union to Latvia.

Pelmeņi Kaļķu 7. Latvians have not made many attempts to compete with the international chains in fast food, but here is one that has succeeded, as the regular midday queues will prove. *Pelmeņi* are dumplings and the proportions of meat to dough are very fair. They can be supplemented with salads, and followed with cakes or ice-cream. Alcohol is of course available too. Nobody lingers here, but for a quick cheap bite when the hotel buffet breakfast has finally been digested, it has few equals in the Old Town.

Pulvertornis (Powder Tower) Vaļņu 3. Two intimidatingly heavy sets of doors 'welcome' visitors to the War Museum but they are worth enduring for the basement café. Few tourists find it and not many Latvians do either but it makes a convenient and cool break during the summer from the crowds elsewhere in the Old Town. Given the size of the War Museum, it can also provide a break in a visit there. Do not expect serious service or an extensive choice but for a cheap and adequate beer and snack, it is ideal.

Smaragds Jāņa 18. There are not many cafés in Riga where anyone over 40 will immediately feel at ease. This is definitely one; absolutely no concessions are made to young people, in the décor, the music or from the menu. The music is in fact usually from a live pianist who would not take kindly to suggestions that he update his repertoire. The tables are polished wood, the paintings formal portraits and the light comes from a chandelier. The location is appropriately under the watchful eye of St John's and St Peter's churches.

For those too young or too modern to come here, the **Dickens Pub** and **Paddy Whelan's** are just around the corner in Grēcinieku.

Entertainment and nightlife

Riga offers not only offers plenty of traditional entertainment, but also a thriving club scene, appreciated by locals and visitors alike. Many clubs are open all day, and often serve food until late as well. At weekends, don't expect much action before 23.00 or so, though on Wednesday nights, dubbed by Latvians as 'little Saturday', everything starts around 21.00. Inevitably, clubs in favour come and go with the seasons, so it's worth checking locally, but current favourites that attract the non-teenage crowd include **Četri balti krekli** – 'Four White Shirts' (12 Vecpilsētas; tel: 721 3885), a cosy cellar club with live Latvian rock bands on a regular basis, and **Casablanca** (Smilsu 1–3; tel: 721 2420; www.casablanca.lv), a rather more stylish venue whose North African cuisine and cocktail menu is proving a popular combination. Cocktails are equally popular at the trendy chrome and glass **Deco Bar** in Berga Bazārs (tel: 728 9241), while at the opposite end of the spectrum is **Pulkvedim Neviens Neraksta** – 'Nobody writes to the Colonel' (26–28 Peldu; tel: 721 3886): loud, dark and thrumming to alternative rock and punk music. There are a number of **casinos**, too, of which the most recently opened – and upmarket – is that at the Radisson SAS Hotel. If you're seeking something calmer, don't despair, but head to one of the **Zen** branches (Stabu 6; tel: 731 6521, and Vāgnera 8; tel: 721 1540), and relax with tea and waterpipes to a background of soothing music.

Concert lovers and opera buffs have plenty of choice. Several churches, including St Peter's, stage regular concerts, and the organ recitals at the **Dome Cathedral** (tel: 721 3213) are world famous. The **Latvian National Opera** is based at 3 Aspazijas bulvaris (tel: 708 3745; web: www.opera.lv), with the annual Riga Opera Festival taking place in June.

Shopping

Shopping in Riga is good: you can buy almost anything you are likely to need. Below, however, are the names of some shops selling items which are peculiar to Latvia or Riga. Amber and jewellery are popular purchases, as are traditional wooden toys and linen. Latvian art is popular, especially ceramics. Consult *Riga in Your Pocket* and the other Riga city guides for details of local commercial galleries and what they are showing. Laima sweets and chocolates and the traditional Black Balsam drink in its distinctive bottle are also popular souvenirs.

Generally, shops are open between 09.00/10.00 and 18.00/19.00 on Mondays to Fridays, closing an hour or so earlier on Saturdays. Most are closed on Sundays, although those catering for tourists now tend to open every day. Food shops open a little earlier and some stay open until 21.00 to 22.00 It is still common, particularly for small shops, to close for lunch, often from 14.00 to 15.00.

Whilst **antiques** are available in the Old Town, most shops are off Brīvības fairly near to the Latvia Hotel. Vecais Grāmatnieks (Lāčplēša 9) has a wide selection of stamps, coins, books, china and brassware. Antikvariāts (Baznīcas 8) has paintings, clocks and a few books.

Central Riga now has about 12 serious **bookshops**. The cheapest for books most likely to appeal to visitors is Pie Doma (Krāmu 3) which has a wide selection of guidebooks, art books and maps. This shop is close to the cathedral and Town Hall Square. Globuss (Vaļņu 26) and Valters un Rapa (Aspāzijas 24) are almost side by side, opposite the Riga Hotel and with just the post office in between. Valters un Rapa is following the trend of attaching a café to a bookshop and it also sells CDs, plus films (including Fuji Velvia). It is probably the largest bookshop in the Baltics. Globuss concentrates on travel books. Jāņa Sēta (Elizabetes 83–85) are best known for their **maps** which cover the whole Baltic area. They produce country maps, town plans and atlases. Prices for their own publications tend to be cheaper at their shop than elsewhere. Their catalogue can be consulted on www.kartes.lv. Jumava (Vāgnera 12, close to the Konventa Sēta Hotel) has a wide selection of antiquarian books in German, English and French, many about Latvia and Riga. The War Museum in the Powder Tower has a wide selection of books, many in English, about the build-up to independence in the late Soviet period.

For **souvenirs**, Sakta (Brīvības 32) is a convenient one-stop shop for amber, glass, linen and copperware. Prices tend to be lower than those in grander Old Town shops. It has a smaller branch at Aspāzijas 30, between the Metropole and the Riga hotels. Sadly both outlets are closed on Sunday, even in the middle of summer. Foreign dignitaries are always taken to A & E (Jauniela 17) for jewellery, in particular amber. Given the uncertain provenance of much of the 'amber' sold on the street, it may well be worth paying the extra here for certain quality. Other good outlets are Rota and Mārx in Konventa sēta. Anti-amber tourists go to Nordwear (Kaļķu 7) which since opening has had the slogan 'amber-free'. It therefore has quite a few humorous souvenirs, including mugs, posters and T-shirts with irreverent slogans, but their main speciality is hand-knitted sweaters. Many hotels hand out their 5% discount cards, so never pay the full price. Their catalogue can be seen on www.nordwear.com.lv. Latvijas Bite (Ģertrūdes 13) sells only honey and beeswax candles. If you're after ceramics or other furnishing accessories, it's worth taking a taxi to Grīvas mēbeles (31k-3 Daugavgrivas Street, tel: 746 8383; web: www.gmebeles.com) about five minutes' drive from the

Radisson. Modern, very stylish and exceptional value, it offers the best in Latvian furniture and decoration.

Berga Bazārs behind the Jāņa Sēta bookshop in Elizabetes iela is beginning to develop itself into a Latvian version of Berlin's Hackesche Höfe, a large pedestrian precinct in a series of courtyards, with cafés and specialist shops. With a hotel likely to be built during 2003, it will then be possible to shop in Riga without crossing a street.

Riga's **Central Market** in a series of hangars near the station (see page 100) is fun to wander in and is a good place to buy for a picnic and to get cigarettes and vodka. The imposition of cash machines on even the smallest stalls has been a major victory of the local tax authorities. The receipts they issue show the VAT that should be paid on all items, including food. The market is open Monday to Friday, 07.00–18.00. Flowers are available everywhere, including the **Flower Market** alongside the park on Turbidas. **Centrs** on Audēju is one of the few shops in Riga to have continued from the 1920s through the Soviet period to the present day. It is a big department store, open until 22.00 every day including Sunday, and the food section on the ground floor sells every Latvian and foreign product likely to be available in Riga.

Medical services
Hospital Gailezeva; Hipokrata 2
Dentist Elladent; Vilandes 18 (open 09.00–23.00 Mon–Fri; 09.00–14.00 Sat–Sun).
Pharmacy There are two 24-hour pharmacies (*aptiek*) in Riga, Rudens Aptieka Ģertrūdes 105 and Vecpilsētas Aptieka Audēju 20, and numerous Drogas branches across the city.

Embassies
Canada Doma Laukums 4; tel: 722 6315; fax: 783 0140.
Estonia Skolas 13; tel: 781 2020; fax: 781 2029.
Lithuania Rūpniecības 24; tel: 732 1519; fax: 732 1589.
Russia Antonijas 2; tel: 721 2579; fax: 783 0209.
UK Alunana 5; tel: 777 4700; fax: 777 4707.

Places of worship
The majority of churches are Lutheran, with Orthodox churches coming in second place. Few offer services in languages other than Latvian or Russian.

Church of England St Saviour's, 2a Anglikāņu iela (service in English 10.00 Sunday).
Lutheran The Dome (Sunday 12.00); St John's (Sunday 10.00); other Lutheran churches abound.
Old Believers Grebenščikova Church, 73 Krasta iela (service in Russian 08.00 Sunday).
Orthodox The Orthodox Cathedral, 23 Brīvības iela.
Roman Catholic St Jacob's, 7 Jāņa iela (the Roman Catholic cathedral); Our Lady of Sorrows, Lielā Pils iela.
Synagogue 6–8 Peitavas iela (Hebrew services at 09.00 and sunset on Saturday).

WHAT TO SEE
It is best to see Riga on foot. The Old Town is a relatively small area and, if pushed for time, you could walk around most of it in a day, although that will

only give you a superficial impression. To see the Old Town more thoroughly and to see something of the New Town, you should allow two days. A car is not much use: access to the Old Town is restricted for cars, and parking in the New Town can be hard to find.

Old Town

The majority of sights are in the Old Town (*VecRiga*), which is the area of the city located between the Daugava River and the city canal (*pilsētas kanāls*). The Old Town contains a wealth of historic buildings, from the medieval town walls dating back to the 13th century to the grey modernity of the flats and offices built when Latvia was part of the Soviet Union. Between the two extremes there are buildings of almost every period and style: classical, Gothic, art nouveau and modern. Much of the Old Town suffered neglect when Latvia was part of the USSR, but a great deal of restoration and reconstruction has been undertaken in the years following independence (the reconstruction of the Konventa sēta area being one of the best examples).

The best way to see the Old Town is on foot: the area is relatively small, but in any event, large parts of the Old Town have been made traffic-free zones (there is access for vehicles, but you have to buy a pass), while other parts consist of narrow streets, making vehicle access impractical. Many of the streets are cobbled and others suffer from lack of maintenance, so you have to keep your eyes open for holes and uneven road and pavement surfaces. Wear sensible walking shoes.

The main sights of the Old Town are described below by reference to two suggested walking routes covering the Old Town sights on either side of Kaļķu iela.

Walk one

Our first walk starts from the Hotel de Rome at the corner of Kaļķu iela and Aspāzijas bulvāris, not far from the Freedom Monument. Take the road leading away from the Freedom Monument and the parks along the side of the hotel and you will find yourself almost immediately at Vaļāu iela, a pedestrianised street of shops, bars and cafés. Turn right into Vaļāu iela. At the end of the street you will see one of the major landmarks of the Old Town, the Powder Tower.

Powder Tower

The Powder Tower (*Pulvertornis*) is one of the oldest buildings in Riga. Its name is derived from the fact that it was once used to store gunpowder, although at times it was also referred to as the Sand Tower after Smilūu iela (Sand Street), the road that leads past the tower and which was once the main road to Pskov in Russia. Records of the tower can be traced back to 1330. The tower is the sole survivor of what used to be 18 towers that formed part of the city fortifications. Because it was used to store gunpowder it had to be dry, well ventilated and secure, hence the walls which are 2.5m thick. They were relatively effective: nine cannonballs are said to be embedded in the walls, relics of the Russian invasions of 1656 and 1710. Only the lower parts of the tower are original. The tower was substantially destroyed by Swedish forces in 1621 and restored in 1650.

Since it ceased to have any military significance, the Powder Tower has been put to various uses. In 1892 it was used as the headquarters of a German student fraternity called Rubonia. After World War I it was turned into a war museum. In 1957 it became the Latvian Museum of the Revolution and functioned as such until independence. Now it houses the War Museum.

Smilšu iela

Smilšu iela itself is one of Riga's oldest streets. Some say it got its name from the sand of which the road was made; others say the name comes from the Kubes Hill and nearby sand dunes which were levelled in the 17th century. If you stand in Smilšu iela facing the Powder Tower and look across Basteja bulvāris you can just see the remains of Bastion Hill (Basteja kalns), one of the fortification towers dating back to the 17th century.

Torņa iela

Behind the Powder Tower is Torņa iela (Tower Street), a well restored, traffic-free street. Next to the tower is the entrance to what is now again the **War Museum** (Latvijas Kara Muzejs) (open 10.00–18.00 except on Monday and Tuesday). The museum is devoted to the military history of Latvia and concentrates heavily on recent history with permanent exhibitions devoted to World War I, the 1905 revolution and the liberation struggle of 1918–20, and the fate of Latvia during World War II.

Texts in these sections are shown only in the original German or Russian. As so often with Latvian museums, the most interesting sections are on the top floor. In this museum, this applies to the Soviet section, which has brochures in English. The museum keeps up to date, so the activities of Latvian forces in Bosnia are covered, and there is an exhibition of military uniforms from around the world.

Further along Torņa iela you come to part of the city wall (best seen from the parallel Trokšņu iela). Riga was protected by a wall from the early 13th century. Eventually it extended to a length of some two kilometres, and by the 14th century the walls were 1.8m thick. The arches between the pillars would be filled with stones and sandbags to provide reinforcement when the city was under siege; in peacetime they were emptied again and used for storage or as stables or even accommodation. The income derived from letting the arches was used to raise money to pay for the upkeep of the city's defences.

Swedish Gate

At the corner of Torņa iela and Aldaru iela (Brewer Street) is the Swedish Gate (*Zviedru Vārti*), so called because it was built when Riga was under Swedish rule and because it was the gate through which the Swedish king, Gustavus Adolphus, entered the city in 1621. It is the only city gate still left intact. According to legend, the citizens of Riga abducted a young Latvian woman who had unwisely fallen in love with a Swedish soldier and was meeting him secretly near the gate, and walled her up in the gate as a warning to others. The Swedish Gate is unusual in that it passes through a whole house (number 11 Torņa iela). The house at number 11 is the first recorded house in private ownership in Riga. It is recorded as belonging to Ivan Martin Serpentin who acquired it on April 2 1679. The first floor was let to a man called Kordu, the town lamplighter, who paid a rent of six taler per annum.

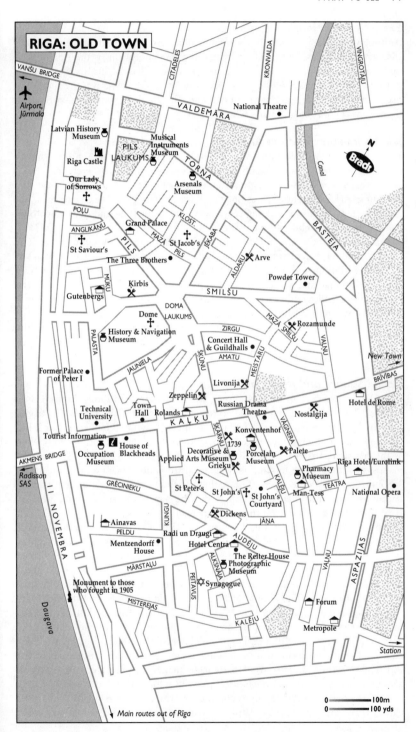

RIGA: OLD TOWN

VANŠU BRIDGE

Airport,
Jūrmala

VALDEMĀRA

National Theatre

CITADELES

KRONVALDA

VINGROTĀJU

N

Bradt

Canal

BASTEJA

Latvian History
Museum

PILS
LAUKUMS

Musical
Instruments
Museum

TORŅA

Riga Castle

Our Lady
of Sorrows

Arsenals
Museum

POĻU

ANGLIKĀŅU

Grand Palace

KLOST.

St Jacob's

JĒKABA

Arve

St Saviour's

PILS

MAZĀ

PILS

Powder Tower

The Three Brothers

MŪKU

Kirbis

ALDARU

SMILŠU

Gutenbergs

DOMA
LAUKUMS

Dome

MAZĀ SMILŠU

Rozamunde

PALASTA

History & Navigation
Museum

ZIRGU

Concert Hall
& Guildhalls

VAĻŅU

New Town

JAUŅIELA

AMATU

ŠĶŪŅU

MEISTARU

BRĪVĪBAS

Former Palace
of Peter I

Livonija

Hotel de Rome

Zeppelin

Technical
University

Town
Hall

Rolands

KAĻĶU

Russian Drama
Theatre

ŠĶŪŅU

VAGNERA

Nostalgija

Tourist Information

Occupation
Museum

House of
Blackheads

1739

Konventenhof

Decorative &
Applied Arts Museum
Grieķu

Porcelain
Museum

Palete

AKMENS BRIDGE

Radisson
SAS

KAĻĒJU

Pharmacy
Museum

Riga Hotel/Eurolink

II NOVEMBRA

GRĒCINIEKU

St Peter's

St John's

St John's
Courtyard

TEĀTRA

Man-Tess

National Opera

Ainavas

KUNGU

Dickens

JĀŅA

PELDU

Radi un Draugi

AUDĒJU

Mentzendorff
House

Hotel Centra

VAĻŅU

ASPAZIJAS

The Reiter House
Photographic
Museum

MĀRSTAĻU

ALKSNĀJA

PEITAVUS

Synagogue

Monument to those
who fought in 1905

MISTEREJAS

Dougava

Forum

KALĒJU

Metropole

Station

0 ▬▬▬ 100m
0 ▬▬▬ 100 yds

↓ *Main routes out of Rīga*

Executioner's House

Although it is not possible to visit them, there are several attractively restored **historic houses** on Torņa iela of which the most notorious is the one now at numbers 7–9, a large pink house that was once occupied by the city executioner until the position was abolished in 1863. Number 5 Torņa iela was the site of the prison built in 1685 by Rupert Bindenschu, the architect who also worked on the reconstruction of St Peter's Church.

Jēkaba laukums and the Arsenal

At the end of Torņa iela you come to Jēkaba iela (Jacob or James Street) and to the right Jēkaba laukums (Jacob or James Square), where concrete barricades were erected during the struggles of January 1991. The square, which was first laid out in the 18th century, was once used for military parades and exercises, but gradually fell into disuse and neglect. It was restored in 1924 and new flowerbeds and a play area for children were added.

On the side of the square closest to Jēkaba iela is a row of low buildings. The middle building, taller than the others, is the former Arsenal. Built in 1828–32 to designs by I Lukini and A Nellinger on the site of what was once part of the town wall, the arsenal that stood here was replaced by a customs house. Now the building is a gallery (the **Arsenals Museum of Fine Arts**, *Mākslas Muzejs 'Arsenals'*) where modern painters exhibit on the ground floor and the first floor exhibits paintings by children. A visit here is refreshing after one too many of the other Riga museums, since it is newly built and has space and light. (Open 11.00–17.00 every day except Mondays.)

Castle Square and Riga Castle

Close to the end of Torņa iela is a green which forms part of Pils laukums (Castle Square). The large building on the corner on your right is the **Bank of Latvia**, built in 1905 to designs by the Latvian architect, Augusts Reinbergs. No 2 Pils laukums was in Soviet times a Red Army Museum but has recently been opened as the **Musical Instruments Museum** (*Mūzikas Muzejs*). It has 19th-century pianos, including some folding ones, wind instruments, organs and records from 1897 through to floppy disks. The staff are friendly and knowledgeable and are happy for the instruments to be played. The top floor has an exhibition on Latvian writers exiled during the Soviet period.

The main building on Pils laukums is **Riga Castle** (*Rīgas pils*), a large yellow building with a red roof. The present structure is the last of three which have stood here. Its predecessors were two Livonian castles, the first of which was built in 1330, the second in 1515. The leader of the Livonian Order lived in Riga Castle up to 1470 when his residence was moved, eventually to Cēsis. The people of Riga destroyed the castle in 1487 but were forced to build a replacement by Walter von Plettenberg, the last head of the Livonian Order. It was completed in 1515 and included the so-called Lead Tower (*Svina tornis*) which still stands. The castle was extended in the 18th century by the addition of a new wing which became the residence of the Russian governor, and from 1918 to 1940 that of the president of Latvia. It also underwent substantial restoration in 1938 which included construction of the 'Three Stars Tower', easily recognised by the three stars on its top. In the early part of the 19th century Wilhelm von Kester built an observatory on the main tower from which Alexander I of Russia observed the solar eclipse of April 23 1818.

Now the castle houses three museums: the **Latvian History Museum**, *Latvijas Vēstures Muzejs* (open 11.00–17.00, except Monday and Tuesday), which traces the course of Latvian history from 9000BC to the 20th century; the **Latvian Museum of Foreign Art**, *Latvijas Ārzemju Mākslas Muzejs* (open 11.00–17.00, except Monday and Tuesday), the biggest collection of foreign art in Latvia; and the **Rainis Museum of Literature and Art History**, *Raiņa Literaturas un Mākslas Vēstures Muzejs* (open 11.00–17.00, except Monday).

Each room in the History Museum takes a different and unrelated theme. It is good to see a museum in Latvia that is keeping up to date and where care is taken over presentation and lighting. Do not judge the museum by the gloomy entrance to the building or by the torn signs on the stairs. One room concentrates on archaeology but sadly the labels are only in Latvian, another covers religious statues in both stone and wood which have been rescued from churches all over the country. Turning to more modern history, there are models and original tools to display 19th-century farming, a school room from the 1930s, a costume room from the same period and another displaying Bidmeyer furniture. When the EBRD (European Bank for Reconstruction and Development) met in Riga in May 2000, a permanent coin room was set up in the museum. Older British visitors, who thought that shillings were abandoned only in 1971 with the advent of decimal currency, will be surprised to read in the catalogue that they were abandoned as being worthless by the Duke of Curland in 1576. The coins on display go back to the 9th century but of most interest, perhaps, are those from the 1914–20 period when German and Russian ones circulated side by side. A hat exhibition opened in 2002.

The Museum of Foreign Art is odd, since many of the oldest exhibits (sculptures from Greece and Rome and artefacts from ancient Egypt) are mixed up with modern works; the more conventional galleries exhibit paintings by 17th century Dutch artists, German works dating from the 16th–19th centuries and Belgian painting of the 20th century. There are almost no works of great distinction.

The Rainis Museum was founded in 1925 and is devoted to Latvian literature. Exhibits include photographs, manuscripts and texts relating to the history of Latvian literature from its earliest times right up to the 20th century. Recent additions are two exhibitions devoted to Gunārs Freimanis (1927–93) and Voldemārs Zariņš (1917–81), both of whom were persecuted by the Soviet authorities. Freimanis spent ten years in the Russian *gulags*; Zariņš was sent to forced labour in the coal mines of Tula. The museum is interesting as an example of how Latvia is trying to emphasise its cultural and national identity after independence. Unfortunately, all the information (except for a short pamphlet) is in Latvian.

To the right of the castle, in the direction of Kr Valdemāra iela, is the old stable block (unused at present).

Our Lady of Sorrows

Leaving Castle Square (Pils laukums) and crossing the cobbled area of the square (the opposite end to the one at which the stables are located, in the direction of Lielā pils iela) you come to a church, the Roman Catholic Church of Our Lady of Sorrows (*Sāpju Dievmātes baznīca*). The location was already the site of a humble Catholic chapel in the 18th century, but the present building owes its existence to the Austrian emperor, Joseph II, who persuaded the Russian tsar, Paul I, and the king of Poland, Stanislav August, to donate money for the construction of the present church which was built in 1784–5.

St Saviour's Church

Just beyond the Catholic church is Riga's only Anglican church, **St Saviour's**, which stands in Anglikāņu iela, just off Lielā pils iela. This red-brick church, the largest Anglican one in the Baltic States, was built in 1857–9 to cater for the spiritual needs of the English seamen and merchants who came to Riga. The main door leads on to a small porch that overlooks the Daugava. The bricks used to build the church were imported from England, as was a layer of soil on which the church was built, although construction was supervised by the Riga architect, Johann Felsko. During the Soviet era the church was used as a discotheque by the students of the Technical University, but it was returned to the Church of England when the Archbishop of Canterbury visited Riga in 1994.

The Three Brothers

Returning to Lielā pils iela, turn right into Mazā pils iela, heading away from the tower of Riga Castle. The three houses at numbers 17, 19 and 21 Mazā pils iela are known collectively as '**the three brothers**' (*Trīs brāļi*). The oldest is the right-hand house with the Germanic step-gable and dates back to the 15th century. It is claimed that it is the oldest domestic building in Riga. Little is known about its history except that in 1687 it is recorded that it was used as a bakery. Numbers 19 and 21 were built later in the 17th and 18th centuries respectively. In 1966 repair work began with a view to restoring the buildings after years of neglect. Number 17 is set back from the street: when it was built there was less pressure on building land in Riga so a small area was left for stone benches to be installed by the main entrance; but by the time the other houses were built land had become more expensive, so they were built closer to the road and with more storeys so as to maximise land use.

The house at number 19 now houses the **Museum of Architecture**, *Latvijas Arhitektūras Muzejs* (open 09.00–17.00 Sunday–Friday, Saturday 12.00–16.00). The museum has no permanent collection on view, being more of an archive, but it has most of the original plans, whether realised or not, from all the famous 19th- and 20th-century architects involved in Riga's expansion. These can all be viewed by specialist groups if prior arrangements are made.

Note also the house at 4 Mazā pils iela where the Baltic historian Johans Kristofs Broce worked from 1742 to 1823 as rector of what was then Riga's imperial *lycée*.

St Jacob's Church

Opposite the three brothers is Klostera iela (Monastery Street) which leads to St Jacob's Church (*Jēkaba baznīca*), the Roman Catholic cathedral of Riga. (The church is also called St James', since Jacob and James are alternative translations of Jēkabs.) Originally built outside the city walls between 1225 and 1226, the church has been rebuilt several times, although the sanctuary and naves are original. The church has changed hands on several occasions: after the Reformation it became a

Lutheran parish church (the first Lutheran service in Latvia was held here in 1522); but in 1582 it was handed over to the Jesuit order; in 1621 it became a Swedish garrison church; it was finally returned to the Roman Catholic church in 1922.

The 73m-high tower shows traces of restoration work carried out in the 16th and 17th centuries. The heavy buttresses are unusual for Riga churches: shortage of land meant that most churches were built with internal buttresses.

Parliament Building

At the corner of Jēkaba baznīca, if you turn right, you come to a formidable brown building with a coat of arms and a balcony over the main entrance. This is the building where the Supreme Soviet of Latvia used to sit. In 1919–34 it was the seat of the Latvian national parliament. Now it functions once again as the Parliament building, the seat of the *Saeima*. It was here on May 4 1989 that parliament passed a resolution on the independence of Latvia. The building itself is in the style of a Florentine palace. Note the decoratively carved double doors and heavy lanterns. In the outbreak of crime which followed independence in the early 1990s, the bronze plaque on the front of the building was stolen.

National Library

Turn right into Jēkaba iela and walk along the back of the cathedral. The small street on the left, Mazā Trokšņu iela (which means 'the street of little noise') has formed the subject matter of many pictures by Latvian artists. Numbers 6/8 Jēkaba iela is a substantial stone building which houses the Latvian National Library.

Turning left back into Smilšu iela, the house at number 6 has a modern front and is now the **Commercial Bank**. The upper storeys are good examples of the Jugendstil (art nouveau) style of architecture for which Riga is so famous. Next to it is Aldaru iela (Brewer Street) with its view back to the Swedish Gate. The large brown building that dominates the rest of Smilšu iela is occupied by ministries and government offices.

House of the Cat

Here the road forks. Take Mazā Smilšu iela (Little Sand Street) and turn right into Meistaru iela (Master Street). On your left is a large yellow building called the House of the Cat. Perched on each of the building's two pointed towers is an arched cat looking down on the city. The origins of this piece of architectural caprice are uncertain but inevitably there is a story. Apparently a Latvian businessman sought admission to the city guild but was refused. To spite the guild he bought the nearest property he could find to the guildhall, built the house that still stands and had two cats put on top so that each directed its backside towards the guildhall. According to the same story the spurned merchant was eventually forced to move them, hence their present position.

Guildhalls

If you continue down Meistaru iela you come to what used to be the Guild Square but is now known as the Philharmonic Park (*Filharmonijas Parks*). On a wet day it can look fairly grim but in better weather it is enlivened by kiosks selling ice-cream and drinks, and by pavement artists. There is also a long strip of wall used for announcements about local musical, theatrical and other cultural events. The **Great Guildhall** (*Lielā gilde*) is the large, dull yellow building at one edge of the square, at the corner of Meistaru iela and Amatu iela (Commercial Street). The **Small Guildhall** is right next to it on Amatu iela itself. These buildings represent the centres of Riga's former glory as a Hanseatic city. The Great Guildhall was the council chamber of the merchants; the smaller one housed the council of the less influential craftsmen's guilds. The Great Guildhall was originally established in the 14th century, but has undergone substantial changes over the years. In 1853–60 it was reconstructed in English Tudor style according to designs by Beine and Scheu. The Old Guild Chamber dates back to the 16th century and is decorated with the emblems of the 45 Hanseatic towns. The so-called 'Brides' Chamber' dates back to 1521: until the 19th century it was still used on the wedding night of children of members of the guild or members themselves. However, a great deal of damage was done by a fire in 1963. Now the building is used as a concert hall. The smaller hall was built (in its present form) in 1864–6. It is also sometimes called the St John's Guild – notice the statue of St John with a lamb in one corner of the façade under the tower. Now it is used as offices.

Continue along Amatu iela to Šķūņu iela (Barn Street). On your right there is a pale green coloured building with white decoration, an excellent example of Riga's Jugendstil (art nouveau). Note the sculptures of a boy reading (at roof level) and of frogs (by the entrance). The nearby billiards/snooker hall was once the site of St Catherine's Church, built between the 14th and 15th centuries.

Riga Dome Church

If you turn right out of Amatu iela, past Zirgu iela, you come to the cathedral square, Doma laukums. The square is dominated by the cathedral, the Dome Church (*Rigas Dome* – the name comes from the German *Dom*, meaning cathedral) or St Mary's Cathedral, as it is sometimes referred to, the largest church in the Baltic States (open for visitors 13.00–17.00 Monday to Friday, and 10.00–14.00 on Saturdays). Groups can arrange private visits in the morning. The foundations of the church were laid in 1211 and consecrated in 1226. It was modelled on the cathedral at Rattenburg at the instigation of Albert, the Bishop of Riga, although he did not live to see his plans come to fruition. The original church was cruciform, but was extended in the 15th century; the central nave was heightened to let in more light, and three chapels were added. Two towers were envisaged, but only one was actually built over what is now the main entrance. It burned down in 1547 and was replaced in 1595. That tower was replaced again in 1775–6 due to fears about its structural soundness (fears prompted by the collapse of the tower of St Peter's). The old tower was 132m high, the tallest in Europe; the new one was much smaller at 90m.

Like many of Riga's churches the Dome became a Protestant church in the Reformation, and much of its elaborate interior decoration was destroyed in 1524 and the church lost its original name of St Mary's. Thus all that remains today as decoration are the tombs of merchants, all purchased, the price set by reference to closeness to the high altar. A whole chapel was devoted to the Tisenhausen family: note the plaque for Mary Tisenhausen who died in 1611, and the stained glass panels donated by the family in the 19th century and made in Munich in 1893.

One depicts the Tisenhausen family with the Virgin Mary and angels, the other Bishop Albert, the founder of the church. In the neighbouring chapel, stained glass depicts Walter von Plettenberg reading the edict proclaiming religious freedom and pledging protection from the Catholic bishops (1525). On the north side there is more modern stained glass (by E Tode, 1902) depicting the life of St Martin, the life of St George and the lives of the apostles, Peter and Paul. The three stained-glass windows above the altar depict stories from the Old and New Testaments. The pulpit, the work of the wood carver Tobias Heincs, dates back to 1641. The angel that surmounts it was added much later in 1817 and is the work of the sculptor Imhof.

The organ of the Riga Dome is world famous: indeed for many people the church is known as a concert hall, and in particular for its organ recitals, rather than as a place of worship. The first organ was installed in the 16th century, but the present instrument was built in 1884 by the firm of Walcker & Co of Ludwigsburg, Germany. It was first used at an inaugural recital and service on January 31 1884 when it was played by three organists, including the cathedral organist, Wilhelm Bergner. It was rebuilt and restored in 1981–4 by the Dutch organ builders, Flentrop Orgelbouw bv Zaandam. With four manuals and pedal board, 6,718 pipes (ranging in size from 10m to 13m) and 124 stops, it is large even by cathedral standards; indeed when it was first built it was the largest instrument in the world. The organ case is older than the organ itself: the work of Jakob Raab, it dates back to the 16th century, although the baroque decorations were added later in the 17th century.

The cloister was reopened in 2000 and reconstruction there will continue for several years. In due course, the garden will have to be replanted to give a true feeling of how it should look. The arches, which date back to the 13th century, are fine examples of Romanesque architecture. The exhibition contains several headstones from the cathedral, the cockerel that used to be on the spire, an exhibition of modern stained glass, and a model of the Peter the Great Statue that was replaced by the Freedom Monument. The Chapter House, attached to the cloisters, dates from 1215 and is crying out for restoration. The panels were covered during the 19th century with stucco, and humidity is now undermining the whole structure. The tiling, which dates from the 15th century, is fortunately still intact. The statue beside the cathedral wall is of Bishop Albert, the founder of Riga. It was unveiled in 2001, to celebrate the 800th anniversary of the city. The entrance to the cloisters is at Palesta 4, and they are open daily from 10.00 to16.00.

The tower of the Dome was used as a lookout post. The watchman would communicate with the guards on the ground below by means of a wooden ball containing a message. (The tower of the town hall was used in the same way.) Now the tower is dominated by a huge weathercock, the predecessor of which can be seen in the church itself where it was placed after 390 years of service in the open air.

Although the Dome is still used for concerts, it now also operates again as a place of worship. The first service in recent times was held there on October 9 1988 to mark the founding of the Popular Front (*Tautas Fronte*). The box office for concert tickets is in the church porch. Tickets can also be bought at the Filharmonijas box office, 6 Amatu iela, and at the Wagner Hall box office at 4 Vāgnera iela. For details of concerts see the posters in the church or consult *Riga in your Pocket* or *The Baltic Times*. They generally take place on Wednesdays and Fridays. Services are held at 08.00 every day and at noon on Sundays.

Around the Dome

Whilst the food in the open-air cafés on Cathedral Square is not exciting, there are a whole range of cafés and restaurants in the nearby streets Jauniela and Šķūņu.

The building at 8 Doma laukums is the **Latvia Radio Building**. It and the nearby Finance Ministry recall the architectural style of Nazi Germany and were built in the late 1930s under the Latvian president, Kārlis Ulmanis. Had his regime lasted, Riga would have had many more similar buildings. The Radio Building was one of the buildings that was barricaded in 1991 by demonstrators resisting communist sympathisers; bullet holes in the building offer a grim reminder of the fighting. Doma laukums was heavily guarded and occupied by people lighting bonfires and erecting tents. From time to time radio staff would appear on the balcony of the Radio Building to announce the news to the people gathered in the square below. It was from the same balcony that President Gorbunovs proclaimed the re-establishment of independence in August 1991.

Opposite the Radio Building is *Rigas Fondu Birža*, the **Riga Stock Exchange**, a green and brown building with ornate statues. It was built in 1852–5 in Venetian style to a design by the architect Harald Bose. Unused for 50 years or so, it now operates again as a stock exchange.

Herder Square

If you leave Doma laukums passing the main door of the cathedral with the Radio Building behind you, you come into Herdera laukums, Herder Square. This small square is dominated by the statue of the German critic, writer and theologian, Johann Herder (1744–1803), which stands on a small green.

Turning out of Herder laukums you come to Palasta iela (Palace Street). The building that was once the clergy enclosure of the abbey attached to the Dome is now the **Museum of History and Navigation of the City of Riga**, *Rigas Vēstures un Kuģniecības Muzejs* (open 11.00–17.00 daily except Monday and Tuesday). Founded in 1773, this is the oldest museum in Latvia. It was originally set up to house items from the private collection of Nicolaus von Himsel (1729–64) whose portrait by an unknown artist hangs in the ground-floor exhibition hall. The main permanent exhibition traces the development of Riga from its beginnings to 1940. It does so by reference to maps, plans, pictures and objects of all kinds from the everyday life of the city's inhabitants.

The collection is weak on the medieval period but particularly strong on 1920–40, showing how affluent and diverse life was for a reasonable number of people at that time. The display covers magazines published in several languages, fans, pottery, glasswork and clothes. In 2002 the Column Hall reopened; it was originally built between 1778 and 1783 but was closed for renovation in 1984 and this has only now been completed. Some of the original brickwork can be seen. It houses a large portrait of Peter the Great arriving in Riga in 1710.

The second main permanent exhibition is devoted to the history of navigation from ancient times to the present day. One room is dedicated to the work of Krišjānis Valdemārs (1825–91), a pioneer in naval education in Latvia. What is displayed here would be more than enough work for most people, but Valdemārs was also active as a short story writer, a newspaper editor and as a constant political campaigner in the National Awakening Movement.

Peter I's Palace

Further on in Palasta iela at number 6 stands a tiny building in which Tsar Peter I (Peter the Great), kept his personal carriage when he visited Riga.

Just beyond it at number 9 is what used to be Peter's Palace, from which Palasta iela derives its name. Peter bought this house from a local merchant called Henaberg and is said to have been especially fond of it because he was able to indulge in his hobby of gardening there, on either the terrace or the hanging garden on the roof. When he lived here in the 18th century it was possible to see the harbour from the windows of the palace (before it was moved further from the centre of the city). In 1745 the palace was rebuilt to designs by Rastrelli, the architect better known in Latvia for his work on the Rundāle Palace. In 1886 it became the Russian school and until recently functioned as a Russian cultural centre. Following extensive restoration, it is now an office building.

Walk Two

Our second walk in the Old Town starts from the Riflemen's Square (Strēlnieku laukums). This large open area used to be a market square, then the site of the town hall of Riga. The most distinguished building is the House of the Blackheads, rebuilt in 1998.

House of the Blackheads

The House of the Blackheads (*Melngalvju nams*), one of Riga's most important monuments, was reopened in January 2000 as a faithful replica of the original, and is open every day except Monday. All the work was carried out and paid for by Latvians; no foreign grants or expertise were involved. The original foundations are skilfully exhibited under glass just inside the entrance. The original house (really a building made up of two houses connected by an enclosed courtyard), with its Dutch Renaissance façade (1620), dated back to 1331 but was badly damaged in World War II.

The first floor of the building was used for shops and businesses; the guildhall of the association occupied the second floor; the upper floors were used for storage and warehousing. The ground floor was a concert hall. The huge step gable was 28m high and highly decorated with statues of people and animals. The building was topped by a large figure of St George which acted as a weather vane.

There had been additions in each century – ironwork from the 17th, baroque sculptures from 18th and panelling from the 19th. Remnants from each era can be seen in the basement museum. None of the paintings in the assembly room on the first floor are original, but they are faithful copies of them. Note the Swedish and the Russian royal families looking across the floor at each other. The silver collection has had the turbulent history which is bound to result from centuries of different occupations. Some of what was here in 1939 is now in Bremen and some in St Petersburg; very little is still in Riga. By helping to rebuild the collection, German Baltic families are able to show that their commitment to Riga did not end in 1939.

The 'Blackheads', first mentioned in 1413, were a group of unmarried merchants who lived in Riga and Reval (Tallinn). Originally a loose association, they grew to become a powerful force. It is believed that they got their unusual name from their black patron saint, St Maurice. The Blackheads left for Germany in 1939 and because of this German association the Soviet authorities blew up the remains of the building in May 1948. The Royal Palace in Berlin and the Castle in Königsberg (Kaliningrad) suffered similar fates. All three buildings could have been restored, had the political climate allowed this.

A statue of Roland used to stand in front of the building. A popular figure in the Middle Ages, and especially in Germany, the Roland statue was erected in 1897 but was damaged in World War II and the original is now kept in St Peter's Church. A replica has been erected in the square.

Next to the House of Blackheads is the **Schwab House**, also rebuilt according to the original, though this only dated from 1890. It now houses the **Riga Tourist Information Centre** which is open daily, 10.00–19.00.

Riflemen's memorial

The present name of the square comes from the memorial to the Latvian Riflemen which was erected in 1970 to commemorate the valour of the Latvian Rifle Regiment during the Russian Civil War. The Riflemen formed Lenin's bodyguard during the 1917 revolution. Plans to change the square provide for the statue to be removed and replaced by something more politically neutral.

Occupation Museum

The ugly black cuboid building behind the memorial was also built in 1970 and used to be a museum devoted to the exploits of the regiment. Now it is the Museum of the Occupation of Latvia, *Okupācijas Muzejs* (open daily, all year, admission free), which contains a permanent exhibition devoted to the history of Latvia during the Soviet and Nazi occupations of 1940–91. Founded in 1993, the museum exhibits photographs and documents, maps and artefacts dealing with the period and contains a replica of a barracks room from a Soviet *gulag*. One display covers the life Latvians led in Siberia after release from the camps but whilst they were still exiled. Another shows the struggle of Latvians in the West to keep the memory of their country alive during the Soviet occupation. The renovation of the Hotel Riga provided a new exhibit for the museum – the bugging equipment with which the hotel staff monitored phone calls during the Soviet era. There is excellent background material in English to all the exhibits and a bookshop which sells most of the publications available in English on the two occupations.

The long-term future of the building is a subject of great controversy. Some Latvians feel that the theme of the museum is so important that even if another building was found elsewhere (unlikely under current financial circumstances) it would suggest a loss of interest in the topic on the part of the city administration. Others feel that a Soviet building, whatever its current contents, should no longer be allowed to disfigure the heart of Latvia's capital. The Latvian-born architect Gunnar Birkerts, who now practices in America, has suggested alterations to the building which might provide an appropriate compromise and which would certainly make it aesthetically acceptable.

Technical University

The west side of the square used to be occupied by lecture halls and laboratories of the Technical University but many of these were torn down by 2002 to make way for the rebuilt Town Hall. As with the House of Blackheads, this building could have been restored but it was in fact blown up in 1954. In due course, most of the Square should look again as it did in 1939. The local administration plans to return to the Town Hall during 2003.

Riga's bridges

The traditional bridge with the large lantern-like lights is the Akmens tilts (Stone Bridge) which replaced the long pontoon bridge that spanned the river before World War II. A more elegant example of 20th century architecture is the dramatic modern bridge, the harp-like Vansu tilts, which crosses the river to the north.

Mentzendorff House

Leave the square by crossing Grēcinieku iela (Sinner's Street) and taking Kungu iela (Gentleman's Street). On the corner of Grēcinieku iela and Kungu iela there is an impressive building called the Mentzendorff House (*Mencendorfa nams*). The museum is open to individual visitors Wednesday to Sunday, 10.00–17.00, but is happy to open by arrangement for groups on Monday or Tuesday.

The building dates from the 1720s when it replaced an earlier one destroyed in the Riga fire of 1677. Wall paintings from that time have only recently been discovered; in some rooms there were as many as five layers of paintings and then 20 layers of wallpaper from the 19th and 20th centuries. Some of the early paintings were modelled on the work of the French artist Antoine Watteau (1684–1721). The house now carries the name of the last Baltic/German family to live here until 1940, though is sometimes still called the 'Merchant's House' in view of the number of trades carried out here. The outlines of the grocery store that the Mentzendorff family ran can be seen on the ground floor, although not all the articles displayed are originals from this house. Note the raised edge of the long wooden table, which prevented coins slipping to the floor. In winter, the kitchen stove was the centre of the household: it was used to cook the food, smoke the meat and heat the whole house. The basement is used for temporary art exhibitions, but the higher floors display furniture, clothes, clocks, playing cards and musical instruments which the Baltic Germans would have enjoyed in the 18th and 19th centuries. In Soviet times 15 different families lived in the building and they were only moved out in 1981 for restoration to begin. It was completed in 1992.

Walk down Kungu iela past the Mentzendorff House to Mārstaļu iela. Number 21 Mārstaļu iela is a fine example of baroque domestic architecture and was built in 1696 for another wealthy citizen of Riga, Dannenstern, and his family. The plaque on 21 commemorates Riga's most famous mayor, James Armitsted, who was of British origin. He held the post from 1901 until his death in 1912.

Reuter House

The house at number 2 Mārstaļu iela is the Reuter House (*Reutera nams*), a building that derives its name from another wealthy Riga merchant, Johann von Reuter. The house was built in 1682. Note the six pillars that decorate what appears to be the front of the house but is, in fact, the side. As with the Mentzendorff House, restoration that started around 1980 revealed a large number of wall and ceiling paintings. It is now largely used for lectures and conferences, but the public are able to see the entrance hall and the balustrade leading to the first floor.

If you backtrack down Mārstaļu iela and turn left into Alksnāja iela (Alder Street) and then left into Vecpilsētas iela (Old Town Street) you may care to take a look at the buildings at numbers 10 and 11–17 which are good examples of some of the 20 or so **medieval warehouses** of the Old Town.

If you bear right around the corner passing numbers 13–15 you come to the house from which the Latvian Popular Front operated in the late 1980s.

Universal Store Building

Turn right into Audēju iela (Weaver Street). The rather grim looking **Centrs department store** was formerly the Universalveikals, the Rigan equivalent of Moscow's GUM or State Universal Store. In fact the building itself predates the Soviet era and was actually built before World War II under the Ulmanis regime. Rīdzenes iela (Rīdzene Street) runs alongside it. The street gets its name from the River Rīdzene which used to flow here. The Rīdzene was originally called the River Riga but became known as the Rīdzene in the 17th century. It flowed through the Old Town and on into the Daugava but eventually became overgrown and disease-ridden so was covered over in the 19th century.

The interior is now a modern department store. The ground floor has an extensive supermarket and a snack bar much cheaper than any of the surrounding cafés. A wide range of foreign newspapers is also sold here.

Convent Courtyard

Turn left into Teātra iela (Theatre Street) at the end of Rīdzene iela. This brings you back to Kalēju iela. Just off Kalēju iela there is a passage that leads you to the **Konventa sēta**, an area of beautifully restored historic buildings between Kalēju iela and Skārņu iela. The 17th-century warehouses and other buildings in this area had fallen into complete decay (the area used to be known as 'the dead town') but have now been restored with the aid of German investment.

The history of the Konventa sēta goes back, like so much of Riga's history, to the 13th century when a castle was built on this site by the Knights of the Sword. The Convent of the Holy Spirit (from which the area then took its name) was also established here, and in due course a number of alms houses and other institutions settled nearby. Eventually commerce superseded religion and the buildings began to be replaced by warehouses. Each warehouse had its own name, but because of the associations the area had with the convent, many were given names with the word 'dove' in them (the dove being a symbol of the Holy Spirit, the third person of the Trinity). The former St George's Chapel became known as 'the white dove', and the building next to it 'the grey dove' and so on. Many of these traditional names have been revived as part of the restoration. One house called Kampenhausen recalls the Riga councillor who founded a home for elderly ladies here. The so-called 'grey sisters' building once served as accommodation for the nuns of the convent.

In 1989 talks began between Latvian and German architects and builders about restoring the derelict area. Before long a German–Latvian joint venture firm, REHO, was formed and the reconstruction of the Konventa Sēta began. The restored complex of buildings reopened in December 1996. A major part of the Konventa sēta is taken up by the Konventa Sēta Hotel, a modern three/four-star hotel occupying a number of the restored buildings. Other buildings in the convent courtyard are taken up by shops and now at Kalēju

Above left Alexander Nevsky
Cathedral, Tallinn (HB)

Above right Viru Gate, Tallinn
Old Town (TH)

Left Pavement café on
Raekoja plats (Town Hall
Square), Tallinn (JS)

Above View towards Riga station and covered market (RR)

Below A train crosses the railway bridge over the River Daugava at sunrise, with Riga's TV Tower in the background (JS)

Below right Art nouveau or Jugendstil door, Riga (SC)

Bottom Old Town Riga (RR)

9–11 by the **Porcelain Museum** (11.00–8.00, closed on Mondays) which opened in 2001. It has three rooms, covering 1840 to the present day. The largest individual exhibit is a vase made to commemorate Riga's 700th anniversary in 1901, but the most extensive collection dates from the Soviet period, when no anniversary could pass without ornamental plates and tea sets. Thus the 100th anniversary of Lenin's birth in 1970 is suitably marked. It is good to see the sophistication of the technique, whatever regime was in power, and the versatility of work now produced without hindrance from a political straitjacket.

St John's Courtyard and Church

Close to the Konventa sēta at the end of Teātra iela there is a part of the city wall. An archway in Kalēju iela leads to Jāņa Sēta (John's Courtyard), a cobbled courtyard with the city wall on one side and a bar, café and restaurant forming the other sides of the quadrangle.

A second arch leads out of the courtyard to **St John's Church** (*Jāņa baznīca*). Built in 1234 for the Dominicans by Bishop Nicolas, the oldest surviving parts of the church are the main door and porch. The original chapel became too small, so in 1330 it was expanded by the addition of a red-brick nave with a choir and apse covered by a tiled roof and decorated with a small tower which still survives. As a result of renovation work in the 15th and 16th centuries the meshed vaulted ceilings came into being. The 35m-high nave dates from the 15th century. The baroque altar is 18th century, the work of J E Meier and K E Apelbaum, and has sculptures depicting the crucifixion and SS Peter and Paul. The altar painting, *The Resurrection*, is the work of the Riga artist, A Stiling. Several paintings of the Passion and of the apostles decorate the organ loft. The stained glass is 19th century. The organ is a gift from the town of Uddevalla in Sweden; the old organ, which dated from 1854, was given to the church of Cesvaine in Vidzeme.

The façade was restored in 1924–26 under the supervision of the architect E Laube. On the outside, at the altar end of the church, is a statue of St John the Baptist (the patron saint of the church), and nearby is one of Salome, the daughter of Herodias who married Herod Antipas, her dead husband's brother. St John preached against the marriage, as a result of which Herodias persuaded Salome to dance for her husband and seek as her reward the head of John the Baptist.

The history of this church again reflects Riga's turbulent past. The Dominicans were ousted in the Reformation, and for some time after 1523 the church was used as stables by the mayor of Riga, Shulte, then as an arsenal, until in 1582 the Polish king, Stephen Bathory, seized it and handed it over to the Jesuits. However, in due course it was returned to the Lutheran church, and is still used as a place of worship, primarily by the Lutherans, but also on occasions for ecumenical services.

The façade overlooking Skārņu iela is decorated with two stone faces which are said to be the faces of two monks. One explanation for their being there is found in the story that they represent two monks who were immured at the time the church was built; the other is that they were put there as an early elocution aid – other monks were supposed to shape their mouths in the same way as the stone examples, thereby improving their own qualities as preachers.

Ekke's Convent

Skārņu iela (Butchers' Street) got its name from the shops that were located in this part of Riga in medieval times. Number 22, next door to St John's Church, is a house known as Ekke's Convent (*Ekes konvents*). It is believed to have been built in 1435 as a guesthouse for travellers. However, in 1592 Nikolaus Ekke, a mayor of Riga, acquired the building and turned it into a home for widows of members of Riga's small guild.

In recent years the building served as a tourist information centre but funds for this ran out in early 1999. It was then reopened in 2000 as a waxworks museum which served as a useful introduction to Latvian history with all the country's heroes portrayed here. This museum in turn closed in 2001 and the future of the building is uncertain.

St George's Church/Decorative and Applied Arts Museum

Further along Skārņu iela, next to number 10, the old white building with brick-lined windows is **St George's Church** (*Jura baznīca*). It was the first stone church and possibly the oldest building in Riga, built at the beginning of the 13th century and generally dated at 1202 or 1204 when it was part of a castle (Wittenstein Castle) belonging to the Knights of the Sword. The castle was destroyed in 1297 after which it became a church until the Reformation. From the 1620s until the 1980s it was used as a warehouse before falling into disuse. In 1989 it became part of the **Museum of Decorative and Applied Arts**, *Dekoratīvi Lietišķās Mākslas Muzejs* (open 10.00–18.00 every day except Monday). The ground floor houses temporary exhibitions of contemporary art. The first floor has large-scale ceramics, leather goods, amber and glass, mostly from the 1880s to the 1960s. The top floor is devoted to tapestries from 1970 to 1990 that in their sombre presentations show the sense of despair that gripped Latvia at the time. Even a sunset is portrayed in grey.

St Peter's Church

On the other side of Skārņu iela stands one of Riga's most famous and distinctive churches, St Peter's (*Pētera baznīca*). It is a large red-brick church with a simple, light interior decorated by coats of arms. The main entrance is located on VecRigas laukums (Old Riga Square). The original church that was built here in 1209 was wooden and, unusually, was built not by foreigners but by the largely Christian Liv people of Riga. No record remains of the original church which was started in 1406, although the reconstruction process went on until the end of the 15th century. A steeple was erected in 1491 but collapsed in 1666 causing considerable damage and killing the inhabitants of a neighbouring building. A replacement was completed in 1690 by the Strasbourg architect, Bindenschu, and was, in its time, the tallest in the world. However, this, too, was damaged by fire caused by lightning in 1721. Tsar Peter the Great was in Riga at the time of the incident and ordered the steeple and spire to be restored yet again. Reconstruction was completed in 1746 under the supervision of Johann Wulbern. His steeple stood for 195 years until it was destroyed along with the rest of the church by German mortar fire in 1941, ironically on June 29, the feast of St Peter.

The latest reconstruction work began in 1963 and was completed by 1973. The present steeple, 123.5m high, is a steel replica of its predecessor. It conceals a lift which takes visitors up to a viewing platform that provides wonderful panoramas of the city. (The lift starts from the gallery in the tower and is open 10.00–18.00 except on Monday; cost Ls1.60.) For many years St Peter's was the tallest building in Riga until Intourist built the Hotel Latvijā, which is about a metre higher.

In 1352 Riga's first clock was installed in St Peter's. One of the church's finest objects was a marble pulpit by the Italian Giovanni Baratta, but it was destroyed in the fire of 1941 along with the German oak altar, the wooden pews and a magnificent organ.

Many of Riga's protestant churches have cockerels as weathercocks, and St Peter's is no exception: a golden weathercock has topped the spire for 200 years. The symbol has a special significance for this church, since it recalls how St Peter denied Christ three times before the cock crowed. The old weathercock is still kept in the church porch.

After restoration, St Peter's functioned initially only as a museum and concert hall, although it has now begun to be used again for church services.

There are two famous stories associated with St Peter's. The first is the story of the blue guard, a civilian volunteer unit formed in the 18th century to guard prominent citizens of Riga. One of the guards is supposed to haunt St Peter's. An old man bet two young men that they would not dare to spend the night of the feast of St Andrew in the church and prove that they had been there by hammering a nail into the altar. On St Andrew's night the two youths entered the church just before midnight, but at the stroke of midnight the old man and his witnesses who were waiting outside the church heard a terrible cry. The people outside soon broke into the church and one of the young men managed to escape through the main door. However, his friend was found hanged from the nail, a victim of the ghost of the blue guard.

The second story concerns Johann Heinrich Wulbern, the steeple builder. There was a tradition that when a new building was being topped off, the architect would go to the top and throw down a glass which was supposed to shatter, the number of shards representing the number of years for which the building would stand. Unfortunately, when Wulbern threw down his glass it was caught by a passing hay cart and therefore suffered only a minor crack. Nothing came of this evil omen, but the glass is preserved in the Museum of History and Navigation.

On leaving St Peter's, return to Skārņu iela and then turn right into Kaļķu iela. This last part of our walking tour of Old Riga will take you past some of Riga's newest shops and bring you back to the Hotel de Rome and a sign that Riga is now a thoroughly 21st-century consumer-oriented city: opposite the hotel and almost in the shadow of the Freedom Monument is Riga's first McDonald's.

New Town

The Old Town and New Town are separated by the city canal (*pilsētas kanāls*) which runs through a series of parks and gardens. The canal follows the line of part of the old city wall which was demolished in the 19th century. Through the centre of the parks, separating the Old Town from the New Town, is Brīvības bulvāris (Freedom Boulevard), a pedestrianised street that is also the site of the Freedom Monument.

Freedom Monument

The Freedom Monument (*Brīvības piemineklis*) dominates the centre of Riga. Known locally as 'Milda', it was erected in 1935 and paid for by public subscription. At 42.7m high it is the tallest monument of its kind in Europe. It was designed by the Latvian architect Kārlis Zāle and consists of a tall granite column surmounted by a 9m high figure of a woman holding three golden stars above her head. The three stars represent the three cultural regions of Latvia - Kurzeme, Vidzeme and Latgale. Engraved in gold letters on the base are the words *Tevzēmei un brīvībai* ('for fatherland and freedom'). Also decorating the monument is a sculpture of Lāčplēsis, the bear slayer, a mythical Latvian hero. The monument was dedicated on November 18 1935, the 17th anniversary of the declaration of independence.

Nowadays the base is often surrounded by flowers, frequently red and white, the colours of the Latvian national flag. Flowers were forbidden during the Soviet era; indeed the Soviet authorities had contemplated removing the monument altogether, since it served as a focus of Latvian nationalistic aspirations, but thought better of the idea, fearing demonstrations and reprisals. Instead they erected a statue of Lenin. The two monuments stood back to back for decades, Lenin facing east towards Moscow, the Freedom Monument facing west. Lenin has now disappeared, but the Freedom Monument remains.

Laima clock
Close to the Freedom Monument (on the Old Town side of the park) stands the Laima clock, another well-known landmark and a popular meeting point. *Laima* is the name of a local chocolate manufacturer and the Latvian word for happiness or good luck (there was also an ancient deity of that name).

National Opera
The building originally dated from 1860 but was largely destroyed by fire in 1882 When rebuilt shortly afterwards, it was one of the first to install electricity instead of gas for lighting. As it was somewhat neglected towards the end of the Soviet period, renovation was begun in 1991 and the interior was completed in late 1995. Extensions have been built since then so that rehearsals can take place in the building and it also now includes storage space for scenery and wardrobes. Backstage tours can be arranged for groups, and these will often coincide with rehearsals. An annual Opera Festival takes place here every June. Full details of the programme, and of all other performances, can be found on the website www.opera.lv.

The parks
The parks on either side of the Freedom Monument were laid out in 1853–63. The one through which Brīvības bulvāris runs is the Bastejkalns Park, so called after the 17th-century bastion that once stood here and formed a vital part of Riga's defences.

If you walk through Bastejkalns Park you will come across a set of engraved stones near the bridge that crosses the canal (most are on the New Town side, one is on the Old Town side of the canal). On the night of January 20 1991 forces loyal to Moscow attempted to capture a number of government buildings including the Ministry of the Interior on Raiņa bulvāris, the street running alongside the canal on the New Town side. Several Latvians were shot, some say by sniper fire from the roof tops. The stones preserve the memory of five victims: Gvīdo Zvaigne, a cameraman who was filming events, Andris Slapiņš, a cinema director and cameraman, two militiamen, Sergejs Kononenko and Vladimirs Gomanovics, and Edijs Riekstiņš, a student.

The park also contains monuments to the writer, Rūdolfs Blaumanis, the composer Alfrēds Kalniņš, and the researcher, Mstislav Keldish.

Next to Bastejkalns Park is **Kronvalda Park** with its monuments to the Latvian writers Sudraba Edzus and Andrejs Upitis. Also set in this park are the Riga Congress House (*Rigas kongresu nams*) and the Riga Council Building (*Rigas dome*).

National Theatre

Close to the canal on Kr Valdemāra iela is the National Theatre, a small theatre with seating for only 890. It was here that Latvia declared independence on November 18 1918. A concert is held here every year to commemorate the event.

If you are interested in the history of Latvian theatre you may care to visit the **Theatre Museum** (37/39 Smiļga iela; tel: 611893; open 11.00–18.00 (12.00–19.00 on Wednesday) every day except Monday and Tuesday). This is housed in the building where theatre director and actor Eduards Smiļgis (1886–1966) lived for all but five years of his life. It was empty for five years after his death before being converted into a museum that opened in 1974. Although his personal theatre here could have accommodated an audience, he always rehearsed in strict privacy, totally on his own. This theatre was modelled on the Dailes Theatre in central Riga. He played every major role in the plays of Janis Rainis and of Shakespeare, and when he gave up acting in 1940, he continued to direct. Both his sons were killed fighting, one in the German army and one in the Russian army. The collections comprehensively cover the history of the Latvian theatre, not only in Riga but also in Ventspils and in Liepaja. No famous actor is missed, nor is any famous stage-set. The private rooms and offices have been left just as Smiļgis would have known and used them.

University

At the New Town end of Brīvības bulvāris, on Raini bulvāris, stands the main building of the **University of Riga**, a Gothic building with elements of the Romanesque. It stands on the site of the ancient Rīdzene River, long since channelled underground, and was originally used by the Riga Polytechnical Institute. It features a stone staircase divided into three parts, the centre section of which is traditionally used only by graduates.

Esplanade Park

The Esplanade Park is the second major park in the town centre. It is the location of a number of important buildings in the New Town. Also in the park is the monument to Jānis Rainis, one of Latvia's most famous writers and translators.

The **Academy of Art** (*Mākslas akademija*) is a fine example of neo-Gothic architecture. In front of it there is a statue by Burkards Dzenis (1936) of Jānis Rozentāls, the founder of the Latvian Realist school of painting.

Next to the Academy is the **State Museum of Fine Arts** (*Valsts Mākslas Muzejs*). The museum has the incongruous address of Valdemāra 10a, which suggests a couple of small rooms, but it is in fact one of Riga's largest buildings.

It dates from the affluent decade at the beginning of the 20th century so flaunts a classical exterior and a Jugendstil interior. The ticket desk is a good source for art books and reproductions and it is worth taking a look at the entrance, even without visiting the galleries. The museum is closed on Tuesdays but otherwise is open 11.00–17.00. It houses a collection of 52,000 paintings and sculptures, including the modern works now displayed in the Arsenals Museum. If funds can be found, it is planning a major refurbishment to celebrate the 100th anniversary of its foundation in 1905. This used to have a superb collection of paintings from all parts of Europe, including works by Ingres, Landseer, Friedrich and various early German, Dutch and Italian masters. However, after World War I its director, Vilhelms Purvītis (himself a prominent landscape painter), began to concentrate on Latvian art, and now its exhibits are almost exclusively works of Latvian and Russian origin. The works of Latvian artists are displayed on the first floor, those of Russian and German origin on the ground floor. Inevitably, there is a great deal of work by Rozentāls (his portrait of the singer Malvine Vignère-Grīnberga painted in the last year of his life is particularly well known), but the majority of paintings are by artists whose names will be known only to experts in Latvian and Russian art. There is a portrait of the Russian writer Turgenev (painted in 1869) by A Gruzdins (1825–91), a bust of the Russian composer Moussorgsky by Teodors Zaļnkalns (1876–1928), a portrait of Kārlis Zāle (the designer of the Freedom Monument) by Ludolfs Liberits (1895–1959) painted in 1934 and showing a relaxed Zāle smoking a cigarette, and a picture of the old harbour when it was located closer to the Old Town by Jānis Roberts Tilbergs (1880–1972). Ludolfs Liberts spent his final years in America and some of his pictures of New York from that time have been given to the museum.

Konrād Urbāns (1893–1981) is Latvia's most famous landscape painter and given the theme of his work, he continued to be active in the Soviet period. Latvia's most famous woman painter, who likewise spanned both the first independence period and its Soviet sequel, is Alexandra Belcova (1892–1981). Many of her portraits are on show.

Orthodox Cathedral
The Russian Orthodox Cathedral, with its distinctive domes surmounted by Orthodox crosses, was built in 1876–84 to designs by Roberts Pflugs and Jānis Baumanis. During the Soviet years it was used as a planetarium and for scientific lectures. Now it has been handed back to the Orthodox church, and although functioning as a place of worship is still undergoing much-needed restoration.

Opposite the cathedral, the large government building is the *Ministru kabinets*, the **Cabinet Office**.

Hotel Latvijā
The skyline of the New Town is dominated by what used to be the huge Soviet-built Hotel Latvijā but is now a modern hotel, refurbishment having been completed in May 2001. With its 27 storeys, it is still the tallest building in the country and has become something of a landmark, although many of Riga's inhabitants used to regard the original hotel as an eyesore. It took about 20 years to complete. There is a story about a travel guide who was asked by someone in her group what the huge building site was. She told the person concerned and bemoaned the inefficiency of Soviet construction. The story got back to her boss

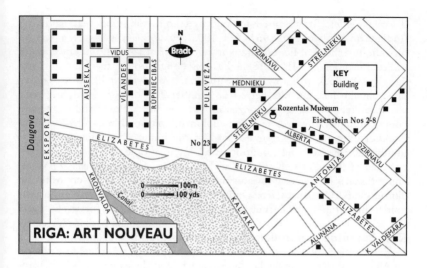

who reprimanded her for her disloyalty. The next time she was asked the same question, by which time building was at a more advanced stage, she simply replied, 'I don't know what it is, but things move fast here: there was nothing there the other day'. The travel writer, Colin Thubron, describes a stay there in the 1980s in *Among the Russians*:

> The hotel itself conformed miserably to expectation. It was huge, charmless, exhibitionist. Latvians joke that these tourist ghettos are made of 60 per cent glass, 30 per cent ferro-concrete and 10 per cent microphones. All their minor fittings, all those things by which a civilization may be gauged by archaeologists after it has gone, were wretchedly poor. When I turned on the light-switch the electricity made a scuttling like rats along the curtain rails, then died. The furniture was of black-varnished pine; the shower curtains chiffon-thin. The lukewarm water which trickled from the shower was augmented by surreptitious leaks in other places, and the rain had enfiladed the double-glazed windows to stream down the frames.

The new Reval Hotel Latvijā has no traces of this former description. It has been fully renovated and offers all the usual facilities of international hotels. Even if you are not staying there, a ride to the Skyline Bar on the 26th floor, using the glass lift, provides wonderful views over Riga.

Art nouveau
If you turn left along Elizabetes iela along the front of the Hotel Latvijā, you come to Antonijas iela on the right; this in turn takes you to Alberta iela. The streets in this area are known for two architectural features. There are a number of **traditional wooden buildings** here, including some on the Brīvības iela itself. There are also some of Riga's finest examples of art nouveau or **Jugendstil** in the surrounding streets. The house at 4a Strēlnieku iela dates back to 1905 and is the work of one of the most famous proponents of the style in Riga, Mikhail Eisenstein (father of the film

director Sergei). It was used by various schools for some years and as a student hostel between 1957 and 1993. In 1993 it was given to the Stockholm School of Economics who restored it in 1993–4. Other examples in Strēlnieku iela are 1b (note the beading design around the windows) and 2a, a simple block of restored flats with attractive balcony rails. At the corner of Strēlnieku iela and Elizabetes iela (number 21a) there is a building with an attractive yellow-grey frieze above the third floor and a plaque commemorating the architect and diplomat, Mārtiņš Nuksa (1878–1942). Another example of Eisenstein's work is the house at 10b Elizabetes iela; number 23 Elizabetes iela, opposite the Ukrainian Embassy, is another good example of the style – the plaque at the top says, *Labor vincit omnia* ('Work conquers all'). Other examples in this area are 3 Ausekļa iela (opposite the Tobago café), 14 Ausekļa iela, numbers 3 and 4 Vidus iela and the two domed buildings at the corner of Vidus and Vīlandes iela.

Jānis Rozentāls and Rūdolfs Blaumanis Memorial Museum

Further examples of some of the area's finest art nouveau houses are to be found on Alberta iela, including the house at number 12, designed by K Pēkūens, flat 9 of which is now the Jānis Rozentāls and Rūdolfs Blaumanis Memorial Museum, *Jāņa Rozentāla un Rūdolfa Blaumana Memoriālais Muzejs* (open 11.00–17.00 every day except Tuesday and Wednesday). The museum is reached from an entrance in Strēlnieku iela. Take the elaborate staircase in the rather neglected hallway to the top floor and ring to gain admission. The ironwork, the tiling and the

JĀNIS ROZENTĀLS

Jānis Rozentāls (1866–1916) was born, the son of a blacksmith, in Kurzeme. In spite of the fact that he enjoyed only a rudimentary education, he studied at the St Petersburg Academy of Arts from which he graduated in 1894. He painted some 300 portraits, landscapes and altarpieces and did a large amount of book illustration as well as producing essays and criticism. He and his wife ran Riga's most famous salon. He moved to Helsinki at the beginning of World War I, where he died on December 26 1916 and was initially buried. However, his remains were removed to be reinterred in the Meža (or Woodland) cemetery in Riga (see page 105) in 1920.

Rozentāls' wife, Elija Forsele-Rozentāle (1871–1943), was born in Finland. After studying at the Helsinki Music School and in Paris, Rome and Milan, she went on to become a renowned mezzo-soprano. She met her husband-to-be when she came to Riga to sing in November 1902. They married in 1903 and lived in the flat that is now the museum together with their children, Laila, Irja and Miķelis. She, too, is buried in the Meža cemetery. Later generations of the Rozentāls family continued to live here until 2001, when his granddaughter Eva died. They were obliged to share the floor with other families during the Soviet era, and the ten layers of wallpaper that inflicted one room, date from then. Most of the items displayed are original, but a few have been added from Finland.

paintings on the ceiling are all original but the windows are of a later date. The architect for the building was Konstantīns Pēkšēns (1859–1928), second only to Jānis Blaumanis for his activity and fame at the turn of the century. He designed it for his own use, but then gave the top floor to Jānis Rozentāls in 1904.

The painter Rūdolfs Blaumanis rented a room in the flat and lived there in 1906–08.

The museum was established in 1973. The living rooms contain pictures, photographs and artefacts connected with the life of its inhabitants. The studio and other rooms on the top floor are an art school and are used to exhibit works by the students who range from young children to mature painters. Good photographs of Alberta iela can be taken from the Rozentāls Museum.

Alexander Nevsky Church
The Alexander Nevsky Church on the corner of Brīvības iela and Lāčplēša iela is another Russian Orthodox church. It is named after the 13th century Russian prince who was canonised by the Russian Orthodox church in 1547 for his efforts to preserve Orthodoxy in Russia against the Germans whom he defeated at Lake Peipus (now in Estonia) in 1242. His story is now famous because of the film made by Eisenstein in 1938 with music by Prokofiev.

St Gertrude's Church
St Gertrude's Church, just off Brīvības iela in Gertrūdes iela, is a large red-brick church built in 1863–7 to designs by J D Felsko. The plain interior and pleasing woodwork and gallery are typical of so many Latvian churches.

Vērmaņu Gardens
Bounded by Elizabetes iela, Kr Barons, Merķeļa and Tērbates iela, the *Vērmaņes dārzs* (as the gardens are called in Latvian) is the most popular of Riga's central parks. Opened in 1817, it was named in honour of the woman who donated the land to the city. Originally it was a refuge for residents of Riga who could not get out to the countryside. It soon acquired attractions, including a bronze fountain cast in Berlin, a playground, an ice rink, a sun dial and the first rose garden in Riga. It has an open-air theatre and a statue of Kriūjānis Barons, the writer and poet.

Berga Bazārs
Not far from the Vērmaņu Gardens, just behind the Jāņa Sēta bookshop in Elizabetes iela, is the Berga Bazārs. This area was originally developed in the late 19th/early 20th century by the builder and property developer, Kristaps Bergs (1840–1907), as a combination of commercial, residential and retail properties: the architect was Konstantins Pēkšēns (1859–1928). The area fell into disrepair during the Soviet period, but reconstruction began in 1992 when ownership was restored to Berg's great-grandchildren. The new development has cafés, shops and restaurants.

The Central Station, Market and Academy of Sciences
If you take Raiņa bulvāris past the university it eventually brings you to the **railway station**. The first station was built here in 1861 and was known as the Orel or Dvinsk station. A second station, Tukum station, served Kurzeme. In 1888 a chapel called the Chapel of Thanksgiving was erected next to it to give

thanks for the fact that the tsar's family escaped with their lives from a train crash near Borki in Kharkov. It was demolished in 1925. The present station was built in 1957–60. The clock tower with its digital clock marks it as a product of the sixties. A major rebuilding of the station started in 2001 and is unlikely to be completed before the end of 2003.

Beyond the station (under the railway bridge) is the **Central Market** (*Centrāltirgus*). In the 19th century this area was full of what used to be called 'red warehouses' (some still stand), so called after the colour of the bricks used to build them. The modern market buildings consist of five large pavilions, each one originally designed to deal with a different product. Each one is 12m high and covers an area of 75,000m^2, and was built in 1930 to a design intended for Zeppelin hangars. Apart from the formal market, the area around the hangars is full of stalls selling all manner of food, clothing and other goods.

If you continue along Gogoļa iela to Turgeneva iela you come to an excellent example of Soviet architecture of the Stalin era in the form of the **Academy of Sciences** building. Built in 1957, its nickname, 'Stalin's birthday cake', reflects its ornateness. Similar buildings can be found in Moscow and Warsaw. Note the Communist hammer and sickle motifs close to the top.

Museums

For a relatively small capital city Riga boasts a huge number of museums covering a wide range of subjects – art, literature, theatre, history and politics, medicine and other specialist topics. The visitor to Riga with little time to spare will not be able to visit all of them, so if time is limited, we recommend the following: the **Ethnographic Museum** (see page 95), the **Motor Museum** (see above), the **Museum of the Occupation of Latvia** (see page 79–80), the **art nouveau houses** in the New Town, especially the **Jānis Rozentāls Memorial Museum** (page 90), and finally the **Museum of the History of Riga and Navigation** (see page 78).

The alphabetical list of museums below is not exhaustive but covers the majority of museums any visitor is likely to want to visit.

The opening hours of the major museums are reliable, but some of the smaller museums suffer from staff shortages, so it may be advisable to check opening hours locally before making a long journey. Smaller museums will open for tour groups on 'closed' days by prior arrangement. The Latvian and English *Latvijas Muzeji* ('Museums of Latvia'), published by the Latvian Museum Association with support from the Dutch Prince Bernhardt Foundation, is a useful booklet giving addresses, opening times and brief descriptions of the main museums in Riga and elsewhere in Latvia.

Jāņa Akuratera Museum 6a O Vāciesa iela, Pārdaugava; tel: 619934. Open 11.00–17.00 every day except Sunday and Wednesday.
Situated across the Daugava River from the Old Town, this museum is devoted to the life of Jānis Akuraters (1876–1937), the popular Latvian writer and rifleman. He wrote poetry and novels, his best known being *Kalps zena vasara* ('The Young Farmhand's Summer') and *Degosa sala* ('The Burning Island').
Krišjānis Barons Memorial Museum (*Krišjāņa Barona Memoriālais Muzejs*) 3–5 Kr Barona iela; tel: 728 4265. Open 11.00–17.00 Tuesday, Thursday, Saturday and Sunday, 13.00–19.00 Wednesday and Friday, closed Monday.

The museum is the flat (number 5) occupied by Krišjānis Barons, the collector of Latvian oral literature, the *dainas*. The museum recreates his life and work. Examples of folk music and videos are available.

Cinema Museum *Rigas Kino Muzejs*, 22 Krāslavas iela; tel: 722 0282. Open 12.00–17.00 every day except Monday.

The building, which is in the old Russian working-class district of Riga, used to house the secret printing press used by the communist newspaper, *Cīņa* ('Battle'). You can still visit the secret passages underneath the building and view the model printing presses.

'Dauderi' Latvian Cultural Museum *Latvijas Kultūras Muzejs*, 30 Sarkandaugavas iela; tel: 391780 or 392229. Open 11.00–17.00 every day except Monday and Tuesday.

This museum is housed in an elegant red-brick building, constructed in 1897–8. During the first independence it was the summer residence of the Latvian president, Kārlis Ulmanis, before he was deported. It contains a vast collection of memorabilia related to the recent history of the country brought together by Gaidis Graundiņš, a Latvian living in Germany. There are also mementos of Latvia's prewar independence, such as banknotes, stamps, photographs and so on, all collected from Latvian exiles.

Museum of Fire-fighting *Ugunsdzēsības Muzejs*, 5 Hanzas iela; tel: 733 3306. Open 10.00–17.00 every day except Wednesday.

The engines displayed go back to 1899 with a Shand Mason and a Chevrolet from America. Many fire crews have been voluntary in Latvia, whatever the nature of the regime, and there are pictures of them in action and also posing very formally. Foreign fires are covered too, from Moscow in 1812 to New York in 2001. The only ones missing are industrial ones during the Soviet period when such accidents were never admitted.

Latvian Museum of Natural History *Latvijas Dabas Muzejs*, 4 Kr Barona iela; tel: 722 5765. Open 10.00–17.00 except Monday and Tuesday.

The museum has permanent exhibitions of geology, zoology, entomology, anthropology, and environmental protection. It also has an exhibition concentrating on the Daugava River and the effect of the construction of the hydro-electric power station on the river basin. Note the herbarium display, the work of the botanist J Ilsters. The ticket offices sells attractive bookmarks for five sentimi each.

Pharmaceutical Museum *Farmācijas Muzejs*, 13–15 Riharda Vāgnera iela; tel: 721 3008. Open 10.00–16.00 every day except Sunday, Monday and Tuesday.

Part of the P Stradiņš Museum of the History of Medicine, this branch is housed in a beautifully renovated house in the Old Town. Given the size of the collection, it seems to display every potion known to the medical world around 1900.

Latvian Photographic Museum *Latvijas Foto Muzejs*, 8 Mārstaļu iela; tel: 722 7231. Open 13.00–19.00 Wednesday and Thursday, 11.00–17.00 Friday, 11.00–15.00 Saturday.

The basic exhibition is of cameras and pictures from 1839 to 1941 and of a studio from 1900 which can still be made to function. The museum is now gradually being extended. At long last, photographs from the War and from the Soviet period can be shown in public and many have been given to the museum. Latvian photographers forced to emigrate have also helped to build up the collection. One gallery is reserved for temporary exhibitions and these usually show the work of contemporary photographers.

Porcelain Museum see page 91.

Latvian Railway Museum (Latvijas Dzelzcela Muzejs) Uzvaras 2 Tel: 583-2849 Open 10.00–17.00 Wednesday to Saturday, although with prior arrangement happy to open at other times. The Museum only dates from 1994 but has accumulated a wide range of materials going back about 100 years, including signals, timetables, track and above all, steam engines. One German engine from the War is fitted out as a snowplough. As late as April 1944, the Germans produced a timetable for the whole Baltics area. It is displayed here and it remains the last one to have appeared. The Soviets regarded such information as too dangerous to impart and the three Baltic railway administrations have been unable to co-ordinate a similar publication. Another branch of the Museum is at Jelgava, and it concentrates on railway safety and training.

Gustavs Šķilters Museum *Gustava Šķiltera Memoriālais Muzejs*, Daugavgrivas iela, (across the Daugava River near Ķīpsala island), tel: 62 5364. Open 12.00–18.00 Wednesday to Sunday only.

This museum, founded in 1971, is dedicated to the life and work of the Latvian sculptor, Gustavs Šķilters (1874–1954). There is a permanent display of his work as well as changing displays.

Museum of Space Exploration also known as Fridrich Zander's Memorial Museum (*Fridriha Candera Memoriālais Muzejs*), 1 F Candera iela; tel: 761 4113. Open only on Wednesday 11.00–16.00.

Established in 1987, this museum is located in the house of the Latvian rocket designer, Fridrich Zander (1887–1933).

Latvian Sports Museum *Latvijas Sporta Muzejs*, 7–9 Alksnāja iela; tel: 722 5127 or 721 1365. Open 10.00–18.00 every day except Monday.

This has a unique collection of bicycles, including a collapsible Peugeot built in 1915 and used during World War I and an English Raleigh ladies bicycle dating from 1895, as well as more conventional exhibits. It is housed in an attractive 17th century warehouse.

P Stradins Museum of the History of Medicine *P Stradiņa Medicīnas Vēstures Muzejs*, 1 Antonijas iela; tel: 722 2656. Open 11.00–16.30 every day, except Sunday and Monday and the last Friday of each month.

This is one of the few museums in Riga that could cross the political divide quite happily in 1991. Without fear or favour, the museum had already acknowledged the equal role played in the development of medicine by Germans, Latvians and Russians. Professor Paulis Stradins (1896–1958) had been a collector all his life and it is sad that the museum could only open in 1961, three years after his death. It shows the simple treatments used by cavemen, a model of Riga's first pharmacy which opened in 1357, the treatment centres run by nuns, vaccinations, and the stained glass used in anatomy lessons for students unable to read. X-rays are covered extensively, One room has the cumbersome equipment of a Soviet operating theatre. The top floor, which is sponsored by a Latvian drug company, covers contemporary medicine both on the ground and in space. The only missing topic is medicine at war, perhaps because there was little street by street fighting in Riga in either World War.

Lattelkom Museum of Telecommunications 33 Brīvības iela; tel: 724 0004. Opening times vary; check locally.

One hundred and fifty years of telecommunications in Latvia.

Theatre Museum see page 95.

By the Daugava River

The wide 11 Novembra krastmala (Embankment of November 11) is the road that runs along the bank of the Daugava between the Vansu and Akmens bridges. It commemorates November 11 1919, the day on which the pre-war Latvian flag was raised over Riga castle. It leads on to 13. Janvara iela which turns away from the river towards the station. On the bank of the Daugava, one can see the

Monument to the 1905 Revolution. It was here that the workers of Riga held a peaceful demonstration in 1905 to show solidarity with their comrades in St Petersburg. Troops opened fire and about 70 demonstrators were killed and some 200 injured, many of them as they tried to escape the gunfire by crossing the frozen river, only to find that the ice was too thin. The statue we now see here was erected in 1960 and is the work of the sculptor Terpilovskis.

It is to the Daugava River that Riga owes its importance. Up to the turn of the century ships still loaded and unloaded their cargoes on the quayside close to the Central Market, but by 1900 the river was silting up at this point, and new docks had to be built further upstream. The new harbour relies heavily on container traffic. The only active sign of shipping that can be seen from the Old Town these days is what comes and goes from the ferry terminal and yacht harbour at the end of Ausekļa iela.

Ķīpsala

From 11 Novembra or its extension, Eksporta iela, you look across the river to the island of Ķīpsala. There is little of interest on the island which is now occupied mainly by industrial and commercial buildings and the campus of the Technical University of Riga. There is also a large swimming pool and sports complex, 'Alex', on the main road, Ķīpsala iela.

In earlier times the island of Ķīpsala was inhabited largely by fishermen and others who made their living from the sea. The island's historical connections with the sea still live on in the names of some of its streets, Balasta dambis (Ballast Dam), Matrožu iela (Sailor Street), Zvejnieku iela (Fisherman Street) and so on. Herder often came here to walk and study the Latvian customs still practised by the inhabitants.

In more recent times the islander Jānis Lipke (1900–87) sheltered 53 Riga Jews in his house on the island during the Nazi occupation. As their number grew, two large cellars were dug to conceal them, and 43 survived the war.

Pārdaugava

Pārdaugava is the name for the area on the 'left bank' of the Daugava, the part of Riga that lies on the river bank opposite the Old Town. There is little in this area to attract the visitor. It began to be inhabited only after the building of bridges across the Daugava (an iron bridge in 1871 and a pontoon bridge in 1896). Gradually it grew into an area of about 120km² of industrial and residential development. If you cross the river using the Akmens bridge you come to Uzvaras bulvāris (Victory Boulevard) which leads to **Victory Park** (*Uzvaras Parks*), so called to commemorate the liberation from German occupation. It was given this name in 1923. The smaller **Arcadia Park** (*Arkādijas Parks*) was created in 1852 by the Prussian consul general, Wehrmann (Vērmans). It was acquired by the city in 1896. Next to it, *Māras dīķis* (Mary's Pond) is a popular place of recreation. It derives its name from the mill attached to St Mary's Church which was acquired by the city of Riga in 1573. The pond is probably the old mill pond and is sometimes referred to as Mary's mill pond (*Māras sudmalu dīķis*).

Other places of interest
Moscow District, Riga Ghetto and Jewish Riga

Beyond the railway station, the Central Market and the Academy of Sciences lies the Maskavas District (*Maskavas Forštate*), so called because it was a Russian area in earlier times (*Moskva* = Moscow in Russian) and the road to Moscow passed through it. Now it is often called the Latgale district, but its history reflects Riga's historical links with Russia. The Russian character of the area is still reflected in the presence of several Orthodox churches, notably the green and white one (used by a congregation of Old Believers) still undergoing restoration in Grebenščikova iela (the street is named after the merchant whose wealth enabled the church to be built in 1814) and the Church of the Archangel Michael in Dricānu iela. The area near the junction of Maskavas iela and Kalna iela used to be known as the New Hill (*Krasraga Gorka*) and was where the Russian population of Riga came to celebrate the first Sunday after Easter, a traditional Orthodox feast day. The traditional Russian name is barely remembered now, but the tradition remains alive in the name Sarkanā iela. Strūgu iela (between Gogoļa iela and Maskavas iela, parallel to Lāčplēša iela) also reflects the area's Russian past: the name means 'Barge Street' and recalls the days when barges and rafts sailed along the Daugava between Riga and ports in Russia. Now the Maskavas area is very run down compared to central Riga, and there are signs of poverty in the dilapidation of so many of the buildings as well as in the faces of many who live there.

This district was where the **Jewish ghetto** was established by the Nazis in 1941. In August 1941 the non-Jewish Rigan citizens who lived in the district were moved to locations closer to the centre of the city, and by October an area of about 750m² had been formed taking in Lāčplēša iela, Maskavas iela, Ebreju iela (Jews' Street) and Daugavpils iela. The total Jewish population of the ghetto was about 30,000. The men in the ghetto who were fit to work were put to forced labour; the others were taken to Rumbula Forest on November 30 1941 and systematically murdered by German guards with the assistance of a significant number of Latvian collaborators. Other Jews were brought in to replace those murdered, only to suffer the same fate in the forests of Biķernieki or in Dreiliņi. The total number of people killed in this way has never been finally ascertained, but estimates indicate it to be around 50,000. On November 2 1943 the Riga ghetto was closed following the Warsaw ghetto uprising, and the few remaining inhabitants were shot or transported to concentration camps.

No trace of the ghetto remains today, although there is a **Jewish cemetery** (*Ebreju kapi*) in the area between Tējas iela and Lauvas iela.

The only **synagogue** that now operates in Riga is in Peitavas iela. The site of what used to be the main synagogue (the Choral Synagogue) on the corner of Dzirnavu iela and Gogoļa iela is marked by a memorial (not a very impressive one) consisting of parts of the old synagogue set in a sort of park. A plaque records the destruction of the synagogue on July 4 1941. Number 29 Dzirnavu iela was also the site of a Jewish school until 1940. It opened again in 1989 as the only recognised Jewish school in the country.

There is a **Jewish Museum** and community centre at 6 Skolas iela, a short walk from the Hotel Latvijā. The exhibition covers Jewish life before World War II and full details of the Holocaust as it hit this community in Riga.

Riga's cemeteries

Riga has three cemeteries that are worth visiting, if time permits, since they reflect something of the history of Latvia and present a number of architectural styles. They are all close to one another in an area directly south of Meža Park and can be reached by public transport.

The Brothers' Cemetery

The Brothers' Cemetery (*Brāļu Kapi*) or Cemetery of Heroes on Aizsaules iela can be reached by taking the number 4 or number 9 bus from Brīvības ilea heading east (bus stops in front of the Hotel Latvijā or at the central bus station) or the number 11 tram from the stop by the National Opera.

The Cemetery of Heroes is a fascinating ensemble of architecture and sculpture in attractive natural surroundings. It was planned in 1915 when thousands of Latvians were dying in the fight against the Germans in Kurzeme, and the same year the first fallen soldiers were buried here. It took 12 years to complete the cemetery, the overwhelming part of the work being done between 1924 and 1936. There are approximately 2,000 graves in Brāļu Kapi, 300 of them simply marked *nezinams* ('unknown'). On March 25 1988 a memorial service for the victims of the years of the Stalin terror was held here, organized by the Latvian Writers' Association, and 10,000 people attended.

In Latvian folklore the oak symbolises masculine strength, while the lime tree symbolises feminine love; both of these powerful symbols are used extensively in the cemetery. The Latvian coat of arms appears over the entrance gate, while on both sides there are sculptured groups of cavalrymen. An avenue of lime trees leads to the main terrace. In the centre an eternal flame burns, flanked by oak trees. Beyond it is the cemetery itself, bordered by trees, shrubs, bushes and walls decorated with the coats of arms of all the Latvian regions and towns.

Especially moving are the *Ievainotais jatnieks* ('The Wounded Horseman') and *Divi brāļi* ('Two Brothers') sculptures. At one end of the cemetery stands the figure *Māte Latvijā* ('Mother Latvia') who looks down in sorrow at her dead, a wreath to honour her fallen sons in one hand, in the other the national flag. The sculptures are the work of Kārlis Zāle who is himself buried here.

The cemetery was allowed to fall into neglect during the Soviet period, but was restored in 1993 and has since then become a focus of Latvian national feeling.

Rainis Cemetery

The Rainis Cemetery (*Raiņa Kapi*), Aizsaules iela, can be reached by taking the number 11 tram from Vermana Gardens/Merķeļa iela near the National Opera or the number 4 or 9 bus from the main bus station. Latvia's best loved writer, Jānis Rainis, died on September 12 1929 and was buried here three days later. The cemetery was renamed in his honour. An avenue of silver birch leads to his grave which is marked by a red granite sculpture. Around the monument there is a semi-circular colonnade entwined with ivy.

Alongside Rainis lies his wife, the poet Aspāzija (Elza Rozenberg who died in 1943). The cemetery is also the resting place for a great number of Latvian writers, artists and musicians, many of whose graves are decorated with a creativity to match the lives they are designed to commemorate.

Woodlands Cemetery

The Woodlands Cemetery (*Meža Kapi*), also on Aizsaules iela, was designed by G Kufelts, the director of Riga's parks, in 1913. Numerous political and government figures from the period of Latvia's first independence are buried here, including the former president, Jānis Čakste, and the government ministers, Zigfrids Meierovics and Vilhelms Munters. In addition, a number of Latvian artists, writers, poets and scientists lie here, among them Jānis

Rozentāls, Anna Brīgadere and Paulis Stradiņš. In April 1988 Latvia's leading human rights activist, Gunārs Astra, was buried here. Astra was sentenced to seven years' imprisonment followed by five years' internal exile by the Soviet regime in December 1983 for the crimes of possessing recordings of radio programmes, photo negatives and subversive books and for writing a manuscript of a personal nature. In his final words to the court he delivered an impassioned speech against the Soviet regime including these words:

> I fervently believe that these nightmare times will end one day. This belief gives me the strength to stand before you. Our people have suffered a great deal but have learned to survive. They will outlive this dark period in their history.

Television tower

The TV tower stands on Hare Island (Zaķusala). The tower is open for tours, viewing and refreshments.

Outside the city centre

Ethnographic Open Air Museum

The Latvian Ethnographic Open Air Museum (*Latvijas Etnogrāfiskaja Brīvdabas Muzejs*) is located on the outskirts of Riga by Lake Jugla about 12km from the centre of Riga (the address is 440 Brīvības gatve). The only way of getting there by public transport is to take the number 1, 19 or 28 bus from the city centre to the stop just by the road leading to the museum (the stop bears the name of the museum, so is easy to spot). Established in 1924 (although it opened in 1932 with only six buildings) the museum now covers 100 hectares and depicts traditional ways of life from the 16th to 19th centuries. It consists of reconstructions of old farmsteads and traditional houses, windmills, fishing villages and exhibits; on occasions there are also demonstrations of traditional crafts.

The **Usma Church** is named after the lake in western Latvia, near Kuldiga, from where it was brought to the museum in 1938. It was built in 1704 and the original used no nails in its construction. Men and women were divided during services and the rich sat at the front with the poor behind them. The landlord had a private entrance behind the altar. The organ accommodates two players, one just concerned with the pumping. The windows are high so that the congregation would concentrate on the service and not be distracted by activity outside. Outside the church, the stocks and the fencing are also original.

The museum is open every day 10.00–17.00. It has an excellent self-service **restaurant** in a traditional wooden building close to the museum entrance which serves excellent typical Latvian food and drink. You should allow at least two hours for a visit, and you could easily spend a half or even a whole day here.

Motor Museum

The Motor Museum (*Rigas Motormuzejs*) is located at 6 S Eizenšteina iela to the east of the Old Town about 8km from the centre along Brīvības gatve. It can be reached by taking the number 15 bus, but this does not run from central Riga (alight at the Pansionāts stop in Mežciems). The number 14 or 18 trolleybuses go from Brīvības iela and Čaka iela respectively to Gaiļezers hospital, about 500m from the museum. The museum is not easy to spot: look out for what appears to be a large Audi dealership and showroom; it is a modern red brick and glass building. The entrance is reached via a bridge from the car park. It is an acclaimed collection of over 100 motor vehicles, including cars which once belonged to the Soviet leaders, Stalin, Khrushchev and Brezhnev, and Erich Honecker, the leader of the former German Democratic Republic. Wax figures of some of these former politicians and motor enthusiasts help to liven up the displays: Stalin sits in his armoured ZIS 115 (said to have done 2.5km to the litre), Brezhnev at the wheel of his crashed Rolls-Royce, Gorky stands next to his 1934 Lincoln.

The first car assembly plant in Tsarist Russia was established in Riga in 1909 and this was followed by no less than 30 bicycle factories during the first independence period. Their products are also exhibited here, as are later Soviet motorbikes. A lot of the cars that form the backbone of the collection were abandoned in 1939–40, firstly by the Baltic-Germans recalled 'home' by Hitler and secondly by the embassies closed after the Soviet occupation. Others are German cars abandoned during the long retreat towards the end of World War Two. One is a Rolls Royce which had been built under licence in Germany. Although the museum is famous for displaying the car that Brezhnev crashed, another one of the 40 or so that he owned is also on display – a 1974 Continental presented by the American government.

The museum is sensibly open seven days a week, a sad rarity in Riga, although on Mondays it closes at 15.00. It opens at 10.00 and on other days closes at 18.00. Private parties are often held there in the evening. Sadly no written material is available on the collection.

Riga Zoo

Riga has had a zoo since 1912. Covering an area of 16.4 hectares it has 2,500 animals and 400 species. It is known for its bears (brown and polar bears are represented), Galápagos turtles and Amur tigers. Rides on horseback or in carriages are alternatives to walking. It is at 1 Meža prospekts in the forest of the Mežaparks and is open 10.00–16.00 every day.

EXCURSIONS FROM RIGA
Jūrmala

Jūrmala is Riga's seaside resort (indeed the name Jūrmala means 'seaside' or 'by the sea' in Latvian) with a beautiful 30km or so of unspoilt sandy beach. Jūrmala is actually the collective name given to a number of small towns and villages along the Baltic coast about 25km from Riga. It can be reached by train, bus, taxi or car. Buses leave from the bus station and taxis from a special stand outside the railway station in summer. If you drive using your own or a hired car you must stop on the outskirts of Jūrmala and pay a toll of Ls1 a day to enter the area. There are frequent trains from the central railway station in Riga, but note that there is no station actually called Jūrmala so you will need to know your destination. Trains run on average every 15–20 minutes, and take about 20 minutes from Riga to the first station at Lielupe, although not all trains stop there. Fares are around Ls0.50 return depending on the destination. The main stop is Majori, about 40 minutes from Riga and the main centre of the Jūrmala area. The writer, Jānis Rainis, had his summer house here (at 5–7 J Pliekšāna iela), and it is now a museum in honour of him and his wife, the poet Aspāzija. There are a number of decent restaurants and cafés in Majori, most of them on or near the main pedestrianised shopping street, Jomas iela, which stretches to Dzintari.

Salaspils

Salaspils is 18km southeast of Riga and can be reached by taking the train to the station at Dārziņa and following the footpath through forest for about 15 minutes. If travelling by car, take the A6 out of Riga, turn left just before Salaspils and follow the granite sign ('Salaspils 1941–44') to the memorial.

Salaspils is remembered largely as the site of the Nazi concentration camp, Kurtenhof. Built in 1941 during the Nazi occupation of Latvia in World War II, the camp operated for three years. In 1944, as the Red Army approached Riga, the camp guards and administrators ordered the inmates to exhume and burn the thousands of bodies buried at the camp; it then was burnt to the ground by the retreating Nazis in an attempt to hide the atrocities committed there. Over 100,000 men, women and children, most of them Jews, were put to death here, among them Austrians, Belgians, Czechs, Dutch, French, Latvian, Polish and Soviet citizens. Today, lines of white stones mark the perimeter of the camp.

The Salaspils memorial, which now dominates the site of the former camp, was erected in 1967 to honour those who died there. A huge concrete wall in the shape of a long beam marks the position of the former entrance; symbolising the border between life and death, it bears the words of the Latvian writer, Eižēns Vēveris, (a prisoner at Salaspils): '*Aiz šiem vārtiem vaid zeme*' ('Beyond these gates the earth moans'). You can actually walk the length of the wall on the inside – there is a door at each end. A series of steps takes you through a number of gloomy rooms, giving the impression of a mausoleum. There is also a small exhibition with photographs of the camp. The seven sculptures which stand in the grounds behind the wall evoke the suffering but also the spirit of defiance and resistance of those imprisoned and killed.

The stillness of Salaspils is broken only by the ticking of an underground metronome beneath the altar-like structure located to the left as you enter the ground. The noise of the ticking is a reminder of the lives spent and ended here. A narrow path leads through the woods to the place where the prisoners were executed.

Rundāle

Rundāle is often billed as the most significant palace in the Baltics. Certainly most visitors will be impressed by its grand exterior, dominating the surrounding flat farmland leading down to the Lielupe River, and the 40 or so sumptuously decorated rooms which have been restored.

Rundāle is about 1¼ hours by car from Riga, along the A7 Via Baltica road to the south. There are yellow minibuses to Bauska, costing Ls2 return, and taking about an hour. From here, a taxi for the last 11km will cost around Ls5 each way.

Rundāle Palace (*Rundāles Pils*) was built in the 18th century as a summer palace for Ernst Johann von Bühren (Biron in Latvian) by the Italian architect Francesco Bartolomeo Rastrelli. Rastrelli, already established as the architect of the Winter Palace in St Petersburg, began work in 1736 and took five years to finish the task. The interiors were mostly completed later, between 1763 and

1768. Among those who worked on them were Italian painters from St Petersburg and Johann Michael Graff from Berlin, whose work includes the artificial marble wall panelling and the decorative moulding in many rooms.

Why was such a lavish palace built by Rastrelli beyond the Russian borders? The link with Russia was Anna Ioannovna, a niece of Tsar Peter I who, in 1710, married Frederick, Duke of Kurland. During the 1720s Ernst Johann von Bühren, a Baltic German baron, became her chief adviser, and some say lover also. In 1730, on the death of Peter, Anna became Empress of Russia and delegated much of the management of the empire to a group of German advisers, von Bühren among them. When von Bühren expressed the wish for a summer palace, Anna complied by sending Rastrelli to Kurland and providing all the necessary money and craftsmen too; nearly everyone involved in the construction – a total of 1,500 craftsmen, artists and labourers – was sent from St Petersburg. Before the palace could be finished, however, Rastrelli began work on another major project, a palace at Jelgava, seat of the Duchy of Kurland. Many of the workmen and the materials needed for Rundāle were transported to Jelgava instead. In 1740, just before Rundāle was completed, Anna died, von Bühren was forced into exile, and the building of the palaces halted. Only in 1763 when the Russian Empress Catherine II restored von Bühren to favour, did he return to Kurland and finish the work on Rundāle. The palace was finally completed in 1767, but von Bühren was only able to enjoy it for a short time until his death in 1772. When Russia annexed the Duchy of Kurland in 1795, von Bühren's son, Peter, agreed to leave taking with him some of the splendid interior items from Rundāle and installed them instead in his properties in Germany. Rundāle itself was given to another favourite of Catherine II, Subov.

Since the incorporation of Kurland into Russia in 1795, the palace has had many uses and owners. Although damaged in the Napoleonic Wars and again during World War II the exterior has been repaired and remains fundamentally unaltered from its original design. The interior has not survived so well. Parts of the castle were used as a granary after 1945, and other areas fell into severe disrepair. In 1972, however, the Rundāle Palace Museum was established and major restoration work began. Artists in Leningrad began the restoration of works of art, and they were subsequently joined by experts from Riga, Moscow and Belarus. As a result the 40 or so rooms (out of 138) restored contain many impressive, but few original, works of art. Particularly interesting are the Golden Hall (the throne room), with beautiful ceiling decoration and chandeliers, the grand Gallery (the banquet room) and the aptly named White Hall (the ballroom), with its intricate stucco. Look out here for the storks! The palace also houses some permanent exhibitions: Treasures of the Rundāle Palace, with furniture, porcelain, silverware and paintings, and 'The Time of Misery', an exhibition about Lutheran churches in Latvia during the years of Soviet power.

Behind the palace, the French-style formal garden has been largely reconstructed. It is surrounded by a canal, beyond which are hunting grounds.

On the south side of the palace is a formal baroque garden, still being reconstructed. A restaurant in the palace is used for formal receptions, and is a favourite place for weddings.

The palace is open daily except on Monday and Tuesday, from 10.00 to 17.00 in winter, and daily from 10.00 to 18.00 in summer (May 1–October 31); tel: 396 2197; fax: 392 2274. In addition to the restaurant/café in the palace itself, there are cafés on the road nearby.

Vilnius

Gordon McLachlan, updated by Neil Taylor

That the name of Lithuania's largest city and national capital exists in several slightly differing versions – Vilnius to the Lithuanians, Wilno to the Poles, Vilna to the Jews and Russians – is a reflection of its eventful history as a melting-pot in which different ethnic groups have competed with one another for predominance. By the vagaries of fate, it is the only one of the many traditionally multi-national and multi-cultural cities of the old Polish-Lithuanian Commonwealth which has preserved a mixed profile right down to the present day. Despite its key role in modern Lithuania, little more than a bare majority of its inhabitants are ethnic Lithuanians; the Russian and Polish minorities are both substantial, while there is also a significant number of Belarussians, and smaller representations of a host of other nationalities.

The diversity of the city's make-up is given a very visible expression in the Old Town, whose outstanding quality has gained it a coveted place on UNESCO's World Heritage List, one of only two places in Lithuania to be so honoured. Although its Jewish quarter is now a sad shadow of its former self, the Old Town is otherwise substantially intact, with the domes of the Orthodox churches competing for attention with the towers of their far more numerous Catholic counterparts. Most of the latter were established by mendicant or missionary orders, and all but a few were either built or totally reconstructed in the baroque era. Vilnius boasts one of the greatest assemblages of baroque monuments outside Rome, having developed over nearly two centuries a distinctively indigenous interpretation of the style.

The re-establishment of Lithuania's independence in 1991 meant that Vilnius regained its role as capital of a sovereign state after a gap of well over four centuries. This development has inevitably led to huge changes. By no means all of these are welcome, but there have been many undoubted benefits, not least the ever-increasing numbers of recommendable hotels, restaurants, bars and cafés which have helped make the city a favourite holiday destination, especially for members of the (predominantly North American) Lithuanian diaspora.

Vilnius' location in the far southeast of Lithuania means that it is not ideally placed for day-trips into the countryside. However, its administrative county does have a few attractive destinations, notably the outstanding medieval town of Trakai, which probably preceded it as the nation's capital.

THE CITY

The city of Vilnius has a population of around 580,000, which is well spread out over a municipal area liberally endowed with areas of greenery; indeed, only about a third of the municipal area is built up. There are two distinct parts to the city centre. The Old Town, which is very large by the standards of its time, lies at the confluence of the Vilnia with the Neris, west of the former and south of the latter. It is now joined seamlessly to the west by the New Town, which grew up in the 19th century. Although the Old Town contains the lion's share of the city's sights, many others, including some of the most important, are scattered all over the inner and outer suburbs.

History

According to legend, Vilnius was founded in 1323 by Grand Duke Gediminas, progenitor of the Gediminian dynasty which ruled Lithuania, latterly in union with Poland, for over 250 years. The story goes that, after a successful day's hunting, Gediminas decided to pitch camp for the night at the point where the Vilnia flows into the Neris, rather than return to his castle in Trakai. On falling asleep, he had a strange dream of a huge iron wolf on the hill above, which howled with the ferocity of a pack of a hundred wolves. The pagan high priest Lizdeika interpreted this dream as a message from the gods instructing Gediminas to build a city on the hill where he had seen the iron wolf in his dream. This city would grow so great that its fame would reverberate around the world with the force of the howls of a hundred wolves.

The truth of the matter is that there was a settlement beside the Neris-Vilnia confluence at least as far back as the 1st century AD. Moreover, a wooden castle was built atop what is now known as Gediminas Hill in the 11th century. Vilnius (which takes its name from the river) was certainly a well-established town by Gediminas' time, though his role in its history is none the less an important one since it was in one of his letters of 1323 that it is documented for the first time, and it was probably he who raised it to the status of Lithuania's permanent capital.

Under Gediminas and his successors Vilnius occupied a small, tightly packed site protected by a fortification system which included three castles. Between 1365 and 1402 it was attacked by the Teutonic Knights on seven separate occasions, but despite inflicting considerable damage they never managed to capture it. In 1387, the year after the royal union with Poland, Vilnius was granted municipal rights, though it was only after the decisive defeat of the Teutonic Knights at the Battle of Žalgiris in 1410 that it was able to expand southwards from the confines of the original site.

Between 1503 and 1522, in response to a threat of invasion by the Tatars, the whole city was enclosed within a 2.4km-long wall. With the advent of more peaceful times, Vilnius flourished as a city of merchants and craftsmen, becoming one of the great book-printing centres of Europe. The year 1569 was one of crucial significance, as the Union of Lublin, which created the Polish-Lithuanian Commonwealth, had the inevitable consequence of Vilnius (like Kraków) losing its roles as a royal residence and administrative capital, as Warsaw, thanks to its central location, became the hub of the huge unified state.

However, 1569 also saw the arrival of the Jesuits in Vilnius, and as a result the city played a leading role in the Counter-Reformation, which saw the Roman Catholic Church recover most of the ground it had lost in Lithuania. The school founded by the Jesuits in 1570 was raised to university status in 1579, and quickly established itself as one of the great academic institutions of Europe.

It was also the Jesuits who were responsible for introducing the new baroque style of architecture, and this soon came to dominate the face of Vilnius' Old Town. Many of Vilnius' early baroque buildings were destroyed in the mid-17th-century wars with the Swedes and Russians, during which the city lost half its population, principally as a result of the plague of 1657–58. None the less, it recovered well, and was embellished with a host of new aristocratic palaces, churches and monastic buildings. Initially, these were inspired by the Roman High baroque style, but in the 18th century a distinctive local style, derived from German and Central European models, was developed.

With the Third Partition of the Commonwealth in 1795, Vilnius, along with most of the rest of Lithuania, became part of the Tsarist Empire. Paradoxically, this led to it regaining its role as a capital, as it was chosen as the seat of a large administrative province. Nevertheless, there were patriotic hopes for a revival of Lithuanian independence, with the French dictator Napoleon Bonaparte, who captured Vilnius in June 1812, seen as the potential saviour. During the 19 days he spent in the city, he showed himself to be no more than a lukewarm supporter, though he did authorise the formation of a provisional government supported by an army. A dispirited Napoleon returned to the city in December of the same year in retreat from the Russians, but stayed for only a couple of hours before continuing to flee. The Russians recaptured Vilnius soon after, ending its hopes of re-establishing itself as capital of an independent Lithuania within the foreseeable future.

Throughout the failed rebellion of 1831, the authorities remained in control of Vilnius, but in the repressive measures introduced in its aftermath the city was made to suffer heavily. Its university, the most venerable in the Russian Empire, was closed down; the religious houses were dissolved, and several churches were transferred to Orthodox congregations. The next unsuccessful revolt, in 1863, resulted in the public executions of the ringleaders.

However, the 19th century also saw Vilnius develop as a major industrial centre, and it expanded greatly in size, with the construction of the New Town and suburban areas. Its population grew from 18,000 to 138,000, an increase which was in part due to an influx of Jews from elsewhere in Russia. Indeed, a census taken towards the end of the century made Jews the biggest ethnic group within the city, accounting for over 40% of the population. Poles were the next largest, at around 30%, with Russians numbering 20%, and Lithuanians little more than 2%. Language seems to have been the determining characteristic in these figures, whose significance is still much disputed: it is likely that many of the Poles (perhaps even the overwhelming majority) were ethnic Lithuanians whose (often distant) ancestors had adopted the Polish tongue.

Despite the paucity of Lithuanian speakers in Vilnius, the city became the focal point of the national awakening which gathered momentum in the early years of the 20th century. The so-called Great Seimas, a gathering of 2,000 Lithuanians, met there in 1905 and demanded autonomy within the empire. Although nothing came of this, the city's long-dormant dream to become a national capital once more was revived as a result of World War I, which saw the Russians abandoning Vilnius to the advancing German Army in September 1915.

A census by the occupying forces the following year produced a somewhat different result from that of the Russians a couple of decades earlier. The percentage of Jewish residents was virtually unchanged, but Poles were now said to number a fraction over 50% of the population. Despite these findings, the Germans allowed a Lithuanian congress to meet in the city in September 1917. This made the formal demand for Vilnius to be made capital of a Lithuanian state, and independence was duly declared in 1918.

However, the city found itself a major bone of contention in the conflicts following World War I, which saw Soviet Russia and the newly resurrected nations of Lithuania and Poland tussle with one another for territory. In July 1920 the Soviets recognised Lithuania's right to Vilnius, and the Poles apparently followed suit by the Treaty of Suwałki of October 7. Two days later, however, ostensibly rebel troops commanded by General Lucian Żeligowski, a Polonised Lithuanian, captured Vilnius and the surrounding area. In this action, they were secretly supported by the Polish leader, Marshal Józef Piłsudski, another ethnic Lithuanian, who was determined that the city where he had grown up would become an integral part of Poland.

Following two years of somewhat half-hearted international mediation, the dispute over Vilnius was resolved in Poland's favour largely by default, there being no readily enforceable alternative to leaving it in the hands of the occupying power. From a purely objective standpoint there is no doubt that the Poles had a strong claim on the city, though for Vilnius itself the result was certainly not fortuitous, as it was reduced to a provincial role within Poland,

REBIRTH OF THE UNIVERSITY

From 'Beyond the Baltic' by A MacCullum Scott, published in 1925

Late in the evening of June 21 1924 I arrived in Vilna. It was the eve of St John's Day, the great pagan midsummer festival throughout the Baltics. Fires were lit beside the river, small boats decorated with lanterns and bearing festive parties were rowed up and down stream. The sound of music and singing floated over the water. From the midst of the city, outlined against the pale northern sky, rose abruptly the Hill of Gedimin like an altar to the ancient gods of the Lithuanian race.

Vilna is now, by the turn of the international kaleidoscope, part of the Republic of Poland, but there has been no revolutionary change in social manners. The old formalities of address still continue. The hotel porter and the barefooted chambermaid both addressed me as 'Barin' or lord. 'Would the Barin like some hot water? Will the Barin be wearing his coat?' It is an old, old work in Vilna.

My hotel was in Adam Michevicius Street, named after the national poet of Poland who was a native of Lithuania and a student at the University of Vilna. The next street on the right was Jagellon Street, named after the Grand Duke who united the thrones of Lithuania and Poland. I passed a 'Kultur' shop, in the window of which was displayed a large map showing the extent of the former territories of Poland and Lithuania, stretching from the Baltic to the Black Sea. The new generation in Vilna feeds its soul upon dreams of the past.

Some day Europe will rediscover Vilna. At present few people in western Europe know that this is a bone of contention between Poland and Lithuania and that it is impossible to make out whether it is inhabited while Kaunas was developed as the showpiece Lithuanian capital in its stead.

Following the carve-up of Poland between Nazi Germany and the Soviet Union at the beginning of World War II, the Soviets restored Vilnius to Lithuania in October 1939 as its capital in return for the right to establish military bases there, a move which paved the way for the annexation of the country the following June. The Nazi occupation of 1941–44 led to the elimination of almost all of Vilnius' large Jewish community, many of whom were murdered in the Paneriai Forest in the outskirts. When the war ended with the Soviets back in control, the city's population had fallen to 110,000, a reduction of around 100,000 on what it had been in 1939. Over the following decade, a large percentage of the local Polish population was deported to Poland. They were replaced by Russians and migrant Lithuanians, and the city's population grew steadily, with most of the newcomers housed in high-rise suburbs constructed according to Soviet principles.

For Vilnius, the Soviet decades did at least offer the compensation of its re-establishment as a national capital, albeit one under foreign occupation. It was therefore inevitable that it was in the vanguard of the successful drive towards independence, and the scene of the most dramatic flashpoint in the largely peaceful struggle – the storming of the television tower by Soviet tanks in January 1991, which resulted in the martyrdom of 14 citizens.

Now the proud capital of an independent nation-state once again, Vilnius is

by Poles, Lithuanians, Russians or Jews. To discover Vilna is to revisit an ancient civilisation which has for centuries been buried under the debris of later and barbarous regimes. However, the Vilna that now emerges is no city of the dead. It fills its lungs with the exhilarating air of freedom. It is full of energy, zeal and effort as if it were determined to make up for the years which have been lost. Europe must learn that Vilna has a personality and that it is a very vivid one.

It was my good fortune in Vilna to spend a day with Professor Rustchuts, Dean of the Faculty of Arts at the university. His reddish-brown hair and beard, as so often amongst the Poles, would seem to indicate a tincture of Gothic blood, which would account for his unfailing energy and for a certain robust quality which shines like a hard grain through the artistic temperament. Following the insurrection of 1832, the Russians closed the university as a dangerous institution. Having been founded in 1578, the tree of 350 years' growth was cut down to the ground. Now after nearly a century, the stump still has a life, and is sending forth strong and vigorous shoots. It already has 2,500 students of both sexes, studying not only the humanities but all manner of practical arts and sciences. The Professor is recovering the university buildings from all kinds of perverted uses. He has the delights of an explorer of a Roman forum in some buried city. The old porticoes and cloister, which the Russians had walled up, are being cleared again. Already the quadrangles, with their shady trees, have that look of scholastic peace which pervades the colleges of Oxford and Cambridge. The old corridors and galleries are trodden by youths and maidens keen on the pursuit of knowledge. Here were the rooms where Adam Michevicius, the great and immortal Michevicius, lived whilst he studied at the university.

THE END OF AN ERA

From 'Lithuania, Independent Again' by Vytautas Landsbergis.
The author, who would subsequently become President and then Speaker,
describes the night of January 12/13 1991 in Vilnius.

The Soviets had decided to act without delay, and a terrible slaughter took place on the streets of Vilnius that night. The disturbance began just after midnight when Soviet tanks and armoured troop carriers loaded with special KGB riot troops came roaring through our streets. They drove straight to predetermined destinations; their orders were to seize the radio and television studios as well as the television tower which stands on the outskirts of Vilnius. As they followed their instructions, the people responded to their manoeuvres and a sequence of events followed which stirred the conscience of the world. Some people had already kept vigil at the television facilities for several days and nights, and now others hurried through darkened streets, often passing the cumbersome tanks as they lurched slowly forward. When they reached the threatened buildings, they linked hands and began to sing the old folk songs of Lithuania or shouted slogans such as 'Lithuania will be free'. Soon they heard bullets passing over their heads as automatic rifles and machine guns swung into action. According to standard Soviet calculations, the crowd should have been scattered under this onslaught, but they did not move and so the strategy was changed with shots being direct at people's legs and then at their bodies. Back at the Supreme Council, I learned what was going on and immediately summoned the deputies to a rally in Parliament. Most

rapidly modernising and transforming itself in the hope and belief that this role will never again be lost. Poland formally renounced any claim to the city in the Friendship and Co-operation Treaty of 1994, though it declined Lithuania's request to apologise for having annexed it in 1920. For the first time in its history, Vilnius can look forward to stability, as both a Lithuanian and a European capital. On the streets Lithuanian is the dominant language, and the lack of any Polish or Russian signs in shops makes it quite clear that the role of these former masters is now very much in the past. When these shops decide to take euros, which could well be during the lifetime of this book, this policy of closer integration with its Western neighbours will for the first time have been decided in Vilnius, and not in Warsaw, Moscow or Berlin.

PRACTICAL INFORMATION
Communications

The *Baltic Times*, published weekly on a Thursday, is the best English-language source of news for the three Baltic republics. It also lists exhibitions and concerts. The *City Paper*, published every two months, also covers the Baltic capitals.

Telephones

Telephone numbers in Vilnius changed in November 2002. Eight-digit numbers always begin with a 5 and seven-digit ones with a 2. Dialling from abroad also requires the Lithuanian code: + 370. Dialling out of Lithuania requires the prefix responded without delay, and as they assembled, they witnessed the volunteer defenders inside the building gathering together to take the oath of allegiance afresh. Many of them went on to make their confessions, in grim recognition of what we might all soon be facing. Our defenders had no other weapons than a few pistols and rifles, sticks and petrol bombs.

The most difficult hours still lay ahead of us. Long before dawn on January 13, the local hospitals began to overflow with the dead and injured. Because Vilnius TV was now in Soviet hands, the Kaunas station replaced it as our chief means of disseminating information. We remained in Parliament awaiting an onslaught. I asked the women to leave us, but they all refused. I then addressed the crowd surrounding the Parliament buildings, imploring them to move away to avoid casualties, but I received the same response. Everyone then knew exactly what to expect, but they all refused to move. Their heroism was unflinching, and later I was told that some had even been angry that I had urged them to leave. I had prepared a videoed speech, which could be transmitted if we were killed. In it, I gave careful directions for a campaign of passive resistance and suggestions about how life could be made difficult for our enemy under a new occupation. Fortunately this did not come about, because the assault ended at daybreak, and although the threat was not over, it was never repeated on that scale. It was a people's victory in the best sense. Indeed, a cynical KGB officer was later overheard to say: 'We did not attack the Parliament because of the excess flesh surrounding it.'

810 and then the relevant country code. The normal 00 for an international line does not yet operate in Lithuania.

Post and telecommunications
Central Post Office Gedimino 7. Open Mon–Fri 07.00–19.00, Sat 09.00–16.00.
Telecommunications Office Vilniaus 33. Open Mon–Fri 08.00–18.00, Sat 09.00–14.00.

Internet cafés
Most hotels now have internet access in every room and even many smaller ones have a computer centre. Before heading for an internet centre, it is worth checking what they charge. It may be nothing, or it may be a fortune; it may be by the day, or it may be by the minute. Outside the hotels, Vilnius does not have as many internet cafés as might be expected, but two places in the town centre can be recommended, both of which are open seven days a week from 08.00 until 24.00. Charges are 8Lt per hour, or pro rata, so you can have 15 minutes for 2Lt.

Collegium 22 Pilies
Spausk Lt 18 Basanaviciaus

Banks and money
The Lithuanian lit is fixed to the euro at €1 = 3.45Lt. In spring 2003 when the euro was stronger than the dollar, approximate exchange rates were US$1 = 3.20Lt; £1 = 5.20Lt.

The bank at the airport is always open for arrival flights and the one outside the railway station operates 24 hours a day. Clearly quite a few rich people turn up at this station office since it gives better rates for those changing $5,000 or more. Exchange rates at most hotels in Vilnius are not very different from those in banks, so for small sums this will normally be more convenient for most visitors.

Banks and exchange bureaux take all major Western currencies as well as the Baltic ones, and Russian roubles. Travellers' cheques can only be exchanged in banks. Cash machines are available all over the city. Most hotels and restaurants accept credit cards.

Tourist information

The English-language magazine *Vilnius In Your Pocket*, which is available from kiosks, newsagents and tourist offices, is a well-nigh essential acquisition, having attained near-legendary status among travellers, as well as the municipally-bestowed designation of The Official City Guide. Published five times annually, it contains comprehensive reviews of hotels, restaurants, cafés and bars; information and dates of forthcoming events and entertainment; and a host of useful listings covering professional services, shopping, transport, communications and many other subjects. Not the least of its attractions is its quirky and irreverent style, the bizarre range of idioms employed being a reflection of the contributions made by the multi-national cast of people who have worked over the years on what was originally a German-Belgian venture. The text of the guide can also be accessed from its website at www.inyourpocket.com. Another highly recommendable purchase is the 1:25,000 map of the city, with an enlargement of the Old and New Towns and A–Z street listings, by the Latvian publisher Jāṇa Sēta.

Tourist offices

Municipal Tourist Office Pilies 42; tel: 262 6470; tel/fax: 262 0762; email: turizm.info@vilnius.lt; web: www.vilnius.lt. Open Mon–Fri 09.00–18.00, Jun–Sep Sat and Sun 10.00–16.00. In addition to selling the usual range of maps and brochures, the office keeps piles of free information leaflets about various aspects of the city and posts up current public transport timetables.

Municipal Tourist Office Vilniaus 22; tel: 262 9660; fax: 262 8169; email/web: as above. Open Mon–Fri 09.00–18.00. Another branch of the above.

In Your Pocket **Information Centre** Airport arrival hall; tel: (8299) 395455. Open Mon–Fri 09.00–17.00, Sat 09.00–15.00. This small booth is the only public office run by the listings magazine. In addition to selling maps and guides, it books accommodation and car rental.

Travel agencies

Baltic Travel Service Subačiaus 2; tel: 2112 0220; email: lcc@bts.lt; web: www.bts.lt

Lithuanian Holidays Juozapavičiaus 6/2; tel: 2563 6064; fax: 272 6864; email: travel@lithuanianholidays.lt

Lithuanian Tours Šeimyniškių 12; tel: 272 4154; fax: 272 1815; email: contact@lithuaniantours.com; web: www.lithuaniantours.com

Wrislit Rūdninkų 16; tel: 25210 7660; fax: 25212 2098; email; wrislit@wrislit.lt; web: www.wrislit.lt

Transport
Airport

Rodūnės kelias 2; tel: 230 6666; web: vilnius-airport.lt. Two bus routes service the airport: number 1 to the train and bus stations, number 2 to the hotels over the river. Tickets cost 1Lt if bought on the bus or 80 cents if bought at the kiosk beforehand. Minibus 18 also links the airport with the bus and train stations. The fare for this is also 1Lt, but tickets can only be bought on the bus itself. Bus route 2 terminates at the airport but the others continue out of town so it is important to check its direction before boarding.

In the arrivals hall in the older front building are a 24-hour currency exchange, the *Vilnius In Your Pocket* information office, and the booths of several car-hire companies. The airline ticket offices are all in the departure hall to the rear, with the exception of LOT, which is in the arrivals building. The arrivals building also has a left luggage office, and a café that is much cheaper than the one in the departures building. Even cheaper refreshments are available between 10.00 and 16.00 at the café in the Lithuanian Airlines building beside the main terminal.

Taxis are strictly regulated at the airport and have meters. To most hotels the cost should not be more than 25 Lt (£4.50/US$7.00).

City trolleybuses and buses

Networks of trolleybuses and buses cover virtually the whole city, though no services actually penetrate the Old Town. Tickets, which are now valid on both modes of transport, can be bought in advance from kiosks (currently 0.80Lt, 0.40Lt for pensioners and bona fide students) or, with rare exceptions, from the driver (1Lt). A few bus routes which run beyond the city boundaries have slightly higher tariffs, with tickets sold by an on-board conductor. Otherwise, tickets – whether bought in advance or from the driver – must be punched in one of the machines positioned throughout the bus or trolleybus. Usually these are primitive devices which make different patterns of holes, though a few buses are now equipped with computerised machines which print out the date and time that the ticket has been validated.

For visiting all but the far-flung parts of the city, the trolleybuses cover most needs, though they are prone to be uncomfortably crowded throughout much of the day, and it is often necessary to jostle with other passengers in order to be able to alight and disembark. Particularly useful services are trolleybus 2, which travels from the train station down the western side of the Old Town, the eastern part of Gedimino, then along the south bank of the Nevis to Antakalnis; and trolleybus 5, which likewise begins and ends at the station and goes down the western side of the Old Town, before continuing northwards over the Green Bridge and past the Calvary Market en route to Žirmūnai. An excellent map of the whole trolleybus network can be found in *Vilnius In Your Pocket*.

Bus 1 links the train station with the airport, while the more frequent bus 2 goes to the airport from the northern inner suburb of Šeškinė via the Green Bridge and the New Town. These and many other bus routes are duplicated by minibuses, which can be flagged down anywhere. Their destination and the fare (which is normally either 1Lt or 2Lt and paid directly to the driver) are displayed prominently on the windscreen.

During the summer of 2002, Gedimino was being closed in sections for rebuilding and a new bridge was under construction across the Neris from the end of Vrubievskio. This work should be completed during 2003 but, whilst it is underway, trolley buses are being rerouted on the far side of the river. The opening of the bridge will bring about many changes in bus and trolleybus routes and in due course it will carry a new tram service to link the suburbs with the Old Town.

Taxis

Taxis are always worth considering, particularly if travelling as a family or in a group, as they are much more comfortable than the alternatives and are also very inexpensive by Western standards. They are often necessary for getting to the airport, as buses are only starting to run at the time it is necessary to check-in for some early flights. Outrageous rip-offs of tourists by taxi drivers, once commonplace, are now largely a thing of the past, though cars without meters or which do not display the name of a company should still be avoided. Ordering a taxi by telephone from one of the companies listed below, rather than picking one up at a rank, is a sure-fire way of avoiding any difficulties. Rates consist of a fixed charge of around 1.30Lt plus upwards of 1Lt per kilometre travelled; the latter figure is invariably increased at night, sometimes to as much as 2Lt.

Denvila Tel: 244 4444 or 244 8182
Ekipazas Tel: 1446
Fiakras Tel: 270 5705
Vilniaus Taksi Tel: 212 8888

Car hire

Autorenta Dariaus ir Gireno 42a; tel: 8698 24795; tel/fax: 216 6822; email: info@carrent.lt; web: www.carrent.lt.
Avis Dariaus ir Gireno 32a; tel: 230 6820; fax: 230 6821; email: avis@avis.lt; web: www.avis.lt. Also at the airport, tel/fax: 232 9316; email: apo@avis.lt
Budget At the airport; tel: 230 6708; fax: 230 6709; email: budget@budget.lt; web: www.budget.lt
Europcar Stuokos-Gucevičiaus 9-1; tel: 212 0207 or 212 2739; fax: 212 0439; email: city@europcar.lt; web: www.europcar.lt. Also at the airport, tel/fax: 216 3442.
Hertz Kalvarijų 14; tel: 272 6940; fax: 272 6970; email: hertz@hertz.lt; web: www.hertz.lt. Also at the airport, tel/fax: 226 0394; email: airport@hertz.lt
Litinterp Bernardinų 7-2; tel: 212 3850; fax: 212 3559; email: vilnius@litinterp.lt; web: www.litinterp.lt
Sixt At the airport; tel: 395636; fax: 395635; email: renbt@sixt.lt; web: www.sixt.lt

Buses

Bus station Sodų 22; tel: 216 2482 or 216 2977. Located just south of the Old Town, this has a comprehensive network of services to other Lithuanian towns. These include at least a couple of buses an hour throughout most of the day to Kaunas, of which the fastest are the minibuses, which leave from stand 37. One or more buses per hour run to Panevėžys, while over 30 per day go to Trakai, often en route to another destination. Other approximate daily frequencies include 12 to Utena via Molėtai, 12 to Šiauliai, ten to Klaipėda, five to Druskininkai and, in season, 12 expresses to Palanga. In addition, a daily bus runs to Nida from June to August.

Among the daily international services are seven to Minsk, five to Riga, two to Tallinn, two to Kaliningrad, four to Warsaw, one to Białystok via Suwałki and one to Gdańsk; there are also four per week to Moscow. For destinations in western Europe, it is normally necessary to change at Warsaw. However, there are also connections to the routes passing through Kaunas as well as a direct weekly service to a range of German cities. There is a left luggage room in the terminal building.

Trains
Railway station Geležinkelio 16; tel: 233 0086; web: www. litrail.lt. This grand old building with a recently refurbished interior is diagonally opposite the bus station. There are 12 trains daily to Kaunas, including two expresses which are far faster than any bus. Among the other daily domestic services are seven (five at weekends) to Trakai, six to Ignalina, six to Šiauliai, four to Marcinkonys, three to Klaipėda via Telšiai, Plungė and Kretinga, and three direct to Šeštokai.

There are also a number of daily international services: four to Daugavpils (Latvia), one to St Petersburg, two or three to Moscow, three to Kaliningrad, three to Minsk and one or two to Warsaw (a daily daytime service in both directions, plus an overnight one on alternate days). Beware that some of the Warsaw trains travel via Grodno in Belarus, necessitating the purchase of an outrageously expensive transit visa. There is an overnight train to Riga, but as this takes about eight hours with border formalities in full swing at two o'clock in the morning, it is hardly a sensible alternative to the bus. In July 2002 a twice-weekly train service started from Tallinn to Minsk via Riga and Vilnius. It leaves Vilnius on Monday and Friday at 15.15 and reaches Riga at 21.59 and Tallinn at 06.13, with many en-route stops in the three Baltic States.

The left-luggage facility is in the station basement, which can only be reached by the stairway in front of the building. There is a 24-hour exchange office just outside the railway station.

Accommodation
There is a wide choice of accommodation in Vilnius, ranging from dorm beds in hostels to super-luxury hotels. Prices are naturally similarly variable, and are usually a fairly reliable indicator of the quality of any particular establishment.

By mid 2004, the hotel scene in Vilnius will have changed over a two-year period more than in any other European capital. About 20 new hotels in all categories will have opened by then, giving an enormous choice of price and location. The deluxe traveller will be able to rely on the chains that prevail elsewhere, but budget travellers will no longer be dependent on a haphazard range of guesthouses. They too can stay in large hotels with a range of facilities. Air conditioning is becoming standard in the more expensive hotels, as are 'light-proof' curtains, specifically tailored to keep out the early morning midsummer sun.

The city now has plenty of highly recommendable upmarket establishments, including many which offer the bonus of an atmospheric Old Town location. However, it is very noticeable that the majority of these are geared primarily towards the business traveller. Promotional leaflets tend to emphasise the provision of conference rooms, computers with email access, fax machines, photocopiers and the like. Room rates in such hotels are often comparable with those in cities of similar size in the West. There is still something of a shortage

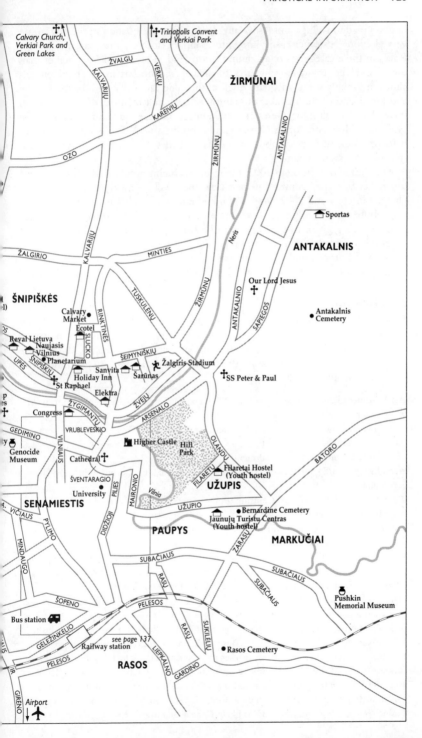

Calvary Church, Verkiai Park and Green Lakes

Trinapolis Convent and Verkiai Park

ŽIRMŪNAI

ŽVALGŲ

KALIVARIŲ

VERKIŲ

KAREIVIŲ

OZO

ŽIRMŪNŲ

ANTAKALNIO

Sportas

ANTAKALNIS

ŽALGIRIO

MINTIES

Neris

ŠNIPIŠKĖS

TUSKULĖNŲ

ŽIRMŪNŲ

ANTAKALNIO

SAPIEGOS

Our Lord Jesus

Antakalnis Cemetery

Calvary Market

RINKTINĖS

Ecotel

SLUCKO

Reval Lietuva
Naujasis
Vilnius
Planetarium

ŠEIMYNIŠKIŲ

UPĖS

ŠNIPIŠKIŲ

Žalgiris Stadium

Sanvita
Holiday Inn

Šarūnas

ŽVEJŲ

SS Peter & Paul

St Raphael

Elektra

ARSENALO

ŽYGIMANTŲ

Congress

VRUBLEVESKIO

OLANDŲ

BATORO

GEDIMINO

VILNIAUS

Higher Castle

Hill Park

Genocide Museum

Cathedral

FILARETŲ

Filaretai Hostel
(Youth hostel)

ŠVENTARAGIO

MARONIO

University

Vilnia

UŽUPIS

UŽUPIO

Bernardine Cemetery

SENAMIESTIS

VIČIAUS

PYLIMO

DIDŽIOJI

PILIES

PAUPYS

Jaunujų Turistu Centras
(Youth hostel)

ZARASŲ

MARKUČIAI

MINDAUGO

SUBAČIAUS

SUBAČIAUS

SUBAČIAUS

ŠOPENO

RASŲ

PELESOS

RASŲ

SUKILĖLIŲ

Pushkin
Memorial Museum

Bus station

GELEŽINKELIO

see page 137
Railway station

PELESOS

LIEPKALNO

RASOS

GARDINO

Rasos Cemetery

Airport

of good medium-range and (especially) budget accommodation in the city; some very dubious customers can almost invariably be found in the cheaper hotels. Prices in these categories of accommodation tend to be at least 50% higher than they would be anywhere else in Lithuania. Receptionists in the better hotels almost invariably speak adequate English; the same cannot be said for the middle and lower end of the market, though there is often a member of staff who can speak basic English or German. Discounts from the standard rates may be available in July and August at the luxury 'business-class' hotels for reservations made through their usual booking agents, but these prices may be difficult for 'walk-in' guests to obtain.

At the time of writing in 2003, the level at which prices would settle was hard to predict but one promise can be made: they will be much lower than those charged in 2001 and 2002. High published rates may well stay in brochures and on websites, and during trade fairs may even be obtained, but the intense barrage of offers being given to tour operators both for groups and for individuals will ensure that very few tourists end up paying these.

For a twin room with breakfast expect to pay £80/US$120 in luxury hotels; £50/US$75 in a medium-sized hotel, and £30/US$45 in a budget hotel.

Luxury hotels

During 2003, two new luxury hotels are due to open, the Congress, beside the River on Zygimantu, the site of the former very unluxurious Green Bridge Hotel, and the Novotel on the corner of Gedimino and Vilniaus. Marriott are planning to take over and rebuild the former Vilnius Hotel on Gedimino, with opening scheduled for 2004.

AAA Mano Liza Ligoninės 5; tel: 212 2225; fax: 212 2608; email: hotel@aaa.lt; web: www.hotelinvilnius.lt.

A small guesthouse in the quiet southwestern part of the Old Town, which will arrange pick-up from the airport. All eight rooms are equipped with satellite TV. The restaurant offers a nicely varied international menu.

Artis Liejykos 11/23; tel: 266 0366; fax: 266 0377; email: artis @centrum.lt; web: www. centrum.lt.

The latest addition to Vilnius' Centrum group of hotels occupies a refurbished Old Town mansion, and is smaller and homelier than its two counterparts. In a very quiet location just at the back of the Presidential Palace, it is still within walking distance of many sites and shops. All rooms are air-conditioned and in summer 2003 the hotel will double in size from 30 to 68 rooms, some with showers, and some with baths. A swimming pool and gym will then be a welcome addition to its facilities. Email printed editions of newspapers from all over the world can be ordered for room delivery.

Astorija Didžioji 35/2; tel: 212 0110; fax: 212 1762; email: reservations.vilnius@radissonsas.com; web: www.radissonsas.com.

This grand early 20th-century hotel in the heart of the Old Town has been refurbished by the Radisson SAS chain, and has a Business Service Centre prominent among its facilities. All rooms have hairdryer, trouser press, telephone, cable TV, safe and hot drinks machine. Prices include either a 'grab and run' or a full buffet breakfast. The Brasserie has an international menu and is among the best restaurants in the city. The buffet lunch for around 50Lt, including drinks, is very popular with both tourists and business visitors. A swimming pool is likely to be added in late 2003.

Atrium Pilies 10; tel: 210 7777; fax: 210 7770; email: hotel@atrium.lt; web: www.atrium.lt.

A large, no-photography sign suggests that many guests might attract paparazzi who have to be deterred. Space is everywhere – in the rooms, at reception and in the Argentinean restaurant El Gaucho Sano, which of course specialises in steak (although it is quite happy to include three vegetarian dishes in its menu). Wooden tables and saddles hanging from the ceiling reinforce the restaurant's theme. The Rio nightclub continues the Latin theme set by the restaurant.

Balatonas Latvių 38; tel: 272 2250; fax: 272 2134; email: info@balatonas.lt; web: www.balatonas.lt.

A Hungarian joint-venture, this hotel occupies a gleaming white historic villa set amid the wooden houses in the heart of the Žvėrynas district. Facilities include a sauna, swimming pool and a small café which serves full meals.

Business Guesthouse Saltoniškių 44; tel: 272 2298; fax: 275 3761; email: bgh@tdd.lt; web: www.tdd.lt/bgh.

Located in the north of the Žvėrynas district, this detached house overlooked by tower blocks looks unassuming from the outside, but has a Scandinavian-style designer interior. Guests can use the sauna and swimming pool without extra charge. There is also a commercial art gallery and the expected range of business services.

Centrum Vytenio 9/24; tel: 268 3300; fax: 213 2760; email: hotel@centrum.lt; web: www.centrum.lt.

Located in the eponymous business centre in the western part of the New Town, this plush hotel is unashamedly modern with its ample use of glass and light colours. It is a very convenient base for business visitors and for groups with a coach since parking is no problem in the surrounding streets. Being beside the Belarus Embassy, peace and quiet around the clock is assured, and for many this is ample compensation for the dreary surroundings and the 15-minute walk to the Old Town.

City Park Stuokos-Gucevičiaus 3; tel: 212 3515 or 261 5123; fax: 261 7745; email: citypark@is.lt; web: www.citypark.lt.

Having opened as a modest tourist-class hotel, in late 2002 it expanded and reinvented itself as a major player at the top end of the market. It is obvious even from a distance why its extension was the major architectural controversy of 2002. The enormous dark glass façade is hardly in keeping with the Old Town around it. All rooms now have air conditioning, baths and lightproof curtains, and many offer a view over the cathedral. An underground car park is an unexpected bonus in the Old Town. The doubles are of a normal size; the singles somewhat mean in space.

Crowne Plaza Čiurlionio 84; tel: 213 6711; fax: 216 3101; email; hotel@cpvilnius.com; web: www.crowneplaza.com.

In Soviet times, there was a hotel on this site called the Draugystė and it briefly housed several embassies during the early 1990s after Lithuanian independence had been re-established. Perhaps because of its former associations, the building was completely demolished and the new one will open in May 2003. Its location in a smart residential area near Vingis Park will set it apart from most other hotels in the town and will be welcome to those wanting space, quiet and country views during their stay. Unusual features will include tea- and coffee-making facilities in all rooms and a complimentary taxi service to and from the airport.

Europa Imperial Aušros Vartų 6; tel: 2161 3333/266 0770; fax: 261 2000; email: reservation@hoteleuropa.lt; web: www.hoteleuropa.lt.

A stylish new hotel in a renovated Historicist building beside the Italian embassy. The baroque views from many of its rooms give a Mediterranean feel during the summer. Bedrooms have satellite TV, air conditioning, minibar and heated bathroom tiles. The restaurant preserves the mock-Arab décor of the fast-food eatery it has supplanted. For tourists, the location could not be better, given the proximity of so many shops and restaurants. Business visitors might find the rooms on the small side and the reception area similarly cramped.

Grotthuss Ligoninės 7; tel: 266 0322; fax: 266 0323; email: grotthuss@takas.lt; web: www.grotthusshotel.com.

Brand-new hotel with cellar restaurant in one of the most peaceful parts of the Old Town. All rooms offer internet access, a safe and a minibar.

Grybas House Aušros Vartų 3a; tel: 261 9695; fax: 212 1854; email: grybashouse@taide.lt; web: www.grybashouse.lt.

A delightful small hotel (there are only 9 rooms) in a refurbished baroque house set in a quiet courtyard at the northern end of the Old Town. The décor includes sculptures from the Congo and the former pier in Palanga. Primarily geared to tourists, it offers full travel agency services. All rooms have telephone, satellite TV, minibar, water filters and heated floors. There is a fine basement restaurant, with live classical music on Wednesday evenings. Do not judge the hotel by the surrounding buildings, where renovation is long overdue. At the entrance, note the plaque in Hebrew commemorating a Jewish hostel that once stood on this site.

Holiday Inn Šeimyniškių 1; tel: 5210 3000; fax: 5210 3001; email: holiday-inn@ibc.lt; web: www.sixcontinenthotels.com.

It is perhaps surprising that it took until May 2002 for such a well-known chain to open its first hotel in the Baltic States. Choosing a site over the river opposite the Old Town was certainly a shrewd move as this area is becoming the new business centre of Vilnius. When the hotel opened, baths, air conditioning and soundproofing in every room were unusual for Vilnius, though competitors are now rapidly following suit. What will keep the hotel unusual is its seventh-floor gym and sauna.

Le Meridien Villon A2 highway; tel: 273 9600 or 273 9700; fax: 265 1385; email: lemeridienvillon@post.omnitel.net; web: www.hotelvillon.lt.

This huge motel and conference centre lies 19km from the centre of Vilnius, beside the main dual carriageway to Panevėžys and Riga. It lays on free shuttle buses to the city, and offers the services of a full holiday complex, including tennis courts, a fitness club, swimming pool, three saunas and a restaurant, Le Paysage, specialising in Gallic-influenced cuisine.

Mabre Residence Maironio 13; tel: 5212 2087; fax: 5212 2240; email: mabre@mabre.lt; web: www.mabre.lt.

Occupies the grand neo-Classical courtyard buildings of a former Russian Orthodox monastery in the quiet eastern part of the Old Town. Its former function perhaps ensures that most clients are quieter and older than elsewhere. The opening of the cellar Steakhouse Hazienda and the granting of free internet access in all rooms is clearly aimed at bringing in younger guests. The swimming pool is a rare bonus for the town centre.

Narutis Pilies 24; tel: 212 2894; fax: 262 2882; email: narutis@post.5ci.lt; web: www.narutis.lt.

This hotel on the Old Town's main artery occupies an originally Gothic mansion that was remodelled in neo-classical style. The bedrooms are tastefully furnished in oak, and some have 19th-century murals. Other facilities include a lounge in the glass-covered courtyard, a sauna, fitness room and a cellar café-restaurant.

Naujasis Vilnius Ukmergės 14; tel: 273 9595; fax: 273 9500; email: office@hotelnv.lt; web: www.hotelnv.lt.
The smaller of the two giant hotel blocks on the north side of the Neris, the former Turistas is now a member of the Best Western group, having been made over by a Swiss joint venture company into a business-class hotel with the usual support services.
Neringa Gedimino 23; tel: 268 1910; fax: 261 4160; email: neringa@scandic-hotels.com; web: www.scandic-hotels.com.
This Communist-era hotel on the main commercial street has been given a Swedish-style makeover by the Scandic chain, and is equipped with a gym, sauna, small pool, library and business centre. The restaurant, however, still preserves some outrageous Soviet décor and this has given it a certain cult status.
Ratonda Gedimino 52/1; tel: 5212 0670; fax: 5212 0669; email: ratonda@centrum.lt; web: www.centrum.lt.
An offshoot of the aforementioned Centrum, this attracts tourists as well as business travellers. It is in fact located just off Gedimino and so is unaffected by traffic noise.
Šarūnas Raitininkų 4; tel: 272 3666 or 272 4888; fax: 272 4355; email: info@hotelsarunas.lt; web: www.hotelsarunas.lt.
This modern business hotel near the Žalgiris stadium is owned by Šarūnas Marčiulonis, president of the Lithuanian Basketball Federation and erstwhile player with the Sacramento Kings of America's National Basketball Association. Sportsgear and trainers worn by leading stars of the NBA decorate the informal Rooney's Bar, which serves Lithuanian and American dishes, while the formal restaurant has an international menu and features live jazz on Friday evenings A fitness room with weightlifting equipment supplements the obligatory sauna. Singles 360–380Lt, doubles 420–440Lt, suites 460–600Lt, apartments 700Lt.
Shakespeare Bernardinų 8/8; tel: 231 4521; fax: 231 4522; email: info@shakespeare.lt; web: www.shakespeare.lt.
This English-style country hotel on an Old Town back street opened with 10 rooms in 1999, expanded to 30 by 2001; in 2002 it opened Shakespeare Too on Pilies, nearby, with a further 11 rooms. Most of the rooms are named after famous writers and contain reading material linked to each. Many offer imposing views of nearby landmarks, such as the Church of St Anne; all have safes, internet connections and underfloor bathroom heating, while the more expensive have air conditioning. The Sonetas ('Sonnets') restaurant is one of the classiest and most expensive in Vilnius. Offering 'scenes' rather than courses, its menu stresses local ingredients, and guests are assured of 'no imported fodder'.
Stikliai Gaono 7; tel: 262 7971; fax: 222 3870; email: stikliai@mail.iti.lt; web: www.stikliai.hotel.lt.
This hotel numbers foreign royalty and other dignitaries among its clients, most of whom have left ostentatiously signed photographs in the lobby. Occupying a 17th-century building in a quiet Old Town back street, it is exquisitely furnished throughout. All bedrooms are soundproofed and air-conditioned, and have satellite TV and telephone. Other facilities include a sauna, swimming pool and fitness room. The hotel restaurant serves pricy French cuisine; close by are several less formal and expensive eateries run by the same management.

Medium-range hotels
Accapella Dariaus ir Girėno 61; tel: 216 7898; fax: 216 7241; email: info@hotelacappella.lt; web: www.hotelacappella.lt.

This new venture is now by far the most attractive of the options in the vicinity of the airport, from which it lies a short distance to the northwest, on the way towards the city centre.

Ambassador Gedimino 12; tel: 261 5450; fax: 212 1716; email: info@ambassador.lt; web: www.ambassador.lt.

By summer 2003, when building work ceases on Gedimino and lime trees, marble and black paving stones imported from China are all in place, this should be an attractive spot. While the bedrooms still have many of the unmistakable hallmarks of the Soviet era and the reception is particularly gloomy, for most summer visitors the relatively low prices and the convenient location on the main business street will be more than ample compensation.

Baltpark Ukmergės 363; tel: 238 8000; fax: 238 8555; email: vilnius@baltpark.com; web: www.baltpark.com.

This new, box-like hotel at the far northern edge of the city was built to plug what was perceived to be a gap in the market – an establishment offering fully modern business-class standards at reasonable prices.

Centro Kubas Stiklių 3; tel: 266 0860; fax: 266 0861; email: hotel@centrokubas.lt; web: www.centrokubas.lt.

If prizes were given for original design, this hotel would certainly win one. The centrepiece of the lounge is a windmill and all rooms are decorated with different agricultural tools. Although it only has 11 rooms, these are scattered across four different floors, linked by a glass lift. Some extra adornments are provided by the linen shop next door. It also has a fine cellar restaurant.

Congress Vilniaus 2/15. On the site of the former Žaliasis Tiltas; tel: 269 1919; fax: 264 9994; email: info@congress.lt; web: www.congress.lt.

Regular visitors to Vilnius will remember the sadly dilapidated Green Bridge Hotel at this location which was allowed to endure a long and painful death. The Congress is due to open during the summer of 2003 and will sensibly aim at a three-star clientele and not chase the business market. The location will appeal to those not quite sure whether to be in the Old Town or the New: being on the river, it is exactly in between.

Conti Raugyklos 7/2; tel: 251 4111; fax: 251 4100; email: info@contihotel.lt; web: www. continhotel.lt.

It was a courageous move to open a private hotel in January 2003 on this site, surrounded by potholes, long-abandoned small factories and temporary car parks. Entering the hotel, however, is to forget this, as guests are faced with a waterfall, a marble lobby and a glass lift. The provision for the disabled, the baths, air conditioning and internet connections in every room, together with lightproof blinds, all reflect its up-to-date design and with luck the neighbourhood will soon follow suit. Telephone charges are much lower than those in most Vilnius hotels. Being behind the synagogue, the hotel is convenient for Jewish groups and it allows them to prepare Kosher food in its kitchens. The eight rooms in the garret are of a lower standard, but are much cheaper. Rooms 506,507 and 508 have the nicest views over the Old Town, but all rooms have prints showing Vilnius around 100 years ago.

Elektra Žvejų 14a; tel: 262 6748; fax: 272 3779; email: hotel.elektra@entra.lpc.lt; web: www.elektra.lpc.lt. The hotel occupies the palatial former headquarters of the electricity company, whose tower is crowned by a statue of the torch-bearing Elektra, daughter of Agamemnon. Rooms all have satellite TV, telephone and minibar, while those facing the front command fine views across the Neris to the Higher Castle. There is also a café-restaurant. Singles 250–330Lt, doubles 320–350Lt, suites 380Lt.

Europa City Jasinskio 14; tel: 266 0770; fax: 261 2000; email: reservation@hoteleurope.lt; web: www.hoteleuropa.lt.
Although under the same management as the Europa Imperial, it would be hard to imagine two more different hotels. This will be a large three-star hotel near the parliament building likely to appeal to tour groups and individual visitors for whom price is more important than an Old Town location. It is due to open in summer 2003.
Reval Lietuva Konstitucijos 20; tel: 210 2570; fax: 272 6270; email: lietuva@revalhotels.com; web: www.revalhotels.com.
When the old Lietuva closed in early 2002, few mourned its passing as none of its various attempts at modernisation during the 1990s were ever able to rid it of its Soviet image. The Reval group will reopen it in May 2003 and, if they follow the pattern they set with similar buildings in Tallinn and Riga, a deluxe successor will emerge but at prices that will tempt many tour operators to include it in their programmes. The surroundings will be disconcerting at first as the new financial quarter over the road is still under construction, but the bar on the 22nd floor will provide a comforting view of the Old Town over the river, which thanks to a pedestrian bridge is now only a few minutes' walk away.
Mikotel Pylimo 63; tel: 260 9626; fax: 260 9627; email: mikotel@takas.lt; web: travel.lt/mikotel.
When this hotel opened in 2000, it became instantly popular amongst budget-conscious travellers. The immediate surroundings, it has to be admitted, are still rather run-down but the hotel itself is very modern. Its location halfway between the bus station and the Old Town enables some visitors never to use transport at all during their stay. Access to the breakfast kitchen during the day and evening enables visitors to self-cater, if they wish. Prices are usually similar to those of hotels well out of town.
Rūdninkp Vartai Rūdninkų 15/46; tel: 261 3916; fax: 212 0507; email: rudvar @takas.
Named after the western gateway to the Old Town that formerly occupied the spot, the hotel is close to the current synagogue, the Jewish and Holocaust museums and the site of the Ghetto. It is built round a courtyard which in summer serves as an open-air extension to its café. All rooms have satellite TV and telephone; some also have a minibar or refrigerator. A sauna and fitness room are the other main facilities.
Senatoriai Tilto 2; tel: 212 7056; fax: 212 6491; email: senator@takas.lt; web: www.senatoriai.com.
This small low-rise hotel profits from an excellent location, being discreetly tucked away down a side street immediately to the rear of Gedimino, just a stone's throw from the cathedral. Its 11 rooms are small, but few visitors mind, and it is often fully booked for long stretches during the summer.
Victoria Saltoniškių 56; tel: 272 4013; fax: 272 4320; email: hotel@victoria.lt; web: www.victoria.lt.
In the mid 1990s this was a very popular hotel amongst British visitors, but sadly it has not moved on. The website still boasts of modernisation in 1993, so the clientele tend to be as unimaginative as the décor. Lower prices or redecoration are really needed to bring back its former supporters.

Budget hotels
Bernardinai Guest House Bernardinų 5; tel: 260 8410; fax: 260 8421; email: info@ avevita.lt; web: www.avevita.lt.
With the avalanche of hotels opening in 2003, it is good to report a new guesthouse as well. As befits the courtyard location in the Old Town, rooms have been renovated rather than rebuilt. Look out for old panelling and wall paintings, but expect modern

furniture too. There are rooms and flats here, all for self-catering. The courtyard provides a secure location for parking a car, sadly now necessary in the Old Town overnight.

Ecotel Sluko 8; tel/fax: 7005 5300; email: hotel@ecotel.lt.

When this hotel with its 168 rooms opens in summer 2003, it may set a trend in all the Baltic States, if only to show what can become of a formerly derelict factory. In the old days it produced shoes; now it will provide basic hotel rooms in a quiet location on the edge of the new financial quarter and within ten minutes' walk of the Old Town. It will not be surprising if many business visitors stay here too. The very tall should note that some rooms have two-metre beds.

Gintaras Sodų 14; tel: 273 8012; fax: 216 3789; email: hotel.gintaras@tdd.lt; web: www.hotelgintaras.lt.

Vilnius' most notorious hotel is a large Soviet-era block opposite the railway station. The oft-expressed fears about room security are much exaggerated and it is a convenient place to spend the night if arriving late or departing early – even if some of the staff seem to have learnt their craft from Basil Fawlty. The renovated rooms are only relatively better than the unrenovated, and not really worth the extra money.

Jeruzalė Kalvarijų 209; tel: 271 4040; fax: 276 2627; email: jeruzale@takas.lt; web: www.jeruzale.com.

A smallish hotel in the northern residential district of the same name, a short distance south of the Calvary Church. It can be reached by buses 26, 35, 36 or 50.

Pušis Blindzių 17; tel: 268 3980; fax: 272 1305; email: pusis@pusishotel.lt; web: www.pusishotel.lt.

The location, within the Agribusiness Training Centre at the far western edge of Žvėrynas, is not terribly convenient, but the rooms are good value at the price asked.

Skrydis Rodūnės kelias 8; tel: 232 9099; fax: 230 6498.

Renovations at the airport hotel are proceeding at a leisurely pace, and many rooms are still of the Soviet era. It is certainly worth considering for at least single-night stays if arriving late or departing early.

Sportas Bistryčios 13; tel: 234 6953; fax: 234 6946.

Originally intended for sportsmen, but now open to all, this large and rather worn hotel is in the Antakalnis district; trolleybus 2 passes nearby. The cheaper rooms lack private facilities.

Hostels

IYHF Filaretai Hostel Filaretų 17; tel: 215 4627; fax: 2112 0149; email: filaretai@post.omnitel.net; web: www. filaretai.8m.com.

Much the larger of the two IYHF-affiliated hostels, situated at the northeastern edge of the Užupis district, and reached by bus 34.

IYHF Old Town Hostel Aušros Vartų 20-10; tel: 262 5357; fax: 268 5967; email: oldtownhostel@delfi.lt; web: www.balticbackpackers.com.

Despite its name, this 23-bed hostel actually lies just beyond the southern edge of the Old Town, and is signposted from the railway station.

Jaunujų Turistų Centras Polocko 7; tel: 261 1547 or 261 3576; fax: 262 7742.

The Young Tourists' Centre is in the eastern part of Užupis, and has a dozen rooms, each accommodating three or four people.

JNN Hostel Konstitucijos 25; tel/fax: 272 2270; email: jnn@lvjc.lt.

A short distance west of the Hotel Lietuva, this is a superior hostel in which all rooms have private facilities. Two swimming pools, a sauna, solarium and massage facilities are also on the premises.

Bed and breakfast

Litinterp Bernardinų 7/2; tel: 212 3850; fax: 212 3559; email: vilnius@litinterp.lt; web: www.litinterp.lt.

Office open Mon–Fri 08.30–17.30, Sat 09.00–15.30. In addition to its own small guesthouse on the premises, this offers rooms in private houses in central Vilnius and Trakai, and also has some apartments for rent. Advance bookings for Kaunas, Klaipėda, Palanga and Nida can be made, and car hire, interpretation and translation services are also available.

Food and drink

In a welcome change from the Soviet years, Vilnius now has a huge range of restaurants, cafés, bars and pubs to choose from, even if it still does not have quite the range of cuisines now taken for granted in Tallinn and Riga. Many of the leading cuisines of the world are represented, though this development thankfully has not (as it has in other capital cities of former Communist countries) resulted in any diminution in the number or quality of establishments specialising in traditional local dishes, such as stuffed dumplings and pancakes. As is the case throughout Lithuania, some places are difficult to categorise, with many bars and cafés offering a full restaurant-type menu. The main concentrations of places to eat and drink are in the Old and New Towns, though there are a few restaurants further afield which well warrant the detour. Most of the places listed below have been around for at least five years; omission of many others should not be seen as a criticism.

For further recommendations, particularly for formal dining, see also *Hotels* above.

Restaurants

Aqua Didžioji 28; tel: 260 8851. Opened early in 2003, Aqua is situated opposite the Radisson Astoria beside St Casimir's Church, and well symbolises the pace of change. The hurried lunchtime tourist can now scoff a wide range of salads in summer, and more substantial food in winter, without missing too many sights. Only in the evening does the pace quieten down.

Balti Drambliai Vilniaus 41; tel: 262 0875. In most Vilnius restaurants, vegetarians are now happily tolerated; at 'White Elephants' they are welcomed, as are non-smokers. At the time of writing, this cellar restaurant with garden was probably still the only 100% vegetarian restaurant in town. Nonetheless, it offers 11 different pizzas and six varieties of *rosti*, the Swiss potato dish. Portions, however, would satisfy even the greediest of Texans. Alongside well-known brands of alcohol, strangely named teas include 'yoga tea' and 'harmonising tea'.

Da Antonio Pilies 20; tel: 261 8341 and Vilniaus 23; tel: 262 0109. Both branches offer serious Italian food, including delicious pizzas made in a wood-fired oven, as well as a range of pasta dishes and other classic Italian fare. The former has the appropriate baroque surroundings in its neighbouring buildings, but the latter one may well be quieter at the height of the tourist season. Diners can see ingredients being put together on the spot – and there's no sign of a microwave.

Fortas Algirdo 17; tel: 265 2526. This New Town restaurant offers an eclectic menu of Lithuanian dishes, pizzas and Tex-Mex fare in a bar-type setting.

Freskos Didžioji 31; tel: 261 8133. Decorated with theatre costumes and posters as well as the frescos which give it its name, this occupies the rear part of the Town Hall, very close to the Radisson Hotel. The restaurant expands outside during the summer when it is tempting to linger until the sun finally sets towards 23.00. The international menu is prepared with a Gallic sense of flair, and must be one of the largest in Vilnius, so check it in advance at www.freskos.lt. While relatively expensive, it is good value none the less, the best bargains being the set lunches and help-yourself salad bar. To save money on wine, go for the dish 'Drinkers' Delight' a risotto drenched in red wine, accompanied by salad with a dressing of whisky and almonds. Although the staff inevitably changes each year, standards of service never seem to suffer.

Geltonoji Upė Stiklių 18; tel: 212 2875. Part of the Stikliai group, the 'Yellow River' is the classiest Chinese restaurant in Lithuania. Its elaborate interior is laid out and decorated in Tang dynasty style. Closed Mon.

IdaBasar Subačiaus 3; tel: 262 8484. The cavernous cellar and the hearty portions successfully invoke the culinary tradition of the German joint-owners. There are some imaginative dishes on the menu, though unfortunately the accompanying vegetables are not invariably fresh. Among the beers on tap is the celebrated Jever, Germany's bitterest brew.

Kaukazo Belaisvė Trakų 7; tel: 261 1663. Dining here is under the watchful eye of Georgian warriors, fortunately all made out of wax. A Georgian menu is sufficiently diverse for choices from elsewhere not to be necessary. First-time diners should go for fried aubergines with pine nuts, followed by chicken in prune sauce.

Literatų Svetainė Gedimino 1; tel: 261 1889. The 'Literary Salon' is a true golden oldie, and was the place from where the Nobel Prize-winning poet Czesvaw Mivosz witnessed the occupation of the city by Soviet tanks in 1940, an episode described in his autobiography, *Native Realm*. Now under Swedish ownership, it serves Scandinavian-style hot and cold dishes at prices which would be low in Sweden but are relatively high for Lithuania. These can be enjoyed either in the formal dining room overlooking the cathedral, or in the more relaxed café alongside.

Lokys Stiklių 8; tel: 261 1889. Occupying a warren of brick Gothic cellars in one of the quietest parts of the Old Town, 'The Bear' is another stalwart of the Vilnius restaurant scene, and the only one which functions much as it did in the Communist era. Game dishes, particularly elk and wild boar, are its main specialities, though it has a fine all-round menu in which salads and desserts also feature strongly.

Marceliukės Klėtis Tuskulėnų 35; tel: 272 5087. A traditional family-orientated hostelry just northeast of the Calvary Market, whose rustic exterior is totally at odds with the surrounding high-rise apartment blocks. Its amazing cluttered décor includes an old wooden bicycle suspended from the ceiling. Most of the staple dishes of the Lithuanian kitchen are featured on the menu, and professional folk groups perform most evenings.

Markus ir Ko Žydų 4a, entrance from Antokolskio 9; tel: 262 3185. Primarily a steakhouse offering a wide choice of succulent cuts, though there are plenty of other options, including salads and sweets, as well as a long drinks list. There is live piano music (usually jazz) most evenings.

Po Saule Labdarių 7/11; tel: 262 4825. The small French community in Vilnius congregate here with their families so this must be a strong recommendation, as is the fact that they had to move to larger premises in summer 2002. Expect to dine at a leisurely pace, with children around all evening. The set lunch is undoubtedly one of the best culinary bargains in the city.

La Province Vokiečių 24; tel: 261 6573. Classy and relatively pricey new restaurant sandwiched between the two constituent parts of Žemaičių Smuklė. Only the prices here are Lithuanian, otherwise everything fits the name in a perfect transplant from the south of France. Expect plenty of fish, salads and above all, varied dressings and sauces.

The Pub see Prie Universiteto, page 136

Ritos Slėptuvė Goštauto 8; tel: 262 6117. This celebrated restaurant founded by Chicago-born Rita Dapkutė, erstwhile spokeswoman for the Sajūdis movement, broke the mould of Vilnius' eating scene. Open until 02.00 (06.00 at weekends), it features all the favourites of American cuisine – including deep-pan pizza, hamburgers, burritos and mud pie – on the long menu, and also has a large choice of breakfast dishes. Adjoining is a bar with a dance floor, while in the corridor opposite the entrance is a take-away bakery, Ritos Krautuvė.

Ritos Smuklė Žirmūnų 68; tel: 277 0786. The sister restaurant to the above is a re-invention of an old-style Lithuanian country tavern, notwithstanding its unpromising setting in a commercial district well to the north of the city centre (take bus 9, 12, 13 or 17 to Žirmūnai). Only traditional Lithuanian dishes (many of which are now rarely found elsewhere) and drinks are served; anything of Russian or Western origin is banned from the menu. Professional folk groups perform in the evenings, Thu–Sun. Reading the website for both Ritos Sleptuvė and Ritos Smulkė, www. rita.lt is almost as much fun as eating at either restaurant. Check out not only the menus and the forthcoming entertainment, but also the customer profiles and the analysis of their questionnaires.

Rojaus Arka Dauksos 3; tel: 212 2803. It is worth passing through the Gates of Dawn and tackling the traffic on Dauksos to reach a restaurant that seems to have managed a transition from the 1930s without any Soviet intrusion. Go inside to discover real flowers on the tables together with copper lampholders. Do not look for sweets on the menu but after an onion and celery soup, herring with apples and mushrooms, and pork chop with prunes, they would in any case be superfluous.

Senoji Pasaga Vrublevskio 2/Tilto 1; tel: 262 7581. The 'Old Horseshoe' is a country-style tavern, complete with a cellar and a back garden with fountain, and serves a typically Lithuanian menu.

Stikliai Aludė Gaono 7; tel: 262 4501. This small basement restaurant has a predominantly local menu and makes a much cheaper but still highly recommendable alternative to the posh French restaurant in the hotel next door.

Stikli Bočiai Šv Ignoto 4/3; tel: 262 5141. This latest addition to the Stikliai group is set in a truly grand dining hall complete with open fires on which various meats are roasted. There is often live folk music in the evenings.

Sue's Indian Raja Ligoninės 7; tel: 261 2614. Offers a wide range of dishes from the Indian sub-continent, whose spiciness may come as a welcome antidote to a surfeit of milder local fare.

Sue Ka Thai Jogailos 11/2; tel: 262 3270. This shares the premises of the above, but serves Thai cuisine.

Tobira Šv Mykolo 4; tel: 260 2952. Lithuania's first Japanese restaurant got off to a sticky start, largely because it adopted a hybrid cooking style borrowing elements from the more familiar Chinese kitchen. Sensibly, it now concentrates on authentic sushi dishes.

Trys Draugai Pilies 25a; tel: 261 6296. The 'Three Friends' is on three different floor levels, and offers a variety of food, including local dishes, steaks and good though rather small-sized portions of Tex-Mex fare. Kapitonas Tenkešas in the cellars has a short menu of deliciously spicy Magyar dishes plus a decent choice of Hungarian wines.

Žemaičių Smuklė Vokiečių 24; tel: 261 6573 An amazing warren of a place, the 'Samogitian Tavern' offers a choice of dining experiences, ranging from the dark intimacy of the cellars (which are adorned with a series of fantastical murals) to the airy al fresco atmosphere of the courtyard's upper storey. A special strong beer is brewed exclusively for the tavern, which serves many traditional dishes and has live folk bands at weekends.

Fast-service restaurants

Afrika Pilies 28. A popular option for an express meal, with plenty of soups, salads and pancakes to choose from.

Čili With its pizzas and pastas, together with some Mexican sidelines, this is the most successful catering business in Vilnius. It now has nine branches all over the city, of which the most useful one for tourists is probably at Ukmergės 3a, opposite the Lietuva Hotel, and close to the Naujasis Vilnius and the Holiday Inn; others are at Didžioji in the Old Town and Gedimino 23 in the New Town. The website www.cili.lt has an up-to-date list of all their outlets.

Keisti Zenkliai Trakų 13. A good choice for a quick and tasty Lithuanian meal: order and pay at the counter before sitting down.

PVM Algirdo 8. An inexpensive daytime restaurant with a good range of hot and cold dishes.

Stikliai Stiklių 14/7. This self-service restaurant is the bargain-price member of the eponymous chain. It offers a limited but enticing array of salads, desserts and cakes.

Cafés

Alumnatas Universiteto 4. Situated alongside the university, this is a particularly recommendable choice for a summertime al fresco drink or snack, which can be enjoyed in the irregularly shaped triple-tier baroque courtyard to the rear.

Banga Vokiečių 26. A cybercafé with fast internet connections, charging 6Lt per hour. Open Mon–Thu 10.00–22.00, Fri and Sat 10.00–23.00, Sun 12.00–22.00.

Bar Italia Gedimino 3a. An Italian-style café, with a good range of coffee, freshly squeezed fruit juices, sandwiches and ice-creams, run by the same management as the Da Antonio restaurants.

Café de Paris Didžioji 1. Situated beside the French bookshop and cultural centre, the Gallic atmosphere continues here. Coffee and pancakes are taken seriously, though one suspects the tapes are shared with a local nightclub. Sit at the back to avoid the music, and to avoid feeling rushed.

Collegium Pilies 22. A combined cybercafé and art gallery, charging 8Lt per hour for internet use.

Gabi Šv Mykolo 6. A delightful café with a rustic interior and a side courtyard, right next door to the Amber Museum. One of the few places in the city to have adopted a strict no-smoking policy, it offers a full menu of homely Lithuanian dishes.

Greitai Totorių 1. In 2002, this was a cheap and cheerful self-service café conveniently situated opposite the main post office. The name means 'quickly' but this describes the speed of service, not the rate at which food has to be eaten. Hopefully when the new, grand Gedimino is opened in 2003, it will not feel the need to gentrify. Currently they do cakes best, but also have a range of filling hot dishes.

Kavos ir Arbatos Namai Presto Gedimino 32a. Serves a wide range of freshly ground coffees and teas.

Klubas Bazė Gedimino 50/2. This new cybercafé, which serves inexpensive snacks, is Vilnius' largest, and is open round the clock. It costs 6Lt per hour, 20Lt for the whole night.

Kolonos Daukanto 2. This cellar café with a small outdoor seating area is a good choice for pancakes, and also serves full meals.

Magdė Basanavičiaus 3. A small country-style café-restaurant at the eastern edge of the New Town.

Poni Laimė Gedimino 31. 'Ladies Happiness' is a mock-Parisian café run by the Stikliai chain. It offers a full menu, but is primarily recommendable for its cakes and desserts, and for the international deli dishes sold in the adjoining shop.

Skaunas Aušros Vartų 9. This café attached to a bakery is primarily of interest for its cakes and sweets, though savoury dishes are also available. Low prices ensure that it also has a Lithuanian clientele eager to try the increasing range of Western snacks now offered. The best souvenir from Vilnius can be bought here every morning – a loaf of black bread, which will keep for several days and which even a long-haul flight will not harm.

Skonis ir Kvapas Trakų 8. Set in a delightful suite of rooms off an old courtyard, this exquisitely furnished café presents a marvellous selection of teas and coffees from around the world. Diners at the Kaukazo Belaisve over the road sometimes adjourn here after their meal.

Soho Aušros Vartų 7 Opened in summer 2002, Soho has added a much-needed touch of irreverence to the eating and drinking scene between Town Hall Square and the Gates of Dawn. It is a convenient halfway house between a restaurant and a café so makes a good lunch stop for those who do not need much after indulging in a hotel buffet breakfast. Beef in coconut is one of several original dishes, but as important as the food are the Impressionist reproductions in each room, both of paintings and of posters.

Užupio Užupio 2. Predictably, the 'local' of Vilnius' bohemian quarter is a favourite with artists and students. Idyllically set by the River Vilnia, it has a spacious beer garden (the only one in Vilnius) and a contrastingly cosy interior. It is hard to predict what this café will be like during the currency of this book, as the area is racing through a transformation from slum to bohemian quarter to chic suburb, although in summer 2002 the shops and cafés had not yet caught up.

V002 Ašmenos 8. What was formerly a live music café-bar has been transformed into a quiet cybercafé charging 6Lt per hour. Open Mon–Fri 10.00–24.00, Sat and Sun 11.00–24.00

Vilanta Gardumynai Totorių 3. This is the nearest Vilnius comes to a British tearoom.

Pubs, bars and café-bars

Amatininkų Užeiga Didžioji 19/2. Plenty of inexpensive Lithuanian dishes, including a wide range of tasty starters, are available in this rambling bar with a snug cellar which remains open until 05.00. This bar closes only between 05.00 and 08.00, but many visitors will probably prefer its sedate air during the day rather than its liveliness in the evening, when the basement attracts large numbers with its wide-screen televisions and music that is loud, even by Lithuanian standards. The food is the Lithuanian answer to 'pub grub' with potato dumplings and plenty of red meat. Anyone on a diet should keep away.

Amerika Šv Kazimiero 3. The main draw here is the large courtyard, one of the most attractive spots for outdoor imbibing in the Old Town.

Angaras Jasinskio 14. One of the hippest addresses in the city, offering internet access from its cybercafé and regular live music.

Avilys Gedimino 5. This new home-brew pub has three products: Avilio, a standard light beer; Medaus, which is made with honey; and Korio, a dark ginseng beer. Plenty of other drinks, including a wide range of Tibetan teas, are also available, and there is a long menu which includes plenty of typical Lithuanian fare.

Betmenas Gedimino 32. The décor of this bar must be the most outrageous in the city, dominated as it is by the life-sized figure of Batman himself.

Bix Etmonų 6. Founded by the eponymous Lithuanian band as a rock music bar, though it also has a cellar with a more sedate atmosphere.

Brodvėjus Mėsinių 4. The beer tap in the guise of a saxophone is the most eye-catching piece of décor in this pub, which presents all kinds of live music, from rock to classical, each evening at 20.00.

Būsi Trečias Totorių 18. A pleasantly rustic bar on two floors. In the basement is Vilnius' first boutique brewery, whose single product can either be enjoyed neat, or mixed with perfumed cordial to make a 'cherry beer'.

Gero Viskio Baras Pilies 34. As its name suggests, this bar is primarily known for its range of whiskies, though it also serves a menu of mostly light dishes.

Jazz Club Vilniaus 22. This new venture in the basement of the Radvila Palace presents live jazz Mon–Sat 20.00–02.00.

Lithuanian Pub Vokiečių 8. Housed in a glass-covered courtyard with minimal décor, this is more like a restaurant than a pub, serving a good choice of reasonably priced national fare, including bargain set lunches. Underneath is the raucous Lithuanian Club.

Pieno Baras Didžioji 21. Seemingly belonging to a bygone age, this traditional milk bar serves hot milk and home-baked cakes at very low prices.

Prie Parlamento Gedimino 46. A convincing re-creation of an English pub, though it was actually founded by a New Zealander. It is regularly full of expats and English-speaking tourists, who come to enjoy juicy steaks, jacket potatoes, and traditional pub grub such as shepherd's pie and hot puddings. Downstairs is the hugely popular nightclub Ministerija, which is open 18.00–02.00 (04.00 on Fri and Sat).

Prie Universiteto (also known as **The Pub**), Dominikonų 9; tel: 261 8393. No competition has yet appeared for any Brit unable to survive abroad without shepherd's pie and a suitable brew to help it down. Lunchtime is pleasantly tame, and there's an attractive galleried courtyard, but the evenings get lively and the over 30s should probably retreat then. Full details of evening entertainment are on the easy-to-remember website, www.pub.lt.

Savas Kampas Vokiečių 4. This popular bar serves a wide range of food, including tasty lunchtime hotpots on weekdays. An atmospheric cellar is open in the evening, while in summer a large pavilion is rigged up outside.

Twins O'Brien Vokiečių 8. Irish pubs have mushroomed all over Europe in the past decade, and this establishment ensures that Vilnius residents do not miss out on draught Guinness and Irish stew. There are various imported beers on tap, plus a range of bistro-style dishes.

Entertainment
Theatres

Lėlė Puppet Theatre Arklų 5; tel: 262 8678. Housed in the baroque Oginskis Palace, this presents entertaining shows, mostly for children, though a few are pitched at an adult audience.

Lithuanian National Drama Theatre Gedimino 4; tel: 262 9771; web:www.teatras.lt. The city's main venue for straight dramatic fare, offering both traditional and avant-garde productions.

Opera and Ballet Theatre Vienuolio 1; tel: 262 0727; web: www.opera.lt. A varied programme of operas, operettas and ballets is staged in this huge concrete and glass building from the 1970s.

Russian Drama Theatre Basanavičiaus 13; tel: 262 7133. As its name suggests, it presents Russian-language performances.

Youth Theatre Arklų 5; tel: 261 6126. Housed in the same building as the Puppet Theatre, this company has gained a high reputation for its innovative stagings, and has made successful tours to the West.

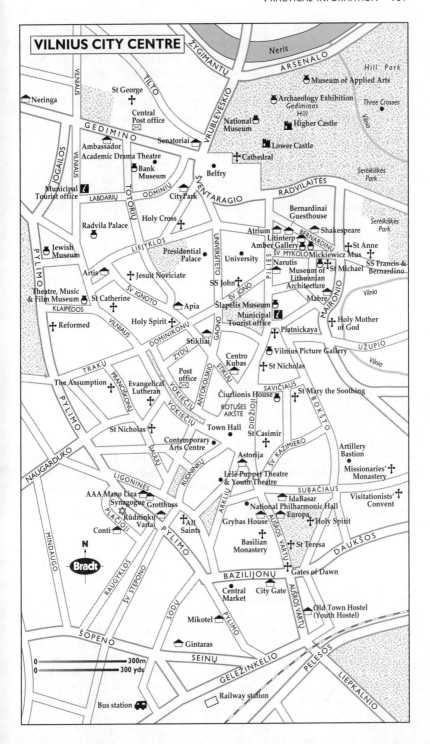

VILNIUS CITY CENTRE

Neris

Hill Park

ŽYGIMANTU

ARSENALO

VILNIAUS

TILTO

St George

Central Post office

Neringa

VRUBLEVSKIO

Museum of Applied Arts

Archaeology Exhibition
Gediminas Hill

Three Crosses

GEDIMINO

National Museum

Higher Castle

Senatoriai

Vilnia

Ambassador Academic Drama Theatre

Lower Castle

Cathedral

JOGAILOS

VILNIAUS

Bank Museum

ŠVENTARAGIO

Belfry

Sereikiškės Park

Municipal Tourist office

LABDARIŲ

TOTORIU

ODMINIŲ

CityPark

RADVILAITĖS

Bernardinai Guesthouse

Sereikiškės Park

Radvila Palace

Holy Cross

LIEIYKLOS

UNIVERSITETO

Atrium

Shakespeare

BERNARDINŲ

PYLIMO

Jewish Museum

Presidential Palace

University

Litinterp
Amber Gallery
SV MYKOLO

St Anne

Mickiewicz Mus

Narutis

SS Francis & Bernardino

Artis

Jesuit Noviciate

SS John

Museum of Lithuanian Architecture

St Michael

MAIRONIO

Theatre, Music & Film Museum

St Catherine

SV JONO

Apia

Šlapelis Museum

Mabre

Vilnia

KLAIPĖDOS

Holy Spirit

Municipal Tourist office

Holy Mother of God

Reformed

VILNIAUS

DOMINIKONŲ

GAONO

Pfatnickaya

UŽUPIO

Stikliai

ŽYDŲ

STIKLIŲ

Vilnius Picture Gallery

Vilnia

TRAKU

Centro Kubas

St Nicholas

PRANCISKONŲ

The Assumption

Post office

ANTOKOLSKIO

SAVICIAUS

St Mary the Soothing

Evangelical Lutheran

VOKIEČIŲ

Čiurlionis House

B.BOKŠTO

PYLIMO

VOKIEČIŲ

ROTUŠĖS AIKŠTĖ

NAUGARDUKO

St Nicholas

SAULIŲ

Town Hall

DIDŽIOJI

St Casimir

SV KAZIMIERO

Artillery Bastion

Contemporary Arts Centre

Astorija

Missionaries' Monastery

RŪDNINKŲ

Lėlė Puppet Theatre & Youth Theatre

SUBAČIAUS

Visitationists' Convent

LIGONINĖS

ARKLIŲ

IdaBasar

MINDAUGO

AAA Mano Liza

Synagogue

Grotthuss

National Philharmonic Hall

AUŠROS VARTŲ

Europa

PLAČIOJI

Rūdninkų Vartai

AH Saints

Grybas House

Holy Spirit

N

Conti

PYLIMO

Basilian Monastery

St Teresa

DAUKŠOS

Bradt

RAUGYKLOS

SV STEPONO

BAZILIJONU

Gates of Dawn

SODU

Central Market

City Gate

AUŠROS VARTŲ

0 ——— 300m
0 ——— 300 yds

Mikotel

PYLIMO

Old Town Hostel (Youth Hostel)

ŠOPENO

Gintaras

SEINŲ

GELEŽINKELIO

PELESOS

LIEPKALNIO

Bus station

Railway station

Music

In addition to the concert halls listed below, concerts and organ recitals are held in several Old Town churches, especially the cathedral, SS John and St Casimir. At the last-named, live music is normally performed every Sunday immediately after the last morning mass ends at around 13.00. Open-air concerts – which take place in the courtyards of the university and the Chodkevičius Palace, among other venues – are a regular feature of the city's musical life in summertime.

Concert and Sports Palace Rinktinės 1; tel: 272 8942. The main venue for large-scale pop concerts.

Congress Centre Vilniaus 6/14; tel: 261 8707 or 261 8127; web: www.lvso.lt. Between mid-September and mid-June, there are regular concerts by the Lithuanian State Symphony Orchestra, usually on Friday evenings.

Music Academy Gedimino 42; tel: 261 2691. In term-time, there are usually several public recitals every week by students and staff.

National Philharmonic Hall Aušros Vartų 5; tel: 212 2290; web: www.filharmonija.lt. The country's leading concert hall presents an enticing programme of orchestral, choral and chamber concerts and organ, piano and song recitals by both Lithuanian and foreign artists. Throughout the season, there are regular concerts by the Lithuanian National Symphony Orchestra on Sunday at 19.00.

St Christopher Chamber Music Club Šv Ignoto 6; tel: 262 3114. The former Jesuit Noviciate is the home of the St Christopher Chamber Orchestra, a versatile and very active body which also performs in other venues.

Festivals

Vilnius hosts an extremely varied programme of festivals throughout the year, including the following:

Užgavėnės The climax of the Carnival season celebrations is held on Shrove Tuesday (variable date in February or March) on Tauro Hill.

St Casimir's Market The feast-day of Vilnius' very own saint is on March 6. Associated with it is a handicrafts market in the Old Town, which lasts for several days.

Skamba skamba kankliai A colourful annual festival of folk-song and dance, held throughout the city, usually on the last weekend in May. It features invited groups from abroad as well as performers from all over Lithuania.

Rasos The midsummer solstice is celebrated on the evening of June 23 on the White Bridge.

St Christopher Summer Music Festival Throughout July and August, there is a wide range of concerts of all types of (predominantly classical) music. They take place at a variety of venues, many in the open air, with the majority given by Lithuanian performers.

World Lithuanian Song Festival This massive six-day event is held in early July, usually at four- or five-yearly intervals, with the next set for July 1–7 2003. The first two days are mainly devoted to rehearsals; on the third, the participating groups assemble in Sereikiškės Park for informal performances. Each of the last three days climaxes in a spectacular open-air concert: the first, held in the Hill Park, is given by song and dance ensembles; the second, in the Žalgiris Stadium, by dance troupes (with no singing); the third, in Vingis Park, by choirs (with no dancing). The last-named makes an awesome climax, featuring up to 12,000 singers on the Song Dome stage at a time.

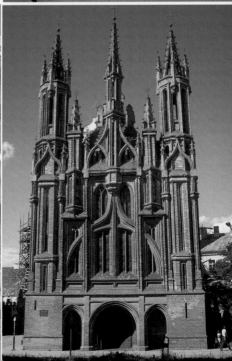

Above University Church, Old Town Vilnius (RR)

Right Calvary Market, Vilnius (GM)

Below left Houses on Town Hall Square, Vilnius (RR)

Below right 16th-century Gothic St Anne's Church, Vilnius (JS)

Above Evening view of the Pregolya River and the old German red-brick Gothic Dom (cathedral), founded in 1333, Kaliningrad (JS)

Right Hammer and sickle emblem on a bridge over the River Pregolya, Kaliningrad, with the cathedral in the background (JS)

Below The red-brick Dohna Tower, part of Kaliningrad's old defensive ring, now housing the Amber Museum (JS)

Day of Statehood On July 6 there is a solemn military procession with banners, followed by an open-air concert of patriotic songs and operatic arias with orchestral accompaniment.
Vilnius International Summer Fair and Street Events Festival The week-long fair in mid-August features a crafts market, complete with an ethnographic village, in Sereikiškės Park. During the last four days, pageants and street theatre are held throughout the Old Town.
Three Days Three Nights A three-day beer festival on the last weekend of August or the first weekend of September in Vingis Park.
Banchetto Musicale A festival of early music, held in September.
Film Festival A week-long cinematic festival in mid-September.
Fire Sculptures Festival A celebration of the September 21 autumn equinox in Kalnu Park.
Jazz Festival Aa festival of avant-garde jazz, held over three days in the first half of October.

Cultural institutes
America Centre Pranciškonų 3-6; tel/fax: 266 0330
British Council Vilniaus 39-6; tel: 261 6607; fax: 212 1602; email: mail@britishcouncil.lt; web: www.britishcouncil.lt
Jewish Cultural Centre Šaltinių 12; tel: 215 0387; fax: 215 0389

Shopping
Competition from shopping malls in the suburbs is forcing town-centre shops to put potential customers before staff. Most shops of interest to tourists are now open seven days a week, although bookshops still stay firmly closed on Sundays. In general, shops stay open until around 19.00 during the week, but tend to close around 17.00 on Saturday and Sunday.

Amber
Amber Gallery Šv Mykolo 8. The excellent gallery has a shop alongside where authenticated pieces of amber and amber jewellery can be purchased.
Sagė Aušros Vartų 15. Another highly reputable dealer in genuine amber artefacts.

Bookshops
Akademinė Knyga Universiteto 4. As its names suggests, this is a good source for scholarly books on Lithuania and they have a wide range of what is published in English. They are the best outlet for books on Jewish Lithuania.
Dalininkų Sajungos Parodu Salė Vokeičių 2. The Painters' Union Exhibition Hall sells not only paintings, amber and ceramics, but also has a large selection of art books, including many in English.
Draugystė Gedimino 2. A general bookstore with some English-language titles.
Littera Šv Jono 12. With its elaborate frescoed interior, the bookshop within the university complex is undoubtedly the most attractive in the city, and has a decent representation of English-language books about Lithuania, as well as journals, magazines and postcards. This is also the best place to obtain copies of the English-language literary magazine *Vilnius*. On the minus side, the staff are rude, the stock is chaotic, and the lighting is poor.
National Museum Bookshop Arsenalo 1. The ticket office to the museum has a reasonable selection of books in English on Lithuanian art and history.

Department stores

Valstybinė Universalinė Parduotuvė Gedimino 18. A typically wide-ranging Soviet-era department store, still going strong.
Vilniaus Centrinė Universalinė Parduotuvė Ukmergės 16. The city's largest department store.

Souvenirs

Dailė Žydų 2/2. Sells a wide range of Lithuanian handicrafts.
Sauluva Pilies 22. Housed in a fine old courtyard, this is the largest souvenir shop in Vilnius, selling ceramics, glassware, woodcarvings, leather goods and many other traditional artefacts, including candle houses which are made to order.

Medical services

Baltic-American Medical and Surgical Clinic Antakalnio 124; tel: 234 2020; tel/fax: 276 7942; email: bak@takas.lt; web: www.baclinic.com. A US joint-venture, this is the only hospital in the Baltic States offering fully Western standards.
Medical Diagnostic Centre Grybo 32; tel: 270 9120. There are English-speaking doctors on the staff.

Pharmacy

Gedimino Vaistinė Gedimino 27. Open 24 hours.

Embassies and consulates

Australia Vilniaus 23; tel/fax: 212 3369; email: aust.con.vilnius@post.omnitel.net; web: www.dfat.gov.au
Belarus Muitinės 41; tel: 213 2255; email: bpl@post.5ci.lt
Belgium Kalinausko 2b; tel: 266 0820; fax: 212 6444; email: vilnius@diplobel.org
Canada Gedimino 64; tel: 249 6853; fax: 249 6898; email: vilnius@canada.lt
Denmark Kosciuškos 36; tel: 215 3434; fax: 231 2300; email: dkemb@taide.lt; web: www.denmark.lt
Estonia Mickevičiaus 4a; tel: 278 0200; fax: 278 0201; email: sekretar@estem.lt
Finland Klaipėdos 6; tel: 212 1621; fax: 212 2441; email: finemb.vilnius@omnitel.net; web: www.finland.lt
France Didžioji 1; tel: 212 2979; fax: 212 4211; email: amba-fr-vilnius@post.omnitel.net; web: www.centrefrancais.lt
Germany Sierakausko 24/8; tel: 265 0272; fax: 213 1812; email: germ.emb@takas.lt
Italy Tauro 12; tel: 212 0620; fax: 212 0405; email: ambitvilnius@post.omnitel.net
Japan Čiurlionio 82b; tel: 231 0462; fax: 231 0461
Latvia Čiurlionio 76; tel: 213 1260; fax: 213 1130; email: lietuva@latvia.balt.net
Netherlands Didžioji 13-13; tel: 212 4085; fax: 212 4084; email: hollandhouse@eunet.lt; web: www.netherlandsembassy.lt
Norway Poškos 59; tel: 272 6926; fax: 272 6964; email: norambvilnius@aiva.lt; web: www.norvegija.lt
Poland Smėlio 20a; tel: 270 9001; fax: 270 9007; email: ambpol@tdd.lt
Russia Latvių 53/54; tel: 272 1763; fax: 272 3877; email: rusemb@rusemb.lt
Sweden Didžioji 16; tel: 268 5010; fax: 268 5030; email: ambassaden.vilnius@foreign.ministry.se; web: www.ud.se
Ukraine Teatro 4; tel: 212 1536; fax: 212 0475; email: ukrembassy@post.5ci.lt; web: www.5ci.lt/ukrembassy

UK Antakalnio 2; tel: 212 2070; fax: 272 7579; email: be-vilnius@britain.lt; web: www.britain.lt

USA Akmenų 6; tel: 266 5500; fax: 266 5510; email: mail@usembassy.lt; web: www.usembassy.lt

Places of worship

Grace Baptist Church Verkių 22; tel: 231 6062. English-language service every Sunday at 11.00.

International Lutheran Church Vokiečių 20; web: www. icvilnius.org. Ecumenical service in English every Sunday at 09.30.

St John's Church (in university) Mass in English every Sunday at 16.00

SS Philip and James Lukiškių aikštė 10. Roman Catholic Mass in English every Sunday at 09.00, with confessions beforehand on request.

Synagogue Pylimo 39. Friday evening at 19.00.

WHAT TO SEE
City walk

Start at the Gates of Dawn (Aušros Vartų) and walk down to the Town Hall Square past the Russian Orthodox church and St Casimir. Continue along Pilies and turn right along Šv Mykolo, passing the Amber Museum. This leads past the Architecture Museum to St Anne's Church. Return to Pilies along Bernadinų, and turn right to face the cathedral. To the right is the castle and the National Museum. Turning left from the cathedral into Universiteto, the Presidential Palace soon comes into view. To the left of the palace are the university buildings. The continuation street of Universiteto is Gaono, which leads into the former Jewish quarter around the Stikliai Hotel. Turning left at the hotel into Stikliu, and Town Hall Square is just a 300m walk.

Old Town

Vilnius' Old Town (*Senamiestis*) is among the most extensive in Europe, occupying a total of 255 hectares, and including over 1,000 protected monuments, among them outstanding masterpieces not only of baroque, but also of Gothic, Renaissance and neo-classical architecture. A great deal of cleaning and other restoration work has been carried out since independence was achieved, though many fine buildings languish in a semi-derelict state, a situation which is likely to persist for many years to come.

There are two distinct parts to the Old Town. The site of the original settlement, which includes the castles, the cathedral and the areas of greenery surrounding them, is no longer inhabited, and now forms an island of calm in the midst of the city centre. Across the bustling Šventaragio and Radvilaitės streets lies the much larger part of the Old Town, which came into being after the threat from the Teutonic Knights had been eliminated. Although it has become a tourist magnet in recent years, it is far from being a museum piece. Some of it is still residential, it retains the main university campus, has plenty of shops and offices, and is well-endowed with places to eat and drink. It preserves its chaotic medieval layout, in which twisting narrow alleys are juxtaposed with a central thoroughfare divided into three distinct parts and several huge open squares. Almost every street is worth a look, and a detailed exploration of all the important sights requires several days. Much of the Old Town is either pedestrianised or has severe restrictions on vehicular access, so it can really only be seen on foot.

Cathedral

Vilnius' cathedral, which is dedicated to SS Stanislaus and Ladislaus, occupies the site of an ancient pagan temple to the god Perkūnas, and originally lay within the fortification system of the Lower Castle. The first church on the site was erected in the 13th century, following the ostensible conversion of King Mindaugas. When the nation officially reverted to heathen ways, the Perkūnas temple was re-instated, but was replaced by another church when Christianity was introduced in 1387 following the royal union with Poland. Under Vytautas the Great, this was supplanted by a more splendid Gothic cathedral, which underwent repeated alterations down the centuries, before being almost totally rebuilt between 1783 and 1801 to plans by Laurynas Gucevičius. Even if its neo-classicism makes it something of an outsider in the predominantly baroque townscape of Vilnius, it is a majestic building none the less, one of the most important churches in the style anywhere in Europe. Under the Soviets, it served as an art gallery for 32 years, but in 1989 was restored to its role as the seat of the local archbishop.

The façade has a portico of six Doric columns and a rosette-encrusted vault. On the tympanum above is a carving depicting The Sacrifice of Noah by an Italian sculptor, Tommaso Righi, who was also responsible for the five small reliefs and the niche statues of the Four Apostles and the Patriarchs Abraham and Moses on the entrance wall. Atop the tympanum, and visible from afar, the figures of SS Stanislaus and Casimir flank St Helena, who bears the gilded True Cross. These huge statues, which were put in place in 1996, are reproductions of the originals, which were destroyed by Soviet decree. The north and south sides of the cathedral are closely harmonised with the façade. Both have colonnades with six columns, with the former having niche statues of saints, the latter of Grand Dukes.

The interior is laid out in the form of a spacious hall, with a grand central area and narrow aisles with chapels. Its focal point is the high altar, which is shaped like the front of a classical temple, and shelters a large painting of The Martyrdom of St Stanislaus by Franciszek Smuglewicz, the founding director of the Vilnius School of Art. On the altar table is an exquisite gilded silver tabernacle from the 1620s, whose panels depict Christ Washing the Disciples' Feet and The Last Supper. A complete series of the Apostles by Smuglewicz forms the upper tier of paintings hanging on the columns of the nave. In the west gallery is the organ, which preserves a splendid 18th-century case; most of the pipework dates from 1969, though some 19th-century registers survive.

It is sometimes possible to visit the vaults underneath the cathedral on application to the shop by the entrance; the best time to try is around 11.00, when pre-booked groups are often escorted round. On view are altars used for pagan worship, as well as fragments of the medieval churches which occupied the site. Particularly intriguing is a late 14th-century fresco of The Crucifixion with the Virgin and St John, the oldest surviving monumental painting in Lithuania. Several royal coffins can also been seen, among them that of the highly esteemed Barbora Radvilaitė, the second wife of Zygmunt August and herself a member of one of Lithuania's most powerful families.

Of the small chapels off the cathedral aisles, the third on the south side is of particular note. It belonged to the Goštautus family, and contains a 17th-century painting of miracle-working properties, *The Adoration of the Virgin Mary* by SS Francis and Bernardino, and two magnificent tombs by 16th-century Italian Renaissance masters. The monument to Albertas Goštautas, Chancellor of the Grand Duchy and Governor of Vilnius Province, was carved by Bernardo Zanobi, and is the oldest memorial sculpture in Lithuania. That to Bishop Povilas Algimantas Alšėniškis is by the most celebrated of the Italians who dominated artistic life at the Polish-Lithuania court, Giovanni Maria Mosca 'Il Padovano'. The first chapel on the same side houses a painted wooden crucifix from the early 18th century, while the second chapel on the north side, which was the property of the Valavičius family, features some impressive stuccowork.

The **Chapel of St Casimir**, which is entered via a resplendent portal from the southern aisle, is the only important part of the previous cathedral which survives in an unaltered state. In order to integrate it into his new design, Gucevičius added a sacristy on the northern side which copies its distinctive outline of a square lower storey surmounted by an octagon supporting a cupola with lantern. The chapel was built between 1622 and 1636 by the Italian Constantino Tencalla in order to house the mortal remains of St Casimir (1458–84), Lithuania's patron saint. Work on the sumptuous interior, which is faced with luxuriant black, white and coloured marble, continued for a century after its construction. Much is by itinerant Italian masters. Hiacinto Campana painted the ceiling frescos, Michelangelo Palloni the side frescos of *The Opening of the Coffin of St Casimir* and *The Miracle of the Coffin of St Casimir*, while Pietro Peretti (or Perti) created the lavish stucco backdrop to the silver shrine. In front of the shrine is a curious little portrait of the saint, dating from the 1520s, in commemoration of his beatification. The only painted sections uncovered by the intricate 18th-century silver frame are Casimir's head – and three hands. Other 18th-century additions to the chapel are the eight niche statues of Lithuanian Grand Dukes, and the unusual movable pulpit, which is shaped like a goblet.

Katedros aikštė (Cathedral Square) is a vast paved space on the south and west sides of the cathedral which makes an ideal starting or finishing point for parades and processions. Since 1996, it has been the setting for the **Monument to Grand Duke Gediminas** – a particularly appropriate location, as it must be close to the spot where he had his legendary dream about the iron wolf. The commission for the statue was entrusted to the veteran sculptor Vytautas Kašuba, who had spent most his career in America and died soon after the monument was erected. That Gediminas is shown with his sword in his left hand is an allusion to his supposed preference for diplomacy over war – though in reality he used both to achieve substantial territorial gains for the Grand Duchy.

The focal point of the square is the **belfry**, a combined bell and clock tower which is a favourite local rendezvous point. It has had a curious history. Its round lower storey, which is pierced by numerous gunports, dates back to the 14th century and belonged to the fortification system of the Lower Castle; indeed, it is the only part of this which survives to this day. In the 1520s it was converted into the cathedral's bell tower by the addition of two octagonal tiers. The following century, a fourth tier was added to house a clock which still preserves its original mechanism. In 1893 it finally assumed its present appearance when it was crowned with a small steeple.

Lower and Higher Castles

The **Lower Castle** (open daily 10.00–17.00/19.00, with guided tours at 14.00 and 15.30), which in the 16th century was transformed into a splendid Renaissance-style Royal Palace for Zygmunt the Old, was the main residence of Lithuania's Grand Dukes. Unfortunately, the finest parts of the complex, which had a stately triple-tiered courtyard as its centrepiece, were pulled down by the Tsarist authorities in 1802, leaving only a number of ancillary buildings. However, highly fruitful archaeological excavations have been carried out on the site over the past decade, uncovering the foundations of the palace, which can now be seen under a protective roof. There is an ambitious plan to reconstruct the building over the course of the present decade, though only time will tell if this actually comes to fruition. In the meantime, visitors can wander around the excavations and also see a small exhibition of the artefacts which have been dug up, including a series of glazed ceramic tiles depicting coats-of-arms and fantastical creatures.

A path to the rear of the cathedral leads up the 48m-high Gediminas Hill to the **Higher Castle** on its summit. The walk is steep but by late 2003 a funicular railway from behind the National Museum should offer an alternative.

The original wooden fortress was replaced in the late 14th century and early 15th century with a brick and stone Gothic castle which featured three towers, a palace, a chapel and various other buildings. Badly damaged in the wars of 1655–61, it was thereafter abandoned, only to be revived as a fortress by the Russians following the 1831 uprising. A wooden superstructure containing an optical telegraph was built on top of the truncated western tower, the only one of the three which was retained. This was removed in 1930, and replaced by a reconstruction of one of the two octagonal storeys which had previously been lopped off.

Nowadays it can be taken for granted that the Lithuanian flag will be raised at the Castle every day. It was first raised on January 1 1919 but by the end of 1920 Poland was firmly in control of the city and it would be 1939 before the flag was seen again. Its appearances over the next five years would be brief as the Nazi and Soviet armies fought for control over Lithuania and from 1944 onwards it would be banned. It was raised again on October 7, 1988 as a courageous act of defiance towards the Soviet authorities who tried to maintain their authority for a further two-three years, giving up only in August 1991. At long last, there seems little threat to its long-term survival.

Nowadays designated the **Castle Museum** (open daily 10.00–17.00/ 18.00/19.00), the tower contains displays of historic arms and armour, plus models showing the changing appearance of Vilnius' medieval fortification system. However, the main attraction is the wonderful view from the observation platform on top. As all the main landmarks of the Old Town are clearly visible (the only publicly accessible place where this is so), it makes an ideal place to begin or end a tour of the city. Looking north, little seems to have changed since Soviet days with endless dreary blocks of flats, straight wide roads and tall factory chimneys. Looking east the Three Crosses stand out (see page 161). Looking west from the castle, beside the river, is St Raphael's Church. The nicest view is clearly to the south, where the Old Town will hopefully remain intact.

Normally, the best light for photography is in the later part of the day. Other than the tower, little remains of the Higher Castle, save for the ruins of the palace and fragments of the outer walls.

National Museum of Lithuania

Just to the north of the cathedral is the 18th-century New Arsenal, which now houses the National Museum of Lithuania (open Wednesday–Sunday 10.00–17.00). The history of the Grand Duchy is evoked in a display of portraits, weapons, books, textiles, prints, liturgical objects, coins and sundry other artefacts. Those of particular aesthetic appeal include the 15th-century treasury door of the nearby Bernardine Friary, the baroque banner of the Handcraftsmen's Guild, the 17th-century vestments of a Uniate bishop, the embossed leather sleigh of the Tiškevičius family, and a Meissen vase decorated with coats-of-arms honouring the dynastic union of Saxony and Lithuania. There is also an extensive folk art section, which is grouped by region and features iron crosses, wooden statues, painted chests, embroidery, costumes, pottery, masks, lace, baskets and decorated Easter eggs.

Next door, in the 17th-century western extension to the Old Arsenal, is the **Archaeology Exhibition** (open Wednesday–Sunday 10.00–17.00; wheelchair access), which was inaugurated in 2000, using modern display techniques which put those of its old-fashioned parent museum to shame. The exhibits are arranged chronologically in two large rooms, the first of which ranges from the Paleolithic Era of the 11th millennium BC up to the time of Christ. Šventoji, the Baltic port which is now part of Palanga, has yielded some particularly rich finds from the third and fourth millennia BC, including a metre-long upturned boat, a clay bowl in the shape of a vessel, a wooden pole statue, ceremonial sticks and ladles with animal and bird heads, and amber jewellery. Upstairs, the era leading up to the formation of the Lithuanian state is documented by thematic displays on barter, agriculture, metallurgy, pottery, horse and rider, arms, spinning and weaving, and silver, all of which are copiously illustrated with excavated objects. There are several impressive silver hordes, notably one consisting of brooches, necklaces and ingots from Štakliškės. The culture of the various different tribes who lived in and around the territory that is now Lithuania is imaginatively illustrated by means of dummies decked out with reconstructions of the clothes, weapons and jewellery they wore, while the intact contents of several excavated graves of the period are also on view. Finally, in the entrance hall is a horde of 15,950 coins, mostly Lithuanian and Polish copper shillings of the 17th century, which were probably stowed away by a local merchant when the Swedes occupied Vilnius in 1702, and only rediscovered in 1999.

Museum of Applied Arts

The original Old Arsenal, a hybrid Gothic-Renaissance building of the 16th century, is now home to the Museum of Applied Arts (open Tuesday–Sunday 11.00–18.00), which at present is entirely devoted to the really marvellous exhibition Christianity in Lithuanian Art. Beautifully displayed and lit, this celebrates both the new millennium and the 750th anniversary of King Mindaugas' coronation in 1253; it was opened in the final days of 1999, and is due to close on October 30 2003. Although some of the exhibits belong to the Lithuanian Art Museum and were previously on view in this building and in its various other branches throughout the city, many others, which have been borrowed from churches and private collections throughout the country (with a few lent from abroad), had seldom or ever been on public view. It must be hoped that some means will be found of keeping at least part of the exhibition on permanent display, as it has given Vilnius the world-class museum it otherwise lacks.

The centrepiece of the first-floor displays is the Vilnius Cathedral Treasury, which has had a decidedly eventful history. Over the centuries, monarchs, nobles, bishops and clergymen endowed it with masterpieces of decorative art made in some of the most prestigious European workshops. It suffered many losses in the 17th-century wars against the Russians and Swedes, but continued to be augmented by important new gifts. In 1939, it was bricked up for safekeeping in a false wall of the cathedral, and for several decades was believed lost. However, it was found in 1985 by three local men who kept their discovery secret from the Soviets for fear it would be carted off to Moscow; only in 1998, when the country's independence was reckoned to be fully secure, was the public officially informed. A 14th-century French ivory diptych of four scenes from the life of Christ was, it is believed, given by Pope Urban to Grand Duke Jogaila on the occasion of the latter's marriage and baptism in 1386, and subsequently donated to the cathedral at the time of its foundation. The oldest chalice on display was made in the 15th century in Danzig (Gdańsk); the stipula or ritual stick used by the cathedral's precentor is of the same era. From the following century are a huge gilded monstrance and a crystal cross-reliquary, both of which were given by the Goštautas family. A particularly rich group of 17th-century artefacts includes a gold monstrance studded with precious stones and enamels given by Bishop Jurgis Tiškevičius, and three pieces donated by Bishop Mikalojus Steponas Pacas – the reliquary of St Mark Magdalene dei Pazzi from Florence, and the spectacularly florid monstrance and chalice made in the German city of Augsburg. Of special note among the 18th-century objects is the sarcophagus-reliquary of Josaphat Kincevitius, a martyred Uniate archbishop.

Displayed alongside the cathedral treasures are items of comparable quality from elsewhere in Lithuania. Notable artefacts from other churches in Vilnius include the 16th-century monstrance from the Church of the Holy Spirit; the ciborium given to the Church of SS John at the end of the same century by Jurgis Radvila, the first Lithuanian to gain a cardinal's hat; and the 18th-century silver-plated antependium or altar front from SS Peter and Paul. From the Church of the Assumption in Trakai are the 17th- and 18th-century crowns made to adorn the surround of The Madonna of Trakai, and an 18th-century monstrance incorporating an ex-voto of the double-headed Austrian eagle donated by Contance von Habsburg, the wife of Zygmunt III, when she visited the town in 1611. There are several treasures from Kaunas Cathedral, notably a 17th-century monstrance made in Königsberg and another by an Augsburg goldsmith of the following century.

On either side of the treasury chamber are halls devoted to the Vilnius and Samogitia bishoprics. These feature galleries of portraits of the bishops themselves, though all are of provincial quality save for that of Povilas Algimantas Alšeniškis, a penetrating example of Italian Renaissance portraiture by Giovanni dal Monte. There are also copious examples of the quite different liturgical garments favoured in the two dioceses down the centuries. The Vilnius gallery features an important piece of furniture in an 18th-century credence made from birch with intarsia, gilded bronze, leather and veneering. Vilnius Cathedral's collection of French and Flemish tapestries – which include mythological and genre scenes as well as religious subjects – are on display throughout the first floor, notably in the Grand Chamber at the northern end, which also features a small display on the background to King Mindaugas's coronation.

Upstairs, the gallery of paintings is mostly devoted to lesser-known masters, though there are a few outstanding works, including two prime examples of Netherlandish Mannerism: *St Ursula and the Martyrs* by Bartholomeus Spranger, court artist to Emperor Rudolf II in Prague; and *An Allegory of the Old and New Testaments*, a Protestant tract by Cornelis van Haarlem. There are also some characteristic 17th-century Italian canvases, such as *Christ in the Tomb* by Lodovico Carracci, *St Paul the Hermit* by Salvator Rosa, *Mater Dolorosa* by Carlo Dolci; a few Spanish works, including *Head of the Crucified Christ* by Luis Morales and *Penitent Mary Magdalene* by Francisco Ximenez; and a fine *Lot and His Daughters* by the leading exponent of Austrian baroque, Johann Michael Rottmayr. Several large and archetypally baroque altarpieces which the Polish artist Szymon Czechowicz painted for various Vilnius churches are also on view.

Likewise on the first floor are areas devoted to Lithuania's religious minorities. A display of icons includes examples from Orthodox, Old Believers and Uniate congregations. The section on Protestantism highlights the crucial role the Reformation played in the development of Lithuanian as a written language, and displays early editions of some of the key books, including the earliest of all, Martin Mažvydas's *Cathechism*. There are also a number of krikštai, the distinctive grave crosses which can still be seen on the Curonian Spit, and some splendidly austere 17th- and 18th-century silverware from the Calvinist stronghold of Biržai.

The exhibition concludes with an outstanding display of folk art in all its many religious manifestations. This is dominated by numerous examples of the wooden crosses which are such characteristic features of rural Lithuania.Around a score of those on view are by the acknowledged master of the genre, Vincas Svirkis (1835–1916), who spent his whole life moving continually from village to village and farm to farm, leaving behind crosses which typically incorporate high reliefs of saints or religious scenes clearly influenced by the baroque art of the 18th century. A set of four dozen coloured drawings by Kazys Šimonis show crosses in their original locations. The pomp associated with local religious festivals is evoked by some splendid processional banners and lanterns mounted on poles, while smaller devotional figures, paintings, embroideries and miscellaneous liturgical objects further illuminate the sheer diversity of the Lithuanian tradition.

Bernardine churches

At the extreme eastern edge of the Old Town, on the far side of Sereikiškės Park, which stretches south from Gediminas Hill, is the **Bernardine Friary**. An offshoot of the Franciscan Order, the Bernardines arrived in Vilnius in 1469. They initially built a wooden church on the site, which was granted to them by Grand Duke Kazimierz, but this was destroyed by fire.

Its replacement, the brickwork **Church of SS Francis and Bernardino**, was erected at the beginning of the 16th century under the patronage of the Radvila (Radziwiłł) family. Unusually large by the standards of medieval Lithuania, it is in the hall church style (with nave, aisles and chancel of equal height), and features some spectacular examples of late Gothic vaulting. Following repeated damage by fire and in war, the church was given a twin-turreted Renaissance façade, though the single tower on the southwest side was restored to its original Gothic form. The baroque Chapel of the Three Kings, which is used for weekday services, was added in 1632. Among several impressive funerary monuments in the nave is that to Stanislovas Radvila by Willem van den Block, the leading Renaissance sculptor of Danzig (now Gdańsk). In the Soviet era, the church was allowed to fall into a dilapidated state. It is now back in Franciscan hands, and for some years past has been the subject of what will be a very long-term restoration programme.

The much smaller and better-preserved **Church of St Anne** in front is undoubtedly the most celebrated building in Lithuania. According to an oft-quoted tradition, Napoleon was so captivated by it that he declared his wish to carry it back to Paris in the palm of his hand, and it has long been an inexhaustible source of inspiration to local painters and photographers. No fewer than 33 different shapes of brick were employed in the construction of its unforgettable flamboyant Gothic façade, which is symmetrical in appearance, being twice as high as it is broad. Its decoration is a bravura medley of extravagant ogee arches, narrow oriel windows, slender pinnacles, openwork octagonal towers and crocket-studded steeples. When lit by the setting sun, the upwardly sweeping lines take on a truly incandescent appearance.

For all its fame, the church is something of a mystery, there being no general agreement as to exactly what its function was in relation to the friary, nor exactly when and by whom it was built. Until recently it was thought to have been constructed by German masters at the very end of the 15th century, though new evidence suggests that the façade, at least, is not older than the mid-16th century and is the work of local craftsmen. In dramatic contrast to the exterior, the inside of the church is disarmingly modest, though it does preserve some fine original vaulting. The detached belfry, which was added in 1873, imitates the elaborate brickwork of the church, but fails to rise above the level of a pastiche.

Directly across the street is the former **Church of St Michael**, built between 1594 and 1625 by order of Leonas Sapieha, Chancellor of the Grand Duchy of Lithuania, to serve as a convent for Bernardine nuns, as well as a mausoleum for his own aristocratic family (also known as Sapiega or Sapiegos). The only important Renaissance building to survive in the city, the church has an elaborate façade with a massive central pediment, twin turrets, and pilasters with capitals bearing stylised depictions of leaves of the rue (rūta), the national flower of Lithuania. In the early 18th century, a wall was constructed round the church in order to create an enclosed courtyard for processions. Entry to the complex is now via a sturdy baroque tower which serves as both belfry and gateway.

Most of the furnishings of the hall-like interior, which boasts a richly stuccoed vault, were stripped away by the Soviets, but several Sapieha memorials remain. The most prominent is a 10m-high red marble monument commemorating the founder and his two wives; also of note is that to Stanislovas Sapieha, which has an eccentric location above the sacristy doorway. Since 1971 the church has housed the **Museum of Lithuanian Architecture** (open Monday 11.00–17.00, Wednesday–Sunday 11.00–18.00). This is divided into two sections, the first featuring plans of the main architectural projects, notably public buildings in Kaunas, undertaken during the inter-war republic. Particularly intriguing are rejected designs for a visionary neo-Gothic appearance for the

Church of the Resurrection. The post-war part of the display concentrates on housing projects and the re-creation of Trakai's Island Castle.

A short walk across the Vilnia River behind St Anne's leads to the area of **Užupis** (outside the Old Town), which only came to fame well after independence. In the early 1990s, as in the Soviet period, it was charitably described as the 'bohemian' quarter if it was mentioned at all. Guidebooks from both periods chose to ignore it given its obvious squalor and years of neglect. The name means 'Beyond the River', but it was beyond much else as well. That it has suddenly become respectable is due to the shrewdness of the mayor of Vilnius, Arturas Zuokas, who not only bought a house there but was happy for this to be known. Suddenly Užupis has been transformed. It advertises itself as the local Montmartre. Though you'll look in vain for artists with long hair, politician and celebrity spotting will be easy – at least for Lithuanians. The designer shops have not yet arrived, nor have expensive restaurants, but architects and builders have certainly been busy.

By declaring itself a republic (naturally on April 1), by granting rights in its 'constitution' to cats and dogs, by erecting a statue of an egg and then two years later by putting an angel on it, and by bringing the Dalai Lama during a visit to Vilnius in summer 2001, the area ensures that it never leaves the public eye. Take a camera and a sense of humour for a stroll likely to last about half an hour. The serious may wish to visit St Bartholomew, a 19th-century church now used by the Belarussian community. It suffered long periods of closure under both the Tsars and the Soviets but the exterior has been restored and work is underway inside.

Rest of the northeastern quarter

Bernardinų, which follows a winding northwesterly course from the Church of St Michael, is one of the best-preserved streets of the Old Town, lined with many splendid urban mansions. The **Mickiewicz Museum** (open Tuesday–Friday 10.00–17.00, Saturday and Sunday 10.00–14.00) at Bernardinų 11 has been set up in the courtyard building where the great Romantic poet Adam Mickiewicz (known to Lithuanians as Adomas Mickevičius), who had previously spent four years in Vilnius as a student at the university, lodged for two months in 1822. It was during this stay that he wrote the Byronic verse tale *Grażyna*. Old editions of Mickiewicz's main works are on display in the museum, as well as paintings and engravings showing Vilnius as it was in the poet's day. A memorial to Mickiewicz can be seen nearby, just a few paces to the south of the Bernardine Friary. Designed in 1984 by Gediminas Jokubonis, this shows the influence of the Socialist Realist style of which the sculptor had long been a favoured practitioner. Just to the north is the gleaming white Orthodox Church of the Holy Mother of God. There has been a church on the site since the late 14th century, though the present building dates mainly from the 1850s.

At No 8 on Šv Mykolo, an atmospheric old street running west from the Church of St Michael, is the **Amber Gallery** (open daily 10.00–19.00). Like its pioneering counterpart in Nida, which is owned by the same family, this offers informative displays on the geology of 'Baltic gold', as well as temporary exhibitions of amber jewellery. There is also a shop selling fully authenticated pieces of amber and amber artefacts.

Both Bernardinų and Šv Mykolo terminate at Pilies, the northern part of the Old Town's central axis. Stalls selling handicrafts can be found all along the street, and these increase greatly in number and quality whenever a festival is taking place. Of particular note among a picturesque jumble of buildings of various dates are the Renaissance mansion at Pilies 4 and the gabled Gothic houses at numbers 12 and 14. Pilies 26 is now designated the **House of the Signatories** (open Monday–Thursday 08.00–16.00, Friday 08.00–15.45), as it was there, on February 16 1918, that Lithuania's declaration of independence was signed, with a similar document signed 72 years later on March 11 1990. On the second floor is a small museum devoted to the event. Due to the lack of any surviving original material, it has to improvise, displaying some furniture of the period plus a set of modern portraits of the signatories based on old photographs. The first and ground floors both have exhibition rooms where temporary artistic and photographic displays are held. The balcony from which Jonas Basanavičius in 1918, and Vytautas Landsbergis in 1990, spoke to the crowds is open to visitors. It offers a good opportunity for taking photographs of St John's Church and of the now very calm Pilies.

The downstairs section of the **Šlapelis Museum** (open Wednesday–Sunday 11.00–16.00) at Pilies 40 is a recreation of the pioneering Lithuanian bookshop established in 1906 by Jurgis Šlapelis and his wife Marija Šlapelienė. Jurgis was born in 1877 and Marija in 1880, so they grew up during the Tsarist ban on Lithuanian literature which was only lifted in 1904. Although there was no such ban under Polish administration from 1920 to 1939, Lithuanian studies were clearly not encouraged. Jurgis was a fully qualified doctor and he combined his medical practice with publishing; Marija was the bookseller. Displayed in the couple's flat above, which is entered from the courtyard, are books and other objects associated with the national cultural revival they did so much to promote. It is one of the very few places in Vilnius that features life during the Polish era, showing attacks on the couple in the local press, and the letters they received from abroad (those posted from Lithuania simply had 'Vilnius' on them; to have added 'Poland' would have been unacceptable).

Backing on to the western side of Pilies is the sprawling university campus whose main public entrance is from Universiteto, the next street to the east.

University

It is fitting that the university is by far the largest and most prominent complex of buildings in the Old Town, as it has played a key role in the life of Vilnius since its foundation in 1570, despite suffering many vicissitudes at Russian hands over the past two centuries – it was closed down altogether between 1832 and 1919, and for most of the Soviet period was forced to tailor its activities to Marxist-Leninist dogma. Grouped around no fewer than 12 courtyards is a picturesque huddle of structures of widely varying dates and aesthetic merit. In a somewhat opportunistic attempt to extract money from the many visitors to the complex, the authorities have recently introduced what are supposedly set opening times (Monday–Saturday 09.00–17.00/18.00) and an entrance charge. However, the only benefit gained by buying a ticket is the woefully inadequate sketch map available in several languages from the cash desk. In practice, anyone can, as before, wander in and look around discreetly.

Payment of the entry fee does not even result in access to the **University Library**, which is entered via the doorway labelled Vilniaus Universitetas on the south side of the courtyard opening directly on the Universiteto. Officially, this is now only open to pre-booked groups, though a sympathetic attendant may grant individual access to the oldest room (reached by taking two consecutive left turns then descending a short flight of stairs), which is known as Smuglevičius Hall in honour of the neo-classical painter Franciszek Smuglewicz, who frescoed the vault. The central scene shows the Holy Trinity blessing the Madonna of Mercy, who shelters a group of Jesuits under her cloak. On the spandrels above the windows are monochrome trompe l'oeil busts of distinguished scholars of Classical antiquity. A small selection of the library's most valuable books and manuscripts is displayed in the show-cases.

Immediately behind the library is the **Astronomical Observatory**, the fourth oldest surviving example of its type in the world. Built between 1753 and 1773 by Tomas Žebrauskas (Thomas Żebrowski), the Professor of Mathematics and Astronomy, it is actually two separate observatories, one of which occupies the entire length of the building, with a smaller one above. No longer in use, the interior is not generally accessible, but the peaceful courtyard to the rear offers a fine view of the building's façade, with its handsome portal, twin turrets and frieze of zodiacal symbols.

A gateway at the northeastern corner of the Library Courtyard leads into the Sarbievijus Courtyard, which is named in honour of Maciej Kazimierz Sarbiewski (1595–1640), who served as Professor of Rhetoric, Philosophy and Theology but is better known as a prolific writer of both sacred and secular Latin verse. At the far end is the **Littera Bookshop**, whose interior is covered with a colourful fresco scheme painted by Antanas Kmieliauskas in 1978–79. Inspired by the Vatican frescos of Michelangelo and Raphael, this pays symbolic tribute to the subjects which have loomed largest in the university's history.

A small hall on the first floor of the **Centre for Lithuanian Studies** next door is decorated by an even more ambitious fresco cycle entitled *The Seasons*, which Petras Repšys completed in 1985 after nine years' work. There are over a hundred different scenes, illustrating episodes from Lithuanian history and mythology as well as work, pastimes and popular customs. Also worth seeking out is the classically inspired coloured stucco frieze of *The Nine Muses* by Rimtautas Gibavičius which can be found on the first floor of the Philology Department in the Daukantas Courtyard immediately to the north.

A large archway on the southern side of the Sarbievijus Courtyard leads into the **Great Courtyard**, which is also known as the Skarga Courtyard in honour of Piotr Skarga, the Jesuit scholar who was the university's first rector. The academic buildings lining three of its sides were erected in the early 17th century in the mannerist style which marks the transition from Renaissance to baroque. All along their lower storey are open arcades which impart a sunny Mediterranean flavour, even if the local climate is only occasionally warm enough for them to be enjoyed to best advantage. Between the pilasters are faded 18th-century frescos portraying important figures in the history of university.

The eastern side of the Great Courtyard is closed by the **Church of SS John**, which was founded by Grand Duke Jogaila immediately after his conversion to Christianity and completed in 1426. A presbytery and apse were added to the original hall church after it was allocated to the Jesuit college in 1571, and much of the Gothic fabric is clearly visible underneath the overlay added between 1738 and 1749 by Jan Krzysztof Glaubitz, the presiding genius of the final phase of Vilnius baroque. The monumental façade, in which the plain horizontal rustication of the lowest storey forms a dramatic counterpoint to the sweeping vertical emphasis of the elaborately contoured tiers above, ranks among the greatest achievements of the style. Almost equally impressive is the assemblage of ten interconnected altars which together make up the high altar. There are memorials honouring, among others, Adam Mickiewicz, Tadeusz Kościuszko and Stanisław Moniuszko, the Polish composer who served as the church's organist from 1840–58. Of the six side chapels, the most elaborate is that dedicated to St Anne, which has both an ornate portal and a carved altar of Christ as the Tree of Life.

Nowadays, the building has a curious double life, serving as the university church once again, yet still retaining its Communist-era role as the **University Science Museum** (open daily 10.00–17.00) – hence the scattering of cases displaying old scientific tracts. The detached **belfry**, one of the Old Town's most prominent landmarks, was built in the first decade of the 17th century and raised to its present height as part of the programme of baroque renovations.

Northwestern quarter

Daukanto aikštė, the triangular space immediately west of the university, is dominated by the vast pile of the **Presidential Palace**. The Bishop's Palace which had stood on the site since the 14th century was remodelled to serve as the residence of the Russian Governor-General, and Tsar Alexander I and Napoleon both held court there in the fateful year of 1812. Between 1824 and 1832 this was expanded and rebuilt by a Russian architect, Vassily Stasov, in late neo-classical style. In Soviet times it served first as a dance-hall for army officers before becoming the Artists' Palace in 1975. In the first years of independence it was the French Embassy, before assuming its present role, following a costly refurbishment, in 1997.

In August 2000 the palace started opening on Fridays and Saturdays for pre-booked groups. A tour showing the main reception rooms, the president's office and the gardens takes about 45 minutes. The furnishings are entirely modern, but the designs are from the early 19th century. Oak and birch are the main woods used. One room has four large portraits of the previous Lithuanian presidents, three from the 1920–40 period and one of Algirdas Brazauskas, in office 1993–98. An even larger painting shows Vytautas the Great riding into the Black Sea, when the Polish-Lithuanian Commonwealth stretched that far in the mid-15th century. American visitors may notice the parallels with the White House in the press room and in the size of the lawns outside. This is not surprising as Valdas Adamkus, president from 1998 to 2003, spent all his working life in America and has aimed to bring many working practices there into both the public and the private sector in Lithuania.

Opposite stands the modest little **Church of the Holy Cross**, a foundation of the Bonifratrian Order, which came to Vilnius in 1635. The original building was remodelled in the course of the first half of the 18th century, and the twin towers, pediment, porch and exterior fresco of The Madonna and Child all date from this period. The Soviets renamed it the Baroque Hall and used it for concerts, but it now functions as a place of worship once more. Beside the church is a monument to Laurynas Gucevičius, architect of the cathedral and Town Hall.

At Vilniaus 22, towards the far northwestern edge of the Old Town, is the **Radvila Palace** (open Tuesday–Saturday 12.00–18.00, Sunday 12.00–17.00). Built in the 17th century for Jonušas Radvila, Grand Hetman of Lithuania, this splendid urban palace has been much altered subsequently, and now serves as a branch of the Lithuanian Art Museum. One room is devoted to a gallery of 165 portrait engravings of members of the dynasty commissioned by Mykolas Kazimieras Radvila from an amateur artist, Herszek Leybowicz (1700–70). Apart from an unexpected collection of Oceanic art, the rest of the display space is given over to old master paintings, graphics, furniture and decorative art. Most of the former are by little-known artists; among the few works of special note are *Venus and Cupid* by Antoine Pesne, the French-born court painter to Frederick the Great of Prussia, and several fine examples of 17th-century Dutch painting, including *The Allegory of the Owl and the Birds* by Melchior d'Hondecoeter, *The Old Mill* by Meindert Hobbema and *The Waterfall* by Jacob van Ruisdael.

A little further up the same street is the **Church of St Catherine**, which originally belonged to a Benedictine convent founded in 1618. Following a series of fires, it was rebuilt between 1741 and 1753 by Jan Krzyzstof Glaubitz. In order to overcome the restricted nature of the site, he adopted an audacious design based on a nave which is as high as it is long. The exterior features an elaborate rear-facing gable as a counterbalance to the majestic twin-towered façade; the interior is richly furnished, but has not been accessible for many years because of ongoing restoration work. A statue of Stanisław Moniuszko stands in the garden in front of the church.

Diagonally opposite, at the corner with Trakų , is a long, low-lying baroque palace which was formerly another of the Radvila properties. For the first 15 years of Tsarist rule, it housed the municipal theatre; nowadays it contains the Lithuanian **Theatre, Music and Cinema Museum** (open Tuesday–Friday 12.00–18.00, Saturday 11.00–16.00). Now one of the largest, but least-known museums in Vilnius, it offers a mixture of temporary exhibitions and permanent displays on the history of the performing arts in Lithuania. The star exhibit is a recently acquired stage curtain painted by Mikalojus Konstantinas Čiurlionis (1875–1911), who has the unusual distinction of being both the best-known composer and the most famous artist Lithuania has ever produced. For those unable to visit the gallery in Kaunas devoted to his work, this seascape is a good introduction to his style. It dates from 1909, his most productive year, just before depression and pneumonia led to his tragically early death. The costumes, stage sets, masks, puppets and photographs cover the whole 20th century and belie the fraught political environment from which the theatre and cinema could sometimes provide relief. The more technically minded will be interested in the gramophones and film-projection equipment. Sadly, labels throughout are only in Lithuanian so it is sensible to visit with a guide.

Šv Ignoto, a block to the east of Vilniaus, is named after the Church of St Ignatius, part of the former **Jesuit Noviciate**, a vast 17th- and 18th-century baroque complex with three large courtyards. Following the suppression of the Order in 1773, the buildings served successively as a seminary and a barracks; they are now home to, among others, a commercial art gallery, a technical library and the St Christopher Chamber Orchestra.

Šv Ignoto leads to Dominikonų, which takes its name from the Dominican friary established there in 1501. Its Church of the Holy Spirit, one of the most extravagant manifestations of Vilnius baroque, was one of the few churches kept open during the Soviet years, and is nowadays the main place of worship for the Polish-speaking community. Although retaining some of the fabric of its fire-ravaged 17th-century predecessor, its main features – the dome, the side gables and the sumptuous array of furnishings and decoration which give the interior an almost Rococo appearance – date from the second half of the 18th century. A sculptor of German origin, Franz Ignatius Hoffer, designed the assemblage of 16 artificial marble altars and the curious pulpit, which is combined with the confessionals below in a single unit. Also of note is the elegant tribune gallery housing an organ whose richly carved case with statues of King David and angel musicians still shelters the original pipework.

Didžioji

The Old Town's central thoroughfare changes its name from Pilies to Didžioji at a little square which has become an open-air gallery. Forming a backdrop to this is the **Piatnickaya Orthodox Church**, the favoured place of worship of the younger members of the Russian community. Although the church's present appearance is the result of a remodelling carried out in the 19th century, it was originally built in 1345 for Marija, the wife of Grand Duke Algirdas, and was the place where the grandfather of the great Russian poet Alexander Pushkin was baptised.

Immediately to the rear is the baroque Chodkevičius Palace, which was adapted to house the **Vilnius Picture Gallery** (open Tuesday–Saturday 12.00–18.00, Sunday 12.00–17.00), a branch of the Lithuanian Art Museum, when the latter was forced to vacate its previous premises in the cathedral. The early 19th-century interiors on the first floor form a setting for period furniture, objets d'art and paintings, including portraits of Mickiewicz by Valentinas Vankavičius, and of the arts patron Duke Mykolas Oginskis by Francois Xavier Fabre. One room on the floor above is devoted to portraits of leading lights of 18th-century Lithuania, including that of Chancellor Jonas Sapieha by Silvestre de Mirys, an artist born in France to Scottish Jacobite exiles. There then follows a large collection of paintings by Franciszek Smuglewicz and his successors at the Vilnius Academy of Arts, plus a display of architectural drawings by Laurynas Gucevičius. The participants in the celebrated exhibitions of Lithuanian art in the first decade of the 20th century dominate the final rooms of the circuit, with the little paintings entitled *Storm* and *Mountains* by Čiurlionis being among the very few works by him outside his memorial museum in Kaunas.

A few paces further on, just before the point where Didžioji broadens out to form Rotušės aikštė (Town Hall Square) is the **Orthodox Church of St Nicholas**, which was originally built in a hybrid Gothic-Byzantine style in 1514. In 1609, the church was granted to the Uniates, remaining in their hands until 1827. Extensive renovations were carried out in the 1860s, when a neo-Byzantine façade and belfry were erected and a new iconostasis added to the interior.

The two wings of the Radisson are split by Arklių Street and it is worth making a short detour to visit the courtyard of the Youth Theatre on the right-hand side. The theatre was the headquarters of the 'Judenrat' – the Jewish Council imposed by the Germans to run the ghetto from 1941 until its liquidation in 1943. Desperately little of Jewish Vilnius now remains, but the modernist sculpture unveiled in the courtyard in October 2000 is meant to be seen as a flame of hope, and not only as a memorial to the 200,000 Jews killed in Lithuania during the Holocaust.

Tucked away in a courtyard at Savičiaus 11, the next street to the south, is the **Čiurlionis House** (open Monday–Friday 10.00–16.00), the home of the composer-artist during his residency in Vilnius. It often hosts recitals of his music, but unfortunately contains no original paintings by him. A little further along the same street stands the **Church of St Mary the Soothing**, which was formerly part of an Augustinian friary. Built between 1746 and 1768, it was among the last of Vilnius' great series of baroque churches, and is dominated by its elegantly tapering single tower which displays clear classicising tendencies. Now in a totally decrepit state, it is awaiting a much-needed restoration.

Coincidentally, the nearby Jesuit **Church of St Casimir** at the southern end of Didžioji marked the debut of the baroque style in the city. It was begun in 1604, just two years after Casimir's canonisation, and completed in 1618. Although probably designed by the Italian Giovanni Maria Bernardoni, it was built by a local architect, Jan Prochowicz. Despite being modelled on the Jesuits' much-imitated mother church of Il Gesù in Rome, the addition of twin towers (which are now lower than when first built) give it a distinctive Lithuanian accent. The crown atop the lantern of the central dome was added as recently as 1942 in recognition of St Casimir's royal lineage. In 1966, in a humiliating affront to Lithuania's Catholics, the Soviet authorities installed a Museum of Atheism in the church's bare interior. However, it was returned to the Jesuits in 1988, and a strong musical tradition has since been established.

Immediately opposite, its grand Doric portico fronting the square named after it, is the former **Town Hall**. Designed by Laurynas Gucevičius, it was built between 1781 and 1799 on the site of its medieval predecessor. The municipal offices have long since moved elsewhere, though the building is still used for receptions. It also functions as an 'Artists' Palace', and as such its foyer is regularly used to show-case contemporary Lithuanian arts and crafts.

Southwestern quarter

Vokiečių, which leads northwest from the Town Hall, was widened considerably as part of a 1950s' planning project, and now has a pedestrianised area down the middle. The new layout necessitated the demolition of part of the former **Ghetto** to the east, including the 17th-century Great Synagogue on Žydų, which lost its roof during the Nazi occupation period but otherwise survived largely intact. In recent years, there has been talk of re-instating it. A monument on Žydų commemorates Eliyyahu ben Shelomoh Zalman (1720–97), otherwise known as the Gaon of Vilna, one of the greatest Talmudic scholars of all time and a virulent opponent of the revivalist Hasidic movement.

At the head of Vokiečių, right alongside the Town Hall, is the concrete and glass **Contemporary Art Centre** (open daily 11.00–19.00). Although an ugly blot on the face of the Old Town, it provides much-needed display space for exhibitions which are predominantly, but not exclusively, of the works of living artists. Upstairs is a permanent display on Fluxus, the experimental art movement founded in the United States by the Lithuanian-born George Maciunas.

Hidden away at the back of a courtyard at Vokiečių 20 is the **Evangelical Lutheran Church**. Vilnius' first Protestant church was established on the site in 1555. The present building, a plain baroque preaching hall which is whitewashed both inside and out, was built in the 1740s by Jan Krzysztof Glaubitz, with the neo-Romanesque belfry being added in 1872. The focal point of the interior is the high altar, which adapts traditional Catholic forms to the requirements of Lutheran doctrine, giving a prominent role to the carved depiction of The Last Supper.

Šv Mikalojaus, the little street immediately to the east, is named after the Church of St Nicholas at its far end. An unassuming example of the Gothic brickwork style, it is the oldest intact church in Lithuania, and the only one pre-dating the official adoption of Christianity in 1387, having been built earlier in the century to serve the German merchants and artisans who had made the city their home.

According to tradition, the **Church of the Virgin Mary**, situated a short distance to the northwest on Pranciškonp, was founded by Franciscan missionaries before the mass conversion of Lithuania. However, the present building, constructed between 1773 and 1785, is in a classicising baroque style, and while it incorporates a few fragments of its Gothic predecessor (notably the façade portal and the crystalline vaults of the south aisle), these appear to be 15th century in date. Having been closed since 1949, the church was handed back to the Franciscans in 1998, leaving them with the massive task of repairing the worn fabric and bringing the faded frescos back to life.

On Rūdninkų, close to the now-vanished western gate to the Old Town, is the **Church of All Saints**, formerly part of a Carmelite friary. The main body of the church was built in 1620–31 and is modelled on the Jesuits' Il Gesù. The single bell tower was not added until 1743 and is somewhat more elaborate in appearance, but none the less blends in well. What would otherwise be a rather plain interior is enormously enlivened by the kaleidoscopic colours of the somewhat folksy carvings and paintings adorning the altars.

Southeastern quarter

The southernmost section of the Old Town's central axis is known as **Aušros Vartų** (Gates of Dawn) after the gateway at which it terminates. On the western side of the street, the first major landmark is the **National Philharmonic Hall**, which was built in 1902. The massive street frontage, built in the fin-de-siècle eclectic style, seems rather out-of-scale in comparison with the concert hall itself, which is of very modest dimensions. None the less, it is the most important venue in the country for classical music, and has also hosted some fateful political meetings, including the 1940 'application' for Lithuania to be admitted to the Soviet Union.

A bit further up the same side of the street is the **Basilian Monastery**, which takes its name from the Uniate monks who settled there in 1608. Access from the street is via the entrance gateway, a swaggering baroque masterpiece built in 1761 to designs by Jan Krzysztof Glaubitz. Its gable bears a carved depiction of the Holy Trinity, this being the dedication of the now very dilapidated church in the courtyard behind, which was originally built in 1514 but much altered down the centuries. A congregation of Ukrainian-speaking Uniates currently worships there. For six months in 1823–24, Adam Mickiewicz was imprisoned in a cell in the monastery for anti-governmental activities, and was shortly afterwards deported from Lithuania, never to return.

Across the street, again in a secluded courtyard, is the Orthodox **Church of the Holy Spirit**. It is the most important Orthodox church in the country, though its external appearance differs markedly from all the others, being very obviously a product of the Vilnius baroque style, with only the merest traces of Russian influence. Indeed, it is in large part the work of Jan Krzysztof Glaubitz, who was entrusted with rebuilding the original 17th-century church following a fire in 1749. Glaubitz is also believed to have designed the colossal lurid green iconostasis, which incorporates baroque paintings of the life of Christ in addition to traditional icons. In front of the altar, a baldachin shelters the miraculously preserved bodies of SS Anthony, Ivan and Eustachius, whose feet can be seen peeking out from under their shrouds. The trio were servants at the court of Grand Duke Algirdas but were martyred for their faith in 1347 as a result of a militant pagan backlash against the previous policy of religious tolerance.

Back on the street a short distance beyond stands Vilnius' most Italianate building, the **Church of St Teresa**, which was designed for the Discalced Carmelites by Constantino Tencalla, and built between 1633 and 1652. The façade, the only part erected under Tencalla's direct supervision, is a strikingly vertical composition culminating in a pediment adorned with the coat-of-arms of the aristocratic Pacas (Pac) family, who provided funds for the construction. Following a fire in 1760, the interior was provided with a new set of furnishings, and the walls were frescoed by Mateusz Sluszczański. The scenes he painted in the nave illustrate the life of the church's patron, the Carmelite mystic St Teresa of Avila.

A stairway to the rear of the church, up which pious penitents hobble on their knees, leads to the so-called **Gates of Dawn**, Lithuania's most famous place of pilgrimage. Disabled people and beggars can almost invariably be found outside the gateway, which once formed part of the city wall and is the only one of the nine it formerly had which survives. When viewed from the south its original defensive function is still obvious, but the northern side looks completely different, having been revamped in neo-classical style in 1829 in order to provide a chapel to house the reputedly miraculous image of The Madonna of Mercy. Despite adopting the form of a traditional icon, this was probably painted in the early 17th century and was later provided with a gold and silver setting which covers the entire picture except for the face and hands. Densely hung ex-votos left by grateful pilgrims are attached to the wall panels of the chapel.

The other significant surviving fragment of the municipal defences is the **Artillery Bastion** (open Wednesday–Sunday 10.00–17.00), which is reached by following Šv Dvasios in a northeasterly direction. This was built in the early 17th century in order to provide extra protection for the nearby Subačius Gate. It consists of three parts: a tower on a round base, a horseshoe-shaped gallery for firing cannon, and an underground tunnel. The bastion encloses a natural hillock, from which there is a good, albeit partial, view over the Old Town.

New Town

In the 19th century, the New Town (Naujamiestis) was built immediately to the west of the Old Town, in the process engulfing a few older buildings which had hitherto stood in isolation. In addition to serving as the commercial and administrative heart of the city, it is also a residential area, its streets lined with large tenements which were originally thrown up to house a rapidly growing population.

Pylimo

Pylimo is the street which marks the boundary between the Old and New Towns. Near its southern end, at the corner with Bazilijon , is the rather cramped **Central Market**. Downhill, on the left-hand side of the street, is the Synagogue, the only survivor of the hundred or so Jewish temples Vilnius had prior to World War II. Built at the turn of the 20th century, it is modelled on Moorish architecture. Above the doorway is a depiction of the tablets of the Ten Commandments.

Somewhat further down, on the opposite side of the street, is the **Reformed Church**, which was built in 1830–35 by Karolis Podčašinskis, the leading local practitioner of the late neo-classical style. It is fronted by a giant Corinthian portico surmounted by a tympanum carved with a scene representing Christ Preaching to the People. The interior, which was converted into a cinema in 1958 but has now been returned to the local Calvinists, is a large hall covered with a coffered wooden vault. Normally it is only open for services (usually on Sundays at 18.00).

Housed in a tenement building at Pylimo 4, a short distance to the north, is the **Lithuanian State Jewish Museum** (open Monday–Thursday 09.00–17.00, Friday 09.00–16.00). On the first floor are displays of liturgical objects, dolls used for theatrical performances during the Feast of Purim, prints and drawings of Vilnius' Great Synagogue, and photographs, supplemented by a few tantalising fragments, of the wonderfully elaborate wooden synagogues, all now destroyed, which once graced several Lithuanian towns. Two rooms on the floor above are dedicated to a photographic record of memorial sites throughout Lithuania to victims of Nazism, and to a gallery honouring those who sheltered or otherwise saved Jews.

Round the corner, at Pamėnkalnio 12, the wooden **Green House** (open same times) serves as an annexe of the museum, with a documentary display focusing on Jewish culture and life in Vilnius and Lithuania immediately before World War II, and its destruction during the Holocaust. Outside stands a monument entitled *Moonlight*, which commemorates Chiune Sugihara, the Kaunas-based Japanese diplomat who is credited with rescuing up to 6,000 Jews.

In autumn 2001, a new Jewish Centre was inaugurated at Naugarduko 10. Dogged by persistent controversy, it is not yet open to the public, though it is likely that it will eventually supplant the two existing Jewish museums.

Gedimino

Gedimino, the New Town's central boulevard, stretches for 1.75km along a straight east–west line. Its name has changed many times since it was laid out in the early 1850s, with the appellations chosen almost invariably reflecting the nationality and ideology of the authorities of the time. Indeed, the present honouring of Grand Duke Gediminas, a historical figure with impeccable Lithuanian credentials, is as politically motivated as some of the names (which include those of Piłsudski, Hitler, Stalin and Lenin) bestowed on the street in the past.

The easternmost of the three large squares which open out from the northern side of Gedimino is Savivaldybės aikštė. On its northern side is the **government building**, which was formerly the seat of the Central Committee of the Lithuanian Communist Party, while on the eastern side are the **municipality** headquarters. Incorporated within the latter complex is a secluded courtyard, round which are the baroque buildings of a former convent of the Discalced Carmelites, centred on the **Church of St George**. Designed by Franz Ignatius Hoffer, this lacks a tower, but has a striking tiered façade; the interior is unfortunately not accessible at present.

Just off the south side of the square, at Totori 2, is the **Bank of Lithuania Museum** (open Wednesday and Thursday 09.00–12.00 and 13.00–14.30, admission free), which has two exhibition rooms. The first of these displays coinage of the Grand Duchy of Lithuania, the earliest dating back to the late 14th century, plus a few maps and plans. In the second room are Ostmarks issued by the German occupying forces during World War I, the currency of the inter-war republic, Soviet-era roubles and the trial printing sheets for the Litas banknotes which were introduced in 1993. Excellent documentary information in English on all the exhibited material is provided free of charge, and commemorative coins, most of which have wildlife themes, are on sale. The coin collection covers the 250 years from the 15th to the early 18th century when Lithuania, as part of the Commonwealth with Poland, was able to mint its own coins. There is then a long gap until 1922 before Lithuania was able to control its currency again, but by then the Poles had occupied Vilnius so the bank had to move to Kaunas with the rest of the government. It is often forgotten how powerful Germany remained in Eastern Europe between 1918 and 1922 since the armistice was only a surrender in the West, not in the East. The exhibition shows a wide range of the Ostmark that circulated between 1915 and 1920 in territory which would later become Poland and Lithuania.

It was fortunate that Lithuania could break from the German financial system just before the hyperinflation of 1923. Many of the litas bank notes and coins on display from the 1922-1940 period were produced in Britain. The Soviet occupation quickly imposed roubles on Lithuania and it was not until October 1992 that they were withdrawn from circulation. The museum shows examples of the temporary 'talonas' that circulated in 1992-93 and then of the new litas that have circulated since June 1993. Several display cabinets are needed to show the range of rejected designs. The bank notes finally accepted are printed in the USA and Japan, but coins are now minted in Lithuania itself.

The next square to the west, Lukiškių aikštė, was where the leaders of the 1863 rebellion were executed. On the far northern side is the baroque **Church of SS Philip and James**, which was begun in 1690 but not completed until 1748, when the twin towers were raised to their present height. A Dominican foundation, the church has a strikingly geometric appearance, with its single nave being exactly as high as it is long. It is the only church in Vilnius to hold regular masses in English.

A statue of Lenin once stood in the little park in the middle of the square, facing the KGB headquarters. The latter, originally built in 1899 by the tsarist authorities to serve as a courthouse, is now designated the **Museum of Lithuanian Genocide Victims** (open Tuesday–Sunday 10.00–18.00). In due course, it is intended to present a full documentary record on Soviet repression against Lithuania (particularly the Siberian deportations), and on the resistance to it. In the meantime, the cells in the basement, which were used for the imprisonment and torture of political opponents until 1991, can be visited. These include an isolation cell which has neither heating nor windows, a special padded and soundproofed cell for suicide risks, and two cells where water torture was administered in order to keep prisoners constantly awake. There is documentary material on some of the most prominent victims, while sacks of incriminating documents shredded by the KGB in the final three years of Soviet rule are also on view. Also open to the public is the former execution chamber. Great efforts were made to conceal this activity from the other prisoners, including naming the area the 'kitchen' and delaying executions until the spring, when removal and burial of the bodies became easier. Labelling throughout the museum is in idiomatic English.

Towards the eastern end of Gedimino is Nepriklausomybės aikštė. Despite its name ('Independence Square'), it is dominated by two of the most prominent buildings of the communist era. The **National Library**, which is built in a debased modern version of neo-classicism, is a typical example of the cultural 'gifts' Moscow was wont to bestow on subsidiary republics and satellites. Ironically the **Seimas** (Parliament) alongside, which is no more distinguished from an architectural point of view, has gained an honoured place in the Lithuanian consciousness, being the place where the restoration of national independence was declared on March 11 1990.

Outside the city centre

Vilnius' suburbs have a generous endowment of sights, and while most of these lie off the beaten tourist track, a few rank among the best-known landmarks of the city.

Rasos, Paupys and Markučiai

The **Rasos Cemetery**, which takes its name from the district in which it lies, is about 1km southeast of the Gates of Dawn, on the opposite side of the rail tracks. Its leafy, undulating site, which looks particularly wistful in autumn, contains the graves of some of Lithuania's most revered citizens. The tombstone of the composer-painter Čiurlionis is directly uphill from the main entrance, while that of Jonas Basanavičius, cultural guru and founder of the newspaper *Aušra*, is just across from the chapel. More controversially, the heart of Józef Piłsudski, who bears the primary responsibility for Poland's annexation of Vilnius in 1920, is buried in the family plot to the left of the entrance; the rest of his body lies in the Polish national pantheon in Krakow's Wawel Cathedral.

Ras leads from the western side of the cemetery to the district of Paupys and the former **Visitationists' Convent**, which directly overlooks the Old Town. At the heart of the complex is the domed Church of the Heart of Jesus, the only one of Vilnius' baroque churches built to a Greek-cross design. Although a prominent feature of the city's skyline, the church can only be seen from afar, as the whole convent is currently a prison enclosed within a high wall topped with barbed wire.

The former **Missionaries' Monastery** opposite is now a hospital and is likewise inaccessible, although at least good close-up views can be had of the exterior of its Church of the Assumption, which was begun in 1695 and remodelled by Jan Krzysztof Glaubitz in 1750–54. As with the Church of St Catherine in the Old Town, which he worked on at the same time, the architect concentrated attention on the monumental façade, so giving the building a sense of grandeur which belies its small size. The slender five-storey twin clock towers are unlike any others in Vilnius, being clearly influenced by those of the German-speaking lands.

Subačiaus leads eastwards from the Missionaries' Monastery to the residential district of Markučiai, at the far end of which is an extensive park in which stands the **Pushkin Memorial Museum** (open Wednesday–Sunday 10.00–17.00), a large wooden homestead which belonged to Alexander Pushkin's son Grigorij (1835–1905) and his wife Varvara (1855–1935). The ground floor is furnished according to Russian upper-class taste of the time, with a large ceramic stove being a feature of each of the main public rooms. Upstairs is a small exhibition on the works of Pushkin and their dissemination in Lithuania.

The wooded **Hill Park** (Kalnų Parkas), which stretches northwards from Užupis to the Neris embankment, is one of the city's most popular recreation areas. Towards its northeastern end is the Song Valley, an open-air auditorium which is regularly used for a variety of folklore events. In medieval times, the Crooked Castle, one of the city's trio of fortresses, crowned the 91m hill above, one of the city's highest points. In its place are the **Three Crosses**, which first appeared there in the 17th century. According to tradition, they were erected to commemorate early missionaries of the Franciscan Order who were martyred for their faith. Substitute concrete crosses were erected in 1916, but these were destroyed by the Soviets in 1950. The present crosses were put in place on June 14 1989 to coincide with the inauguration of the annual festival of the Day of Mourning and Hope, which commemorates Lithuanians deported to Siberia after World War II.

Church of SS Peter and Paul

Situated in splendid tree-framed isolation at the edge of the Antakalnis district, immediately east of the Hill Park, is the Church of SS Peter and Paul, which was founded in 1668 by Mykolas Kazimieras Pacas (Michał Kazimierz Pac), Grand Hetman of Lithuania and Governor of Vilnius, and granted to a congregation of Lateran Canons. The design of the church, whose main external features are a squat, twin-towered façade and a large central dome, was entrusted to a Polish architect, Jan Zaor, who supervised the construction work for several years before being replaced by Giambatista Frediani, who worked simultaneously on the Pacas dynasty's other prestige project, the Pažaislis Monastery outside Kaunas.

When the fabric was completed in 1675, local sculptors were commissioned to make the façade statues. Pacas was dissatisfied with the results, and accordingly invited two masters from the Lake Como region of northern Italy, Pietro Peretti (or Perti) and Giovanni Maria Galli, to take charge of the decoration of the interior. Between 1677 and 1685 the Italian duo created a stuccowork scheme of stupendous richness and variety, in the process transforming the pleasant but unexceptional shell of the building into a high baroque masterpiece, one which has been regarded ever since as among the crowning glories of Lithuania's cultural heritage.

There are over 2,000 human figures, each of them differently characterised, though these form but a small part of the overall scheme, which also features carvings of plants (including accurately depicted local species), flowers, trees, mythological creatures, grotesques and purely decorative elements. The iconographic programme behind the decoration is highly complex and often symbolic. For example, the many battle scenes are a reference to Pacas's status as Lithuania's most senior soldier, while the recurrent fleur-de-lis was his family emblem, and several of the saints depicted in hagiographic fashion were those with whom his dynasty had a special affinity.

Instead of aisles, there are two chapels on either side of the nave. Those on the north are dedicated to the Holy Queens and to St Augustine, the patron of the Lateran Canons; those to the south to the Warrior Martyrs and to St Ursula and the Virgin Martyrs. The last-named chapel, with its coolly beautiful statue of St Mary Magdalene alongside a virtuoso relief of a palm tree, stands out even among the magnificence all around it. To appreciate the decoration to the full, it is necessary to come on a sunny day, when the shafts of light penetrating the clerestory and dome windows illuminate the stucco-work in a magical series of ever-changing reflections.

Among the church's most notable furnishings are the pulpit and the main chandelier, both of which adopt the form of a boat. At the entrance to the chancel is another curiosity, an impassioned Ecce Homo statue in the Spanish manner, which was carved in Rome in the late 17th century. A large painting of *The Parting of SS Peter and Paul* by Franciszek Smuglewicz has taken the place of the original unfinished high altar.

Antakalnis

Antakalnis itself was formerly the estate of another prominent dynasty, the Sapieha family. A short distance to the north along Antakalnio are the two main buildings, both dating from the 1690s: the **Sapieha Palace**, an Italianate palazzo, and the **Church of Our Lord Jesus**, which formed part of one of the city's two Trinitarian foundations. The latter is a domed octagon fronted by a porch flanked by two towers placed at strikingly oblique angles. It apparently still preserves stucco decoration by Pietro Peretti, but there is little prospect of seeing this as the building is boarded up with no sign of any much-needed restoration work.

The **Antakalnis Cemetery** to the east encapsulates Vilnius' complicated modern history. Close to the entrance are rows of identical tombstones of Polish soldiers killed in World War I. At the heart of the complex is a large circular memorial containing the graves of the nationalist martyrs of the 1991 standoffs with the Red Army at Vilnius' TV tower and the border post of Medininkai. Further on, colossal Socialist Realist statues guard an eternal flame which no longer burns, while a pantheon of the leading lights of Soviet Lithuania is laid out in tiers alongside.

Šnipiškės

From the New Town, the **Green Bridge** (Žaliasis tiltas) leads across the River Neris to the district of Šnipiškės. Adorning each of its four corners are Socialist Realist sculptures of happy workers and peasants. These now seem somewhat comical, but have been left in this prominent location as a deliberate reminder of the 'heritage' of the communist era.

Just over the bridge is the **Church of St Raphael**, which was built by the Jesuits in the first decade of the 18th century. A typical example of the baroque architecture of the period, it has a monumental high altar with a large painting of the Archangel Raphael by Szymon Czechowitz. The church now stands at the edge of a pedestrian precinct which was something of a Soviet-era showpiece. Its facilities include the **Planetarium** (shows Monday–Friday 09.30–18.00, Saturday 12.00–16.00), the city's largest department store and two gargantuan hotels.

At the foot of Rinktinės, just over 0.5km east of the Green Bridge, the **Žalgiris Stadium** and the **Concert and Sports Palace** occupy the site of the city's main Jewish cemetery. This was levelled by the Soviets in 1950 in order to make way for the stadium, which hosts large-scale open-air events, including international football matches and the dance programme of the four-yearly Song Festival. Its indoor counterpart, which is two decades younger, stages everything from basketball tournaments to rock concerts.

A short distance further north, with entrances on Rinktinės and Kalvarija, the long street running northwards from the Green Bridge, is the **Calvary Market** (open Tuesday–Sunday 06.30–16.30). Like all the best Lithuanian markets, this has an almost bazaar-type atmosphere. Although dominated by stalls offering a huge choice of fresh fruit and vegetables, hardware items and clothing can also be bought, while a poignant touch is added by the people who stand in rows day after day, and somewhat desperately try to sell individual plastic bags or a few odd garments.

Northern suburbs

From Kalvarija, buses 26, 35, 36 and 50 run to the northern suburbs, which are primarily high-rise housing estates separated by large areas of greenery. In the district of Jeruzalė, some 5km north of the market, the **Calvary Church of the Rediscovery of the Holy Cross** can be seen on a hillock to the right of the road. One of Lithuania's most important pilgrimage sites, this one-time Dominican friary was among the few Vilnius churches kept open during the Soviet era. In its present form, it was built between 1755 and 1772, and features a characteristic twin-towered façade and a richly decorated interior. The most notable features of the latter are the combined pulpit and font and the illusionistic ceiling frescos on the theme of the Holy Cross and its rediscovery by St Helena, mother of the Emperor Constantine. Outside the church are four pilgrimage chapels, the only original ones remaining from the 19 which, together with a ceremonial archway which also still survives, formed a processional way similar to that in Žemaiči Kalvarija, one of Lithuania's best-known pilgrimage sites.

The others, which were razed by the Soviets but are gradually being reinstated, were scattered along a route which leads 1.5km southeast through the woods to the **Trinapolis Convent**, a Trinitarian foundation overlooking the River Neris. Designed by Pietro Putini, one of the architects of the Pažaislis Monastery, it was built between 1695 and 1709. It has been re-settled by a small community of nuns, and is now a popular retreat centre. Although the façade of its Church of the Holy Trinity is a characteristic example of Lithuanian baroque, the interior, an irregular octagon with highly complex spatial arrangements, is untypical, being modelled on the Trinitarian church of San Carlo alle Quattro Fontane in Rome by Francesco Borromini.

The landscaped **Verkiai Park**, a former estate which nowadays functions as Vilnius' Botanical Garden, can be reached from the Trinapolis Convent by the road alongside the Neris, or from the Calvary Church by continuing northwards along Kalvarija. At its heart is the **Verkiai Palace**, a late 17th-century complex remodelled in neo-classical style by Laurynas Gucevičius as a summer residence for the Vilnius bishops. Unfortunately, the main building was demolished in the

1850s, but the two wings, which are themselves of palatial dimensions, both survive. One serves as the headquarters of the Botanical Institute, and is not accessible to the public. However, regular art exhibitions are held in the other, whose reception rooms were plushly decorated in the late 19th century with oak panelling, marble and stuccowork.

Bus 36 continues northwards from Verkiai to the **Green Lakes**, a hugely popular recreation area. On summer weekends especially, it swarms with day trippers who come to go boating or swimming in the chain of lakes and to have a relaxing picnic or barbecue by one of the shores.

Western suburbs

The setting for many of the big nationalist rallies during the final years of Soviet rule, **Vingis Park** is bounded on three sides by a loop of the River Neris, and to the east by the New Town, one of whose major thoroughfares, Čiurlionio, leads straight to the main entrance. In the middle of the park is the Song Dome, whose covered auditorium, which can seat 20,000 people, can serve two completely different functions. On the last day of the four-yearly Song Festival, it serves as the stage for the concert by the massed choirs, which the audience watches from the field alongside. However, the roles can be reversed, in order to have open-air performances watched by an audience seated under cover.

A footbridge at the northern end of the park leads to **Žvėrynas**, a residential suburb of wooden houses and grand villas, which can also be reached from the New Town via the bridges at the end of Gedimino and Jasinskio. Just west of the latter, on Liubarto, is the **Kenesa**, an early 20th- century temple whose vaguely Oriental appearance reflects the exotic origins of the Karaites (see page 163) who worship there.

In 1957 a Jewish graveyard, the only one in Vilnius, was established within the **Šaltoniškių Cemetery** in Viršuliškės, the next suburb to the west, which can be reached by trolleybuses 11 (from the city centre), 16 (from the station) and 19 (from Žvėrynas). This contains tombs brought from razed Jewish cemeteries, notably the large burial chamber of the Gaon of Vilna, though many gravestones were pillaged in the Soviet era and recycled as masonry in the construction of new buildings.

Lithuania's tallest building, the 326m-high **Television Tower** (open daily 10.00–21.00), rises above the apartment blocks of Karoliniškės, the suburb immediately south of Viršuliškės, which is likewise on the routes of trolleybuses 11 and 16. Outside the entrance, crosses commemorate the 14 unarmed civilians who were mowed down by Soviet tanks on January 13 1991 in the single most tragic episode in the run-up towards independence. A lift goes up as far as the observation deck at 165m, which rotates slowly on its own axis and offers sweeping views over the city.

The **Gariūnai Market**, which lies just off the Kaunas highway, 10km west of the centre, is by far the most notorious in the country. All manner of secondhand and imported goods are sold there, and it is best-known for its huge array of used motor vehicles (not all of which have an impeccable provenance). Trading takes place every morning except Monday.

Paneriai

The name of the southwestern suburb of Paneriai has become synonymous with the killing fields of the Nazis, who murdered around 100,000 people there, including almost all of Vilnius' large Jewish population, between 1941 and 1944. There are several memorials to the dead. The earlier of these adopt the Communist practice of paying tribute to 'Soviet citizens' massacred as a result of 'Fascist terror'; the more recent, which date from 1990, make proper acknowledgement of the fact that 70,000 of the casualties were local Jews. A path round the site leads to the pits where the dead bodies were burnt, and to another where the bones where crushed. There is also a branch of the Lithuanian State Jewish Museum, which contains a photographic record of the site, as well as some of the retrieved personal effects of the victims. Inexcusably, it has no set opening times, and is regularly shut.

By far the quickest and easiest way to reach the site is by rail. All trains to Trakai and Marcinkonys, and most of those to Kaunas, stop at Paneriai station. From there, it is a straight ten-minute walk onwards along a dead-end road which runs parallel to the rail tracks.

EXCURSIONS FROM VILNIUS
Trakai Historical National Park
The one unmissable short excursion from Vilnius is to the Trakai Historical National Park. With an area of just 8,000 hectares, this is by far the smallest of the country's national parks and – as the additional word 'Historical' in its title implies – it differs markedly from its four counterparts. Whereas the conservation of the landscape is their primary purpose, this one is mainly concerned with preserving the monumental heritage of Trakai, Lithuania's best-known and most impressive small town. That said, the scenery is an integral part of Trakai's charm, and is archetypally Lithuanian, with forests accounting for 33% of the park's area, lakes for 18%.

Trakai
Although its current population is a modest 7,000, Trakai has played an important role in Lithuanian history and is one of the country's oldest towns, perhaps dating back to the 12th century. The original settlement was the capital of one of the duchies into which early medieval Lithuania was divided, and at one time it rivalled Vilnius in importance. Indeed it may have served as capital of the whole country for a couple of years during the reign of Grand Duke Gediminas. Now known as Senieji (Old) Trakai, it lies 4km southeast of the replacement town founded some time around the middle of the 14th century by one of Gediminas's sons, Duke (later Grand Duke) Kęstutis. This occupies a highly strategic site on a peninsula bordered to the west by Lake Totoriškiai, to the east by Lake Luka (or Bernardinai), and to the north by the islet-strewn Lake Galvė. These lakes, and others beyond, are interconnected by narrow channels.

Trakai fell briefly to the Teutonic Knights in the internecine wars which led to Kęstutis's death. Under his son, Grand Duke Vytautas the Great, it was transformed into one of the strongest fortresses in Europe. Vytautas also encouraged Karaites, with whom he had made contact during his eastern military campaigns, to come and settle in the town, and they have made a distinctive mark, retaining a presence there to this day.

Trakai's multi-ethnic character was boosted in the 16th century, when Jews arrived in numbers. However, the 17th-century wars with Russia left the fortresses in ruins. As a result it lost its strategic importance and went into

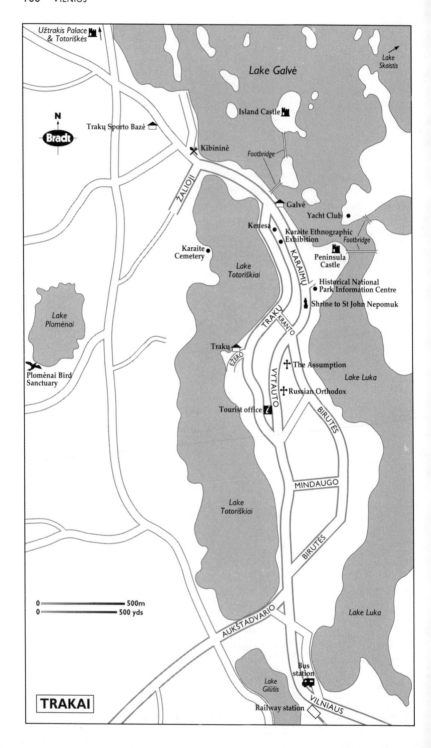

Lake Galvė

Island Castle

Footbridge

Užtrakis Palace & Totoriškės

Lake Skaistis

N

Bradt

Trakų Sporto Bazė

Kibininė

ŽALIOJI

Galvė

Kenesa

Karaite Ethnographic Exhibition

Yacht Club

Footbridge

Karaite Cemetery

Lake Totoriškiai

KARAIMŲ

Peninsula Castle

Historical National Park Information Centre

Shrine to St John Nepomuk

Lake Plomėnai

TRAKŲ KRANTO

Trakų

EŽERO

VYTAUTO

The Assumption

Russian Orthodox

Lake Luka

Plomėnai Bird Sanctuary

Tourist office

BIRUTĖS

MINDAUGO

Lake Totoriškiai

BIRUTĖS

0 ___ 500m
0 ___ 500 yds

AUKŠTADVARIO

Lake Luka

TRAKAI

Lake Gilūšis

Bus station

Railway station

VILNIAUS

economic decline, becoming just another small provincial town. Only in the late 19th century, when the nationalist movement stimulated interest in Lithuania's medieval past, did it begin to make something of a come-back.

Telephone numbers
As for Vilnius, different dialling codes apply when calling from abroad or from within Lithuania. From abroad, Trakai numbers are reached by dialling 528; from within Lithuania, the code is 82 and then the local number.

Information and maps
Historical National Park Information Centre Karaimų 5; tel: 28 55776; fax: 28 51528. A 1:50,000 map of the Historical National Park, with a panorama of the town on the reverse, is available. Open Mon–Thu 08.00–12.00 and 12.45–17.00, Fri 08.00–12.00 and 12.45–15.00.
Tourist office Vytauto 69; tel/fax: 28 51934; email: trakai@is.lt; web: www.trakai.lt. Accommodation can be arranged; some English is spoken. Open in summer Mon–Fri 09.00–18.00, Sat 10.00–15.00, in winter Mon–Fri 08.00–17.00.

Public transport
Bus station Vytauto 90; tel: 28 51333. Located immediately south of the peninsula. There are over 30 services daily to Vilnius, two direct to Kaunas via Rumšiškės, and seven to Prienai via Aukštadvaris and Birštonas.
Railway station Vilniaus 5; tel: 28 51055. Situated a short walk south of the bus station, this is the terminus of a branch line from Vilnius via Paneriai, on which seven trains run daily in each direction.

Restaurants
Kibininė Karaim 65. The Karaite restaurant has a decent drinks list, including a freshly made *gira*, but there are only two dishes to choose from (with only the former always being available): *kibinai*, which is a meat pie resembling a Cornish pasty, and *troškinta mėsa*, a meat and vegetable stew.
Pilies Smuklė This daytime restaurant in the courtyard of the Island Castle is an offshoot of Ritos Smuklė in Vilnius.
Prie Pilies Karaimų 53. This classy restaurant on the quayside directly opposite the Island Castle has a formal dining room and an outside terrace. The food is imaginatively prepared, and there is a particularly good choice of fish dishes.
Židinis Vytauto 91. This basic town-centre café-restaurant, which serves standard Lithuanian fare, has a small terrace overlooking Lake Totoriškiai.

Festivals
The Island Castle makes a dramatic backdrop for a number of annual events, including the Medieval Festival in late May, the Festival of Lithuanian National Opera and Ballet throughout July, and the Trakai Festival in August. On a weekend in early July, the Peninsula Castle is the setting for the Archaeology Festival, with demonstrations of knightly combat and medieval handicrafts.

The town
Trakai's peninsula is bisected by a snaking main street. The southern part of this, known as Vytauto, leads past the 19th-century **Russian Orthodox**

Church to the **Church of the Assumption**, which is set in splendid isolation on a hillock overlooking the street. One of Lithuania's oldest churches, it was founded by Grand Duke Vytautas around the turn of the 15th century. It was originally fortified, but was remodelled in the baroque style in 1718. Inside, the high altar has as its centre-piece a venerated image usually known as The Madonna of Trakai. This was painted in the 16th century, though the gilded silver surround was only added in the 18th century. From the church, Vytauto sweeps round to the east, terminating in what is effectively an open square, in the centre of which is another baroque monument, a pillar topped by a **shrine to St John Nepomuk**.

By the lakeside immediately to the east is the **Peninsula Castle**, the outer part of the elaborate defensive system begun by Kęstutis and completed by Vytautas. Destroyed by the Russians in 1655, it has been left as a ruin, though one of the towers, a gateway and the lower parts of the walls have all been restored.

Yachts, rowing boats and water bicycles can be hired at the various quaysides to the north of the castle or from the **Yacht Club**, which lies on the opposite side of the channel between Lake Luka and Lake Galvė. By road, it is several kilometres away, but it can be reached in a couple of minutes via a rustic wooden footbridge which commands fine views over the town and its lakes.

The northern section of Trakai's main street is named Karaimų in honour of the Karaite settlers, and is lined with their colourful wooden houses. At Karaimų 22 is the **Karaite Ethnographic Exhibition** (open Wednesday–Sunday 10.00–18.00), a permanent display on the life of the community. The Karaites's military background is evoked in a collection of swords, knives, daggers, helmets, armour, shields and guns; other aspects of their culture are illuminated by displays of historic photographs, books, costumes, textiles, household goods and liturgical objects. A little further up the street is the Karaite prayer house or **Kenesa**, a late 18th-century building with a distinctively Oriental look. It was recently given a thorough restoration, but the chances of finding it open are slim.

Karaimų continues northwards across the bridge at the tip of the peninsula which spans the channel between Lake Galvė and Lake Totoriškiai. The wooden building at Karaimų 65 houses **Kibininė**, a Karaite restaurant which has gained cult status, in spite of its abbreviated menu (see page 167). Just before it, Žalioji leads up to the **Karaite Cemetery**, which overlooks Lake Totoriškiai, with a fine view back towards the Kenesa. The older tombs are scattered among the grass on the higher ground, while the more recent graves are clustered more closely together on a promontory by the lakeshore.

Island Castle

One of Lithuania's most famous sights, Trakai's Island Castle (open daily May–September 10.00–19.00, October–April 10.00–17.00) occupies almost the whole of one of the islets in Lake Galvė, and is linked by footbridge to the tiny Karaite Isle, from where another footbridge provides a connection to the eastern shore of the peninsula. The most secure and prestigious part of the town's medieval fortification system, it suffered the same fate as the Peninsula Castle in the mid-17th-century wars with the Russians, and was left as a ruin, albeit a substantial one, whose relatively isolated setting meant that it survived in better

THE KARAITES (KARAIM)

Founded in the 8th century, the Karaite sect is often regarded as an offshoot of Judaism, adhering as it does to the authority of the Old Testament. In reality, it differs considerably, rejecting both Talmudic interpretations of the Word and oral religious laws. Moreover, the Lithuanian Karaites are not a Semitic people. They are of Turkish origin, and spread from their original base in the Byzantine Empire into the Crimean Peninsula. There, some were taken to Lithuania by Vytautas as prisoners-of-war, while others came of their own volition.

Granted freedom to practise their own religion, they were settled in Trakai, where they served as guardians of the fortresses and as Vytautas's personal bodyguards. In 1441, Vytautas's successor, Grand Duke Kazimierz, granted the Karaites the right to administer their own affairs, a privilege most unusual in medieval Europe for a non-Christian denomination. Although Lithuania's Karaite community remained small, it retained its own faith, language and identity and produced several distinguished scientists and writers. However, in the 20th century numbers declined sharply, and with a population now under 300 there are fears that it will die out within a generation.

shape than any of the country's other medieval castles. Plans to rebuild it were mooted in the late 19th century, and brought to fruition between 1951 and 1962, although it seems positively bizarre that the Soviet authorities were prepared to countenance the phoenix-like reappearance of a monument symbolising Lithuania's past as a great military power.

Although this type of conjectural restoration is now very unfashionable, it is hard to judge the result as anything other than a spectacular success. When seen from across the water – and there are marvellous views from all over Lake Galvė's shoreline – it looks an awesome sight, one which must have struck fear into the heart of any medieval attacker. Close up, it is not quite so impressive, mainly because of the very obvious difference between the original bricks and rough stonework of the lower parts of the walls, and the modern machine-made bricks used to reconstruct the missing sections.

There are two parts to the fortress, which has a highly irregular ground-plan. The Outer Castle, whose walls are up to 3.90m thick, is entered via a gateway with drawbridge. This is flanked by massive towers, with a third tower guarding the northwest corner. All round the trapezoid-shaped inner courtyard are casements, which were used as residential quarters and storage rooms. Those on the western side now contain a somewhat quirky collection of applied art, including furniture, amber, ceramics, snuff-boxes and pipes.

A short bridge connects the Outer Castle to the palace, whose dominant feature is a 25m-high keep. From its inner courtyard, there are steps down to the basement, where the treasury was housed, and stairways to the upper chambers, including the Great Hall on the first floor. These contain displays on the castle (including a series of archive photos showing how it looked prior to and during the reconstruction work), plus sundry historical artefacts.

Elsewhere in the Historical National Park

Outside Trakai itself, the main set-piece attraction in the Historical National Park is the 19th-century **Užtrakis Palace** on the eastern shore of Lake Galvė. Built in neo-Renaissance style for the Tiškevičius (Tyszkiewicz) dynasty, it is set in a formal park laid out by the French landscape gardener Édouard André, whose work for the same family can also be seen in Palanga. Unfortunately, the palace has been allowed to fall into dereliction, but will doubtless be restored in the future. The quickest way to reach Užtrakis from Trakai by road involves circumnavigating the entire shoreline of Lake Galvė in an anticlockwise direction from the northern tip of the peninsula; approximately 7km in total.

Just to the west of Lake Totoriškiai is the **Plomėnai Bird Sanctuary**. This consists of the small, almost circular Lake Plomėnai, together with the much larger area of marshland to the west.

The Centre of Europe

The point which the French National Geographic Institute deemed in 1989 to be the Centre of Europe lies some 25km north of Vilnius, down a signposted dirt track from the main A101 road to Molėtai. There are plans to erect a suitably grandiose monument on the spot, consisting of a sundial and a giant map, but these have yet to come to fruition.

A rather more substantial attraction inspired by the Centre of Europe theme is the **Europe Park** (open daily 10.00–sunset), which lies much closer to the city, some 5km north of the Green Lakes. It can be reached by a 3km walk from the terminus of bus 36, but a better alternative is to take bus 92 from the Žalgirio terminal (one stop north of the Calvary Market). This service never runs more than four times a day, but it does stop at the side road leading to the park entrance. The Europe Park is an open-air museum of modern sculpture in a woodland and meadow setting, with exhibits specially created for the site by artists from all around the world. Chair Pool by the American Dennis Oppenheim is the most popular work – and also the most humorous, its subject being exactly what the title suggests, a giant chair with a small pool instead of a seat. Other sculptures which are guaranteed to catch the eye are Jon Barlow Hudson's Cloud Hands, which consists of four granite blocks seemingly suspended in the air; and the 6m-high Woman Looking at the Moon by the Mexican Javier Cruz.

There are currently 90 sculptures and regular donations are increasing this figure all the time. It is hard to take many of them seriously, although the on-site guides most certainly do. The central monument gives distances to a range of worldwide capitals, including the furthest from Vilnius, which is Wellington. Dublin disguises itself from most visitors by being spelt in Gaelic.

Before leaving, stop at the Television Information Tree, made up of nearly 3,000 sets. The exhibit ensured an entry for the museum in the Guinness Book of Records, which may well be why it was set up. The park publicises itself brilliantly so receives many more visitors than easily accessible sites in the town centre.

Kernavė

Kernavė, which lies on a terrace high above a bend on the River Neris, 40km from Vilnius down a minor road, is nowadays an insignificant village of just over 300 souls. However, its now-vanished medieval predecessor, which was situated by the riverside and abandoned in 1390 following repeated sackings by the Teutonic Knights, was almost certainly Lithuania's original capital, a status it may have gained under King Mindaugas, and is securely documented as having held throughout the reign of Grand Duke Traidenis (1269–82).

At the southern end of the present-day village is its dominant monument, a bloated neo-Gothic parish church completed in 1920. Alongside is the entrance to the **Historical and Archaeological Museum-Reserve** (open Wednesday–Sunday 10.00–15.00/17.00), the only one of its type in Lithuania. From the observation platform there is a magnificent view over the protected area, with its five large mounds, and the Neris valley beyond. The mounds, which can be ascended via wooden stairways, were formerly girded with ramparts and fortifications, and formed a unified defensive system. To the southeast of the platform is Castle Mound, which according to legend was linked by an underground tunnel to Trakai and Vilnius. However, the ducal castle was actually situated on Hearth Mound, which lies immediately south of the platform; its name comes from the tradition that a pagan temple formerly stood there. The central Hearth Mound is the oldest of the group; the others are the steep Lizdeika Mound, which protected its approaches, and Kriveikiškis Mound, which is further to the southeast, on the right bank of the Kernavelė stream.

Kernavė, which was first settled around 9000BC, has proved to be a fruitful hunting ground for archaeologists. Many of the artefacts they have unearthed are on view in the exhibition building. These range from Stone Age arrowheads via Bronze and Iron Age tools to medieval cult objects and jewellery. The extensive trade networks are well illustrated by a string of 400 beads of Russian origin which also includes ten shells which originated in the Maldive Islands in the Indian Ocean.

In honour of Kernavė's status as the likely setting for the coronation of King Mindaugas in 1253, the Living Archaeology Days festival is held there over a weekend in early July, around the time of the public holiday commemorating the event. It consists of a series of tableaux re-creating different aspects of life from the Stone Age to medieval times, and the emphasis is firmly hands-on, with visitors given the opportunity to sample ancient methods of cookery, metalwork, handicrafts and even fighting.

There are usually five daily buses to Kernavė from Vilnius; the terminus is at the northern edge of the village. Each immediately turns round and travels back to the capital, necessitating a wait of several hours for the next service, though it is easy enough to fill the time.

Aukštadvaris Regional Park

West of the Trakai Historical National Park lies another very pretty protected landscape, the Aukštadvaris Regional Park. Within its boundaries are no fewer than 77 lakes, and it is seen at its best in September or October when cloaked in glorious autumnal colours. Buses from Vilnius to Alytus, or from Vilnius to Birštonas and Prienai, travel all the way through the middle of the park, enabling a good cross-section of its scenery to be seen. En route they pass through the village of **Aukštadvaris**, which lies on the northern shore of Lake Nava and has a fine twin-towered wooden parish church. In the woods some 4km to the north, and reachable by footpath, is the so-called **Devil's Cave**, a mysterious hole 40m deep and 200m in diameter which has been the inspiration for a host of legends.

Kaliningrad

For 46 years between 1945 and 1991 the Soviet Union occupied the Baltic States of Estonia, Latvia and Lithuania and also incorporated part of the former German province of East Prussia, renaming the town of Königsberg as Kaliningrad. Confusingly they used this name, too, for the surrounding region or *oblast*. A cultural and political uniformity was quickly imposed on all these territories and most former links with the outside world curtailed. Kaliningrad suffered most in this respect, with travel there even for Soviet citizens being difficult or impossible. Its history as a major German city was ignored; in the town centre British bombing in August 1944 and the final battle for the city in April 1945 left many buildings totally or largely destroyed. Much of what could have been restored was subsequently removed to make the break with the long German past even stronger. Tallinn, Riga and Vilnius were still granted a history, albeit a distorted one as the Soviet Union was unhappy to publicise the period between 1920 and 1940 when these towns were not part of it. Many of their pre-war inhabitants, however, were unable to enjoy it, having been murdered in the Holocaust, or deported to Siberia in 1941, or having fled west ahead of the Soviet army in 1944.

From around 1960, the Soviet authorities allowed travel to Tallinn, Riga and Vilnius but with a maximum stay of three nights. Travel between the cities was by air or on overnight trains. Longer stays were rarely granted to prevent serious contacts being established with the local populations. Tours always started and finished in Leningrad (now St Petersburg) or Moscow to stress the Soviet nature of the programme and to minimise the Baltic element. Travel outside the capitals only became possible in the 1980s toward the end of the Soviet period. Tourists first came to Kaliningrad from 1990 as the Soviet Union fell apart and the military were no longer able to prevent this. As Kaliningrad was a major naval base on the front line with NATO, admitting tourists was out of the question before then. The occasional visitor from Scandinavia came in the 1950s and 1960s but, in comparison, Tibet, North Korea or Albania seemed wide open in those days. Many former East Prussians were desperate to return and 60,000 Germans came to visit in 1992. Their largely hostile reports, and continued bitterness at what many regarded as an illegitimate occupation of their homeland, initially discouraged more general tourists. Now with many business, academic and voluntary organisations working towards reconciliation and with the successful rebuilding of several pre-war monuments, the image of Kaliningrad has greatly improved and visitor numbers are likely to increase again.

THE STATUS OF KALININGRAD

Independence in Estonia, Latvia and Lithuania brought an immediate influx of tourists to their capitals from all over the world, many taking tours that visited all three. Arrivals came to be counted in millions rather than in thousands. This added to the determination of the local town councils to eradicate the recent Soviet past. Cyrillic road signs were torn down, hard currencies introduced and visas abolished for most visitors. Active tourist boards were established, eager to work with the travel industry and with travel writers. In these capitals, the new private sector quickly adapted to tourism so that by 1994 visitors had no problem in finding a luxury hotel or a small two-star one, eating Chinese or Italian food, and reading a Western newspaper on the day of publication. Tourist visits are now similar to those in Stockholm, Lübeck or Kraków, with ample scope for specialist and general groups or individuals preferring to stay on their own.

World War II left savage human scars across the region but fortunately there was little fighting in the three other Baltic state capitals so an architectural heritage stretching back for eight centuries welcomes all visitors. Many of the sites are within walking distance of each other and of the hotels which visitors are likely to use. Others are cheaply and easily reached by public transport.

The transformation in Kaliningrad would be, and remains, more ambivalent. British bombing and bitter fighting in April 1945 left the town centre a shell. By the end of the Soviet period most of the inhabitants were from Russia, a few from the other Soviet Republics. In 1991 they were suddenly cut off from home by three foreign countries – Lithuania, Poland and Belarus. Renewed contact from Germany with this former part of East Prussia was as much a threat as an opportunity. The year 1992 brought visions of Kaliningrad becoming the 'Hong Kong of the Baltics' but realism on the spot and hostility in Moscow soon put paid to this. A new role has still to be found.

The problems the rest of Russia faces are equally acute in Kaliningrad: nearly half the working population earns less than £65/US$100 a month, a sum which is regarded as a realistic minimum wage. The old age pension, if it is provided on time, is £33/US$50 a month. Tourists will appreciate the massive grants the Germans have provided in the last ten years as they admire the restored cathedral, the enlarged History Museum and the repainted seaside resort of Rauschen. They will enjoy the restaurants and the many 24-hour shops. Königsberg is methodically and aesthetically returning to many parts of Kaliningrad. Yet the abandoned fields in much of the countryside and the dismal blocks of flats in many of the suburbs show that little has changed for much of the local population. In some ways, Russia has left Kaliningrad behind. Those who never knew the Soviet Union can still take the chance to see Lenin looking down on most town hall squares. They can still do serious shopping in local markets as peasants prefer to bypass the official distribution structures. They can wonder why the name of the town has not been changed, since Kalinin, as a close associate of Stalin, hardly inspires reverence any more. Kant would be the obvious person to choose in renaming the town as he is respected by both the Germans and the Russians, but some local residents claim that the town is not yet worthy of his name. Tourists need not worry whether it is or whether it is not, but for the sake of the local residents let us hope for not too long a delay.

HISTORY

The history of the former German town of Königsberg began with bloodshed in 1255 and ended with bloodshed in 1945. The establishment of the first settlement by the Teutonic Knights was to lead by 1283 to the complete annihilation of the Prussian tribes. In 1945 the Germans would in turn be annihilated by Soviet troops at the end of World War II. In the intervening 700 years, war would generally pass the town by, its few temporary occupiers having established their authority in battles elsewhere. Membership of the Hanseatic League from 1340 ensured close relationships with all the other large ports along the Baltic coast and a common adherence to Lutheranism after the Reformation. It also ensured extensive trading links with Britain. During this long period of time, Germany and Russia would usually be friends, uniting just as easily against the French as against the Poles. Loyal former residents always refer to 700 years of German history, yet such rule can hardly be seen as continuous. For much of the 15th century, local rulers had to swear allegiance to the Polish crown. The Swedes followed in the 16th century and were only finally driven away in 1679. The first Russian occupation lasted four years, between 1758 and 1762. In 1807 Napoleon occupied the town for 39 days. Far worse than any occupation was the plague that killed a quarter of the population in 1709.

Learning and culture

Albertina University, founded in 1544, was a constant feature of the town's history. Foreign occupiers always respected it and eagerly encouraged its work. It was equally well-known throughout Germany. It pioneered in many fields, being one of the first to lecture in German instead of Latin, to introduce science degrees and to admit women students. Throughout its 400-year history, any prominent writer, historian or scientist living in Königsberg had a post at Albertina. Its academic standards were only to slip twice during this time. An honorary degree was awarded to Napoleon's General Pierre Daru who led the forces that occupied Königsberg. In the university's final 12 years between 1933 and 1945, the teaching was as dominated by Nazi ideology as it was in all other German universities.

The original 16th-century buildings of the university were beside those of the cathedral in the heart of the old town. These were all destroyed during the fighting at the end of World War II, including a library of over half a million books. As part of the 300th anniversary celebrations in 1844, further faculties were built on the northern side of the Pregel River and some of the buildings survived the war and are still in use. These followed other institutions that had been founded earlier in the century, such as the botanical garden and the observatory built by Germany's most famous astronomer, Friedrich Wilhelm Bessel (1784–1846).

The philosopher Immanuel Kant (1724–1804) was undoubtedly Königsberg's most famous resident and probably the only one ever to achieve fame outside Germany. He stayed loyal to the town throughout his life and never accepted posts elsewhere. In fact he went further than this and hardly left the town, indicating in many of his writings that travel would not have broadened *his* mind. Marxist philosophers see him as a precursor to Hegel and then to Marx himself. Because of the Russian occupation he was, like all other residents for that four-year period, a Russian citizen. One hundred and fifty years later these two factors would be crucial. During the Soviet period between 1945 and 1990, he was the one famous former resident who could officially be commemorated. His tomb outside the cathedral, erected in 1924 on the 200th anniversary of his birth, was not destroyed and his work continued to be published.

Kant was renowned for his rigid schedule and his regular companions. His butler always woke him at 04.45 each morning and he was always in bed by 22.00. He never married, to his regret, but he consoled himself with the thought that staying single kept his mind more alert. He held the Chair of Logic from 1770 until his death in 1804, the year of which he had actually predicted. He had a regular circle of friends whom he entertained each Sunday. Amongst the latter were two Englishmen, Joseph Green and Robert Motherby, whose shipping business, originally based in Hull, brought grain and herrings to Britain. They had lunch with him every Sunday for about 20 years. In the 19th century their successors started a regular steamer service between Hull and Königsberg, profiting in particular during the Crimean War when Königsberg was the only source of Russian goods.

The most famous visitor to Königsberg was Peter the Great, who came in 1697 en route to western Europe. A Russian trading community had already been settled in the town for over a hundred years and was sufficiently large to hold regular church services. Officially he came incognito, but being some two metres tall (well over six feet) and bringing an entourage of 400, this pretence was impossible to maintain. He did enjoy disguising himself in a range of unlikely occupations but wildly drunken behaviour was on several occasions to let him down. On his visit to Königsberg the German court presented him with amber jewellery and horses from the famous breeding centre in Eastern Prussia, Trakehnen. Later they would present him with the Amber Chamber, which would adorn the summer palace at Tsarkoye Selo for two centuries, before being brought back to Königsberg by German troops in 1942. After his 1697 visit, Peter the Great continued his journey to Holland and England, settling in Deptford for several months to study shipbuilding. He would send students from St Petersburg to study at Albertina University but this link was broken in 1720 as too few Russian students had sufficient knowledge of German to follow the courses. It was restored during the tsarist occupation (1758–62) when Russian students attended Kant's lectures.

Expansion and prosperity

The 19th century was one of fame in every commercial and intellectual field for Königsberg and the city enjoyed peace and prosperity throughout these hundred years. 'First' and 'largest' are adjectives that need to be used again and again. At the beginning of the century, in 1809, the famous Königsberg marzipan was first produced. At the end of the century, in 1895, Germany's first electric trams operated here and then, two years later, the first 11 women graduated from Albertina. Well before the end of the century, the port handled more grain and wood than any other in Germany whilst at the same time 'Gräfe und Unzer' had become the country's largest bookshop. Shipbuilding, printing, railway engineering and textiles were the industries that enjoyed particular success. The opening of the railway link with Russia in 1861 greatly expanded the scope of the port, as did the construction of the canal to Pillau (Baltiysk) on the coast.

Uniquely it could guarantee ice-free access throughout the winter. The first British steamer had in fact arrived seven years earlier in 1854 and trade with Russia through the port would greatly increase following the completion of the railway link.

Culturally, Wagner, Schumann and Liszt paid several visits for performances of their works; Bizet's *Carmen* was successfully performed in 1879 after its initial failure in Paris. In architecture, the Luisenkirche and the Stock Exchange are the most famous of a wide range of impressive 19th-century buildings that are still in use.

Königsberg remained untouched by World War I, although it was sufficiently close to several battles for it to be used as a military relief station and for its hospitals to be greatly expanded. Under the Versailles Treaty of 1919, independence was restored to Poland after over a century of German and Russian occupation. This led to the division of East Prussia and its capital Königsberg from the rest of Germany. Although links with the 'mainland' were assured, Königsberg was forced to look for closer trading links with the new Baltic States of Lithuania, Latvia and Estonia and also with the Soviet Union. There are few realistic portrayals of the 26 years Königsberg was still to exist as a German city. The many memoirs that the exiles would produce after World War II present an idealised picture of a prosperous town with no crime, no tension and where the sun always shone. One writer does in fact admit that she cannot recall a rainy summer's day, so happy are her recollections of her childhood in Königsberg. There is no doubt that much was achieved there and evidence of this can still be seen in many parts of the town, despite the later bombing. One mayor, Hans Lohmeyer, was in office from 1919 to 1933 and he relentlessly drove the town forward. In Carl Gördeler, his deputy from 1922 to 1930, he had an equally active supporter. (Gördeler then become Mayor of Leipzig and, had the July 1944 plot to kill Hitler succeeded, he would have been nominated as German Chancellor. He and several other East Prussians were among the many executed for their role in the plot.)

Lohmeyer built a new main railway station, probably the first in Germany with non-smoking waiting rooms, and with a bowling alley. He foresaw the role air travel would play so gave his city a large airport. He realised the need for close links with the new Soviet government so helped to establish Deruluft, a joint venture with them which operated regular flights to Moscow. The two-storey road and rail bridge across the River Pregel, which is still in use, was built at his instigation. His most famous achievement was the annual *Ostmesse*, the export trade fair that dominated trade to and from the city throughout the inter-war period. First opened in 1920, by 1923 it was attracting 2,500 exhibitors and continued operating until the autumn of 1941.

Yet an honest portrayal of the city between 1919 and 1939 has to reflect the developments that hit the whole of Germany. The rampant inflation of 1923 destroyed many long-established businesses and then unemployment in the early 1930s provided the breeding ground for Nazism. The Nazis' main opponents both on the streets and in the ballot box were the communists. None of the centre parties appeared to offer solutions to the ever-worsening crisis. At the *Ostmesse* in 1932, many stands were empty and an art exhibition had to fill up the empty space.

The Nazi era

In the last free election to be held in Königsberg the Nazis were elected on March 5 1933, with 54% of the vote. Democracy and racial tolerance died that night throughout Germany. Opposition to the Nazis was dealt with as ruthlessly in Königsberg as elsewhere. Mayor Lohmeyer was sacked on March 9. On May 10 a book burning was organised on the Trommelplatz, the main parade ground. Any books which could be stigmatized as 'Un-German, Jewish or Bolshevik' went up in flames. Sixteen staff at the university were immediately sacked on account of their political views or racial background.

The most famous Jew who left Königsberg in 1933 was the song-writer Max Colpet who wrote 'Where Have All the Flowers Gone' for Marlene Dietrich. In his American exile he went on to write for Charles Aznavour and to translate *West Side Story* into German. A five-year old Jewish girl who also left in 1933 later achieved prominence as Lea Rabin, wife of the Israeli Prime Minister. By the end of the year, the Hansaring had been renamed Adolf Hitler Strasse, to mark the supposed permanence of the Nazi regime.

On November 7 1938 a junior diplomat Ernst von Rath was shot in the Paris Embassy and died two days later. He had joined the Nazi Party in 1932 whilst a student in Königsberg. His assassin, Herschel Grynzpan, was a young impoverished Polish-Jewish refugee who had just been expelled from Germany with all his family. This murder gave the Nazis a pretext for launching a new wave of attacks on all Jewish businesses and synagogues in Germany, on what later became known as *Kristallnacht*. November 9 was already a symbolic date in German history since on that day the Kaiser had abdicated in 1918 and in 1923 Hitler had launched his unsuccessful 'Beer Hall Putsch'. Because of von Rath's links with East Prussia, these attacks were particularly brutal in Königsberg and the main synagogue was totally destroyed. Destroyed, too, were any hopes some maintained that Nazism could be tamed. For those happy to support the Nazi regime, Königsberg would survive for another six years. For anyone else, Königsberg as a cosmopolitan, racially diverse city, rightly proud of its past and present, died in November 1938.

Until 1944 one can almost say that Königsberg 'enjoyed' the fruits of World War II. The destruction of Poland reunited East Prussia with the *Reich* and the advance into Russia again brought the Baltic States under German influence. 'Bombing' was what relatives in Hamburg or Berlin suffered, but it did not initially touch Königsberg. Food supplies were ample and prisoners provided cheap labour on the farms and in the factories. With most opponents of Nazism having been exiled by 1939, there could be no focus for any opposition and little need for it given the high standard of living enjoyed by most of the population. 1944, however, was a turning point. The defeat at Stalingrad in early 1943 and continuing German losses on all fronts after that could no longer be concealed from the population at large.

August 1944 presented the local authorities with an acute dilemma – how should the 400th anniversary of the founding of Albertina University be celebrated? In the past such celebrations had been particularly flamboyant and had been well documented for posterity. To continue in a similar vein might be seen as tasteless in the middle of an increasingly desperate war, yet to ignore the occasion could be termed as defeatism. Gauleiter Erich Koch took the second option, even sanctioning new buildings for the university. He probably bore in

ROYAL AIR FORCE REPORT ON KÖNIGSBERG RAID OF AUGUST 29–30, 1944

1900 miles, 176 aircraft, 485 tons of bombs, 16 minutes and 400 acres of devastation. This calls, and without apology, for yet another misquotation of the Prime Minister's famous epigram. Never has so much destruction been wrought by so few aircraft at so great a distance, in so short a time. Königsberg, the capital of East Prussia, the greatest port in Eastern Germany, and the base for nearly 50 enemy divisions, is practically no more. Königsberg, the administrative centre of that province of Germany which has been the malignant breeding ground of the arrogant military caste, a town which has stood unchanged for 600 years, has to the benefit of mankind, been wiped out overnight.

The effects of this blow cannot be measured merely in acres, it is a pincer movement on the grand scale. Königsberg may have been just another strategical target to Bomber Command, though a large an important one at that, but it was also a tactical target for the Russians of absolutely first-class importance. The Russian victories of June and July brought them to within 100 miles of the town and within sight of the German frontiers; so did this great port with its ample dock facilities, miles of marshalling yards and modern factories, become of paramount importance to the armies desperately trying to stem the Russian advance.

With the few railways between Berlin and the front choked with supplies in one direction and the evacuation of such of the frightened populace as were allowed to go in the other, the port became the only means of relieving this bottleneck. Through its docks came the armour, the supplies and the reserves so urgently needed to re-equip the tattered divisions after their long retreat. Through its docks must go such of the much needed agricultural produce as could be salved from this fertile but threatened area. Meanwhile the armament and engineering works were ideally situated for the maintenance and repair of unserviceable armour brought back from the front.

The Königsbergers, busily engaged in digging trenches, with their eyes turned fearfully towards the east, and the British heavily committed nearly a thousand miles away in the opposite direction, can have had little thought of danger from the west. The shock of discovering that Bomber Command could meet the needs of the western armies, engage in the battle with the flying bombs and at the same join in on the Russian front, will not have been confined to those who actually felt the blows.

Indeed to judge from the lack of comments in the press and on the wireless, it has left the enemy speechless.

Perhaps the best way of all of considering the effect of this raid is to ponder on what would have been the reactions of the Germans, and indeed of this country, had the Russians flown to Bremen before us and utterly destroyed it.

mind Hitler's interest in Frederick the Great and the commitment the emperor had shown to the 200th anniversary in 1744. At one of the formal ceremonies, Koch presented three statues, of Kant, Copernicus and Hitler. In the British air raids that followed two weeks later, most of the university was destroyed, but two of these statues survived intact. Hitler did not.

The Royal Air Force launched two major bombing attacks, on the night of August 26–27 1944 and again on August 29–30. The desolation these caused can still be seen all too clearly in the former Old Town by the river. All the streets were destroyed and only the shells of the cathedral and the castle remained. The cathedral is still being rebuilt, but the castle was torn down in the late 1960s; none of the university buildings survived. Refugees from Lithuania started to come into East Prussia. Wild cattle, abandoned by their owners, drifted across the countryside. The Russians slowly encircled the town, the last train to Berlin leaving Königsberg on January 22 1945. The next one would not leave until August 1991.

Even during the following two months, reality was evaded. Food and fuel supplies were adequate, the zoo sold annual season tickets valid until December 1945 and hairdressers required clients to make appointments two weeks in advance. Children, as normal for January, built snowmen at the side of the streets and passing soldiers handed out chocolate bars to them. Officially nobody could plan to escape, but 100,000 East Prussians did so via the port of Pillau which stayed in German hands until the end of the war.

The occupation of Königsberg came quickly and brutally; after a three-day siege the German commander, General Otto Lasch, formally surrendered to the Russians on April 10 1945. He spent the next ten years in prison and then wrote his memoirs, which still remain contentious amongst the *Vertriebene*, the exile community who fled to West Germany. With 35,000 troops and no air cover against the 250,000 Russian force, the result of the battle could not be in doubt. Some argue that, with an earlier surrender, there would have been less suffering in the town as the Russians would not have felt so vengeful. Others argue that Lasch could have disobeyed Berlin earlier and arranged for a more orderly civil evacuation, as happened in other East Prussian towns. Cynics claim that he fought until his own life was in danger and then surrendered. Hitler had ordered him to fight to the last man, but he was one of many German commanders not to carry these orders out, even though he pursued such a policy further than was necessary.

The defence of Königsberg did not prevent war crimes being carried out to the last minute. In early April 1945 resources were still found to force-march 5,000 Hungarian prisoners from Königsberg to Pillau. Some 2,000 perished en route and most of the remaining 3,000 drowned in the sea or were murdered on the beach. Only 13 were rescued by extremely brave local villagers.

Soviet rule

Although leaflets dropped by Russian aircraft before the final attack promised a quick and pleasant return to civilian life, the population of Königsberg was exposed to every possible form of human depravity as the Russian troops arrived. Women were 'lucky' if they were only raped by one soldier. Men forced into work brigades were similarly fortunate in that this ensured just enough rations to survive. Stalin is alleged to have encouraged his troops with the slogan, 'Take these blonde German women. They are all yours.' Soldiers could loot at will and understandably took the chance to do so. If there was one German word that they all learnt it was *Uhr* ('watch') but their interests could not be expected to stop there. Most had spent the last years seeing town after town destroyed by the German Army and few would not have had many relatives killed. Despite the siege and the earlier bombing, Königsberg still had a modern vibrant feel to it. Russian troops expecting an impoverished German proletariat found thousands of townhouses full of clothes, china, furniture and jewellery. One soldier wrote home, 'It is hard to know where to look first when you enter a German house. Do you realise that they all have pianos the size of tables?' Some items were unknown to them, particularly to soldiers from Central Asia. They had never seen bicycles or flushing toilets and were equally inept with both.

For about a week, Russian troops were allowed to rampage as the German Army had done on their territory for the previous four years. Under the circumstances their behaviour was perfectly comprehensible, even though it can in no way be condoned. Königsberg was the first major German town to surrender. The soldiers knew that it was going to be incorporated into the USSR. Like Berlin and Dresden, in 1945 the town was to pay a particularly high price for its Nazi past. It would soon pay an even higher one.

If law and order were quickly restored, food supplies were certainly not and mere survival became a total preoccupation for the German population of around 100,000 who remained in May 1945. Survival was only possible through ingenuity and barter. Elderly relatives were abandoned so that their clothes could be sold and then their corpses would be cannibalised. (Only those who died of typhus could expect a burial.) Pets had to be eaten, as did any non-poisonous plants. Everyone turned their hands to thieving as honesty could only lead to starvation. The three letters LSR daubed across makeshift air-raid shelters were a familiar sight in the town since this was the German abbreviation for such cellars (*Luftschutzräume*). Under the occupation it soon came to mean *Lernt Schnell Russisch* ('quickly learn Russian').

In the early days of the occupation, it was assumed that the remaining German population would be allowed to stay. In fact, some German refugees who had reached what was now western Poland were returned. By 1946, though, the German population in the city had dropped to around 25,000. Relations between the Russians and the Germans became remarkably cordial and reminiscences from both sides dating from that time testify to this. The Russians needed the Germans for their skills and for their local knowledge. They admired their resilience and cleanliness. No Russian would regularly clean the doorstep and pavement outside his house, let alone outside a bombsite. Only the Germans could find the sewers, operate the drainage systems and restore production in the amber mines. When the Königsberg trams started to operate again in the summer of 1946, there were 400 German staff and only 70 Russians. The Germans needed the Russians for regular supplies of food and money, so became the workers, tradesmen and nannies that could ensure this.

The early Russian settlers had mixed backgrounds. Some soldiers simply stayed on, attracted by a potential lifestyle unlikely to greet them elsewhere in the Soviet Union. Those who had been imprisoned by the Germans, and could therefore be judged as traitors by the Red Army, felt less threatened here as their past could be more easily falsified or ignored. New settlers were positively encouraged from summer 1946. Those from a country background admired the asphalt and cobbles which were as novel to them as bicycles and flush toilets had been to the troops a year earlier.

The Germans still went to church, although the Russians by and large did not. There were of course no orthodox churches and many Russians feared that expressions of religious belief might prejudice their future careers. A German club was founded in February 1946 and some Russians also attended. Genuine relationships between both communities started to be formed. There were again grounds for optimism. Such hopes were shattered in July 1946. Königsberg was renamed Kaliningrad (Калининград) in honour of Michael Kalinin who had just died (of natural causes). He had been a senior member of the Soviet Politburo, a man of little vision, but of great staying power. Confusingly, the same name was given to the new surrounding region (*oblast* in Russian). Although every other town and village in East Prussia, and all the streets, would now receive Russian names, many were better honoured. Insterburg, the second largest town in the former East Prussia, was renamed Chernyakhovsk after a noted commander, Ivan Chernyakhovsky, who fought heroically in many battles on the Eastern Front and died of his wounds in February 1945. Only the rivers and the town gates kept their German names after 1947 so the Pregel still ran through the town centre, overlooked by the Brandenburg Gate.

In the same month, the whole *oblast* of Kaliningrad was declared a military zone. A barbed-wire fence along the entire length of the new border with Poland went up in September 1946, dividing families and cutting the link with Germany. The following winter was, as elsewhere in Europe, a bitter one, and many were to suffer almost as badly as they had done in the summer of 1945. Many older people felt there was no alternative to suicide particularly as rations were often restricted to 'specialists'. ('Parasites' were expected to fend for themselves.) In the countryside, conditions were worse as the months of hard frost and deep snow prevented any cultivation. Yet some Russians started to learn German and in June 1947 a German newspaper, *Neue Zeit* ('New Times'), was founded with six Russian staff and four Germans. Its contents were largely translations from Russian papers, but its publication did suggest a long-term future for the German community.

The complete opposite was made clear on October 10 when Stalin suddenly ordered what would now be called ethnic cleansing. On October 22, the first special train left for Germany and many others were to follow. By March 1948, the policy had by and large been carried out, with only a few specialists allowed to stay a little longer because their expertise was still needed. Kaliningrad became a unique region of Europe in many ways. It had been ethnically cleansed with total success and with the full agreement of the wartime Allies. It became a community with no past and with minimal links to the outside world. Guidebooks and school textbooks would talk of Kant being born in Kaliningrad in 1724, but no other reference was made to the German era or even to the Seven Years War when the Russians previously occupied Königsberg. Lhasa, Pyongyang and Tirana suddenly appeared cosmopolitan in comparison as they did at least see regular delegations from abroad and occasional groups of tourists. Public displays of religion ceased as the German churches closed in 1948 and were only restored 40 years later when the Russian orthodox church took over some of the churches whose fabric could still be saved.

We must hope that those settlers who came in their twenties and are now retired will write up their experiences. For the time being, our knowledge of the next 40 years is restricted to the few official documents that have entered the public domain since the downfall of the USSR. Because of the military sensitivity of the area, minimal information was published during the Soviet era and there was no way in which it could be checked. We now know the background to the dynamiting of the castle ruins in 1969 which aimed to remove a clear visual link to the German past, but with the re-opening of the university in 1967 skilful students would in due course track this history down. The Bunker Museum was also opened in 1969, at the site of the German surrender. It displayed large-scale models of the fighting in Königsberg. In 1974 came a museum dedicated to Immanuel Kant which could not conceal his German surroundings, although he was portrayed as a 'citizen of all Europe' because of his fame. In 1975 a second German was commemorated, the astronomer Friedrich Wilhelm Bessel (1784–1846) when a memorial plaque, was erected on the site of his former observatory written in both Russian and German. (In 1989 Kaliningrad again had a Bessel Street, as it had before the war. A crater on the moon also bears Bessel's name.)

The destruction of churches continued until 1976. The last one to be blown up was the Lutherkirche, a beautiful neo-Renaissance building dating from 1907 which had not been seriously damaged during the war. The stagnation and inertia that took over during the later Brezhnev years in the USSR did not particularly affect Kaliningrad, any more than the earlier Khruschev thaw had done in the 1960s. The military maintained such a tight grip that political changes in Moscow were largely irrelevant. For the same reason, Kaliningrad was hardly to enjoy the *perestroika* ('reform') and *glasnost* ('openness') that characterised the final years of the Soviet Union in the late 1980s. Had visitors been allowed then, they would have found some lighter reading in the bookshops and a few Russian orthodox services taking place in the former Lutheran churches. That tourists were still not allowed, under any circumstances, speaks volumes.

After the failed military coup in Moscow in 1991, Kaliningraders were polled by a local newspaper and asked for their views: 25% were saddened at its failure, 25% were glad and 50% did not care. An older generation had known political terror under Stalin and then years of political inertia following his death in 1953. Younger people had only known the inertia, being totally cut off from foreigners and the more radical outbursts that flowered from time to time elsewhere in the Soviet Union.

Modern problems

1991 should have forced a break with this tradition. With the formal demise of the USSR at the end of December and the establishment of the various independent republics, Kaliningrad was now cut off from the rest of the Russian Federation by three foreign countries, Lithuania, Belarus and Poland. It had to adapt to new circumstances in the same way that Königsberg/East Prussia had done in 1919. Yet no new Hans Lohmeyer was forthcoming who could successfully maintain links with Moscow whilst at the same time achieving the local economic autonomy needed to trade successfully with western Europe. There was talk of the town becoming the 'Hong Kong' of the Baltics but Moscow did not grant the full range of tax-free privileges that such a project needed.

Initially the sudden influx of high-spending nostalgic German tourists saved the town from making serious economic decisions. Some 60,000 came in 1992 and similar figures lasted for several more years. Many German charities became active and some businesses from Germany started to invest as low labour costs compensated for all the bureaucratic hurdles that still needed to be overcome. There are other resources, too. Amber is a unique and valuable local product and the legal sales abroad guarantee a regular income. Other export products such as timber have to compete against those from Poland and the Baltic States where an efficient business ethos has quickly taken root. Income is clearly also derived from smuggling as local cigarettes are known to have worldwide distribution networks.

Ten years after the fall of communism, there is still no alternative to take its place in Kaliningrad. The private sector, being so corrupt, does not contribute sufficiently to a tax base that could in turn drive the public sector out of its torpor. There is a general expectation that either Moscow or the EU will in due course bail out Kaliningrad; there is certainly no attempt to turn to self-reliance, nor are closer links being established with other potential markets beyond Germany. The EU is seen as a threat, not as a possible stimulus.

2002 brought Kaliningrad to the attention of the West in the context of imminent EU membership for its two neighbours Poland and Lithuania. Kaliningrad residents, unlike other Russian citizens, did not need visas to travel to either country and this enabled them to travel to other parts of Russia. EU policy, however, dictated that visas would be required in accordance with practice on other borders. In the autumn, it looked as though a compromise would be reached and that transit arrangements through Lithuania would be allowed. Germany remained the major trading partner in the West and the major supporter of any charity work. Whether for ringing bells in the cathedral or for ringing birds at the Rybachy Sanctuary, it is German money that is being provided.

Yet 'Königsberg' will never take over Kaliningrad as so few people on any side would wish for this. 'Königsberg' has returned and is making its presence felt where it is most welcome: in the churches, on the farms and in the factories. History begins again in 1255 and not in 1945. 'Königsberg' remains sensibly absent from the civil administration, from education and above all from the military. Agnes Miegel (1879–1964), Königsberg's most famous poet, wrote during her final years in exile: 'Königsberg, you are NOT mortal,' and she has turned out to be right.

Königsberg and Kaliningrad began to cooperate in 1990. They now happily coexist, as Russians and Germans have so often done in the past, but it is safe to predict that they will never embark on cohabitation.

PRACTICAL INFORMATION
Communications
Telephones

Calls from Kaliningrad to foreign countries require an international access code of 810 and then the relevant country code and foreign number. Calls made to Kaliningrad from abroad require the country code for Russia which is 7 then the Kaliningrad area code 0112 and the local number. The '0' is still used when dialling from abroad.

Direct dial is available abroad from some hotels but charges vary widely and should be checked before using the phone. There is often a three-minute minimum charge, even if the line is engaged or not answered. At telephone centres around the town, charges are lower and English or German are usually spoken. There are telephone centres in the main railway station, the Central Post Office, and in the Kaliningrad Hotel. All have extensive opening hours. In 2002 they charged around 60p/$1.00 per minute for calls to western Europe.

Post

The postal service out of Kaliningrad has greatly improved in the last two to three years even though everything goes via Moscow. Allow two weeks for cards to reach western Europe, slightly longer for elsewhere. Charges are very cheap, even for air mail. Stamps are not sold at kiosks or hotel reception desks though larger souvenir shops do sell them with postcards. The two main post offices in Kaliningrad are not in the town centre; the main one is near the Zoo at Leonova 22 and another is in the main railway station to the south of the town centre.

Internet cafés

This idea has not yet caught on in Kaliningrad but most telephone centres provide internet facilities. Expect to pay around 75p/$1.20 an hour.

Tourist information

There are no tourist information offices anywhere in Kaliningrad. It is therefore advisable to prebook a transfer on arrival and a guide for a day or two to get used to the town layout, public transport and to be up to date on concerts. Kiosks sell town plans in Russian, but these can be several years out of date so may not show new hotels. A local publication *Welcome to Kaliningrad* is distributed through the larger hotels. It consists mainly of advertisements in Russian but there are short descriptions in English of the major attractions and a helpful map with roads given in both Cyrillic and transliteration. *Kaliningrad in Your Pocket* is no longer available in print but can be consulted on the website www.inyourpocket.com

Public transport

An efficient and extensive network of buses, trams and trolleybuses cover the town with very low fares. A ticket will usually cost the equivalent of £0.10/US$0.15, however long the journey. Tickets are bought on board, not beforehand in kiosks. The main bus station, beside the railway station serves other towns and villages in the region. Timetables are clearly listed there, as they are in the railway station, but there is no written guide to these services. Do not expect English or German to be spoken either in the bus station or in the railway station.

Taxis

These are now metered and are cheap by western standards. A short journey within the town centre, should not cost more than £0.75/US$1.20 or around £1.50/US$2 to the more distant hotels.

Airport

There is no public transport to the international terminal, which is about two kilometres from the domestic terminal. Whilst some taxis wait for the LOT flights from Warsaw, it would be unwise to rely on them and a transfer should be prebooked through a travel agent abroad.

Banks and money

Roubles can easily be obtained in the Baltic States, in Poland and also through some banks in western Europe. At the Lithuanian and Polish borders, these local currencies can be exchanged into roubles, otherwise it is difficult to change anything apart from American dollars and euros. The few exchange bureaux will accept other currencies such as British pounds but give very poor rates. Travellers' cheques can only be exchanged at a few banks so are best avoided. ATM machines are few and far between so remain unreliable. Credit cards are accepted by the main hotels and restaurants. The rouble has been very stable since 1999, maintaining a rate of around US$1 = RUB27. In autumn 2002, the €1 was therefore worth around RUB28 and £1 sterling around RUB45.

Accommodation

Hotels (see also pages 209–10)

Visas are issued only with confirmed accommodation and approval from the Ministry of the Interior. Local agents arrange this through tour operators abroad who then in turn arrange for visas to be issued by the local Russian Embassy. To avoid extra visa charges, bookings should be made at least six weeks before the planned date of arrival. It is therefore not practical to book hotels directly since they cannot offer this visa service. Prices given are those likely to be charged abroad by specialist travel agents who work with Kaliningrad. They usually include breakfast. There is little seasonal variation although hotels get very heavily booked from mid-June to mid-August, the German holiday season. Most hotels have a dual pricing system, with Russians paying much less than foreigners. This distinction is strictly enforced and it is, of course, the higher prices applicable to foreigners that are listed below.

Chaika Pugacheva 13; tel: 21 0729; fax: 21 2816.
This was a hotel in German times and was renovated in 1995 to what must have been its former standards. The surrounding area was and is a quiet, affluent suburb, largely untouched by bombing or fighting during the war. The décor remains German in all the 25 rooms and German is the only foreign language spoken by the staff. Breakfast is adequate, but not generous, and the menu is limited. The main road into town is a walk of 500m or so away, but then there are plenty of bus routes and passing taxis. It also has several 24-hour shops. Nearer at hand are several bars and restaurants, all with a calm, elderly clientele. Visitors who want to turn the clock back to the Königsberg era will be very happy in this hotel. Singles US$55, twins US$70.
Deima Tolstikova 15; tel: 71 0814; fax: 71 0700; email: hotel_daima@mail.ru.
The location of this hotel could not be more dire – in the middle of a dreary housing estate about 3km from the town centre – but standards inside are more than adequate compensation. Furnishings are modern and the staff welcoming, although only in German as none seem to speak English. The hotel is on several bus routes, but as taxis rarely cost more than US$1 into town, this is hardly a major bonus. Singles US$55, twins US$65.
Kaliningrad Leninsky 81; tel: 35 0500; fax: 53 6021; email: market@hotel.kaliningrad.ru; web: www.hotel.kaliningrad.ru.

This hotel sells on the basis of its location in the town centre. It also has on site a choice of shops, bars and restaurants enabling business visitors in winter to spend their whole stay within the building. These all, however, charge about double or treble the prices available within a few hundred metres of the hotel so are best avoided. The one exception is the newspaper kiosk which has a good range of maps and postcards. The exchange bureau handles currencies other than US dollars and German marks but not at competitive rates. For the time being, this is by far the largest hotel in the whole region, with over 200 rooms. All are adequately furnished and many have good views towards the cathedral. Phones in the rooms each have separate numbers not linked to the main switchboard, so if calls are expected from abroad, these numbers should be passed to relevant contacts on arrival. Hotel staff and those in the shops speak good English. Singles US$75, twins US$90.

Komandor Schastlivaya 1, tel/fax: 34 1815 and 34 1820; email: comandor@gazinter.net; web: www.comandor.gazinter.net.

This is without doubt Kaliningrad's best hotel, situated 20 minutes drive north from the town centre in a new smart suburb. It will suit those determined to have no contact with contemporary Russia: a portrait of Peter the Great dominates the reception area and all prices are quoted in US dollars. Anyone paid in roubles is unlikely to be able to afford to enter. The hotel has an underground car park, several private dining rooms, satellite television in all rooms and a large swimming pool. Singles US$90, twins US$110.

Moskva Mira 19; tel: 35 2300; fax: 35 2400.

Tourists and business visitors were all greatly relieved when renovation here was finally completed in spring 2002. Kaliningrad now has a normal hotel, with all the facilities that tourists and business travellers require, and perhaps even more important, staff who appear committed to their job. Care too has been taken with the design of both the rooms and of the public areas. The location, opposite the zoo, is very convenient for many sites, for public transport and for shops. Singles US$20, twins US$30.

Patriot Ozernaya 25; tel: 32 8707; fax: 27 5023.

For visitors on a budget this hotel is ideal. It is clean, well-maintained and adequately furnished. Most rooms have a fridge for families wishing to prepare picnics. It is a high-rise surrounded by others, about 2km to the north of the town centre. Locals who can afford it come for dental treatment here as the surgery is regarded as one of the best in town. The café has an unexpectedly wide menu with most main dishes costing around £0.75/US$1.20. Singles US$20, twins US$25.

Food and drink

Francis Drake Sovietsky 19; tel: 21 8353. Only the names of the dishes here and the pictures on the walls have any link with Britain. A Sir Drake salad for £0.90/US$1.40 is a mixture of meats, tomatoes and mayonnaise. A Manchester for a similar price is a fillet of pork, mushrooms, sour cream and garlic. The ice-cream has fortunately no hint of Britain in it. Transportation problems have prevented the flow of British beer so far but hopefully this will be resolved before long.

Kulinaria in the Kaliningrad Hotel. On the ground floor with a street entrance to the right hand side of the hotel, the colours of the ingredients and of the décor at this self-service establishment make a refreshing contrast to the drab exterior surroundings. Although a wide choice of cold meats is offered, vegetarians will not be made to feel a nuisance here. Lingering is not possible as no tables are provided, only stools and a counter. However, a quick filling meal here can be followed by a leisurely coffee in the hotel at one of the upstairs bars which overlook the cathedral.

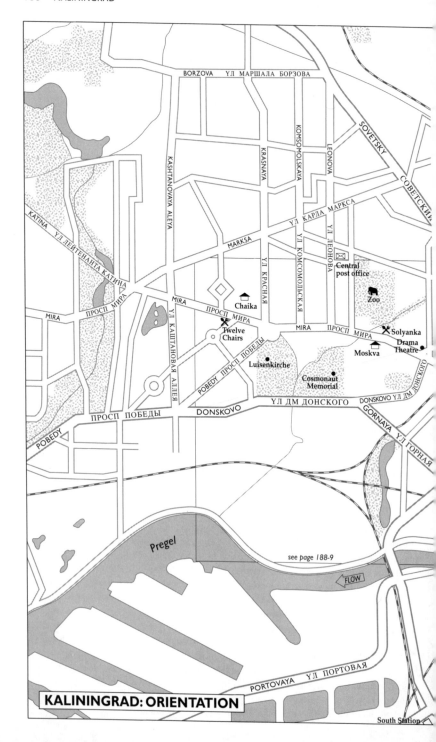

KALININGRAD: ORIENTATION

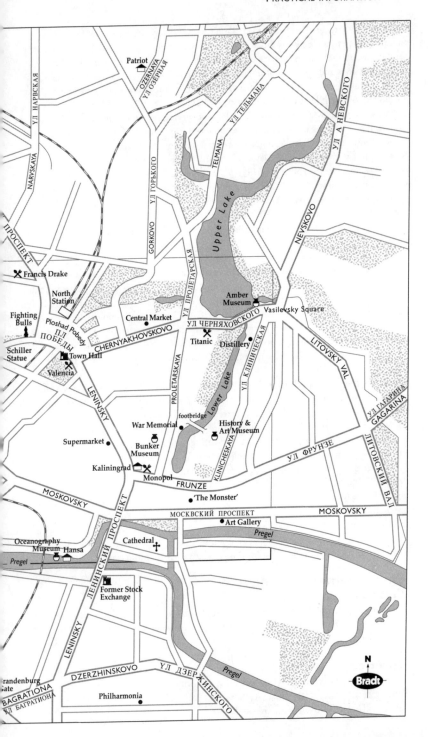

Patriot

УЛ ОЗЕРНАЯ / OZERNAYA

УЛ НАРВСКАЯ / NARVSKAYA

УЛ ГОРЬКОГО / GORKOVO

TELMANA

УЛ ТЕЛЬМАНА

Upper Lake

УЛ А НЕВСКОГО

NEVSKOVO

ПРОСПЕКТ

✗ Francis Drake

North Station

Fighting Bulls

Ploshad Pobedy
ПЛ
ПОБЕДЫ

Central Market

Amber Museum

Vasilevsky Square

УЛ ЧЕРНЯХОВСКОГО

CHERNYAKHOVSKOVO

✗ Titanic   Distillery

УЛ ПРОЛЕТАРСКАЯ

УЛ КЛИНИЧЕСКАЯ

LITOVSKY VAL

Schiller Statue

♟ Town Hall

✗ Valencia

LENINSKY

PROLETARSKAYA

Lower Lake

УЛ ГАГАРИНА
GAGARINA

ЛИТОВСКИЙ ВАЛ

Supermarket

War Memorial

footbridge

History & Art Museum

Bunker Museum

Kaliningrad

Monopol   FRUNZE

KLINICHESKAYA

УЛ ФРУНЗЕ

'The Monster'

MOSKOVSKY

ЛЕНИНСКИЙ ПРОСПЕКТ

МОСКВСКИЙ ПРОСПЕКТ

● Art Gallery

MOSKOVSKY

Pregel

Oceanography Museum Hansa

Cathedral †

Pregel

Former Stock Exchange

LENINSKY

N

Bradt

Brandenburg Gate

BAGRATIONA
УЛ БАГРАТИОНА

DZERZHINSKOVO   УЛ ДЗЕРЖИНСКОГО

Pregel

Philharmonia

Monopol Frunze 17-21; tel: 46 8311. Don't be put off by the awesome décor that dominates the entrance just as much as the restaurant itself. Although the table-cloths are starched, as are the waiters' collars, and the builders were given free rein with the marble, a fairly standard range of international dishes is offered at normal Kaliningrad prices. It will be hard to pay more than £3/US$4.50 for a substantial lunch or £5/US$8 for dinner. Allow at least two hours for proper indulgence.

Solyanka Prospekt Mira 26; tel: 27 9203. Self-service restaurants in Russia tend to be basic, but the Solyanka has definitely broken with this pattern. Cleanliness is taken to an obsession, in the toilets as much as in the restaurant itself. Menus are only in Russian, but with the clear displays, this hardly matters. A wide range of hot main courses is available for about £1/US$1.50 each and there are also even cheaper snacks, while beer is around £0.40/US$0.60 depending on the brand. Smokers are segregated into a glass-covered alcove. A board at the entrance invites job applications from potential waitresses and cooks. The salary offered of 5,000 roubles a month, about £100/US$150, clearly gives the management a good choice as service always seems to be friendly and efficient.

Titanic Chernyakhovskovo 74; tel: 53 6768. The décor was meticulously planned before this restaurant opened in the summer of 2000. The designer clearly did more than see the film to have constructed the 'life-boat alcoves', to have reprinted the old menus, and to have varnished the wood on the stairs. If the food is not quite first-class, it is well above steerage. The veneer is almost April 1912 and certainly a complete contrast to the rugged surroundings of the nearby market where the elderly attempt to supplement their minimal pensions by selling knitwear and vegetables. On the opposite side of the road are exchange bureaux with long opening hours and usually the best rates for dollars and euros.

Twelve Chairs Prospekt Mira 67; tel: 21 09031. Named after one of the few satirical novels published in Soviet times, this small cellar-bar mixes the old and the young, locals and tourists. The menu is a mixture of German and Russian, the décor and music likewise, so perhaps this is a portent of future collaboration. Whilst vodka is the usual £0.50/US$0.75 for a large measure, it is worth spending a little more on one of the fifty cocktails in which the restaurant specialises. Salmon salad accompanies them well. A bucolic evening here can happily be concluded with ice-cream drenched in a liqueur.

Valencia Ploshad Pobedy 1; tel: 43 3820. Most tourists visiting the Baltics want to forget previous holidays in Spain, but for those who cannot, southern warmth and a predictable menu of pancakes, *paella* and strong red wine are always on offer here. Their hours, too, are Spanish, as they only close at 02.00 and happily serve both late lunches and late dinners. Local people always recommend it to Western visitors, on the assumption that they are looking for the familiar rather than the unusual.

Entertainment and nightlife
Clubs and casinos

As clubs and casinos are the centres for criminal activity, they are best avoided by visitors, except for those in hotels, which restrict entry to guests and carefully vetted local people.

Theatre

The Drama Theatre at Mira 4 performs only in Russian but its repertoire is international and with cheap tickets. An enjoyable evening can be spent there even without following all the dialogue.

Music

Most concerts take place at the Philharmonia, converted from the former Church of the Holy Family. Over the next few years, more will take place in the cathedral, now that the roof is complete and the interior largely restored.

Medical services

Klinicheskaya Hospital Lower Lake, near Amber Museum; tel: 43 4556
Emergency telephone numbers Fire: 01; Police: 02; Ambulance: 03

Pharmacy

Apteka Mira 98; tel: 21 7883

Consulates

A Swedish Consulate was due to open late in 2002 to represent all EU countries, as the only other consulates in Kaliningrad are those of Lithuania and Poland.

Places of worship

There was no public worship in Kaliningrad until the end of the Soviet era in the late 1980s when some of the former German churches were taken over by the Russian orthodox community. Some services are now held in German in the cathedral.

WHAT TO SEE

A one-day walking tour is suggested, then other sites are described separately. A day excursion to the coast is also outlined. About four or five days are needed to do justice to the town and the surrounding area. Other places in the Kaliningrad region (*oblast* in Russian) are beyond the scope of this book but offer a worthwhile extension to visitors with the extra time.

One-day walking tour

A sightseeing tour of Kaliningrad has to start at the lobby of the Kaliningrad Hotel. Little has been done to remove its 30-year past. In the small shops there will be an incongruous array of goods, many of which have probably spent almost this length of time pressed up against the glass windows. Prices are absurdly low or absurdly high, never sensible. The staff will be polite and will speak reasonable English, probably more than happy to be in work in comfortable surroundings and to be paid on time. Lighting and décor is adequate but hardly enticing.

Those who came in the early 1990s, when the town was first open to tourists, might really have wondered whether such a visit was worthwhile. The hotel lobby could perhaps be passed off as mediocre. When they went outside, what stood before them and beside them was the Soviet Union at its very worst. Concrete was the sole building material and it was abused in many forms. To the left, the view was of an abandoned sixteen-storey tower block, an unfinished bridge and an enormous parking lot for trucks. Ahead was a wide straight road across a small island leading towards anonymous suburbs. To the Germans who had lived here before the war, sacrilege had been committed. This was their beloved Kneiphof, the island that had been the heart of Königsberg with the cathedral, castle, university and a cluster of surrounding lanes. Only the shell of

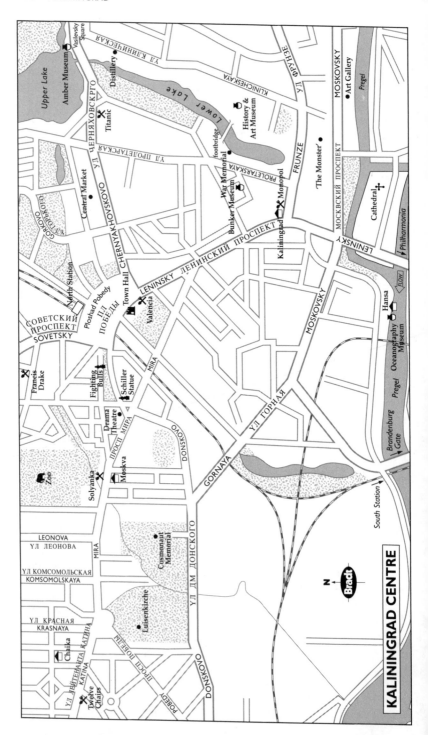

KALININGRAD CENTRE

the cathedral then remained, surrounded by an unkempt garden; its sole use was as a playground for local children, who could enjoy many variants of hide and seek. To the right a slightly less nondescript road offered a few shops with the relief of stone and granite. Few would imagine that it had once been the location of Germany's largest bookshop, Gräfe und Unzer.

The mood of the exiled Germans on their return – 60,000 came in 1992 – is perhaps best summarised by their most famous representative Marion Gräfin Dönhoff who became well-known as the publisher of the weekly *Die Zeit*. After her visit in 1991, she wrote, 'If I had been parachuted into this town and asked where I was, I would have perhaps replied Irkutsk. Nothing, absolutely nothing, reminded me of old Königsberg.'

The contemporary visitor will be much happier, mainly thanks to the fund-raising and reconciliation initiated by Marion Dönhoff since that visit. Through her paper, and by lobbying the German government and private foundations, funds have been raised to rebuild the cathedral and many other former churches. The **cathedral** (Кафедральный, open daily 09.00–17.00) must be the first port of call on any tour as it has been largely rebuilt to its pre-war format thanks to this support. Königsberg has returned to the heart of Kaliningrad.

Construction of the cathedral started in 1333 and was completed in the comparatively short period of 50 years. The first organ was installed in 1535. The early site bore an uncanny resemblance to the vista that greeted tourists in the early 1990s – an austere stone building with little decoration surrounded by greenery. It had as much military as religious significance, proving the power of the Teutonic Knights over the Prussian heathens. The oak piles, topped with copper, which form the foundations, are a credit to the advance in civil engineering at that time. They continued to support the increasing weight of subsequent builds, although it has been calculated that the cathedral has sunk 1.7m over 700 years. Finance was soon a problem and had to be resolved by the sale of Papal indulgences. In 1410 there was the first service of remembrance, to those who had died at the Battle of Grunewald, which saw the end of the Teutonic Knights as a major force in the area. The Reformation was eagerly taken up in the 1520s with Christmas 1523 being celebrated in German, a very popular move according to surviving reports. A second 58m tower was added in 1540.

Much of the interior was destroyed by fire in 1544 but it was again quickly rebuilt within six years and then expanded over the next century, when a larger organ was added and the clock built on the South Tower. It became the aim of every famous resident to be buried behind the gold altar.

However Kant, as a non-believer, never entered the building and his funeral procession stayed outside. The last restoration of **Kant's tomb** was carried out in 1924 and it was little damaged during the war. It can be seen beside the cathedral wall. (The Nazis left it intact after exhuming his skull to check on Kant's Aryan origins.)

There was minor damage to the cathedral during the French occupation at the beginning of the 19th century, when it was variously used as a stable, a prison and a hospital. Whilst Königsberg expanded in every other field over the next 100 years, it was only between 1903 and 1907 that the cathedral received much needed maintenance and rebuilding. It was the first time it had been cleaned since 1695 and many frescos were discovered as a result. The devotion of the population to the cathedral is best summarised in the writings of the poet Agnes

Miegel, born in Königsberg in 1879, who stayed until she was forced to flee in February 1945. 'You are always part of my life, like my father and my mother. Your bells wake me in the morning and send me to sleep in the evening.'

The RAF raids in August 1944 seriously damaged the cathedral but in no way destroyed it. The library, for instance, remained intact. There was no direct hit but fire spread from neighbouring buildings, which destroyed all the woodwork and led to the collapse of the roof. The site was abandoned after the war and some of the bricks were casually looted; others were specifically taken for use in various Soviet cities. The cobbles from the surrounding streets were relaid in Moscow's Red Square. The surrounding area was cleared in 1972, probably in preparation for the destruction of the site.

During the Soviet era, there was considerable dispute about the future of this ruin. Some felt it symbolised both the powerlessness and irrelevance of both Germany and religion. Others felt it was an inappropriate reminder of these former phenomena. In Kaliningrad en route to Britain in 1973, President Brezhnev certainly expressed his eagerness to destroy it, having just four years previously ordered the destruction of the castle ruins. Perhaps it was Kant's tomb that saved it, a complete and restored monument to the precursor to Marxist philosophy, beside a ruin to what he opposed.

Much of the vaulting collapsed in 1975 and some minimal restoration was done in 1976. Arguments went on as late as 1994, well after the demise of the Soviet Union, when views were still expressed that the whole area should become a sculpture park. However, that year saw the first service being held since the war and the burial of joint Russian and German capsules which included a memorial to the suffering of the German population. Four bells were restored during the following year and since then the roof has been completed and a museum has opened in the South Tower. An orthodox chapel has been built in the North Tower, a compromise from the original Russian demands that the whole cathedral should be orthodox. In mid-2002, work was concentrating on the interior windows and walls. The baptistry was completed early in 2000 with four stained-glass windows. The original designs were followed by local Russian glaziers and they depict John the Baptist, Konrad von Tierberg, the founder of Königsberg and Martin Luther. Services and concerts now take place regularly. With considerable local enthusiasm and ample German money, the cathedral should be completely restored by 2004. Both Lutheran and Orthodox services are now held in the Cathedral.

The **Cathedral Museum** already occupies several rooms in the South Tower and is regularly being extended. It shows the 1903–07 rebuilding plans, as well as others proposed earlier which were not in fact carried out. It also outlines plans for the next few years, including archaeological excavations under the former castle and university. One room is devoted to Königsberg city life around the cathedral and shows an extensive china and postcard collection. Several rooms are devoted to Kant. It is fortunate how much material on these subjects survived during the Soviet period or was taken west by refugees in 1945. The whole collection is well lit and generously displayed. Labelling is, however, only in German and Russian.

German visitors always look east from Kneiphof island, to the former Lindenstrasse, now Oktyabraskaya. The remaining brick building facing the bridge dates from 1905 and was a Jewish orphanage for around 45 children. The

Synagogue, which had been built a decade earlier, was destroyed by the Nazis on *Kristallnacht*, November 9 1938.

The street was also famous for the house of Käthe Kollwitz, an artist born there in 1867. Although she moved to Berlin in 1891, she kept close links with Königsberg until the rise of the Nazis. She never made a secret of her left-wing views, and her paintings – similar in many ways to those of the English artist L S Lowry – show the suffering of working-class people under various regimes. She was invited to Moscow in 1927 as part of a delegation to the celebrations of the tenth anniversary of the Russian Revolution. She courageously stayed in Germany during the Nazi era, feeling she would be more of an embarrassment by staying than by going into exile. Her work was banned from public exhibition during this time. Despite this political background, her house was not restored during the Soviet period and she was never mentioned in local publications of that era.

Looking south from the island, the former **Stock Exchange**, painted in a light-blue pastel, stands out on the riverbank. As a contrast to German Gothic and Soviet concrete, it is a welcome Florentine Renaissance façade and was built in the 1870s, when the town's prosperity was at its height. Like the cathedral, it is built on a foundation of deep piles, the exact number used was 2,202 and they are mostly 4.5m (15ft) deep. Statues were erected beside the four corners of the building, which depicted four continents, and hence the extent of Königsberg trade at the time, but these did not survive the war. The ground floor of the building is now a pretentious restaurant, Monetny Devor, one of the few places where the local rich like to flaunt themselves. Unlike their counterparts in other Russian cities, successful business people in Kaliningrad tend to enjoy their wealth discreetly.

Walking north, back across the river, an incomplete Soviet-era office block, the **'Monster'**, as it is usually now called, dominates the skyline. It is built over the foundations of the famous castle (*Schloss* in German) that has haunted contemporary Kaliningrad. The castle dated from 1257 and dominated the German town throughout its history. All major ceremonies of state took place in its main reception room. Peter the Great stayed there and Frederick the Great accepted the surrender of the Russian Army there at the end of the Seven Years War. In 1904 Russian and German Social Democrats were tried there, accused of smuggling Lenin's fledging journal *Iskra* ('The Spark') into Tsarist Russia. The castle housed the Prussian Museum and then, during World War II, the Amber Chamber, which had been brought back from Tsarskoye Selo, outside Leningrad, by German troops. The museum curator, Dr Alfred Rohde, vowed he would not leave Königsberg in 1945 without his treasure but neither he nor the Chamber was ever seen again. One mosaic panel was finally rediscovered in Bremen in 1997 and was sent back to Russia in April 2000 in return for paintings taken by the former Soviet government which had belonged to the Bremen Art Gallery before the war. A small panel has been rebuilt for the Amber Museum in Königsberg but a full restoration is planned for Tsarskoye Selo by 2003.

The former Amber Museum, which was also housed in the castle, boasted about 100,000 items, of which 11,000 were fortunately taken to Göttingen University in late 1944 for safe keeping and therefore survived. The rest of the collection was either destroyed or disappeared.

Much of the correspondence between Moscow and courageous local architects about the proposed destruction of the castle and a suitable replacement

RETURN TO KÖNIGSBERG

My family left East Prussia in 1938 when I was aged 7: refugees from Hitler's Germany. We were to settle in New Zealand, on the opposite side of the world. My father had a globe of the world, and I was worried about where we were going, because looking at New Zealand on the globe, it seemed people had to walk upside down. My father said that wouldn't be a problem, and it wasn't; not being able to speak the same language was a greater worry, for a while. But New Zealand turned out to be a great choice for our new home.

Exactly 60 years later I returned to the place of my birth for the first time. My wife and I flew to Vilnius, then were driven to Kaliningrad, the city where I had been to kindergarten and (for two years) to school. As we crossed the border and moved deeper into the former East Prussia a number of memories came back. The light blue of the sky, the shape of the clouds, captured by pictures my grandfather used to paint, some of which we still have. Farmers haymaking, stacking the hay in round haystacks and transporting it by horse-drawn carts. Storks nesting on telegraph poles, some with large chicks. Swallows. Cobbled streets. As it grew dark, the road sweeping through avenues of trees in the countryside, the headlights catching reflector paint; vague childhood recollections of trips with my grandparents from Königsberg to Insterburg (Chernyakhovsk) to visit my grandparents there. We reach our hotel in Kaliningrad late at night and, despite the excitement, sleep well.

The next day, with our guide, we set out to look at Kaliningrad. The guide assures us that the trams have been replaced, but they seem to have been modelled on the ones I knew. I have a book with me, *Königsberg in 144 Pictures*, and recognise many of the buildings, although others have been destroyed. Some of the streets are familiar to me, Steindamm where my father had his office. Here the buildings have all gone, but the former shape of the streets is clear and unchanged. We come to the Hufenallee with its distinctive winding stretch and instantly I know where we are. I say to our guide, we are close to the Zoo – around the next corner we come to the Zoo entrance through which I was often taken as a child; it seems unchanged. A few minutes later, an unforgettable indescribable moment, we are outside the apartment building where my family was living in 1938.

Thomas Eichelbaum

has recently come to light. To the politicians, the building represented 'centuries of German militarism and plunder' which should be replaced by a large modern civic building to display Soviet power in what had been the heart of the German city. The political activities of the exiled East Prussians in West Germany clearly influenced the final decision to remove all traces of the castle in 1969. They used the castle tower as the logo on all their campaign literature that lobbied vocally and frequently for the then West German government to continue its policy of regarding East Prussia as being 'temporarily under Soviet administration' rather than as being lost for good. It therefore made political if not aesthetic sense for this symbol of former German power to be eliminated. Architects pointed out the many historical links the building had with Russia, as outlined above, and how a Soviet war memorial could be incorporated into a restored building. Their pleas were ignored and a budget agreed for a new town hall.

The 25-year saga that followed showed Soviet planning and political bigotry at its very worst. An initial budget of 1.6 million roubles (about £500,000 or US$1 million at the official rate of exchange in 1969) was agreed for a 16-storey building. Over the first two years, around 1,100 concrete pillars, each eight metres in length, were dug into the marshy ground beside the castle. Cynics were soon to point out that they did not have the firmness of those laid by the Germans 700 years before. Twenty workers were employed on the site between 1972 and 1976 and they completed six storeys. The next ten storeys took a further five years so the basic structure was finished in 1981. By then costs had increased to 9 million roubles, a surprisingly capitalist problem in a country that had been cut off from a market economy for 30 years. There was no money for moving the local government and none for installing electricity and heating. In 1988 money was found to furnish half the building but this work was not completed by the time the Soviet Union collapsed in 1991. Nothing has been done to the building since and there are still no plans for it, not even just to tear it down.

Turning right along Moskovsky for about 100m, leaving behind the Monster and the Kaliningrad Hotel, the first major building on the right hand side is the **Art Gallery**. Soviet money fortunately did not run out here and the gallery opened in 1989, so just in time to give a final overview of art throughout the USSR at that point. Every former Soviet republic is represented, both by paintings and by applied arts. Ceramics and glass are both well covered, but more surprising are the copies of imperial china and lacquer. This style of china with its gold leaf represents a style of life to which few in Kaliningrad can or could ever relate. The gallery holds many exhibitions of children's art. They are now encouraged to paint Königsberg as well as Kaliningrad. The exploits of the Teutonic Knights provide ample material for them to portray happily. One of the most famous local artists is Boris Bulkagov, born in 1944, whose pictures are marked by his almost total use of dark colours. The gallery closed for rebuilding in summer 2002 and the reopening date was at that time uncertain.

Cross Moskovsky and head towards the Lower Lake, called *Schlossteich* or 'Castle Lake' in German times. The surroundings of the lake had been made communal in 1900 and the path around it built in 1937. The History and Art Museum, on the eastern side of the lake, can easily be identified as a former German concert hall.

The nondescript five-storey building on the western side used to be the town's most famous hotel, the Park, where on different occasions both Hitler and Molotov regularly stayed. Because of the notoriety of its former guests, this is now an office building.

The **History and Art Museum** (Историкохудожественный музей) has been totally transformed since the Soviet period. Most labels are in English and German. It originally consisted of the remains of the Prussian Museum collection, which had previously been housed in the castle. This was largely an archaeological collection, so did not cause political problems. It in fact enabled Soviet historians to claim a Slavic rather than a German origin for many of the artefacts. The museum has recently undergone considerable expansion, showing not only extensive material from pre-war Königsberg, but also from the early Soviet period in the 1950s. One can only hope that what is portrayed as a typical apartment from the 1950s is no longer typical of homes in the town outside. Fabrics, furniture, paintings and crockery from both eras have been salvaged. Some 'bourgeois' exhibits such as refined table linen and advertisements are displayed, as well as examples of the inflation banknotes from 1923 when they had to be constantly recycled and overprinted. Programmes and layouts are displayed for the major annual trade fair, the *Ostmesse*, which took place every autumn between 1920 and 1941.

The Königsberg room in other respects still shows considerable political bias. Far more is shown of the rise of the Communist Party than that of the Nazi Party, but no attempt is made to assess the communists' failure to overcome the Nazis in the years prior to 1933. The banners, the photographs and the pamphlets all date from earlier. Some items would seem more appropriate for a car-boot sale than for a serious town museum. Beer mugs and ashtrays seem an odd choice of exhibit but anything gathered from former Königsberg has a magical significance for those who still remember it.

The Soviet room is now frank about issues that were formerly taboo. There are photographs of the destruction of the castle, and portraits of both Stalin and Khrushchev, leaders whose pictures were not shown elsewhere in the later Soviet times. Other exhibits have not been changed since the 1980s and are reminiscent of the Moscow 'Exhibition of Economic Achievements'. Several spacemen came from Kaliningrad so photographs of them with the Politburo abound and a display case is devoted to the presents given to them by visiting foreign statesmen, such as a cigar from Fidel Castro and a ring from Le Duan, the Vietnamese Prime Minister. The **shop and stalls** within the museum offer a variety and value impossible to find elsewhere in the town. They offer good selections of amber, lacquer, woodwork and paintings and some books likely to be of interest to foreigners.

Cross the lake on the footbridge and note the modest **war memorial** to the left. It commemorates Colonel Tulan and his French regiment that fought as part of the Soviet air force in 1942–44. In February 1944 the regiment was named Normandy Neman, the Neman (or Niemen) being the river that traditionally divided Russia from Germany (and which now divides Lithuania from Kaliningrad). The memorial notes that the regiment made 5,000 sorties, fought in 869 battles and destroyed 273 German aircraft.

Next cross Proletarskaya which leads into the **university**. The buildings here date from the 19th century and were designed by August Stüler, one of the pupils of Karl Friedrich Schinkel, Germany's most famous architect of the early 19th century. They were all completed within a year between 1858 and 1859. Although seriously damaged at the end of the war, they could have been restored to show the original Italian façade but this was not done. It is necessary to wander inside for any memories of the 19th century. In the square which the university buildings surround, old sculptures are being restored and new ones being built. The original statue of Kant disappeared at the end of the war, but Marion Dönhoff paid for a replacement to be provided in 1992. This replaced a statue of Ernst Thälmann which had been there for most of the Soviet era. He was the leader of the German Communist Party during the 1930s and he died in a concentration camp in 1944.

In the centre of the square is the entrance to the **Bunker Museum** (Блиндаж Ляша, open daily 10.00–17.00), sometimes called the Lasch Bunker after General Lasch, who had it built as his headquarters for the final defence of Königsberg in 1945. Several of the rooms are much as he would have left them on April 10 1945 after signing the capitulation and surrendering himself to what would turn out to be ten years imprisonment. The heating pipes, the telephone wires and the electric cables have all remained intact. When the museum opened in 1967, it provided the only picture of former Königsberg that local residents were allowed to have, with detailed models of the town layout and of the military formations. Even a German slogan (*Wir kapitulieren nie* – 'We will never surrender'), daubed on a wall, is included. The smallest exhibit is a ticket for the last train to Berlin that left on January 22 1945. The leaflets dropped by the Russians stressed the futility of continued fighting and promised food supplies and family reunions to all who surrendered. Recently the museum has been extended to show the burial sites of troops from both sides.

Leave the museum in a westerly direction towards Lenin Prospekt. On the far side of the road is the town's major supermarket (ВЕСТЕР), open daily until 23.00. Turning left takes one back to the Hotel Kaliningrad after 100m. Readers of Russian will find the **kiosks** along here a good source of books, maps and magazines.

Another site within walking distance of the hotel is the **Oceanography Museum** (Музей истории мирового океана, open daily except Monday, 11.00–17.00) based in and around the ship *Vityaz*. This is now permanently moored on the Pregel about 700m from the hotel. During 2000 and 2001 the exhibitions were considerably extended and now include new buildings on the shore. *Vityaz* was built as a cargo boat in Bremerhaven in 1939 and launched with the name *Mars*, after a river in western Germany rather than the planet. It was never used as a cargo carrier, being taken over as a troop ship on the outbreak of war. In March and April 1945 it made several trips between Pillau, the port on the coast nearest to Königsberg, and Denmark, rescuing about 20,000 civilians from the oncoming Russians. When the British liberated Denmark from the Germans, they took over the boat and renamed it *Empire Forth* but it only stayed in British hands until February 1946 when it was 'returned' to the Russians, being seen as based in territory now belonging to them. This British name would have been most appropriate for the Russians in view of the territory they seized at the end of World War II, but they renamed it firstly *Equator* and then *Vityaz* ('Noble warrior').

It was moved to Vladivostok and between 1949 and 1979 made constant oceanographic expeditions to the Pacific Ocean. It also made pioneering visits to Osaka and to San Francisco in 1958, the first in each case since the start of the Cold War. Jacques Cousteau was invited on board in Mombasa in 1967, again a symbol of an easier political climate. Its last expedition finished in Kaliningrad harbour where it would rot for ten years, becoming known as the 'rusty tin' until a restoration programme began in 1990. This was completed in 1994, partially with the help of surviving members of the *Mars* crew. (Meanwhile another *Vityaz* was built in 1981 and is now part of the Russian Black Sea fleet based at Novorossisk.)

The exhibitions are not limited to the life of the ship. One room covers the history of oceanography, the laboratories ships included, and two earlier boats that carried the name *Vityaz*. Pictures show the startled reaction of the inhabitants of New Guinea in 1870 to a white man when the captain of an earlier *Vityaz* landed. They assumed he had come from the moon, as his skin was a similar colour. The researches beneath the Pacific, including the measurement of the Marianas Trench, are covered extensively. The new political climate means that life on board in any era can be shown honestly, and where appropriate, ridiculed. The whims and needs of all former commanders, Tsarist, Nazi or Soviet are not hidden, be they for an absurdly large piano, a shredding machine or a portrait of Lenin. Mess rooms, too, with appropriate memorabilia, have been rebuilt. The museum authorities hope to set up a British room, if enough material from the 1945–46 period can be provided.

The 60th anniversary in 1999 of the building of the ship was a suitable pretext for further enlargement of the collections. One theme is 'Maritime Königsberg' showing the expansion of the harbour, firstly in 1901 when the canal to the sea at Pillau was widened, and secondly in the 1920s when Königsberg became eastern Germany's major port, following the loss of Danzig and Memel (now Gdansk in Poland and Klaipėda in Lithuania respectively) at the end of World War I. Many of the buildings dating from those times, such as the grain silos, can still be seen along the riverside. In 2000 a miniatures gallery was added with replicas of ships from Egypt, Greece, Japan and Fiji. More familiar to British visitors will be the models of the *Revenge* and of Elizabeth I knighting Francis Drake. Columbus and Queen Isabella have not been forgotten, nor has the *Santa Maria*. April 2000 also saw the conversion of several cabins into displays of coral reefs, sharks jaws and underwater geological discoveries.

In July 2000 the opening to the public of a B-413 submarine greatly increased the scope of the museum. Originally built in 1969, it then travelled almost as much as *Vityaz*, being a frequent visitor to Cuba. The B-413 was the Soviet answer to the NATO Foxtrot submarines, being able to carry 22 torpedoes and to launch them from a depth of 100 metres. Only the small and the agile will be able to enjoy the displays on board as the interior has been maintained as closely as possible to the original. It is hard to believe that it housed 80 men for three month journeys; only the captain and the KGB agent had single rooms. An exhibition honestly portrays the history of the Russian/Soviet navy from 1834 until the present day. Tragedy and triumph are covered in equal measure.

The museum complex around *Vityaz* is probably the most dynamic institution in the whole Kaliningrad *oblast*. Each year there is expansion, the exhibits are regularly updated and the publications show a professionalism totally lacking elsewhere. In 2001 the Whale Pavilion was opened; it displays a whale17 metres long which was captured in 1975 but which was then buried in the sand along the Baltic coast for the next 25 years. A completely new museum will open in 2003, covering in greater detail the whole field of oceanography and also introducing the theme of global warming. Other plans are to restore a fishing trawler and to cover the field of space exploration as several of the leading USSR cosmonauts were born in Kaliningrad. The museum website www.vitiaz.ru provides current information on the whole site. By 2004 a whole day will be needed to do justice to the whole collection.

Further afield

Many other sites within the city are just too far to walk from the Kaliningrad Hotel but can be easily reached by bus or taxi. Tour operators abroad can pre-book English-speaking guides with their own cars and this is the most convenient way to visit other sites in the town and also for visits along the coast. The following itinerary can be done in a long day, or be divided into two days.

The first port of call must be at the **Amber Museum** (Музей янтарья, open daily, except Monday, 10.00–17.30) housed in the Dohna Tower, one of six similar 19th-century fortifications that still dominate the city skyline. General Dohna fought against Napoleon. It replaced an earlier museum, which had been beside the mines at Yantarny on the coast. A few items come from the pre-war museum, which had been housed in the former castle.

Amber has formed the one thread that binds together the history of the region. Since 90% of the world's amber production comes from this area, its value was an incentive for many generations of conquerors and would-be conquerors. The Prussian tribes traded it with the Romans, who saw magical and practical value in it. Tacitus and Pliny the Elder both refer to it and gladiators wore it. Amber would become an important ingredient in medicine, in agricultural fertilisers, and in varnish. It would strengthen fishing nets and be used in fumigation. The museum therefore presents a two thousand year artistic and political history of the region through the 6,000 amber products displayed. The natural history goes back millions of years to the formation of fossilised resin, which is the basis of amber.

The most interesting exhibits are those from the Soviet period; models from Aesop's fables such as *The Fox and the Grapes* are a surprising legacy but more obvious ones are the model Kremlins, dams, pylons, nuclear icebreakers and power stations with smoking chimneys. Examples of gifts to foreign dignitaries include jewellery boxes with the hammer and sickle emblem and statues of Soviet leaders. None have been deposed from the museum so Lenin, Stalin and Khrushchev sit peacefully side by side. There are some replicas of famous pieces in the Hermitage and Kremlin collections. The largest of these weigh over a kilo. Clearly the lost Amber Room cannot be forgotten in these surroundings, so some of the original panelling has been copied and paintings show how the complete original looked when it was displayed at Tsarskoye Selo, outside St Petersburg.

Do not miss the **museum shop** before leaving. Its lack of taste rivals that of much of the collection and the use of amber dust enables 'pictures' to be sold very cheaply. Leonardo di Caprio and Diana, Princess of Wales both cost little more than £1/US$1.50 in 2002.

The museum is on Vasilevsky Square, named after the commander responsible for the final victory over the Germans. The **memorial** at the centre of the square commemorates this victory, in particular 216 Heroes of the Soviet Union and 20 who received this award twice. On the opposite side of the road from the museum is a **distillery**; its shop sells vodka liqueurs at prices low even by Kaliningrad standards. Perhaps it is just as well nobody can really tell how dependent the local economy is on drink and cigarettes smuggled out to Poland and then on to the rest of Europe.

Proceeding west from the museum, along Chernyakhovskovo, the **Central Market** (Центральный рынок) is on the right hand side of the road after about 800m. Between the First and Second Wars, the halls housed the famous *Ostmesse*, an annual trade fair which brought together major traders from East Prussia with their opposite numbers in the Baltic States and the Soviet Union. Being the largest building in Königsberg, it was also the centre for all political rallies during both the Weimar Republic (1920–33) and the subsequent Nazi era. President Ebert opened the building and the first fair in 1920 and Hitler and Himmler spoke here on several occasions.

Now it has a largely local function and for tourists gives a clear indication of what is available and what is fashionable. The 2000 stands within the halls are clearly regulated with prices listed and satisfactory hygiene. Those outside bring together sellers and buyers both of whom look equally desperate. A guide is useful since, when prompted, an otherwise banal stand can suddenly produce caviar or silk at prices much lower than elsewhere. Good picnic ingredients available here include German sausage, Polish ham, Lithuanian fruit, local cheeses and the famous Russian black bread. Few tourists can take advantage of all the fresh fish that arrives here at least once a day.

Chernyakhovskovo continues to **Ploshchad Pobedy** (Площадь Победы; 'Victory Square') the former Hansaplatz, which Gauleiter Erich Koch renamed after himself in 1933. It had by then become the business and administration centre of the town. On the north side of the square, a dominating statue of Lenin makes it clear who are now the masters here but is being overshadowed by the first Orthodox cathedral now being built in Kaliningrad. Boris Yeltsin laid the foundation stone. For the time being, there is a small wooden Orthodox chapel at the side of the building site. There are no chairs as believers stand through the service. In the garden to the southeast of the square stands a statue of Mother Russia; she replaced Stalin on this plinth in 1974.

The former **North Station/Nordbahnhof** built in 1930, still functions as such but it now also includes offices of several government departments and private businesses. Foreign businesses such as the Hamburg Chamber of Commerce are in a new building behind the station on Sovietsky Prospekt (Советский проспект). The town hall building on the south side of the square dates from 1923 and is one of very few to have served the same function both in German and in Soviet/Russian times.

Leaving Victory Square to the west, along Prospekt Mira (Проспект Мира; 'Peace Avenue') note first the bronze **statue** of the fighting bulls on the right-hand side of the road. They are the work of a sculptor August Gaul whose bronze animals became famous all over Germany before World War I. In early Soviet days the statue was moved to the zoo, but it was returned here to its original location in the late 1970s. Local people now read a contemporary theme into the statue, seeing it as a representation of Kaliningrad locked into battle with Moscow. Behind the statue note the baroque entrance of the former courthouse which dates from 1913. Beside the courthouse are the former postal headquarters constructed in 1924. This building now houses the senior staff of the Baltic Fleet so is one of the best maintained in the whole town centre.

The next major building on the right hand side is the Drama Theatre, built in 1927 but given its current bolshoi façade by the Soviet regime. In the six years prior to the Nazi regime every German actor of note played here and the Soviets continued the high standards, once it was finally reopened in 1980. On the other side of the road is a statue of the German writer Friedrich Schiller (1759–1805) which was allowed to stay during the Soviet period, probably because his work was regarded as very 'progressive'. A rather implausible story is told to explain its survival at the end of the war: the words 'don't shoot' were allegedly daubed across it in both German and Russian.

Prospekt Mira now widens and soon the entrance to the zoo (Зоопарк) comes up on the right hand side. It is open daily at 09.00, closing at 21.00 between May and September, at 17.00 during other months. It was founded in 1896 and is the only institution in Königsberg/Kaliningrad to have had a continuous history through German, Soviet and now Russian times. It might well be the world's first theme park; its early posters were decades ahead of their time, the funfair was always as crucial as the collection of animals and no secret was ever made of its commercial intent. Slot machines competed with donkey rides, cycle races and tennis tournaments. There were free family days when cooking facilities would be provided, thereby encouraging long stays and extensive patronage of the fairground attractions. Within two years of its opening, it sold 25,000 annual season tickets, a present for which every young Königsberger yearned at Christmas. Its flamboyant first director Hermann Claass stayed in charge until his death in 1914, never letting his commercial flair interfere with the expansion and maintenance of the collection. Within a year of the opening there were 983 animals and by 1910 this number increased to 2,126, including two Siberian tigers donated by Moscow Zoo.

It closed on the outbreak of war in August 1914 but popular demand and the elimination of any threat from Russia enabled it to reopen in July 1918, before the end of that conflict. It was completely rebuilt during the 1930s and these buildings largely remain despite the zoo being a battleground in April 1945. The zoo stayed open throughout the war this time and the Soviet government even presented two elephants in 1940, while the cynical Nazi–Soviet Pact was still in effect. Annual season tickets were printed for 1945 and were sold from Christmas 1944 until the following March. The director throughout the war was Dr Hans-Georg Thienemann whose father Johannes was founder of the bird sanctuary at Rossitten (see page 208).

Many stories circulate about the number of animals who survived through May 1945 – most of course were killed by the starving residents. Four is the most quoted figure, representing a hippopotamus, a deer, a fox and a badger. Several Russian soldiers tried to feed the hippopotamus which had apparently lost its appetite. Conventional nourishment failed, but a fortnight of vodka, allegedly four litres a day, succeeded in reviving it. The hippopotamus is now therefore the zoo's logo. In the midst of the tragedy that engulfed Königsberg in the summer of 1945, it is good to find one amusing story.

The zoo reopened in 1947, it is claimed with a collection of 2,000 animals, though this figure is now doubted. For the local population, it is again a major attraction although they must feel frustrated at the rather run-down air it now presents. Around 300,000 come each year and a pet shop has been added to the traditional attractions. With a brochure printed in colloquial English, it is, however, well in advance of other Kaliningrad tourist sites in attracting foreign visitors. They are promised 'baboons with colourful bottoms' and 'apes who so closely resemble humans that they look like someone you have probably met before.' Hermann Claass would be proud of the marketing flair shown by his Russian successors.

Almost opposite the zoo south of Prospekt Mira is the **Cosmonaut Memorial**, its circular format with the space in between portraying the journeys around the globe that Kaliningrad's most famous sons accomplished in the 1970s. One, Alexei Leonov, was the first to leave a spaceship whilst it was in orbit. Another, Victor Patzayei was killed in a failed landing when his rocket returned to earth.

Leaving the zoo and continuing along Prospekt Mira out of town, Germany begins to take over the architecture from the Soviet Union. After 200m on the left, the **Luisenkirche** makes this point emphatically. It was built around 1900, paid for largely by one benefactor Louis Grosskopf. He founded a cigar factory in 1857 but expanded the business so successfully that by 1900 he was employing 400 people there and had opened 18 shops around the town. The consecration of the church in 1901 commemorated the 200th anniversary of the crowning of King Frederick I in 1701. The German community worshipped here until 1948 when it was turned into a storeroom for gardening tools used in the surrounding park. Its conversion into a puppet theatre in 1976 possibly saved it from destruction as that was the last year in which German churches were still being pulled down.

A further kilometre along the same road brings up on the left the first new church to be built since the war. It uses the German name **Auferstehungskirche** ('Church of the Resurrection') and was completed in 1999 on land that had earlier been a German cemetery. The large Lutheran exile community in Germany had wanted to re-establish a church in Kaliningrad, theirs having been the predominant religion in the former East Prussia since the 16th century – both Martin Luther's son and daughter had been active in the area and were buried in Königsberg. Every former church considered for this gave rise to considerable difficulties. The current Russian organisation was in some cases not willing to move, in others the bureaucratic and financial hurdles in rebuilding turned out to be too great.

The church now serves a local Russian community, the Volga Germans, who have settled in Kaliningrad with the hope of eventually being resettled in Germany, and the increasingly large number of Germans who now work in Kaliningrad. Attending a service or a concert, or seeing all the voluntary activities that take place during the week shows how strongly German/Russian reconciliation can work. The altar is of great significance, being assembled from bricks taken out of eight different ruined churches.

The oldest church in East Prussia, the **Juditterkirche**, is another kilometre or so along Prospekt Pobedya, but on the right hand side. The Juditter suburb, (renamed Mendeleevo (Менделеева)) was as sought after by successful Germans as it now is by successful Russians. The area offers space, greenery, cleanliness and above all privacy. The public parks near to the church rivalled the zoo as an attraction for children. Reminiscences from former East Prussians tell of collecting anemones in spring and acorns in autumn, of climbing trees, of open-air concerts, and the climax of the afternoon, buying peppermint drops and lemonade at the sweet-shop. The church dates originally from the 13th century with the tower being added at the turn of the 14th/15th century. It was extensively restored in 1906 and this revealed wall paintings which had been hidden for centuries. Although the church was totally untouched by the war and fighting, much of the intricate woodwork was plundered in the immediate aftermath and then 35 years of complete neglect left little of the former interior. Germans were allowed to continue worshipping here until their expulsion in 1948.

The ruins were given over to the Orthodox Church in 1984 and a basic restoration was completed in 1988. Services started in 1986, the first to be held in the Kaliningrad region since 1948. Official atheism had therefore lasted 38 years. It would take another two or three years before any other churches reopened. Given the vigorous support that the local Orthodox community gives to the church, the building is unlikely ever to return into Lutheran hands. However, the German cemetery beside the church is being slowly restored and a memorial plaque is planned to all Germans killed in Königsberg at the end of the war.

Another visit should be made within the town and that is to the **Brandenburg Gate** (it has kept the same name in Russian) situated south of the river on Ulitsa Bagrationa (Улица Багратиона) near to the main railway station. Architecturally, it has nothing in common with its Berlin namesake although being as large, trams and cars also go through it. Like six other similar gates that date from the early 19th century, it is a redbrick structure built so well that it survived both the RAF bombs and the subsequent Soviet onslaught. It even retains two statues, of General von Boyen and General von Aster, two prominent 19th century commanders.

If Lenin dominates the square in front of the North Station, Kalinin has to have his glory here in front of the **South Station** (Южный Вокзал). As most visitors, whether local or international, will arrive here or at the neighbouring bus station, he can perhaps claim to be more prominent. There are now slow attempts to bring back some of the fame that the station rightly deserved in German times although a wooden roof still takes the place of the former glass one. A small **railway museum** was opened in summer 2000 with two restored steam engines and the promise of more. A large post office is at the western end of the station complex and beside it an antique shop, full of Königsberg and Soviet memorabilia. There is another antique shop on the opposite side of the square, beside which is one of the larger bookshops in Kaliningrad.

The current home of the Kaliningrad Philharmonic Orchestra is in the former **Kirche zur Heiligen Familie** ('Church of the Holy Family') known as Philharmonia in Russian. It is on the same road as the Brandenburg Gate, Ulitsa Bagrationa, and it is a walk of about 700m from there or from the station. Originally one of four Catholic churches in Königsberg built around 1900, it was saved from serious damage at the end of the war because it was surrounded by narrow streets. It therefore avoided the worst of the fighting and the bombardments. In the early 1970s, whilst other churches in Kaliningrad were still being pulled down, restoration started here and in 1980 it opened as a concert hall. An organ was added in 1982 and good standards of maintenance have been upheld ever since, together with equally good standards of catering in the crypt-café underneath.

OUTSIDE THE CITY

If time only allows for a one-day trip outside the town of Kaliningrad, this must be to the coast and along the Curonian Spit (Курщская коса) towards the Lithuanian border. It should be done by car and with a guide since it involves a number of stops and signing in many places is not good. Such a trip can start in **Yantarny** (Янтарный), which will very likely be the backbone of the Kaliningrad area's economy for the next 100 years, when the amber mine there is expected to run out. Known as Palmnicken in German times, the village is on the coast about 35 kilometres from Kaliningrad. Its wealth is well disguised since the village houses have a forlorn look and its roads are poorly maintained. Bomb damage was minimal so older German tourists can recognise the layout and again enjoy Sunday afternoons along the beach.

There is now just one large open-cast mine in use, producing about 450 tons of amber a year, about 90% of world production. Water has now seeped into the others, although Russian children follow their German predecessors in collecting amber pieces from the beach when they have been washed up after storms.

There is a somewhat precarious viewing point from which the whole mine can be seen; strong footwear is necessary to reach it and an equally strong constitution to tolerate the dire environmental pollution that it causes. The site was privatised in 1990 and then re-nationalised three years later with the hope of returning most of the profits into government hands. The Baltic Germans in the 13th century had similarly tried to control this trade and although they publicly hanged private traders, they were as unsuccessful at controlling it as their contemporary Russian successors. A small **shop** near the site is sometimes open for the purchase of amber; otherwise the Amber Museum in Kaliningrad is the best source.

If ever a reward could be made for the town in the Kaliningrad region least affected by the Soviet occupation it must go to **Rauschen** or as it is still officially called **Svetlogorsk** (Светлогорск). Its role as a seaside resort did not alter, and having official Soviet status as a spa town, money could always be found for maintenance. The Russian name translates as 'bright city', the German one as 'to rustle'. Both are equally appropriate for a well-designed spacious town full of trees and shrubs. A good regular train service operates from Kaliningrad and the town is small enough to be explored *in toto* on foot. It was the introduction of this train service in 1900 that brought day-trippers from Königsberg to Rauschen and so made it less exclusive than it had been in the 19th century. The Soviet Union, rather than Russia, intrudes with the street names. Marx, Lenin, Kalinin, Gagarin and the October Revolution are all remembered but, unique for the region, the statue of Lenin has been removed. Perhaps he may in due course be replaced by Prussia's King Friedrich Wilhelm I who first made the town famous in the early 18th century. Otherwise one could be in any small German town on the Baltic coast. At weekends, the town is as lively in the winter as it is in the summer. Its year-round population is around 4,000 compared to 2,500 before the war, but this trebles in the summer season when Russians come from all over the federation for their holidays and for medical treatment. Svetlogorsk likes to think of itself as the Sotchi of the north, rivalling this Black Sea resort in its facilities and in its prestige.

The red-brick Gothic church was designed by August Stüler, famous for many grander buildings in Berlin. It was consecrated in 1907, converted into a sports centre after the war but was then given to the Orthodox Church in 1990. Chamber music concerts are held there throughout the year. A second church was built in 1994 as a memorial chapel to 25 children killed when a military aircraft crashed into their kindergarten in May 1972. Following normal Soviet practice, no official mention of the crash was made at the time. The photographs inside are of the children and their teachers, but there are none of the air crew who also all died.

The promenade by the sea, with its funfair, sundial and stairway decorated with mosaics has survived largely intact. Some villas and sanatoria are newly built but most of the grand wooden villas with their intricate window designs and elaborate roofs date from around 1900. They are all at a discreet distance from each other, allowing for extensive shrubbery and flower gardens between them. Some are now in private hands, some still belong to state organisations, but all can be proud of their paintwork and varnish.

Sculpture from Rauschen's most famous artist, Hermann Brachert, (1890–1972) has survived throughout the town. He fell out of favour with the Nazi regime on account of the pessimistic tone of many of his pieces. They did not allow him to teach or exhibit but fortunately they did not destroy his work and some of his most moving sculptures date from that era. He worked with equal effect in marble, limestone and bronze. His house in the neighbouring village of Otradnoye (Отрадное), formerly Georgenswalde, is now a museum.

Oktyabrskaya Ulitsa (Октябрьская Улица) is the main shopping street and it is very clear which shops are for the German tourists and which for the local population. Number 13 has the best bookshop in the whole region with excellent and cheap English–Russian dictionaries. The street also has a very Soviet cafeteria with tin trays and poor lighting. As a full meal from an extensive menu can, however, be had for about £0.25/US$0.40, it seems churlish to complain. Those who do can turn instead to a pretentious café with the surprising name of the Lame Horse (Хромая лошадь) where a mediocre German meal can be obtained for around £6/US$9.00. Cynics might claim that 'lame' refers to the level of service and cuisine.

A 20km drive from Svetlogorsk is needed to reach the start of the Curonian Spit at **Zelenogradsk** (Зеленоградск), formerly Cranz. Not being granted any special status during the Soviet period and having been the scene of serious fighting in April 1945, what was once a glamorous, vibrant resort is now a neglected village best driven through as quickly as possible. The young people drifting around the streets clearly do not represent the success stories of the new regime. The Russian name translates as 'Green City' which perhaps aptly sums up the weeds growing in the streets and the moss that has gripped the former villas. A grotesque concrete walkway along the coast offers no consolation after seeing the main street through the town.

The **Curonian Spit**, however, will without doubt be worth the drive from Kaliningrad. Visitors with more time may well consider continuing their tour to Nida, just over the Lithuanian border. It is also possible to start a tour in Nida as Kaliningrad tour operators can bring visas over the border and then drive back their passengers.

The spit is an 80km tongue of land which divides the Baltic Sea from the Curonian Lagoon. Half the territory belongs to Kaliningrad and half to Lithuania. The history of the Spit shows nature at its most brutal. Humans fought the elements rather than each other in this area. Most visitors travelling on a calm summer's day will see an alternation of dunes and forests, interspersed with the occasional village. It is hard to believe that a graveyard of whole villages lies beneath the sea and sand just a few hundred metres away.

That nature was finally controlled here is due to one man, Franz Epha (1828–1904) whose plans for forestation took 40 years to implement between 1860 and 1900, but which finally made the area secure. The Prussian regime encouraged the work initially to safeguard the road to the end of their empire and also to provide good communications with St Petersburg. If the rail network had developed sooner, this work might never have been carried out. Epha's work has been respected by all the governments that have ruled here since, by Nazis as much as by communists, and now by the new independent regimes. A sand dune that was named after Epha shortly before he died has retained its name throughout the subsequent century, not being changed in the Soviet era. The isolation of the area at that time also spared it from development so animals roamed at will. Wild boar, beavers and elk now predominate in the pine forests, which take up 71% of the land on the Russian side. The Spit is designated by both Russia and Lithuania as a national park and a small tax is charged for entry by car. Cars were banned from the Spit between 1920 and 1940 so access was then by boat, bicycle or on horseback.

There are two main villages on the Russian side of the Spit between Zelonogradsk and the Lithuanian border, **Lesnoy** (Лесной) and **Rybachy** (Рыбачий), Sarkau and Rossitten in German. In Lesnoy new money flaunts itself behind formidable metal grilles. One of the villas belongs to the Moscow Central Bank. It shows reasonable taste in architecture though one must regret the passing of many of the former more modest houses in the village.

Halfway between Lesnoy and Rybachy is the **Spit Museum**, founded in 1987 in what had formerly been a communist party guesthouse. The first German guidebook to the area, produced in 1996, tells visitors not to be put off by the austere concrete exterior and that it really is worth entering. This is true. 1987 was sufficiently into the *glasnost* era for a detailed and honest history of the area to be given. An extensive collection of photographs, models and stuffed animals covers contemporary and past natural history.

More unexpected is the history of the gliding centre which was founded in **Rossitten** in 1920. This resulted from the ban on motorised aviation in Germany stipulated by the Versailles Treaty at the end of World War I. Although neither German nor Russian historians like to dwell on the matter, there was close cooperation between the USSR and Germany throughout the early interwar period here. Soviet pilots came for training and Germans were in return invited to the Soviet gliding school in the Crimea. There had been similar cooperation between Imperial Germany and Tsarist Russia for a time after 1895 when gliding first began in this area. A recently-erected plaque commemorates a world-record eight-hour flight undertaken in 1925 by a local pilot, Ferdinand Schulz. The inscription, carved in both German and Russian, proclaims that 'gliding should overcome frontiers and bring nations together.'

Seven kilometres further along the road towards Rybachy, the **bird sanctuary** founded by the German Ornithological Society in 1901 continues its work. It welcomes visitors and helpers. It broke an earlier culture amongst the fishing community of killing local birds, mainly crows, for food. Now they are ringed and then released. The first and most famous director, Johannes Thienemann ringed 103 himself in 1903. By 1936 this annual total had reached 140,000. The larger birds included seagulls, sparrow-hawks, kestrels and buzzards. Regular smaller ones were robins, thrushes and wagtails. Thienemann was soon able to work out the migratory routes of the white stork through Hungary, Egypt and Kenya to South Africa. He remained as director until 1929. The German staff all fled in 1945 and it was not until 1956 that the sanctuary was reopened by the Russians. They gave it the name Fringilla, from the Latin for chaffinch which is one of the most common birds to be found there. In 1991 the very precise statistic was provided that 1,672,071 birds had been ringed since the re-opening. Its traps are thought to be the largest in the world, one being 100m deep, 30m wide and 15m high. The birds fly in totally unaware that they are in a trap so around 60,000 can be ringed each year. The traps are relocated each season, facing north in the spring and south in the autumn to catch the birds on both their outward and return migrations. The large nets are renewed each year; song-birds in cages entice the migrants. By 2002, a lot of the exhibition material had been translated into English as well as into German. British and German researchers are now regularly at work there. Electronic chips are beginning to replace rings but the enormous cost of tracking them is limiting this research.

Just outside the sanctuary, the **Museum of Russian Superstition** opened in May 2002 with a collection of 70 wooden carvings of spirits linked to water, forests and fields. It is planned to broaden the field of carving, so soon should also have domestic utensils. The building is of course totally wooden.

In Rybachy/Rossitten itself, several wooden houses have preserved their original 19th century carvings. The main building of interest is the red-brick village church, consecrated in 1873, and like the one in Svetlogorsk/Rauschen, it was designed by August Stüler. None of the building was ever damaged and the vicarage beside it is still intact. Even the bell and the windows remain. It was not used between 1945 and 1963 when it was taken over by the 'Dawn of Communism' fishing collective as a storage depot for their nets. In 1990 it was given to the Orthodox Church.

The Lithuanian border is a further 16km from Rybachy so this village is an appropriate point to finish the tour. By the summer of 2003 it may well be possible to return from Rybachy to Zelenogradsk by boat along the sea-coast or along the lagoon. Another likely route is across the lagoon to Polessk. This second route would offer a semicircular journey starting to the west of Kaliningrad and then finishing in the east. In the summer of 2002 it was still necessary to retrace one's steps by road but the variety of tracks through the forest or along the dunes offer so many tempting stops that this is hardly an imposition.

Hotels in Svetlogorsk/Rauschen

It is quite possible to visit Kaliningrad on a daily basis from Svetlogorsk by local train or vice versa. Svetlogorsk is developing as a health centre and as a summer holiday resort, both for Russian and for German tourists. It is attractive in winter, too, particularly after a snowfall, as temperatures rarely drop much below freezing point and day-trippers from Kaliningrad keep it lively year-round. The dialling code for Svetlogorsk is 01153 and the '0' is still used when phoning from abroad.

Azur Coast Dynamo 1a; tel: 21523; fax: 21522.
This large villa was opened as an exclusive hotel in 1999. It only has six rooms, two singles, two twins and two suites, but offers the full range of hotel services. Its private grounds are sufficiently extensive to ensure privacy and tranquillity. With prices not being much higher than those in conventional hotels, the luxury is well worth the modest extra cost. Singles US$45, doubles US$60, luxury US$80.

Baltic Pearl Baltiskaya 15a; tel: 21351.

Without doubt, this is the most pleasant hotel in the whole Kaliningrad region. It is surrounded by woodland but is only ten minutes walk from the town centre. The family feel is unexpected and most welcome. There are only 20 rooms but the hotel offers ample grounds, a large indoor swimming pool, a sauna and a billiard room. Prices for meals and refreshments are very low, tea in spring 2002 costing 10p/16c a cup and coffee 15p/20c. Singles US$45, twins US$75.

Rauschen One and **Rauschen Two** Kaliningradsky 70; tel: 21580, 21564; and Lenina 48; tel: 33452.

These two hotels are within a few hundred yards of each other and were formerly Soviet trade union hotels. They are now largely used by German tour groups spending a night en route to the Baltics. This is why they have only a German and not a Russian name. They have both been sufficiently modernised to make a longer stay possible but neither has any really appealing features. Singles US$45, twins US$75.

Rus Verestschagin 10; tel: 21445; fax: 21418; email: hotel_rusy@baltnet.ru; web: www.rus-hotel.narod.ru.

This new hotel is *the* place to be seen for young successful Russians. Everything is built on a lavish scale and its private grounds stretch to the sea. A winter garden is the most novel feature. It of course has a casino, tennis courts and a restaurant with an extensive wine list. The hotel achieved notoriety in February 2000 when Anatoly Sobchak, the former mayor of St Petersburg, died there from a heart attack after an evening of over-indulgence. He had been helping with Vladimir Putin's presidential campaign. Singles US$80, twins US$130.

Appendix 1

LANGUAGE
Of necessity these are only basic words and phrases. Consult a dictionary if you would like to learn more.

Useful expressions

English	Estonian	Latvian	Lithuanian
hello	*tere*	*sveiki*	*laba diena*
goodbye	*nagemiseni*	*ata*	*viso gero*
good morning	*tere hommikust*	*labdien*	*labas rytas*
good evening	*head õhtust*	*labvakar*	*labas vakaras*
goodnight	*head õõd*	*ar labu nakti*	*labanakt*
yes	*jah*	*jā*	*taip*
no	*ei*	*nē*	*ne*
please	*palun*	*lūdzu*	*prašau*
thank you	*tänan*	*paldies*	*ačiu*
How much?	*Kui palju*	*Cik?*	*Kiek tai kainuoja?*
When?	*Millal?*	*Kad?*	*Kada?*
Where?	*Kus?*	*Kur?*	*Kur?*
Excuse me please	*Vabandage palun*	*Atvainojiet, lūdzu*	*Atsiprasau*
I do not understand	*Ma ei saa aru*	*Nesaprotu*	*As nesuprantu*

Useful words

English	Estonian	Latvian	Lithuanian
airport	*lennujaam*	*lidosta*	*aerouostas*
bus station	*bussijaam*	*autoosta*	*autobusu stotis*
railway station	*raudteejaam*	*dzelzceļa stacija*	*geležinkelio stotis*
toilet	*WC*	*tualete*	*tualet*
beer	*õlu*	*alus*	*alus*
coffee (with milk)	*kohv (piimaga)*	*kafija (ar pienu)*	*kava (su pienas)*
drinking water	*joogivesi*	*ūdens*	*vanduo*
juice	*mahl*	*sula*	*sultys*
mineral water	*mineraalvesi*	*minerālūdens*	*mineralinis vanduo*
wine (red, white)	*wein (pumane, valge)*	*vīns (sarkans, balts)*	*vynas*
sugar	*suhkur*	*cukurs*	*cukrus*

NUMBERS

English	Estonian	Latvian	Lithuanian	Russian
1	üks	viens	vienas	один [adeen]
2	kaks	divi	du	два [dva]
3	kolm	trīs	trys	три [tree]
4	neli	četri	keturi	четыре [chyetiyryeh]
5	viis	pieci	penki	пять [pyat]
6	kuus	seši	šeši	шесть [shest]
7	seitse	septiņi	septyni	семь [syem]
8	kaheksa	astoņi	aštuoni	восемь [vosyem]
9	üheksa	deviņi	devyni	девять [dyevyat]
10	kümme	desmit	dešimt	десять [dyesyat]

English	Russian
hello	Здравствуите [zdrahstvooytyeh]
goodbye	До свидания [dasvidanya]
good morning	Доброе утро [dobriy dyen]
good evening	Добрый вечер [dobriy vyechyer]
goodnight	Спокойной ночи [spahkoynigh nochee]
yes	да [da]
no	нет [nyet]
please	Пожалуйста [pazhalsta]
thank you	Спасибо [spahseebah]
How much?	Сколько? [Skol ka?]
When?	Когда? [Kagda?]
Where?	Где? [Gdyeh?]
Excuse me please	Извините, пожалуйста... [Izveeneetye, pazhalsta]
I do not understand	Я не понимато [Ya nye panimayu]

English	Russian
airport	аэропорт [aeroport]
bus station	автовокзал [avtovokzal]
railway station	вокзал [vokzal]
toilet	туалет [tualyet]
beer	пиво [peeva]
coffee (with milk)	кофе (молоком) [coffee (molokom)]
drinking water	питьевая вода [peetyeva-ya vada]
juice	сок [sok]
mineral water	минеральная вода [meenyeralna-ya vada]
wine (red, white)	(красное, белое) вино [(krasna-yeh, byela-yeh) veeno]
sugar	сахар [sahar]

Appendix 2

FURTHER READING
General books

Baltic Approaches by Peter Unwin is the result of many visits to the area and much research. Writing in 1995 he is able to put the sudden transition of 1990–1 into a longer-term perspective and the book has in no way dated. His chapter on Kaliningrad is one of the very few sources in English on this area. Summer 2002 saw the publication in paperback by Routledge of *The Baltic States, Estonia, Latvia, and Lithuania* bringing together in one volume three books that had previously been published separately and which provide short general histories on each country and then greater detail on the Soviet occupation and the transition to independence. For more detail on the 20 years of independence the Baltic States enjoyed between 1920 and 1940, *The Baltic States, Years of Independence* by George von Rauch is recommended. Earlier history is covered in *The Baltic World 1772–1993* by David Kirby.

Vytautas Landsbergis is the first Baltic independence leader to have written his memoirs. *Lithuania, Independent Again* was published in Britain in July 2000. Walking the calm streets of Vilnius now, it is all too easy to forget the struggles needed to remove the Soviet occupiers. Music and politics have always been linked in his life so it is not surprising that two chapters in this book are called 'Debussy and Despair' and 'The Power of Music'. A third has the title 'Čiurlionis' in recognition of Lithuania's most famous composer.

The literature on their former *Heimat* produced by East Prussians is voluminous. Much of it is tendentious and superficial. An exception, and fortunately one that has been translated into English, is *Before The Storm: Memories of my Youth in Old Prussia* by Marion Dönhoff. She has written many other books about both Königsberg and Kaliningrad but these are only in German. Those with knowledge of German are also recommended to read *Spaziergange einer Ostpreussin* by Agnes Miegel. She was a famous poet who lived in Königsberg before the war and these are her recollections of the 1920s there. The definitive book on German architecture appeared in early 2000. *Königsberg, Architectur aus Deutscher Zeit* by Baldur Koster was the result of four years work there and shows how much has remained. The best account of life and death in Königsberg at the end of the war is *Zeugnis vom Untergang Königsberg*, by Michael Wieck, a Jew who was under equal threat from both the Nazis and then from the Russians. *Königsberg* in the Merian Live series is the best German guidebook. The many still in circulation that date from the early 1990s should be treated with great caution. The writers are still embittered about the loss of the area and the whole Soviet period is described in totally hostile terms.

Travel guides

Individual guides to Estonia, Latvia and Lithuania have been published by Bradt, offering in-depth coverage of each country. New editions of these books were published in summer 2002.

Estonia Neil Taylor. A practical guide to Estonia's complex history and many attractions: Tallinn; the unspoilt countryside and islands; German manor houses and elegant resorts.

Latvia Stephen Baister and Chris Patrick. All corners of Latvia, from the capital, Riga, to the 13th-century town of Cesis, Sigulda National Park, the lakes of Latgale and the coast at Jurmala.

Lithuania Gordon McLachlan. Highlights of this rapidly changing country include medieval cities, national parks, pristine beaches and colourful local festivals.

Maps

Jāņa Sēta in Riga publish atlases of the Baltic States and individual town plans for each capital and for many smaller towns as well. Their maps are available at Stanfords in London and Bristol and all over the Baltic States. Their shop in Riga is at 83–85 Elizabetes iela. The Estonian map specialists are Regio, whose main outlet is the Apollo Bookshop at Viru 23, close to the Viru Gate. They publish historical as well as contemporary maps of Tallinn. They do not, however, sell abroad or cover the other Baltic States. There are no similar publishers to these two in Vilnius or in Kaliningrad, although a wide selection of locally produced maps is available. In Kaliningrad it is possible to buy bilingual maps produced in Germany giving both the former and the current names of all the streets in the town centre.

Local publications

Tallinn In Your Pocket and the parallel publications for Riga and Vilnius are essential purchases on arrival. They only cost about £1.50/US$2.50 and this cover charge enables them to comment freely on local restaurants, museums and shops without being beholden to advertisers. They are all on the website www.inyourpocket.com so this should be consulted for up-to-date information before departure.

Kaliningrad has still to realise the potential of providing tourists with nice books as souvenirs of their visit. A locally produced guidebook in Russian has still to appear, let alone one in German or English. Sets of postcards are easily available, both of pre-war Königsberg and of the contemporary Kaliningrad. The cathedral has produced, in German only, a few booklets on its history.

The other three capitals have suddenly produced a plethora of large photographic albums and manageable booklets. In Tallinn the little book *The Living Past of Tallinn* by Elena Rannu skilfully portrays the high life and the low life of the Upper Town throughout its history. Gustav German's *Estonia* published in 1996 in fact concentrates on photographs of Tallinn just before new building, rather than just restoration, took over in parts of the town. Sulev Maevali's *Architecture and Art Monuments in Tallinn* was first published in 1986 but it is regularly updated and has no equal in its detailed descriptions of church interiors. Tallinn deserves a lively book on its history but for the moment has to do with the rather ponderous *History of Old Tallinn* by Raimo Pullat published in 1998.

Most visitors to Riga return with the two books written by Andris Kolbergs called *The Story of Riga*. One covers the history of the Old Town, the other Riga's expansion in the 19th century. Both are well illustrated with prints and contemporary photographs. A worthy extravagance is *Art Nouveau in Riga* by Janis Krastins which covers every building in this genre. *Riga, a City to Discover* by A Bruders, manages to include 300 original photographs in a book almost pocket-size. Riga's 800th anniversary celebrations in 2001 gave rise to a wide range of publications, many of which will probably be updated for Eurovision in May 2003. One of the best is *Riga in Images* by Janis Lejnieks. *The Jews in Riga* published by the Jewish Museum in 1991, covers all buildings linked with their history, both those still in use and those destroyed during the war. It also has a very useful history of their community.

It would be impossible to leave Vilnius without buying a baroque book. The best is *Baroque in Lithuania* which concentrates on architecture. *Baroque Art in Lithuania* covers porcelain, tapestry and painting. *Lithuania, Past, Culture, Present* does manage to do justice to all three ambitious themes within the space of 270 pages, both in the text and in the illustrations. The title *Lithuania, Facts and Figures* hardly sounds inviting but, although it is an official publication, it is written in a lively manner and has far more photographs than statistics. *Vilnius*, an annual publication in English of the Lithuanian Writers Union, translates the best writing of the previous year and also has commentaries on art and film. *Vilnius 13.01.91* is a grim photographic reminder of the violence the capital had to endure in defending its independence from Soviet forces. (No individual authors are listed for these books as they all have several contributors.)

2001 saw the publication of two new English-language guidebooks to Vilnius by native English speakers clearly aware of the needs of foreign visitors.. Joseph Everatt's *A Guide to Vilnius* has lively architectural detail on all the major buildings; Tomas Venclova's *Vilnius* has a wider canvas, with an excellent historical introduction and a large number of drawings and photographs.

The various chapters earlier in this book include details of local bookshops with the best selection of recent English-language publications. The www.amazon.com and www.amazon.co.uk websites are always up to date on material in English on each of the Baltic countries and the parallel www.amazon.de site similarly covers books published in German.

Useful websites

Baltic Times	www.baltictimes.com
City Paper	www.balticsworldwide.com
Estonian Tourist Board	www.visitestonia.com
Eurolines buses	www.online.ee/eurolines.com
In Your Pocket	www.inyourpocket.com
Latvian Tourist Board	www.latnet.lv
Lithuanian Tourist Board	www.tourism.lt

Index

Page numbers in *italics* indicate maps.